Victorian Sexual Dissidence

Victorian Sexual Dissidence

Edited by
Richard Dellamora

THE UNIVERSITY OF CHICAGO PRESS

CHICAGO AND LONDON

Richard Dellamora is professor of English and Director of the graduate program in
Methodologies for the Study of Western History and Culture at Trent University. He
is the author of several books, including *Masculine Desire: The Sexual Politics of
Victorian Aestheticism.*

The University of Chicago Press, Chicago 60637
The University of Chicago Press, Ltd., London
© 1999 by The University of Chicago
All rights reserved. Published 1999
08 07 06 05 04 03 02 01 00 99   5 4 3 2 1

ISBN (cloth): 0-226-14226-4
ISBN (paper): 0-226-14227-2

Library of Congress Cataloging-in-Publication Data

Victorian sexual dissidence / edited by Richard Dellamora.
    p.   cm.
    Includes index.
    ISBN 0-226-14226-4. — ISBN 0-226-14227-2 (pbk.)
    1. English literature—19th century—History and criticism.   2. Homosexuality
and literature—Great Britain—History—19th century.   3. Gays' writings,
English—History and criticism.   4. Sex customs in literature.   5. Lesbians in
literature.   6. Gay men in literature   I. Dellamora, Richard.
PR468.H65V53   1999
820.9'353—dc21   98-44262
                                                                 CIP

⊗ The paper used in this publication meets the minimum requirements of the
American National Standard for Information Sciences—Permanence of Paper for
Printed Library Materials, ANSI Z39.48-1992.

This book is printed on acid-free paper.

CONTENTS

ACKNOWLEDGMENTS

This collection began with the presentation of three panels on the topic of Victorian sexual dissidence organized by myself on behalf of the executive committee of the Victorian division of the Modern Language Association at the annual meeting held in Washington, D.C., in December 1997. I would like to thank my fellow members on the executive committee for their support.

I would also like to thank the contributors to this volume, who proved to be exemplary collaborators. Doug Mitchell and Matthew Howard at the University of Chicago Press have been engaging, professional, and efficient from the start. The anonymous external readers of the volume made a valuable contribution. I would also like to acknowledge the financial support of the Social Sciences and Humanities Research Council of Canada, who have enabled this and much else of my work.

In addition to the pleasures of collaboration, editing a volume holds open the prospect of sharing new work with other readers as the date of publication approaches. I enjoyed this opportunity when I presented the introduction of this volume in a session of the Victorian Seminar at the Center for Literary and Cultural Studies of Harvard University in April 1998. To my interlocutors, whose intensity and incisiveness I admire, and to Jonah Siegel, Ann Pellegrini, Mary Wilson Carpenter, Gail Weinberg, and Patrick O'Malley, who helped make the occasion a memorable one, I trust that this book makes a suitable return.

Introduction

RICHARD DELLAMORA

I

The "gaying" of critical studies of the late Victorian period has been under way now for more than a decade. Indeed, if one starts not with pioneering essays by Eve Kosofsky Sedgwick, D. A. Miller, Christopher Craft, and Ed Cohen, but with the template of these studies in the New Left, "gay liberation" approach to social history that Ken Plummer and Jeffrey Weeks developed during the 1970s, the work has been ongoing for over two decades. This writing continues to provoke, at times to offend, some readers while simultaneously providing a powerful impetus to the work of others. Chris Craft's essay on *The Importance of Being Earnest* is just as likely to spark disagreements among actors, producers, directors, and theater critics now as when it was first published. Young scholars such as William Cohen continue to mine Miller's insight as to the importance of personal secrets in defining the (male) subject. And Sedgwick's appropriation of René Girard's theory of the triangulation of mimetic desire has enjoyed a half-life beyond its original context in the explorations that feminist critics are currently pursuing into the ways in which female same-sex ties are subtly sexualized in a host of apparently conventional texts.

As a result of this work, university teachers can no longer unselfconsciously pursue the heterosexual thematics even of such marriage-destined genres as Victorian realist fiction. Instead they are likely to stumble over the erotically charged antipathy that results in violence between Eugene Wrayburn and Bradley Headstone in Charles Dickens's *Our Mutual Friend* (1864–65) or between David Copperfield and Uriah Heep in the earlier novel.[1] In a number of essays in *Victorian Sexual Dissidence,* heterosexual representation is reactive in character.[2] For example, in Thaïs Morgan's contribution, the drift of the meaning of the word "effeminacy" toward male homosexuality in Robert Buchanan's attacks on the Pre-Raphaelites in the early 1870s appears to be necessitated by *his* need to define a straight male-identified position against the explicit perversities of A. C. Swinburne's poetry, the male–female eroticism of D. G. Rossetti's poetry and painting, Simeon Solomon's slumberous evocations of male and female same-sex desire, and prominent coverage in the *Times* of the prosecution of two young men for cross-dressing in the West End.[3] In another essay, Dennis Denisoff considers George Du Maurier's changing representations of effeminate Aesthetes from the pages of *Punch* in the late 1870s to the novel *Trilby*, published in 1894 shortly before the Wilde trials, to his final novel, *The Martian*, in 1897. Du Maurier's shifting relation to the category of the emergent male homosexual—at times satiric, at other times condescending and tolerant, but ultimately harshly condemning—indexes the development of male heterosexual identity as constituted in relation to the emergence of a public, proscriptive homophobia.

Morgan's and Denisoff's essays exist within a line of work prompted by Michel Foucault's assertion that "homosexuality appeared as one of the forms of sexuality when it was transposed from the practice of sodomy onto a kind of interior androgyny, a hermaphrodism of the soul. The sodomite had been a temporary aberration; the homosexual was now a species."[4] Sedgwick elaborates this view in *Epistemology of the Closet* (1990): "So, as a result, is the heterosexual [a species], and between *these* species the human species has come more and more to be divided."[5] Both Denisoff and Morgan show additionally the connection between consciousness-effects of legal and medical discourses at the end of the century and the politics of high, middlebrow, and mass culture. Indeed, as one learns more about these aspects of Victorian culture, one becomes ever more impressed by the speed with which avant-garde artistic practice was communicated to the world of fashion and middle-class consumption. Already by the late 1860s, Oxford Aestheticism was shaping public perceptions of domestic and social life.[6] The connections earlier drawn by Regenia Gagnier between sexual dissidence, celebrity, and middle-class consumption in the career of Oscar Wilde now appear to have been widely shared features of the relationship between Aestheticism, the Decadence, and mainstream Victorian culture.

While these thoughts suggest why one can speak of the gaying of Victorian studies, they do not address another remarkable development within literary criticism: namely, the tracing of sexual attraction between women in the work of female Aesthetes, female modernists, and even women writing at the very heart of the Victorian canon.[7] Critics are beginning to recognize the affirmation of dissident desire between women as a feature shared between male and female literary tradition. In an important new book, Ruth Vanita argues that this affirmation occurs both in a Christian tradition that she calls Marian and in a Classical one that she terms Sapphic. Although the publication in 1866 of "Anactoria," Swinburne's dramatic monologue in the voice of Sappho, is obviously a key moment in the history of the latter, Vanita specifies the importance of male Aestheticism as an important point of crisscrossing influences between male and female evocations of what was beginning to be designated as lesbian desire. Vanita remarks that this realization came to her when she discovered that Walter Pater draws attention to something that she herself had noticed, namely, that Leonardo da Vinci's painting *The Virgin Mary and Child and St. Anne* is, in Vanita's words, "a compelling lesbian image." Vanita quotes Pater's remark that, in handling this subject, Leonardo, "the most profane of painters," "carries one altogether beyond the range of its conventional associations" (quoted in Vanita, 65).

Distancing herself both from gynecriticism, which traces a self-contained female literary tradition, and from positions such as Sedgwick's in *Between Men: English Literature and Male Homosocial Desire* (1985), which assume that historical tradition is patriarchal,[8] Vanita argues that such a view is a post-Freudian imposition upon a reality earlier experienced in much more variable terms. "I began to realize," she writes, "that Sapphic writers did not operate within a tradition of their own, but were integrated with and constitutive of mainstream traditions. Sapphic love was not always silenced, invisibilized, or exoticized by the English literary imagination but was rather one of its central components. Love between women creators has functioned as an enabling element in the writings of both male and female authors at least since Romanticism" (1). Vanita's book is so wide-ranging in its explorations that experts in a particular area are likely to find themselves in disagreement with her on specific points. The general thesis, however, is well argued; and Vanita adduces important new evidence. Perhaps most significantly, she suggests a way of imagining dissidence within culture without arguing either its existence as a representation coded for a minority audience or its status as an epiphenomenon (as the Other within) of hegemonic culture.[9]

Foucault's argument that the homosexual came to be recognized as a "species" between 1870 and 1900 specifies that the constitution of the homosexual/heterosexual is a historical phenomenon. In his well-known sentence, "was now" functions as a performative: the definition of homosexuality creates a new ontological category. By the same token, within this period, before, and presumably afterward, same-sex desire was experienced and construed in other terms as well.[10] Moreover, the view, based in Darwinian theory[11] and shared both by intellectuals such as George Henry Lewes and in popular culture, that the term "species" does not refer to a fixed entity but rather to what were referred to then and now as variations, indicates that the speciation of the homosexual occurred at a time when species themselves were considered to be variable. In the words of a turn-of-the-century children's book: "It . . . is for reasons of convenience that men have invented species. Nature knows no such distinction."[12]

The literary critical renaissance that I referred to at the outset did not call itself gay. Rather, its practitioners sought to place a distance between themselves and the efforts made by literary critics such as Robert K. Martin during the 1970s to introduce an explicitly gay thematics into literary criticism. The preferred term was "antihomophobic inquiry," a phrase that implicitly located the overt homophobia of traditional literary criticism while specifying an agenda of undoing such effects.[13] Sedgwick's main contribution to the history of sexuality has been the concept, introduced in *Between Men*, of the regulative function of homophobia within what she refers to as the male homosocial continuum. In chapter four of the *Epistemology of the Closet*, she summarizes her view: "Because the paths of male entitlement, especially in the nineteenth century, required certain intense male bonds that were not readily distinguishable from the most reprobated bonds, an endemic and ineradicable state of . . . male homosexual panic became the normal condition of male heterosexual entitlement" (185). The result is a double bind in which "the most intimate male bonding" is prescribed at the same time that "the remarkably cognate homosexuality" is proscribed (186). *Epistemology of the Closet* focuses on "the self-ignorance that this regime constitutively enforces" (186), an ignorance or rather a set of ignorances summed in the phrase "epistemology of the closet." This epistemology is thoroughly ironic since Sedgwick demonstrates how ignorance functions as a set of discursive practices that determine what can and cannot be known. In the epistemology of the closet, silence is as important as speech. As Foucault writes: "There is no binary division to be made between what one says and what one does not say; we must try to determine the different ways of not saying such things. . . . There is not one but many silences, and they are an integral part of the strategies that underlie and permeate discourses" (quoted by Sedgwick, 3). She continues: "'Closetedness' itself is a performance initiated as such by the speech act of a silence."

Antihomophobic critique focuses on sexual panic within the institution of heterosexuality; where it ventures further into consideration of sexual and emotional ties between men, it tends to read these as manifestations of closeting processes.[14] Even when a critic such as Craft argues, uncharacteristically, that in *Earnest*, for example, "the object of . . . derision is heterosexual representation itself," emphasis falls on what might be termed processes of uncloseting, e.g., the use of plays on words and inside jokes referring to Wilde's sexual transactions in order to signify "a jubilant expression of homosexual desire" (23). In an essay in *Victorian Sexual Dissidence*, Eric Haralson traces dissidence in relation to male sexual panic in Henry James's *The Tragic Muse* (1890). Haralson shows how anxiety about male intimacy motivates the representation of Victorian Aestheticism as both asexual and apolitical. In James's novel, desire between men is subject not so much to silence as to disappearance.

The *Epistemology of the Closet* is best known for Sedgwick's proposition that knowledge in the twentieth century has been constituted within the terms of a heterosexual/homosexual binary. As she says in the introduction: "The book will argue that an understanding of virtually any aspect of modern Western culture must be, not merely incomplete, but damaged in its central substance to the degree that it does not incorporate a critical analysis of the modern homo/heterosexual definition; and it will assume that the appropriate place for that critical analysis to begin is from the relatively decentered perspective of modern gay and antihomophobic theory" (1). This provocation has been of immense value in enabling work in sexuality studies during the past decade. There is, however, good reason to question whether sexual dissidence is always structured within binary terms.[15] The evidence presented in many of the following essays suggests that it is not. Additionally, antihomophobic inquiry tends to ignore other aspects of dissidence; for example, the connections between sexual and cultural dissidence in cultural production by women. The emphasis on homophobic representation in effect de-emphasizes also the expression of desire between men as a mode of cultural dissidence (Sedgwick, 48–59). It is rarely emphasized, for example, that subjects of same-sex desire devoted attention to considering precisely how homophobic consciousness-effects are induced, both among male homosocial elites and among others, including women and the general populace. Whether in specifically sexual terms, in terms of class analysis and resistance, or in terms of defining and contesting concepts of national and ethnic difference—or in combination as these terms usually occur—both male and female critics have put in question the processes of subject-formation posited by Sedgwick.

II

Antihomophobic critique is written under the signature of a number of theorists: Gayle Rubin, Jacques Derrida, and, in particular, the Foucault of *Discipline and Punish* (1975, trans. 1977).[16] This Foucault is the one who is expert in the ruses whereby the constitution of individual subjectivity is the prime mode in which power effects occur in human subjects. In the words of D. A. Miller: "Disciplinary order relies on a subjectivity that, through a rich array of spiritual management techniques, it compels to endless self-examination" (*Novel and Police*, 18). This aspect of Foucault's thinking renders double-edged the concept of reverse discourse that he proposes in *The History of Sexuality*, Volume 1 (1976, trans. 1978), specifically in relation to the invention of male homosexuality in late Victorian sexology:

> There is no question that the appearance in nineteenth-century psychiatry, jurisprudence, and literature of a whole series of discourses on the species and subspecies of homosexuality, inversion, pederasty, and "psychic hermaphrodism" made possible a strong advance of social controls into

this area of "perversity"; but it also made possible the formation of a "reverse" discourse: homosexuality began to speak in its own behalf, to demand that its legitimacy or "naturality" be acknowledged, often in the same vocabulary, using the same categories by which it was medically disqualified. There is not, on the one side, a discourse of power, and opposite it, another discourse that runs counter to it. Discourses are tactical elements or blocks operating in the field of force relations; there can exist different and even contradictory discourses within the same strategy; they can, on the contrary, circulate without changing their form from one strategy to another, opposing strategy. We must not expect the discourses on sex to tell us, above all, what strategy they derive from, or what moral divisions they accompany, or what ideology—dominant or dominated— they represent; rather we must question them on the two levels of their tactical productivity (what reciprocal effects of power and knowledge they ensure) and their strategical integration (what conjunction and what force relationship make their utilization necessary in a given episode of the various confrontations that occur). (101–2)

Foucault argues that readers need to question what "reciprocal effects of power and knowledge" are ensured by the deployment of particular discourses at particular moments. The predicate that he uses *(ils assurent)* is equivocal.[17] Like the English word *assure,* the verb can mean "to declare or promise confidently." It can also mean "to guarantee" or "to make certain of." Like the English word *insure,* the verb can mean "to [contract to] protect against damage or loss."[18] There is a difference between promising an outcome and making it certain. The distance between the two makes it possible to detour and derail discursive practices.

In subsequent writing, Foucault came to advocate the practice of an "aesthetic 'care of the self,'" which is partially aesthetic, partially ethical, partially invested in sexual practices, especially sado-masochistic, between men.[19] This discussion has contexts in nascent male homosexual apology of the late nineteenth century. Foucault's phrase "aesthetics of existence," for example, echoes John Addington Symonds, who, in the chapter "The Genius of Greek Art" in volume two of *Studies of the Greek Poets* (1875), commends a return to an eroticized ideal of *aesthesis* as a guide to moral conduct. Symonds makes this proposal in defense of desire between men against Christian disapproval and the belief, deeply embedded in Western culture, that sexual inversion implies gender inversion.[20]

In the second volume of *The History of Sexuality* (1984, trans. 1985), Foucault implicitly addresses the dilemmas facing those who, in the terms of hegemonic culture, are liable to be termed homosexual.[21] He does so within a larger view of what he refers to as the "individualizing power" whereby institutions define personal subjectivity in the modern state.[22] Foucault has reservations about the sexual politics of ancient Greek culture: "The Greek ethics of pleasure is linked to a virile society, to dissymetry, exclusion of the other, an obsession with penetration, and a kind of threat of being dispossessed of your own energy, and so on. All that is quite disgusting" ("Genealogy of Ethics," 346). Nonetheless, the search for an alternative leads Foucault into Greek tradition, in which he finds a technology of the self in relation to male–male sexual practices that is aesthetic rather than confessional in character. In this context, the term "aesthetic" refers to a specific set of practices, especially apt for gay men, that have potential for being articulated in resistance to "individualizing power."[23] Foucault conceives this resistance as creative—in the use of bodily pleasures and in the use of becoming-gay to invent new modes of personal and social relationship:

> I should like to say "it is necessary to work increasingly at being gay," to place oneself in a dimension where the sexual choices that one makes . . . must be at the same time creators of ways of life. To be gay signifies that these choices diffuse themselves across the entire life; it is also a certain manner of refusing the modes of life offered; it is to make a sexual choice the impetus for a change of existence.[24]

Again, I am ahead of myself since while the word "gay" can connote male–male desire in the 1890s, usually it does not; and the term as Foucault uses it is usually anachronistic in relation to Victorian society. More to hand was the struggle by men who enjoyed sexual and emotional ties with other men to resist having them defined within the new terms of criminal and sexological definitions of homosexuality. In *De Profundis*, for example, Wilde, who today is often casually referred to as gay, explicitly states his unwillingness to become either the exponent or the abjected signifier of homosexuality. Wilde reproaches his former lover, Alfred Douglas, who wished to portray him as such in a feuilleton to be published in the *Mercure de France*. With an acute sense of how he, signs of dissidence, and members of the *lumpen* reflected each other while being reflected in the mass-circulation press, Wilde asks: "What was your article to show? That I had been too fond of you? The Paris *gamin* was quite aware of the fact. They all read the newspapers, and most of them write for them" (*De Profundis*, 137).

While Wilde's defensiveness on this occasion is readily understandable, Douglas would have been correct to claim that, in the 1890s, Wilde did in fact make "sexual choices" that were "creators of [new] ways of life." These choices implied refusals of contemporary mores and manners. And, as is witnessed in the plays, they did "diffuse themselves across the entire life." The stimulus of both negation and appeals to live differently account for Wilde's appeal to women such as Ada Leverson, who responded to his provocations immediately and critically but with great fellow-feeling in the pages of *Punch*. The mutual attraction between Wilde and dissident women has often gone unmarked or unexplained. In approaching Aestheticism, feminist critics have tended to emphasize the subordinate position of women, the cruelty with which their often ingenuous enthusiasm was received by men whose sexual attitudes were more conventional than they pretended even to themselves or by men who were weakly sexed or by men whose sexual interests, whether closeted, repressed or manifest, went towards members of the same sex.[25]

As readers of Thorstein Veblen's *Theory of the Leisure Class* (1899) will be aware, the relationship between "ladies" and connoisseurs put them at odds economically. A prime responsibility of male tastemakers was to ensure that taste continued to be determined by men—while women were to remain its leading enforcers. Nonetheless, one of the important things that *Victorian Sexual Dissidence* does is to show how women drew on the tactics of same-sex desire in male cultural production in order to (re)present women beyond the limits of the bourgeois sexual economy. Kathy Psomiades shows how Vernon Lee in her novel *Miss Brown* (1884) uses the occasion of a satirical critique of straight male–identified Aestheticism to evoke the "clammy" sublime of disreputable female–female attraction. In her subsequent development of a formal aesthetics, Lee appropriates the homoerotic critical impressionism of Walter Pater to validate the female appreciation of the beauty of the female body and its capabilities of aesthetic hypersensation. Yopie Prins demonstrates how, as the turn of the century passes and Victorian obsessions begin to be converted into the templates of modernism, the Cambridge anthropologist Jane Harrison's influential readings of myth and ritual lend a further shade of mauve to Pater's charged readings of the myth of Dionysus. And, in a classic essay, Martha Vicinus shows how the trope of the attractive adolescent male transports "a double desire—to love a boy and to be a boy" between Aesthetic and early modernist work, between men's writing and women's, between nascent male homosexual and nascent lesbian texts that convey "an unnamed sexual subjectivity."

Other essays pursue routings through articulations of male–male desire. Following the lead of Douglass Shand-Tucci's work in *Boston Bohemia, 1881–1900* (1995), Eric Haralson and Christopher Lane consider sexual dissidence in the fiction and aesthetics of Henry James and George Santayana, respectively. Shand-Tucci demonstrates that Boston was the North American center of an Aestheticism closely related to the English variety and shaped not only by men but also by women such as Sarah Orne Jewett and Louise Guiney. *Boston Bohemia* is especially good at evoking sexual dissidence not so much through the lens of sexual anxiety or even in relation to particular sexual relationships or practices—although Shand-Tucci does that work too—but in diverse modes of cultural revision and innovation—e.g., in chapel, church, and house design; in interior decoration; in Anglo-Catholic worship; in the turn-of-the-century fascination with theosophy; in Platonic philosophic interests; the cult of male chivalry; etc.

III

Male poets and writers of nonfiction prose during the Victorian period use the discursive space afforded within a number of aesthetic genres to begin to imagine embodied, intimate, at time sexualized ties between men. Working in critical relation to an Aestheticism from within which they write, Lee, Katherine Bradley and Edith Cooper, George Egerton, and others imagine women similarly. *Victorian Sexual Dissidence* provides detailed opportunities to consider these processes. The contributors show how an investment in same-sex desire can transform genres and disciplines while provoking a range of new aesthetics that are eventually summed (and at times effaced) in the term modernism. In his book, Shand-Tucci is at pains to emphasize that self-conscious Aesthetes and Decadents identified their sexual and cultural interests with modernity, an emphasis that has often been lost sight of.[26] Prins in her discussion of Harrison's anthropology; Julia Saville in exploring the painting of Henry Scott Tuke; Robert Sulcer in tracing how the symptomatic reading of signifiers within late Victorian sexology infects the moralizing practice of close reading endorsed by modernist critics such as T. S. Eliot, I. A. Richards, and F. R. Leavis; and Andrew Hewitt in arguing the importance of the body of the male dancer in Vaslav Nijinsky's choreography each add another side to the story, by now familiar, of how male and female homophobia are constitutive of literary and critical modernism. True, they are. But so is the affirmation of same-sex desire and its association with a range of radical cultural politics—for example, in the writing of Virginia Woolf, who in *Three Guineas* (1938) repudiates marriage as a profession for middle-class women at the same time that she rejects the statist and imperial definition of manhood.

Critics such as Rita Felski and the recently deceased Charles Bernheimer have argued that the (misogynistic) representation of the female body is central to modernism.[27] But Saville and Hewitt demonstrate the cultural radicalism of representations of the male body in painting and dance, respectively. These contradictory observations indicate that it is inappropriate to identify or associate a genre or period with global terms such as gender construed in binary terms or with words such as misogyny and homophobia. More likely, within genres and styles, contest is under way. Not the least significant, for contributors to and readers of this book, is the continuing struggle within English studies itself.[28] The essays in *Victorian Sexual Dissidence* attest to the ways in which revisiting the history of the cultural institutions in which we find ourselves can remind us of the political choices we daily make as well as those that are incessantly made for us whether we recognize them to be political or not.

Although in part 1 above I describe a wide range of meanings for sexual dissidence, the particular meaning the term has in Dollimore's book marks a good point of departure for *Victorian Sexual Dissidence*. In its emphasis on what it refers to as Wilde's transgressive aesthetic, Dollimore's study shares the tendency of the present collection to emphasize affirmative aspects of cultural dissidence. At the same time, problems arising from his use of historicizing terms indicate by contrast new directions that are opened by writers such as Prins and Hewitt. Dollimore's book is well known for the connection that he makes between Wilde and Terry Eagleton's classic characterization of the postmodern subject of our own fin de siècle. Eagleton's subject is "a dispersed, decentered network of libidinal attachments, emptied of ethical substance and psychical interiority, the ephemeral function of this or that act of consumption, media experience, sexual relationship, trend or fashion" (Dollimore, 71). Dollimore contends that in his essays Wilde portrays the subject in much the same way as part of his campaign against the unified subject of bourgeois ideology. Wilde's dispersed subject is both inverted and perverse. "Deviant desire reacts against, disrupts, and displaces from within; rather than seeking to escape the repressive ordering of sexuality, Wilde reinscribes himself within and relentlessly inverts the binaries upon which the ordering depends."[29] Dollimore contrasts this mode of sexual dissidence with the tendency—which he associates with homosexual apology within literary modernism—to assert that sexuality constitutes the truth of a subject's being.

This schema is highly attractive insofar as it makes Wilde our contemporary. Nonetheless, it is caught within the terms—modernist versus postmodern, authentic versus dispersed subject—of its own analysis. To stay for a moment within the terms of a negative deconstruction, the binary opposition between centered and decentered subject that one finds in Eagleton and in Fredric Jameson's even more influential presentation operates within the heterosexual/ homosexual binary as described by Sedgwick. The subject of political agency, whose passing is mourned by Jameson, is both gendered (as masculine) and sexed (as heterosexual); conversely, the subject immersed in sensation is a displaced figure of the (male) homosexual in a moment of abandon.[30] The opposition implies a need to rethink sex and gender in other ways, but Jameson does not draw this inference. As a result, he is able to see no way out of the impasse of agency that he posits. Even staying within the terms of the heterosexual/ homosexual binary, however, the postmodern subject may be characterized not as a dispersed but as a split or even as a schizophrenic subject.[31] The posthistory of Wilde's transgressive subject underwrites the plausibility of Dollimore's identification. But this history also suggests the need to demystify Jameson (and Eagleton's) account of the loss of masculine agency. Furthermore, since Luce Irigaray, one of the most important poststructuralist feminist theorists, likewise has argued that women are, by definition, schizophrenic subjects, further analysis requires rethinking the place of both men and women (including the place of same-sex desire) within a sex/gender system.[32]

The link that Dollimore draws between modernism and commitment to the concept of a unified self makes sense with reference to literary critics such as Richards, whose writing is closely associated with the academic appropriation of male literary modernism (68–70). It also makes sense within the canon of minority identity-formation in gay and lesbian social studies. When Ken Plummer, for example, offers a three-part model for the coming-out narratives of gay and lesbian subjects in the 1970s, he calls these stories "modernist tales."[33] Nonetheless, Stephen Gordon, the presumably authentic lesbian protagonist of Radclyffe Hall's *The Well of Loneliness* (1928), is just as schizophrenic as Simone de Beauvoir's modern woman and Luce Irigaray's postmodern one. The binary oppositions centered/decentered, modernist/postmodern are inadequate to characterize texts and the actualities they imply.

As Oliver Buckton argues in his contribution to the book, this conceptual limit is suggested again in a key misreading by Dollimore of a text by Wilde. Dollimore argues that, at the end of his career, Wilde in his letter from prison relapses into conventional views of the subject. For Dollimore, the Wilde of *De Profundis* exemplifies the Foucauldian confessional subject, wholly subordinated within the play of discursive practices. *De Profundis* "involves a conscious renunciation of [Wilde's] transgressive aesthetic and a reaffirmation of tradition as focused in the depth model of identity" (95). In this text, however, Wilde's play of masks continues unabated while the roles he does play—both his own and Bosie's—provide yet one more example of a split, possibly schizophrenic, subject. To make this suggestion is implicitly to argue for the importance of remembering the links that join a Wilde to a Virginia Woolf and a Radclyffe Hall—and Victorian Aestheticism to modernism. Recalling that in the 1890s the term "decadence" was linked to what one participant later referred to as "ultra-modernism," Shand-Tucci adapts Richard Ellmann's suggestions that the decadents were "'not decadents but counter-decadents'; for did they not deliberately go 'through decadence to come out on the other side'? and was not the other side modernism?"[34]

Sexual dissidents of the 1890s, who lapsed into conformity as they grew older, often thought that their efforts to create a new culture had come to naught. Yet as one of the friends of his youth wrote to Ralph Adams Cram, architect of the Cathedral of St. John The Divine in New York City, in 1936: "What remains with me is the vision itself, and the firm belief that we would now be living in a better world had we been able to make the vision a reality."[35] Had artists such as Wilde and later Hall been successful in evading the violent effects of the discursive construction of homosexuality, then modernism too would have been different. It would have been: more open to the reworking of accessible genres such as those in which Wilde wrote; less pressured to represent heterosexual culture; much less defensive about articulations of sexual dissidence; less liable to represent sexual desire in ontological terms; and although doubtless still homophobic, differently and less relentlessly so. While this alternative future of modernism is in a sense hypothetical, in another sense it escapes the nostalgic defeat of Cram's correspondent. The history of sexual and cultural dissidence not only could have been but indeed is otherwise than we recognize. The resilience and inventiveness of the writers and artists who figure in the following pages make me think so.

Notes

1. Eve Kosofsky Sedgwick, *Between Men*, 161–79.

2. In a classic formulation, Weeks writes: "The concept of heterosexuality was invented (*after* the former [i.e. after homosexuality]) to describe, apparently, what we now call bisexuality, and then 'normality'" (*Sexuality and Its Discontents*, 69). See also Jonathan Katz, *Invention of Heterosexuality*.

3. Kathy Alexis Psomiades, *Beauty's Body;* William A. Cohen, *Sexscandal*, 73–129.

4. Michel Foucault, *History of Sexuality*, vol. 1, 43.

5. Eve Kosofsky Sedgwick, *Epistemology of the Closet*, 9. Unless otherwise noted, page references to Sedgwick in this introduction are to this volume.

6. For example, contemporary attacks on Aesthetic "luxury" were immediately translated into complaints about the current generation of middle-class *jeunes filles*. See Eliza Lynn Linton, "Girl of the Period," 172–76; Linda Dowling, *Hellenism and Homosexuality*.

7. For example, Kathryn Bond Stockton, *God between Their Lips*.

8. Eve Kosofsky Sedgwick, *Between Men*, 20; Gayle Rubin criticizes this assumption in "The Traffic in Women": "It is important . . . to maintain a distinction between the human capacity and necessity to create a sexual world, and the empirically oppressive ways in which sexual worlds have been organized. Patriarchy subsumes both meanings into the same term." Rubin goes on to argue that the term should be confined to a specific context: "Patriarchy is a specific form of male dominance, and the use of the term ought to be confined to the Old Testament–type pastoral nomads from whom the term comes, or groups like them. Abraham was a Patriarch—one old man whose absolute power over wives, children, herds, and dependents was an aspect of the institution of fatherhood as defined in the social group in which he lived" (168). As Yopie Prins points out in her essay, Sedgwick's introduction in later writing of terms such as "the

avunculate" indicates a changing sense of the possibilities of literary and other genealogies (Sedgwick, "Tales of the Avunculate"). See also the introduction to Sedgwick, *Novel Gazing.*

9. My reservation is not about the validity of either argument but about the assumption that difference is *always* articulated in a binary structure.

10. I consider some of the possibilities of sexual-aesthetic discourse in 19th-century writing in England in *Masculine Desire.*

11. Robert Young, *Colonial Desire,* 11.

12. Richard Jenkyns, "Points of Order," 38.

13. Sedgwick, *Epistemology of the Closet,* 14, 48–59; see also *Between Men,* 19–20.

14. For example, Sedgwick, *Between Men,* 201–17.

15. Cf. Gayle Rubin's remark: "As soon as you get away from the presumptions of heterosexuality, or a simple hetero–homo opposition, differences in sexual conduct are not very intelligible in terms of binary models. Even the notion of a continuum is not a good model for sexual variations; one needs one of those mathematical models they do now with strange topographies and convoluted shapes. There needs to be some kind of model that is not binary, because sexual variation is a system of many differences, not just a couple of salient ones" ("Sexual Traffic," 70–71).

16. D. A. Miller, *Novel and Police,* 17–18. The routing of antihomophobic inquiry through critical theory can also be drawn in relation to the movement in literary criticism associated with the name of Stephen Greenblatt and known as the New Historicism. Much of the work in antihomophobic inquiry was carried on by writers at Stanford or Berkeley—where Greenblatt teaches; and major articles by Miller, Craft, and Sedgwick were first published in *Representations,* a journal closely associated with this critical practice. Jonathan Dollimore's earlier work in Renaissance studies is also New Historicist in character. In *Sexual Dissidence* (1991, 285–86), he indicates how his shift to an emphasis on what he terms a "transgressive aesthetic" occurred as a result of a critical rereading of Greenblatt's chapter on Christopher Marlowe in *Renaissance Self-Fashioning* (1980).

17. The clause reads: "quel effects réciproques de pouvoir and de savoir ils assurent" (*Histoire de la sexualité,* vol. 1, *La volonté de savoir* [Paris: Gallimard, 1976], p. 135). I would like to thank Linda Dowling for puzzling over this sentence with me.

18. *Webster's New World Dictionary of the American Language* (Cleveland: World Publishing Co., 1959), s.vv. "assure," "insure" (modified).

19. For Foucault's interest in sado-masochism, see David Halperin, *Saint Foucault,* 85–91. It is a sign of the times that, in this 1995 book, Foucault's interest in SM is dubbed *"queer praxis"* (86); in an important interview that Foucault gave in 1982, he discusses SM within the context of gay politics (Foucault, "Sexual Choice, Sexual Act").

20. Foucault, *Use of Pleasure,* 12, 18.

21. Regenia Gagnier defines hegemony in *Subjectivities,* 5–6.

22. Foucault, *Politics, Philosophy, Culture,* 59.

23. I addressed the need to (re-)claim Foucault as a specifically gay theorist in a panel, in which Sedgwick and I presented papers, at the annual meeting of the Modern Language Association in San Francisco on December 29, 1987.

24. Quoted in Cohen, "Foucauldian Necrologies," 93. Cohen's study of representation during the Wilde trials, *Talk on the Wilde Side,* is more in the vein of the Foucault of *Discipline and Punish.*

25. Judith R. Walkowitz, *City of Dreadful Delight,* 135–69; Elaine Showalter, *Daughters of Decadence,* x.

26. Douglass Shand-Tucci, *Boston Bohemia,* 414.

27. Felski, *Gender of Modernity,* 112–113.

28. Dollimore, *Sexual Dissidence,* 68–70; Richard Dellamora, *Apocalyptic Overtures.* On the latter, see Robert Sulcer, *Victorian Studies* 39 (winter 1996): 241–42. Subsequent references to Dollimore in the text, unless otherwise noted, refer to this book.

29. Jonathan Dollimore, "Different Desires," 31.

30. Dellamora, *Apocalyptic Overtures,* 129–53.

31. Ibid., 151–53.

32. The difficult, contradictory relationship between being-woman and becoming-woman otherwise is central to French feminist theory as it emerges in the aftermath of World War II in Simone de Beauvoir's *The Second Sex* (1949). See Butler, "Variations on Sex and Gender," 128–34.

33. Ken Plummer, *Telling Sexual Stories,* chapter four, "Coming Out, Breaking the Silence and Recovering: Introducing Some Modernist Tales," 49–61.

34. Shand-Tucci, citing the onetime Harvard Bohemian composer Daniel Gregory Mason writing in 1936, and also Richard Ellmann, in *Boston Bohemia,* 413.

35. Ibid., citing Thayer Lincoln.

References

Bernheimer, Charles. *Figures of Ill-repute: Representing Prostitution in Nineteenth-century France.* Cambridge: Harvard University Press, 1989.

Butler, Judith. "Variations on Sex and Gender: Beauvoir, Wittig, and Foucault." In *Feminism as Critique: Essays on the Politics of Gender in Late-capitalist Societies,* ed. Seyla Benhabib and Drucilla Cornell, 128–42. Cambridge: Polity Press, 1987.

Cohen, Ed. "Foucauldian Necrologies: 'Gay' 'Politics'? Politically Gay?" *Textual Practice* 2 (1988): 87–101.

———. *Talk on the Wilde Side: Toward a Genealogy of a Discourse on Male Sexualities.* New York: Routledge, 1993.

Cohen, William A. *Sex Scandal: The Private Parts of Victorian Fiction.* Durham, N.C.: Duke University Press, 1996.

Craft, Christopher. "Alias Bunbury: Desire and Termination in *The Importance of Being Earnest. Representations* 31 (summer 1990): 19–46.

————. *Another Kind of Love: Male Homosexual Desire in English Discourse, 1850–1920.* Berkeley and Los Angeles: University of California Press, 1994. [The book includes essays, in revised form, originally published in journals in the preceding decade.]

————. "'Kiss Me with Those Red Lips': Gender and Inversion in Bram Stoker's *Dracula.*" *Representations* 8 (fall 1984): 107–33.

Dellamora, Richard. *Apocalyptic Overtures: Sexual Politics and The Sense of an Ending.* New Brunswick, N.J.: Rutgers University Press, 1994.

————. *Masculine Desire: The Sexual Politics of Victorian Aestheticism.* Chapel Hill: University of North Carolina Press, 1990.

Dollimore, Jonathan. "Different Desires: Subjectivity and Transgression in Wilde and Gide." *Genders* 2 (summer 1988): 24–41.

————. *Sexual Dissidence: Augustine to Wilde, Freud to Foucault.* Oxford: Clarendon, 1991.

Dowling, Linda. *Hellenism and Homosexuality in Victorian Oxford.* Ithaca: Cornell University Press, 1994.

Eagleton, Terry. "Capitalism, Modernism, and Postmodernism." In *Against the Grain,* 131–47. London: Verso, 1986.

Felski, Rita. *The Gender of Modernity.* Cambridge: Harvard University Press, 1995.

Foucault, Michel. *Discipline and Punish.* Trans. Alan Sheridan. New York: Pantheon, 1977.

————. *The History of Sexuality,* vol. 1, *An Introduction.* Trans. Robert Hurley. New York: Vintage, 1980.

————. "My Body, This Paper, This Fire." Trans. Geoff Bennington. *Oxford Literary Review* 4 (1979): 9–28.

————. "On the Genealogy of Ethics: An Overview of Work in Progress." In *The Foucault Reader,* ed. Paul Rabinow, 340–72. New York: Pantheon, 1984.

————. *Politics, Philosophy, Culture: Interviews and Other Writings 1977–1984.* Trans. Alan Sheridan et al. and ed. Lawrence D. Kritzman. New York: Routledge, 1988.

————. "Sexual Choice, Sexual Act: An Interview with Michel Foucault." With James O'Higgins. *Salmagundi* 58–59 (1982–1983): 10–24.

————. *The History of Sexuality,* vol. 2, *The Use of Pleasure.* Trans. Robert Hurley. New York: Vintage, 1986.

Gagnier, Regenia. *Idylls of the Market Place: Oscar Wilde and the Victorian Public.* Stanford: Stanford University Press, 1996.

————. *Subjectivities: A History of Self-representation in Britain, 1832–1920.* New York: Oxford University Press, 1991.

Girard, René. *Deceit, Desire, and the Novel: Self and Other in Literary Structure.* Trans. Yvonne Freccero. Baltimore: Johns Hopkins University Press, 1972.

Greenblatt, Stephen. *Renaissance Self-fashioning from More to Shakespeare.* Chicago: University of Chicago Press, 1980.

Halperin, David M. *Saint Foucault: Towards a Gay Hagiography.* New York: Oxford University Press, 1995.

Jenkyns, Richard. "Points of Order." *New York Review of Books* (November 20, 1997): 38.

Katz, Jonathan. *The Invention of Heterosexuality.* Foreword by Gore Vidal and afterword by Lisa Duggan. New York: Plume, 1996.

Linton, Eliza Lynn. "The Girl of the Period." In *"Criminals, Idiots, Women, and Minors": Victorian Writing by Women on Women.* Ed. Susan Hamilton, 172–76. Peterborough, Ont.: Broadview Press, 1995.

Martin, Robert K. *The Homosexual Tradition in American Poetry.* Austin: University of Texas Press, 1979.

Miller, D. A. "'*Cage aux folles*': Sensation and Gender in Wilkie Collins's *The Woman in White.*" *Representations* 14 (spring 1986): 107–36.

———. *The Novel and the Police.* Berkeley and Los Angeles: University of California Press, 1988. [The book reprints a number of essays delivered as papers and/or published earlier in the decade.]

Plummer, Ken. *The Making of the Modern Homosexual.* London: Hutchinson, 1981.

———. *Telling Sexual Stories: Power, Change and Social Worlds.* London: Routledge, 1995.

Psomiades, Kathy Alexis. *Beauty's Body: Femininity and Representation in British Aestheticism.* Stanford: Stanford University Press, 1997.

Rubin, Gayle. "The Traffic in Women: Notes on the 'Political Economy' of Sex." In *Toward an Anthropology of Women.* Ed. Rayna R. Reiter, 157–219. New York: Monthly Review Press, 1975.

———. "Sexual Traffic." Interview with Judith Butler. *Differences* 6 (2–3) (1994): 62–99.

Sedgwick, Eve Kosofsky. *Between Men: English Literature and Male Homosocial Desire.* New York: Columbia University Press, 1985. [The book reprints, in revised form, a number of essays delivered as papers and/or published earlier in the decade.]

———. *Epistemology of the Closet.* Berkeley and Los Angeles: University of California Press, 1990.

———, ed. *Novel Gazing: Queer Readings in Fiction.* Durham, N.C.: Duke University Press, 1997.

———. "Tales of the Avunculate: Queer Tutelage in *The Importance of Being Earnest.*" In *Tendencies,* 52–72. Durham, N.C.: Duke University Press, 1993.

Shand-Tucci, Douglass. *Boston Bohemia, 1881–1900: Ralph Adams Cram: Life and Architecture.* Amherst: University of Massachusetts Press, 1995.

Showalter, Elaine, ed. *Daughters of Decadence: Women Writers of the Fin-de-Siècle.* London: Virago Press, 1993.

Stockton, Kathryn Bond. *God between Their Lips: Desire between Women in Irigaray, Brontë, and Eliot.* Stanford: Stanford University Press, 1994.

Symonds, John Addington. *Studies of the Greek Poets.* Vol. 2. New York: Harper and Brothers, 1880.

Vanita, Ruth. *Sappho and the Virgin Mary: Same-Sex Love and the English Literary Imagination.* New York: Columbia University Press, 1996.

Veblen, Thorstein. *The Theory of the Leisure Class.* Introduction by Robert Lekachman. New York: Penguin, 1979.

Walkowitz, Judith. *City of Dreadful Delight: Narratives of Sexual Danger in Late Victorian London.* Chicago: University of Chicago Press, 1992.

Warner, Michael. Introduction. In *Fear of a Queer Planet: Queer Politics and Social Theory,* vii–xxxi. Minneapolis: University of Minnesota Press, 1993.

Weeks, Jeffrey. *Coming Out: Homosexual Politics in Britain, from the Nineteenth Century to the Present.* London: Quartet Books, 1977.

———. "Inverts, Perverts, and Mary-Annes: Male Prostitutes and the Regulation of Homosexuality in England in the Nineteenth and Early Twentieth Centuries." *Journal of Homosexuality* 6 (1980–81): 113–34.

———. *Sex, Politics, and Society: The Regulation of Sexuality since 1800.* New York: Longmans, 1981.

———. *Sexuality and Its Discontents: Meanings, Myths and Modern Sexualities.* London: Routledge and Kegan Paul, 1985.

Wilde, Oscar. *De Profundis and Other Writings.* Introduction by Hesketh Pearson. London: Penguin, 1986.

Young, Robert J. C. *Colonial Desire: Hybridity in Theory, Culture and Race.* London: Routledge, 1995.

PART ONE

Re-gendering Aestheticism

ONE

"Still Burning from This Strangling Embrace": Vernon Lee on Desire and Aesthetics

KATHY ALEXIS PSOMIADES

As far as women are concerned, to read the scholarship on the sexual politics of aestheticism produced over the last ten years is to encounter two very different aestheticisms. On the one hand, critics like Richard Dellamora and Jonathan Dollimore describe a liberatory homo-apologetic aestheticism that ultimately benefits both men and women, through its realization that "motives of desire imply the emancipation of women as well"[1] and through its tendency to destabilize the dominant paradigms of bourgeois subjectivity.[2] On the other hand, feminist scholars like Griselda Pollock and Elaine Showalter see an aestheticism that, rather than liberating women, insists on their status as objects of a heterosexual masculine desire and misogynistically devalues them.[3] True, these different approaches tend to deal with very different authors, so that one might argue that there really are two aestheticisms, a liberatory one produced by Walter Pater and Oscar Wilde that disrupts gender norms, and a conservative one produced by Dante Gabriel Rossetti and the decadent poets that reinforces the status quo. But other scholars, like Thaïs Morgan, have argued that a liberatory homo-apologetic aestheticism might, but does not necessarily, invest itself in women's emancipation; or they have gone much further, to claim as Rita Felski does that aestheticism's liberatory sexual politics rely on a devaluation of the feminine and occur at the expense of "real" women.[4] In these readings, aestheticism's sexual politics may be liberatory, but more for men than for women.

In this essay, I will show how the work of Vernon Lee (Violet Paget, 1856–1935) complicates any easy opposition between liberatory and conservative aestheticisms and complicates too our ideas about Victorian sexual dissidence. Vernon Lee violently repudiated what she called "art for art's sake," the Pre-Raphaelite aestheticism of D. G. Rossetti, Algernon Charles Swinburne, and Edward Burne-Jones, but she made that repudiation a part of her own claim to aesthetic expertise. She was a friend and admirer of Walter Pater and seems to have constructed her relations with her many female admirers on a pedagogic model, yet she insisted on the Platonic idealistic nature of these relationships. She is described by admirers and enemies alike as eschewing physical contact with the women she admired, yet she produced a theory of the aesthetic grounded in the congress between female bodies. Many who knew her described her as suffering from her refusal to acknowledge the sexual nature of her attraction to other women, yet she seems to have lived quite openly in her romantic friendships, appearing always in man-tailored clothes and short hair, exercising, despite her "plainness," considerable fascination for her admirers for much of her life. She was also a successful and respected writer of both fiction and cultural criticism.[5]

In this essay, I address two central moments of engagement with aestheticism in Vernon Lee's writing: her engagement primarily with "straight" Pre-Raphaelite aestheticism in *Miss Brown* (1884) and her engagement with Paterian impressionism in her collaborative efforts with Clementina Anstruther-Thomson to ground the category of the aesthetic in the feminine perception of a feminine body in "Beauty and Ugliness" (1897) and *Art and Man* (1924). My focus in these texts is on how aesthetic experience is linked to desire between women, a desire specifically defined through and against a purity polemic that condemns and reimagines sexual activity. Rejecting Pre-Raphaelite aestheticism's heterosexual imperative, Vernon Lee is nevertheless fascinated and inspired by its depictions of the female body as the object of aesthetic/erotic desire; embracing Pater's location of the aesthetic in individual sensation and same-sex desire, she approaches the body of the beloved obliquely. Her work broadens our notion of aestheticism and our sense of the possibilities it offers both women and men; it also reminds us that sexual dissidence takes many, sometimes contradictory, forms.

Miss Brown

Vernon Lee's 1884 anti-aestheticist novel, *Miss Brown*, explicitly criticizes Pre-Raphaelite aestheticism's sexual politics, particularly its use of the female body as the raw material for an art that exploits women as objects of heterosexual masculine desire. Its heroine, Anne Brown, remains cold to the solicitations of aesthetes who would eroticize and corrupt her but cannot halt their attempts to turn her into images and texts that alienate her from her own appearance. Yet Anne's "real" body—the body that isn't a visual object, but rather a subject constituted by physical sensation—also owes much to Pre-Raphaelite aestheticism. When Anne finally experiences herself as embodied, she experiences that body as the location of a lesbian desire at once insistently textual and insistently perverse. All sex in this novel can only be brought forth on the condition that it is loudly condemned—and the only sex that moves the ever-pure Anne is her bodily contact with another woman.[6]

The novel begins with a male artist, Walter Hamlin: it is through his eyes that we first see Anne Brown, the nursery governess who has the misfortune to possess the full lips, "hair of dark wrought-iron," pale skin, "neck round and erect like a tower," and monumental stature depicted in Dante Gabriel Rossetti's paintings of Jane Morris.[7] Hamlin sees these features as a motive for art, a beautiful surface under which should lie beautiful depths: indeed, he pays for the education to create these depths. But inhabiting this body, according to Vernon Lee, is far different from looking at it. By shifting the novel's point of view to Anne, Lee is able to develop a feminist critique of aestheticism based on the distance between aestheticized femininity and embodied female existence. Dressed by Hamlin in aesthetic attire, Anne can barely recognize herself:

> Miss Brown was by this time tolerably accustomed to the eccentric garb of aesthetic circles, and she firmly believed that it was the only one which a self-respecting woman might wear; but when she saw the dress which Hamlin had designed for her, she could not help shrinking back in dismay. It was of that Cretan silk, not much thicker than muslin, which is woven in minute wrinkles of palest yellow white; it was made, it seemed to her, more like a night-gown than anything else, shapeless and yet clinging with large and small folds, and creases like those of damp sculptor's drapery, or the garments of Mantegna's women. . . . Anne walked to the mirror. She was almost terrified at the figure which met her. That colossal woman, with wrinkled drapery clinging to her in half-antique, half-medieval guise,—that great solemn, theatrical creature, could that be herself? . . . Why did that dress make such a difference to him? Why did he care so much more for her because she had it on? Did he care for her only as a sort of live picture? she thought bitterly. (1:305–9)

Anne shrinks from the image of herself that masculine desire has made because it elevates the textual body (theatrical, costumed, pictorial, sculptural) over the natural body (herself) and at the same time opens both bodies up to the erotic gaze of masculine desire. The clinging wrinkles, creases, and folds of the gown are indecent both in that they highlight the shape of the natural body, and in that they substitute for it, figuring the fold of the female sex itself. Later, Anne thinks with a chill of "that line of Rossetti's which Hamlin admired more than any other—'Beauty like hers is genius,'" because it implies that Hamlin wants from her "that sort of passion which he had spoken of to revive him and his art" (2:277). Like the speaker of Christina Rossetti's "In an Artist's Studio," Vernon Lee here implies that aestheticism is based on an erotic theft, a feeding off the bodies of women that vampire-like wastes the real body (in Rossetti's words "wan with waiting") for the sake of the textual body and for the satisfaction of what Lee sees as a rapacious masculinity.[8] Yet believers in the value of the real over the textual fair no better in *Miss Brown* than aesthetes do. The representative of political economy, Anne's burly, hypermasculine, factory-owning and social-reforming cousin, Richard, who wants to take Anne away

from aestheticism and into the world of politics and social action, is not ultimately invested with more moral authority than the artist. For Anne is as re-
pulsed by Richard Brown's declaration of love as she is by aestheticism's ex-
cesses:

> Richard Brown loved her, wanted her; it was the old nauseous story over
> again; the sympathy, the comradeship, the quiet brotherly and sisterly
> affection had all been a sham, a sham for her and for himself. . . . Her
> cousin Dick had preached against selfish aestheticism, had talked her into
> his positivistic philanthropy . . . what for? that he might satisfy his whim
> of possessing her. (3:75–76)

Male avant-garde sensibility and normative bourgeois masculinity both participate in the nauseous story of masculine heterosexism, a selfish urge to possess
women as gratifying objects, to use them to satisfy needs Anne finds both perverse and trivial.

Paradoxically, it is the very extension of the novel's critique of eroticism beyond aesthetic eroticism to heterosexual eroticism more generally that swings
the novel round to an extraordinarily aestheticist refusal of the "natural" body:

> Some few women seem to be born to have been men, or at least not to
> have been women. To them love, if it come, will be an absorbing passion,
> but a passion only of brief duration, the mere momentary diversion into a
> personal and individual channel of a force which constitutes the whole
> moral and intellectual existence, whose object is an unattainable ideal of
> excellence, and whose field is the whole of the world in which there is
> injustice, and callousness, and evil. . . . They are indeed sent into the
> world (if any of us is ever sent for any purpose) to be its Joans of Arc—to
> kindle from their pure passion a fire of enthusiasm as passionate, but purer
> than it is given to men to kindle: they are not intended to be, except as a
> utilization of what is fatally wasted, either wives or mothers. Masculine
> women, mere men in disguise, they are not: the very strength and purity
> of their nature, its intensity as of some undiluted spirit, is dependent upon
> their cleaner and narrower woman's nature, upon their narrowness and
> obstinacy of woman's mind; they are, and can only be, true women; but
> women without woman's instincts and wants, sexless—women made not
> for man, but for humankind. Anne Brown was one of these. (2:307–9)

From its opening sentence, the passage struggles to convey the blurring of genders in these women, not masculine, but true women, who nevertheless are
born to be men, or at least not to be women, or at least not for men, or at
least not with "woman's instincts and wants." In the end, "sexless" conveys the
destabilizing effect this new kind of woman has on gender categories (sexless =
neither one sex nor the other), a refusal of reproductive heterosexual femininity
(sexless = as if without reproductive organs), and a refusal of sex itself (sex-

less = without sexual instincts and wants). Yet in the context of aestheticism, "sexless" refers not merely to the absence of sex, but to the presence of idealized same-sex desire, as in Walter Pater's essay on Winckelmann:

> The beauty of the Greek statues was a sexless beauty: the statues of the gods had the least traces of sex. Here [in Winckelmann] there is a moral sexlessness, a kind of ineffectual wholeness of nature, yet with a true beauty and significance of its own.[9]

Winckelmann's "sexlessness" gives him an affinity for the sexless Greek statues, allows him to "deal with the sensuous side of art in the pagan manner," to "finger those pagan marbles with unsinged hands."[10] By using the word, Vernon Lee propels Anne Brown into an alternative aesthetic-erotic realm in which "purity" signals sexually dissident desires. But whereas Winckelmann remains unsinged and unfevered, Miss Brown and the novel that bears her name burn. "Want," "corruption," and "shame," the absence of which constitute Winckelmann's serenity,[11] characterize Anne's same-sex erotic experience in *Miss Brown*.

For when Anne Brown is forced to feel herself a "real" body, rather than an image: a feeling, breathing body with sensations of its own, that body is fevered, panting for breath, shaking—not normal, not healthy. These sensations are awakened, not by any male representative of aestheticism, but by the novel's snaky villainess, Walter Hamlin's cousin, Sacha Elaguine:

> "I want *you*," and Sacha flung her arms round Anne's neck, and drew her dark head close to her own little pale yellow one. Anne felt her arms tighten passionately round her, her little hand tighten convulsively around her neck, as if the half-fainting woman would throttle her,—but she felt no fear, only a vague, undefinable repulsion. Madame Elaguine sighed a long sigh of relief, and loosened her hold; but she kept Anne's face near hers, and kissed her with hot lips on the forehead. (2:292–93)

Even as she describes Anne's recoil, Vernon Lee evokes her physical sensations, the feeling of arms tightening passionately, the heat of lips on her forehead. Described always in a language of heat, shudder, scent, and strangling, Sacha's repeated embraces leave Anne's face burning and make her struggle to take breath: "A sort of shudder passed through her as her own lips touched that hot face, and grazed the light hair, which seemed to give out some faint Eastern perfume" (2:190). Masculine desire, in *Miss Brown*, tends toward the disembodiment of women, their reduction to images that can be possessed; in her relations to men, Anne reacts chiefly to her own textualization in their speech, writing, or painting. By contrast, Anne's relation to Sacha is always a relation between bodies: it is problematic for Anne precisely because in making her focus on her own physical sensations, it embodies her. Richard Brown and

Walter Hamlin disgust Anne with words—"the old nauseous story"—, Sacha Elaguine with touch, "like the contact of some clammy thing" (3:198). Of course "clammy" here signifies Sacha's lamia-like qualities, mentioned several times in the text, as when, for example, Sacha is described as "putting her arm around Miss Brown's neck, in her childish way, and which yet always affected Anne as might the caress of a lamia's clammy scales" (3:136). But "some clammy thing" is also Sacha's body and Sacha's sex, the clammy thing that makes Anne hot, rather than cold, "her face still burning from this strangling embrace" (3:202), the clammy thing that is the most decidedly NOT the old nauseous story of heterosexual marriage.

Ostensibly, Anne decides at the novel's end to marry Hamlin because she feels an obligation to save him from Sacha's evil influence. But there is another, more compelling reason:

> To become, therefore, the wife of Hamlin, was an intolerable self-degradation—nay a pollution; for it seemed to her, and the idea sickened her whole soul, that the moral pollution of Sacha Elaguine would be communicated to her. To become the wife of Sacha's lover! Her limbs seemed to give way, to dissolve, a horrible warm clamminess overtook her; she could not breathe, or breathed only horror. (3:280)

The "horrible warm clamminess" that Anne now feels in her own body, the orgasmic dissolving of limbs that takes her breath away, are figures both for disgust and desire. What awakens these feelings is the thought that sleeping with Hamlin will be sleeping with Sacha by proxy, in the novel's logic both the reason not to marry him, and the reason to marry him. When Hamlin finally does embrace Anne at the end of the novel, a startling last-minute substitution occurs:

> "You love me, Anne; you love me!" cried Hamlin, louder; and pressing closer to her, he put out his arms, and drew down her face to his, and kissed her, twice, thrice, a long kiss on the mouth.
>   It seemed to Anne as if she felt again the throttling arms of Sacha Elaguine about her neck, her convulsive kiss on her face, the cloud of her drowsily scented hair, stifling her. She drew back and loosened his grasp with her strong hands. (3:298)

The climactic moment of heterosexual union is spectacularly displaced by yet another experience of the arms, the kiss, the drowsily scented hair of Sacha Elaguine.

My point here is that these embraces are profoundly aestheticist at the same time as they stand in opposition to aestheticism's heterosexual plots, profoundly textual at the same time as they are visceral. Sacha has "the hands that stifle and the hair that stings" of Swinburne's dark Venus, in "Laus Veneris" (line 310).[12] Anne, "feeling her face with all her eager hair / Cleave to me clinging as a fire that clings" (lines 403–4) is Swinburne's reluctant Tannhäuser, torn between desire and the sense of damnation. Until Sacha, Anne's aestheticism is purely external: try as he might, Hamlin cannot provide her with an aestheticist subjectivity to go along with her aestheticist exterior. But Sacha makes Anne a sexually dissident aestheticist subject—not the aestheticist artwork, but the subject who consumes that artwork, who has aesthetic/erotic experiences. Like Pater's aesthetic critic, Anne is "deeply moved" by the presence of a beautiful object (Sacha is described in the language of *The Renaissance* as "curiously fascinating"). Like Tannhäuser, she knows beauty in the flesh; she can claim as the knight does, "I knew the beauty of her, what she was . . . / And in my flesh the sin of hers, alas!" (lines 310–12). Lesbian desire gives Anne a Swinburnian body in *Miss Brown*, the body of the perverse desiring subject, the body of Tannhäuser, but also of Anactoria, embraced by Sacha-Sappho, "with such violence that Anne felt her lips almost like leeches and her teeth pressing into her cheek" (3:201).

Of course Vernon Lee's stated purpose in *Miss Brown* is to condemn, not celebrate, aestheticism's perversity. But by insistently and graphically recounting the sexual sins of the aesthetes, by locating Anne's reactions to Sacha Elaguine in her body, the novel becomes a lesbian text in the only way open to it, namely by being a perverse aestheticist text. That it can only be so by claiming to be the reverse is part of the logic of purity, a logic recognized both by Vernon Lee's nineteenth-century critics and by herself. The novel scandalized its first readers both because it seemed to accuse specific writers and artists of depravity, and because it seemed to reveal its author's obsession with the sexual matters she claimed to deplore. Henry James, to whom, embarrassingly, the novel was dedicated, wrote to Vernon Lee:

> You take the aesthetic business too seriously, too tragically, and above all with too great an implication of sexual motives . . . you have impregnated all those people too much with the sexual, the basely erotic preoccupation: your hand was over violent, the touch of life is lighter.[13]

What Vernon Lee has done is to project onto the lives of the aesthetes in Bohemian London the world these aesthetes created in their art and poetry, a world in which art can never be taken too seriously, too tragically, or too erotically. What James hints here is that she herself is the source of the perverse eroticism she attributes to the aesthetes; she impregnates them with her own sexual preoccupation, a notion enforced by the masturbatory trope of the violent hand. The prude is just a pervert who refuses to admit it.

Vernon Lee herself considered this possibility in a journal entry written in 1885:

Here I am accused of having, in simplicity of heart, written, with a view to moralize the world, an immoral book; accused of having done more mischief by setting my readers' imagination hunting up evil, than I could possibly do by calling on their sympathies to hate that mischief: accused, in short, of doing, in a minor degree the very things for which I execrate Zola or Maupassant. . . .

Am I not perhaps mistaking that call of the beast for the call of God; may there not, at the bottom of this seemingly scientific, philanthropic, idealizing, decidedly noble-looking nature of mine, be something base, dangerous, disgraceful that is cozening me? Benn says that I am *obsessed* by the sense of the impurity of the world and that in transferring this obsession to my readers, I am really enervating not strengthening them. May this be true? may I be indulging a mere depraved appetite for the loathsome while I *fancy* that I am studying diseases and probing wounds for the sake of diminishing both? Perhaps. . . .

The question is, which of these two, the prudes or the easy-goers, are themselves normal, healthy?[14]

Lack of self-consciousness, the unpardonable feminine sin, makes the writer think her book is pure when it is really perverse. But its perversity is then, paradoxically, a sign of her own unacknowledged perversity. *Miss Brown* would then be a lesbian text both because of the scenes it describes, and because of the authorial obsessions it reveals. The final question makes the prude not the opposite of the pervert, but rather the opposite of the easy-goer, the person who doesn't care about the sexual practices of others. What makes prudes and perverts alike, the passage seems partly to acknowledge, is caring too much.[15]

Furthermore, the medical language of studying disease and probing wounds situates the body in question as always other to the writer/critic/artist, who remains at a remove. It seems significant here that the character in the novel with whom Vernon Lee reportedly identified was not the pure Anne Brown, but rather the perverse artist, Walter Hamlin.[16] Without arguing the merits of this claim, I would point out that it acts as a claim to be outside the bodily activity of the novel and yet inside it. Hamlin is in many ways beside the point, a figure only made exciting by his snaky unacknowledged double; a figure who disappears at the point of bodily contact. Yet insofar as to be Hamlin is also to be Sacha, it means having a physical effect on the otherwise chilly and impervious Miss Brown, and yet to be able to distance oneself from that effect. The possibilities for cross-gender identification are increased by the novel's insistence that Anne, Sacha, and Walter all mingle masculine and feminine qualities in an androgyny repeatedly associated with the figures depicted in aestheticist painting.

Miss Brown draws on aestheticist articulations of perverse and lesbian sexuality to imagine what an aestheticism based in female bodies and their desires might look like, but it must do so under the guise of a condemnation of perverse eroticism. Its purity ethos is both a sign of the violence performed by sexism and homophobia, and a sign of resistance to that violence, as it allows the novel to tell its shocking story anyway. Sexual dissidence emerges in the novel's refusal to exclude normative heterosexual desire from its general condemnation of sex, and in its insistent descriptions of the physical sensations occasioned by the only bodily contact it narrates, contact between women.

Art and Man

As we turn from *Miss Brown*'s dark eroticism to the more rarified world of Lee's aesthetic theory, we turn paradoxically to the question of Lee's own sexual practice. For in "Beauty and Ugliness" and especially in the introduction to *Art and Man,* Lee revises the connection between same-sex desire and the appreciation of art put forth in Pater's "Winckelmann" to base aesthetic appreciation in women's same-sex desire. Yet Lee faces complications Pater does not, because the purity polemic labels sexual desire "bestial" and considers this bestiality the sole province of men.[17] Lee's weaving together of a liberatory aestheticism on the one hand and a seemingly antithetical purity ethos on the other complicates our reading of aestheticism's sexual politics.

Burdett Gardner's 1954 Harvard dissertation on Vernon Lee is centrally and obsessively concerned with how her lesbianism affects her work and as such is filled with the speculations of various of Lee's contemporaries on her actual sexual practice.[18] Gardner quotes from Ethel Smyth's memoirs:

> The tragedy of her life was that without knowing it she loved the *cultes* humanly and with passion; but being the stateliest and chastest of beings she refused to face the fact, or indulge in the most innocent demonstrations of affection, preferring to create a fiction that to her these friends were merely intellectual necessities.[19]

He also quotes Irene Cooper Willis, Lee's companion and executor, who insists "Vernon was homosexual, but she never faced up to sexual facts. She was perfectly pure. I think it would have been better if she had acknowledged it to herself."[20] Willis calls Lee "prudish" and "frustrated" and agrees that she shunned physical contact. In chapter 6 of Gardner's dissertation, Smyth's and Willis's hypotheses are supplemented by letters to and from Lee from many of her "cultes" and friends all complaining of her coldness and her tendency to intellectualize her passions, many advising her to be more human in her relations to the women she loves. For Gardner, the documents of Vernon Lee's numerous friendships (Gardner says he has actually only discussed "fewer than one quarter of her 'romances' with women") all add up to a picture of a woman thwarted by the demands of Victorian morality from getting what she must have really wanted. Yet looked at in another light, these documents depict a woman at the center of a remarkable community, based in Italy and England, in which women's romantic attachments to each other exist openly. Lovers come and go in droves, partings are often stormy, but two constants remain: there are always people to be in love with, and (perhaps more importantly for real happiness) there are always people with whom one can discuss and analyze new relationships in minute detail.

What's remarkable about these many discussions of Vernon Lee's "refusal" of "sexual facts" is the way in which that refusal itself is hotly eroticized for the women who know her. Lee's "purity" becomes invested with everyone else's erotic desire, and the occasion for the production of erotic discourse about her. The accusation that her desires are really sexual (Vernon thinks she loves ——'s mind, but *really* she wants to boink her) is also a way of insisting that one's own desires might, but for this, be realized (I want to boink Vernon; and she (really) wants to boink me). The "problem" of Vernon's purity thus becomes a solidarity discourse for the lesbian community that surrounds her.

Gardner is thus partly right: the purity polemic is, as I said above, in part a sign of the violence of sexism and homophobia. But Lee's tendency to "intellectualize" love relationships, her refusal of physical or emotional demonstrativeness, is less a denial of sexuality than it is a sexual style. It is this sexual style that governs the conflicted and interesting relation of Vernon Lee's aesthetics to the female body.[21]

Vernon Lee's interest first in physiological, then in psychological aesthetics grew out of her relationship with Clementina Anstruther-Thomson, with whom she collaborated to produce "Beauty and Ugliness" and *Art and Man*. The process of collaboration is described in detail in the introduction to the latter work:

> I so well remember the alacrity of spirit and weariness of body—for I had neither Kit's splendid muscles nor her painter's habit of standing indefinitely looking at things—with which one early winter in London we would trudge evening after evening to the plaster casts, then still at South Kensington, and in the atmosphere of gas and fog walk and squeeze round the Hermes of Olympia, almost as if expecting him to make us, like some wonder working Madonna, a sign. . . . A sign which would be the revelation of his innermost being; and the revelation of that antique statue's being would also be—as the revelation of the primrose should have been, but wasn't—to Peter Bell, the revelation of one half of life, of the ways of the spirit. . . . Nay even much later, even in the first war-years, I have rarely returned to the Elgin Rooms, alone and full of such different thoughts, without the high lights on the polished seats, the brownness of gleams and of mists which seems immanent in that place, bringing a sudden feeling—more than a mere recollection—of our expectant wandering

among the statues in what, comparatively speaking, had been our distant
youth; a sense of the presence of Kit—a goddess among goddesses, poised
in intent contemplation before her broken and battered antique sisters;
while I sat wearily hunched up and longing for tea at the Viennese Bakery
in Holborn, but waiting with patient faith for the mystery of art to be
solved.[22]

This is less a passage about two women looking at art, than it is about a woman
watching another woman experience art. Vernon Lee, the watcher, characterizes herself as spiritual, intellectual, and existing in a state of bodily insufficiency and lack. Kit, by contrast, experiences art through her "splendid
muscles": she is athletic, physical, a creature of bodily plenitude. "A goddess
among goddesses," Kit becomes in Vernon's memory like the statues she sur-
veys, the bringer of revelation. The collaboration is based in Kit's bodily congress
with art, which forms the empirical and imaginative base for Vernon's scientific
theories. Vernon is thus both part of the scene of aesthetic contemplation and
outside of it; she awaits the same revelation Kit does, but for her that revelation
must come through Kit's body, the body that is sensitive to art and like it.[23]
    Aesthetic experience is thus based in lesbian desire, both Vernon's desire for
the embodied Kit, and both women's desire for the statues' revelation. Vernon
both inserts herself into the congress between Kit and the statues—by describing the statues with the vocabulary of bodily insufficiency as "broken and battered"—and absents herself from it—by insisting that her own desire is for tea
and cakes. Kit becomes a second Winckelmann; her body, like his hands, connects aesthetic and erotic appreciation.[24] Kit, however, doesn't finger the goddesses: her bodily congress with them is both more distanced and more intimate. When Kit looks at statues, she does so in order to ascertain how they
literally make her *feel:* what happens to her pulse, respiration, temperature,
equilibrium. Vernon provides the "psychological framework" (46) for Kit's observations from her extensive research in mental science. As imagined in *Art
and Man,* the contrast between their complementary roles is clear:

> Thus, while in galleries or museums Kit was filling book after book (usu-
> ally humble account books with ready reckoners and the year's almanac
> attached) with half-legible pencil jottings, I was wading through mental
> science. . . . The result of my readings was, however, that when Kit would
> come home after a morning in the galleries, saying, with ill-repressed ex-
> citement: "Do you know, I think I've found out something, after all" I was
> often able to tell her that she really had done so, and even the other things
> which she must set about discovering. (47)

Kit keeps an account of her physical sensations, which she communicates to
Vernon, who makes theories about those sensations and sends her out to have
more and different sensations. Unlike her bodily congress with the statue, Kit's

bodily congress with Vernon is a matter of the body made over into writing, although that writing (half-legible pencil jottings) retains more of the body's trace than the precis and abstracts Vernon makes of scientific books. Vernon's reading allows her to interpret Kit's body back to Kit so that what's exchanged here is always Kit's body, the location of both women's aesthetic/erotic experience.

Between 1888, when the two women met, and 1898, when Anstruther-Thomson broke off the relationship, they spent a great part of every year together, both at Lee's villa in Italy and travelling in Britain and on the continent. Their aesthetic experiments took place primarily in the 1890s and culminated in the publication in 1897 of their jointly authored article "Beauty and Ugliness," which uses Kit's bodily sensations to propose a theory about the biological basis of the aesthetic instinct. Lee and Anstruther-Thomson argue that the perception of form is itself a physical act: a physiological change must occur in us to produce the sense of form, so that we should say, for example, "I feel height" rather than "the object is high." In looking at a chair and perceiving its form, we make movements of the eye, we breathe, we shift our weight, and all these movements make up the act of perceiving. Some movements are more favorable to animal life than others—the body adapts to them well, enjoys them, and is made better by them: these movements occur when we perceive the beautiful. The human animal thus has a biological and a bodily need for art's healthful effects.

Physiological aesthetics translates Paterian impressionism into physiological terms. Pater's statement that art comes to you seeking nothing but to give quality to your moments as they pass is translated as follows:

> The various fine arts are arrangements, spontaneous and unconsciously evolved, for obtaining the maximum of agreeable activity on the part of our perception of Form. . . . This agreeable arrangement of agreeable movements in ourselves, this harmonious total condition of our adjustments, is, moreover, not fugitive; the presence of the work of art, its continuous or renewed perception, enforces the continuance of this agreeable total condition, obliging the simultaneous or consecutive repetition of its whole or of its parts, and excluding thereby the possibility of any other mode of being. It is to this latter fact that works of art owe their strange power of ridding us of the sense of the passing of time. The stress of partial existence is forgotten, we are no longer being driven onwards. We are safe and serene in what seems like a little railed off or mysteriously guarded circle of existence, the circle in reality of our own balanced organic functions, of a mode of life complete and satisfactory in itself.[25]

What happens here is a medicalization of the aesthetic, in which perception is not merely a physiological process, but one that produces health or sickness.

The enclosure art creates is rather like that attributed today to aerobic exercise, where the movements of the body pull the practitioner into the body, into a hypnotic state that is paradoxically closer to life, rather than farther from it. Physiological aesthetics means that art is not life's other, but rather life at its best, the organism functioning at its most perfect.

Perception is thus primarily physical, rather than purely mental. It requires knowledge of the body. The body in question is however, a very limited one—more athlete than aesthete; a body not of desire but of temperature, pulse, and respiration; a body that moves not with sex but in order to balance its equilibrium to that of a statue, or to see a landscape as it was meant to be seen. Through the movements of our bodies, we make form exist in us. Taking the art object into our bodies by miming it, we have congress with it that is physical yet pure. What allows for this is a medicalized platonism, in which the value of pure form is written on the body, so that before Greek statues we become Greek statues, developing better posture, balance, breathing, pulse, living through our own repeated movements in the world of form. Furthermore, it is through our bodily movements that we appreciate the beauty of beautiful forms, we achieve pleasure when our adjustments of balance and breathing are vitalizing. We are literally *moved* by the presence of the beautiful objects—it is our movement in their presence that allows us to perceive them as beautiful. We become the beautiful through perceiving the beautiful, and perhaps even more importantly, we become healthy.

Read as part of a trajectory that stretches from Paterian impressionism to the psychological aesthetics of I. A. Richards, "Beauty and Ugliness" is a disturbing essay. Its utilitarian aesthetics with their connections to evolutionary biology translate aestheticism's focus on same-sex erotic/aesthetic investment into an objective, scientific process. Same-sex desire is sublimated into the healthy body that appears in so many *fin de siècle* nationalist discourses.[26] Later, Lee further disembodies this aesthetics as she moves toward psychological rather than physiological aesthetics, making perception the activity of the nervous system, rather than the body as a whole, and the motion that produces it more mental than physical. So "Beauty and Ugliness" seems to be part of a fin-de-siècle tendency to biologize and psychologize experience that leads ultimately to I. A. Richards's *Principles of Literary Criticism,* which seems, physical movement aside, not very different from it.[27]

Yet although Lee's writing on aesthetics continues to be heavily invested in the connections among art, health, and purity, she herself works to undo the sublimations that occur in "Beauty and Ugliness," by insisting on making those sublimations visible. *Art and Man,* published in 1924, the same year as Richards's *Principles,* restores the production and exchange of Kit's body to the history of psychological aesthetics, making explicit the bodily base of same-sex erotic/aesthetic investment that supports it. *Art and Man* acknowledges that "Beauty and Ugliness" engages in an ultimately damaging erasure of Kit's specificity, hypothesizing that "Kit may have felt as if her very personal and living impressions were being deadened under what perhaps struck her as philosophical padding . . . when she saw her notes solidly built into my blocks of scientific matter . . ." (53–54). By framing Kit's essays and fragments with an introduction that purports to explain their theoretical basis and implications and to give an account of the collaboration of which it makes them a part, Vernon Lee writes Kit's body once again, this time for an audience to whom that body will always be visible. Indeed one of the tasks of the introduction is to place that body before the reader as a necessary accompaniment to Kit's words, as if they could not be understood without reference to her physical form. In addition to providing several portraits as illustrations, Vernon Lee begins her account with an extensive description of Kit's physical appearance:

> Besides her great height and evident great strength, that resemblance to the Venus of Milo was the first thing almost everyone remarked about her. It was the more complete that her hair was of no very noticeable color, though I think it was then light brown; and that she had the smooth whiteness of skin which goes with very deep brown eyes. . . . Her finely chiselled, rather statuesque features, and a certain—I can only call it— virginal expression made one think rather of a very beautiful and modest boy, like some of the listeners of Plato, than of a very independent woman who had mixed a great deal in a particular society which, although rich in good looks, did not pride itself upon modesty. (7–8)

Even before Vernon meets Kit, she hears her described as being like the Venus de Milo: art seems already built into her body. Physically she is statue-like; her beauty is coded as Platonic both in the sense that it seems an avatar of ideal beauty, and also in the sense that it points to an ideal same-sex desire. Indeed her body seems to connect her to all of Greek art, both the goddesses and the young men, and, in her combination of masculine and feminine traits, it connects her to Greek art's sexlessness. Furthermore, she has the same effect on Vernon that art is supposed to have, enclosing one away from the world in some higher place: "She seemed to envelop one, but always from some cool upper sphere, and quite without weight and personal warmth" (21). This is a disembodied envelopment, a disinterested nurturing, like that provided by the enclosure of art.

At the same time at which Kit's body is art object to be enjoyed at a remove by Vernon and her readers, Kit also stands in for "the real." Vernon claims to have learned from her "to make sure of what I really saw and felt, and say it, regardless of whether it had or had not been said by other writers" (32). Part of the exchange of Kit's body involves a performance of the "real body," of a blithe innocent authenticity. Much of the quoting of Kit that occurs in the introduction is this quoting of the "authentic" Kit, for the effect of contrast to the more worked and considered prose of Vernon Lee, as in the following description of Kit's sensations before the Venus de Milo:

> My connection with her is through my motor impulses, and so I feel just as much connected with her drapery as with her body; both of them balance and have movement. She does not look like an alive woman wearing inanimate drapery; but she and her drapery are one. The pressure on my feet on the ground is pressure that I see in the feet of the Statue. The lift up of my body I see done more strongly and amply in her marble body, and the steadying pressure of my head I see in a diminished degree in the poise of the statue's beautiful head. These movements I may be said to imitate, but I should find them and imitate them equally in a Renaissance monument or a medieval chalice. They are the basis of all Art. (94)

Here, once again, physiological aesthetics is located in the congress between two feminine bodies, one made of marble (she) and one of flesh (I). Kit makes her body live for us in her account of her body's likeness to a statue to which she has always been compared. Her imitation of "movements," her physical activity before art turns all art, whether it be statue, monument, or chalice, of all periods, into a feminine body with which she has congress and all aesthetic experience for a moment becomes a bodily exchange between women. That Kit is an active part of this exchange may be seen in her production of passages like this one, in which she displays her sensations before an audience as she reportedly did when giving gallery tours.

The story of collaboration told in *Art and Man* does not have a happy ending. Kit withdraws, her health giving way under the strain of collaboration. Lee reluctantly considers the possibility that Kit's central attachment to art and to herself is essentially narcissistic:

> So that the only personality in the matter was her own ways of feeling, her own modes of being, but stripped of all personal circumstances and motives, which she projected into the sights and sounds of nature and of art, only to receive them back, as if no longer her own, rather as one receives one's voice and words back from an echoing hill. Putting aside her great practical helpfulness and protective tenderness, this was the real, maybe the only, way she gave herself and received herself back; at least, so I am tempted to believe. This was the essential intercourse of her soul; and with it was perhaps connected that aloofness of hers, which suggested that she shut the doors of her own sanctuary. For this, it seems to me, rather than any personal secret thing, was what was happening therein. (14)

For Kit, Vernon Lee implies in this passage, the central pleasures of the aesthetic are narcissistic. Kit's helpfulness and tenderness are mentioned to

counter the suggestion that her self-absorption is frustratingly total and complete, the essential intercourse of her soul merely a kind of talking to herself.
In the texts of aestheticism—D. G. Rossetti's "Body's Beauty," Swinburne's
"Before the Mirror," for example—feminine narcissism often functions as a
trope for aesthetic autonomy; the woman gazing into a mirror becomes a figure
for art for art's sake. The Kit of *Art and Man* follows in the tradition of these
figures, her narcissism signifying both a certain kind of pleasure in images, an
enviable self-sufficiency, and a certain chilliness. For Vernon, this narcissism
constitutes Kit's frustrating, alluring purity.

Massive, sculptural, and chilly, Kit seems to embody the qualities attributed
to Miss Brown, but unlike her she cannot be made to burn in the embrace of
a Sacha/Hamlin/Vernon. She remains untouched and unfevered. Yet at one
point in *Art and Man,* the specter of Sacha comes into view. One of Kit's most
delightful essays is on the Venus de Medici, whose hand gestures and posture
Kit explains by the notion that she is "a creature steering herself on the waters."
A photograph of the statue accompanies the essay, which takes the form of a
gallery talk, leading us around the statue and enthusing about its qualities. Kit
exclaims, "What a delightful and wonderful game this way of sailing must have
been, and what fun this wonderful goddess is having!" (330). In her introduction, Lee acknowledges that the essay is fanciful but sees in it "a kind of truth
different from that of history and archaeology, but just as valuable and incon-
trovertible" (102). She asks, "After all, was this not a gain upon what archaeology tells us of the venerable obscene gesture of all the little Aphrodites, and
Istars and Ashtaroths?" (100). Where Kit sees a sailing goddess, Vernon Lee
must point out to us an obscene gesture, in a move that sexualizes both statue
and woman. The experience of reading Kit's essay after Lee's introduction is
one of watching Kit being solicited by a Venus whose one hand points toward
her genitals and whose other hand fingers a nipple, a solicitation Kit both refuses and acknowledges in her detailed study of the goddess's pose and the
"fun" she is having. Once again, purity makes sex visible. What fun indeed.

Even one of Vernon Lee's contemporaries, Irene Cooper Willis, speculated
that her "absorption in psychological aesthetics must have been some kind of
sex sublimation."[28] *Art and Man* complicates this statement. Although it describes a congress between the body of the beloved and the art object that substitutes for physical contact with the beloved's body, that substitution affirms
rather than denies same-sex attachment. Knowing the beloved's bodily sensations substitutes for a carnal knowledge of that body; aesthetic practice substitutes for erotic practice. Yet after the substitutions are made, the attractions of
Kit's body, Vernon's love for her, the centrality of that body to Vernon's and
the reader's aesthetic experience remain visible. Indeed, rather than acting as a

substitute for sex, aesthetics in *Art and Man* is a body-centered erotic practice in its own right.

* * *

I began this essay with two different ways of looking at aestheticism's impact on women. Even from this brief discussion of Vernon Lee's work, it must be clear that aestheticism could be both enabling and oppressive for the women who produced and consumed it, and not necessarily in obvious and predictable ways. For example, whereas Lee criticized aestheticism's eroticized images of women in *Miss Brown*, she clearly found these images aesthetically and erotically compelling. We tend to assume, unlike the Victorians themselves, that these images can only be consumed in one way, with the effect of strengthening the structures of heterosexual romance, whereas actually a range of different viewers might consume them in very different ways. Similarly, aestheticism's conjoining of same-sex desire and aesthetic attitude were clearly important to Lee's aesthetics, although her feminist purity polemic brought her to a more contradictory form of expression of the connection between aesthetic and erotic. When she writes of Pater, "After all he was a saint, an idealist in the true sense, the sense of choosing what was beautiful and charming and neglecting the rest,"[29] she makes him over into an avatar of purity, but this purity does not for her erase Pater's investment in same-sex desire, as her tribute to his vision of Dionysus clearly shows.[30] As an aestheticist writer who criticized art for art's sake, and an anti-sex polemicist who produced a sexually dissident lesbian aesthetics, Vernon Lee challenges us to broaden our definitions both of aestheticism and of Victorian sexual dissidence.

Notes

I am grateful to Richard Dellamora for his editorial comments and suggestions.

1. Richard Dellamora, *Masculine Desire: The Sexual Politics of Victorian Aestheticism* (Chapel Hill: University of North Carolina Press, 1990), 132.

2. Jonathan Dollimore, *Sexual Dissidence: Augustine to Wilde, Freud to Foucault* (Oxford: Oxford University Press, 1991), 3–18, 64–73.

3. See Griselda Pollock, *Vision and Difference: Femininity, Feminism and Histories of Art* (New York: Routledge, 1988), 120–54, and Elaine Showalter, introduction to *Daughters of Decadence: Women Writers of the Fin de Siècle* (New Brunswick, N.J.: Rutgers University Press, 1993), vii–xx. Showalter writes of New Women writers' need "to purge aestheticism and decadence of their misogyny" (x).

4. Thaïs Morgan, "Violence, Creativity and the Feminine: Poetics and Gender Politics in Swinburne and Hopkins," in *Gender and Discourse in Victorian Literature and Art*, ed. Antony H. Harrison and Beverly Taylor (DeKalb: Northern Illinois University

Press, 1992), 84–107, and "Lesbian Bodies: The Construction of Alternative Masculinities in Courbet, Baudelaire, and Swinburne," *Genders* 15 (1992): 37–57; Rita Felski,
The Gender of Modernity (Cambridge: Harvard University Press, 1995), 91–114.

5. For biographical information see Burdett Gardner, *The Lesbian Imagination (Victorian Style): A Psychological and Critical Study of "Vernon Lee"* (New York: Garland,
1987); Peter Gunn, *Vernon Lee/Violet Paget, 1856–1935* (London: Oxford University
Press, 1964).

6. I discuss this novel with a different focus in *Beauty's Body: Femininity and Representation in British Aestheticism* (Stanford: Stanford University Press, 1997), 165–77.

7. Vernon Lee, *Miss Brown* (1884; reprint, New York: Garland, 1978), 1:24. Further
references by volume and page number in the text.

8. Christina Rossetti, *The Complete Poems of Christina Rossetti*, ed. Rebecca W.
Crump (Baton Rouge: Louisiana State University Press, 1986), 3:264.

9. Walter Pater, *The Renaissance: Studies in Art and Poetry*, ed. Donald Hill (Berkeley
and Los Angeles: University of California Press, 1980), 176.

10. Ibid., 177.

11. Ibid., 176.

12. Algernon Charles Swinburne, *The Poems of Algernon Charles Swinburne* (London: Chatto and Windus, 1904), 1:146–61.

13. Quoted in Gunn, *Vernon Lee*, 105.

14. Quoted in Gunn, *Vernon Lee*, 106 and Gardner, *Lesbian Imagination*, 376–77.

15. In *The Spinster and Her Enemies: Feminism and Sexuality 1880–1930* (London:
Pandora, 1985), Sheila Jeffreys describes the ways in which nineteenth-century women
employed the notion of women's sexlessness as a means of resisting marriage and com-
pulsory heterosexuality. Conversely, the insistence that women as well as men are sexual
creatures was used against unmarried women, lesbians, and feminists to regulate and
normalize women's sexual behavior. Thus, although later nineteenth-century purity
discourses often served the interests of the state by policing the social body, these discourses could also have oppositional effects. For example, Vernon Lee tried to dissuade
her lover Mary Robinson from marrying by pointing out that she and her husband-to-
be would have to be married in name only because they were both so physically degenerate that to have children would be a crime, almost as bad as the crime of using birth
control, which brings marriage to the level of prostitution. Here, as in *Miss Brown*, the
discourse of purity is directed against the institutions of heterosexuality itself. See Gardner, *Lesbian Imagination*, 181–202.

16. Gardner, ibid., 366–67.

17. Ethel Smyth records the following statement: "In short, dear Mr. C——, wom-
en's love is so essentially *maternal* that it were tedious to enumerate possible deviations
from this basic character; whereas man's love, as obviously and invariably, is *triune;* that
is acquisitive, possessive, and BESTIAL." *As Time Went On* (London: Longmans, Green,
1936), 244.

18. Gardner's work is very much shaped by mid-century Freudianism—i.e. he calls Lee's lesbianism a neurosis, he seeks its "causes" in a blocked Oedipal attachment to her mother. But the dissertation, republished by Garland in 1987 as *The Lesbian Imagination (Victorian Style)* is exhaustive in its treatment of Vernon Lee's writing and her life and contains many excerpts from her personal papers and statements by people who knew her not available elsewhere. For Gardner, same-sex desire and the problems of the body pervade Lee's writing. His polemic is aimed against the repressive Victorian convention that he holds responsible for blocking Lee's expression of physical desire for the women she loved.

19. Quoted in Gardner, ibid., 77, from Ethel Smyth, *What Happened Next* (New York: Longmans, Green, 1940), 28.

20. Gardner, ibid., 85.

21. We might indeed read Vernon's denial of her own body, her repeated references to its insufficiency and lack, compared to the huge, beautiful, sculptural bodies of the beloved women as part of the sort of butch stance of the "bodiless lover" analyzed by Teresa de Lauretis in her discussion of lesbian fetishism in *The Practice of Love.* De Lauretis's description of "striving after the fantasmatic female body, the intrapsychic image that is the lovers' common object of desire, the female body they can find to-gether, always for the first time" resonates with the scenes of collaboration described in *Art and Man.* Teresa de Lauretis, *The Practice of Love: Lesbian Sexuality and Perverse Desire* (Bloomington: Indiana University Press, 1994), 296.

22. Clementina Anstruther-Thomson, *Art and Man: Essays and Fragments,* edited and with an introduction by Vernon Lee (London: John Lane, 1924), 33. Further references by page number in the text.

23. I am not, here, interested in the actual historical Clementina Anstruther-Thomson, but rather in Kit as she appears in texts Vernon Lee produces about her. To avoid confusion, I refer to Vernon Lee and Anstruther-Thomson when I am referring to the authors of texts, and to Kit and Vernon when I refer to the characters who appear in the introduction to *Art and Man.* For a wonderful treatment of the collaboration between Vernon Lee and Anstruther-Thomson that pays close attention to the latter's independent projects, see Diana Maltz, "Lessons in Sensuous Discontent: The Aesthetic Mission to the British Working Classes, 1869—1914," Ph.D. dissertation, Stanford University, 1997.

24. For an extended discussion of Pater's affirmation of the body in "Winckelmann," see Dellamora, *Masculine Desire,* 102–16.

25. Vernon Lee and Clementina Anstruther-Thomson, "Beauty and Ugliness," *Contemporary Review* 72 (October and November 1897): 559. Vernon Lee later expanded upon and changed the arguments of this essay in *Beauty and Ugliness and Other Studies in Psychological Aesthetics* (London: John Lane, 1912).

26. For a discussion of Pater and Wilde's critique of the sublimation of same-sex desire into the service of nationalist projects, see Richard Dellamora, *Apocalyptic Over-*

tures: Sexual Politics and the Sense of an Ending (New Brunswick, N.J.: Rutgers University Press, 1994), 42–64. It should be noted that in comparison to the work of physiological aestheticians like Grant Allen (*Physiological Aesthetics,* 1877), Lee and Anstruther-Thomson's physiological aesthetics are far more egalitarian in their implications and far less darwinist in their claims. By making aesthetic perception a whole-body experience, rather than an experience of sight and hearing merely, they connect it to the vital functions, making it a human need, rather than a luxury for the leisured classes.

27. For example, Richards's discussion of the effect of art on the nervous system sounds very much like "Beauty and Ugliness": "Everybody knows the feeling of freedom, of relief, of increased competence and sanity, that follows any reading in which more than usual order and coherence has been given to our responses. We seem to feel that our command of life, our insight into it and our discrimination of its possibilities is enhanced, even for situations having little or nothing to do with the subject of reading." *Principles of Literary Criticism,* 2d ed. (1926; reprint, London: Routledge and Kegan Paul, 1960), 235.

28. Gardner, *Lesbian Imagination,* 226.

29. Ibid., 560.

30. Vernon Lee, "Dionysus in the Euganean Hills," *Contemporary Review,* 120 (September 1921): 346–53. Here Dionysus becomes a figure for masculine and feminine same-sex desire: "Dionysus is a seducer of women, though little more than a woman himself; his effeminacy is like that of those beautiful languid Arabs one has seen lolling under awnings, and who strike one as women in disguise, the beard against their jasmine cheeks seeming like some kind of ritual half-mask" (346).

References

Allen, Grant. *Physiological Aesthetics.* London: H. S. King, 1877.

Anstruther-Thomson, Clementina. *Art and Man: Essays and Fragments.* Edited and with an introduction by Vernon Lee. London: John Lane, 1924.

de Lauretis, Teresa. *The Practice of Love: Lesbian Sexuality and Perverse Desire.* Bloomington: Indiana University Press, 1994.

Dellamora, Richard. *Apocalyptic Overtures: Sexual Politics and the Sense of an Ending.* New Brunswick, N.J.: Rutgers University Press, 1994.

———. *Masculine Desire: The Sexual Politics of Victorian Aestheticism.* Chapel Hill: University of North Carolina Press, 1990.

Dollimore, Jonathan. *Sexual Dissidence: Augustine to Wilde, Freud to Foucault.* Oxford: Oxford University Press, 1991.

Felski, Rita. *The Gender of Modernity.* Cambridge: Harvard University Press, 1995.

Gardner, Burdett. *The Lesbian Imagination (Victorian Style): A Psychological and Critical*

Study of "Vernon Lee" (Ph.D. dissertation, Harvard University, 1954). New York: Garland, 1987.

Gunn, Peter. *Vernon Lee/Violet Paget, 1856–1935.* London: Oxford University Press, 1964.

Jeffreys, Sheila. *The Spinster and Her Enemies: Feminism and Sexuality 1880–1930.* London: Pandora, 1985.

Lee, Vernon [Violet Paget]. "Dionysus in the Euganean Hills," *Contemporary Review* 120 (September 1921): 346–53.

———. *Miss Brown.* 3 vols. Edinburgh: W. M. Blackwood and Sons, 1884. Reprint (3 vols. in 1), New York: Garland, 1978.

Lee, Vernon, and Clementina Astruther-Thomson. "Beauty and Ugliness." *Contemporary Review* 72 (October and November 1897): 544–69, 669–88.

———. *Beauty and Ugliness and Other Studies in Psychological Aesthetics.* London: John Lane, 1912.

Maltz, Diana. "Lessons in Sensuous Discontent: The Aesthetic Mission to the British Working Classes, 1869–1914." Ph.D. dissertation, Stanford University, 1997.

Morgan, Thaïs. "Lesbian Bodies: The Construction of Alternative Masculinities in Courbet, Baudelaire, and Swinburne." *Genders* 15 (1992): 37–57.

———. "Violence, Creativity and the Feminine: Poetics and Gender Politics in Swinburne and Hopkins." In *Gender and Discourse in Victorian Literature and Art,* ed. Antony H. Harrison and Beverly Taylor, 84–107. DeKalb: Northern Illinois University Press, 1992.

Pater, Walter. *The Renaissance: Studies in Art and Poetry,* ed. Donald Hill, Berkeley and Los Angeles: University of California Press, 1980.

Pollock, Griselda. *Vision and Difference: Femininity, Feminism, and Histories of Art.* New York: Routledge, 1988.

Psomiades, Kathy Alexis. *Beauty's Body: Femininity and Representation in British Aestheticism.* Stanford: Stanford University Press, 1997.

Richards, I. A. *Principles of Literary Criticism,* 2d ed. 1926. Reprint, London: Routledge and Kegan Paul, 1960.

Rossetti, Christina. *The Complete Poems of Christina Rossetti,* edited by Rebecca W. Crump. 3 vols. Baton Rouge: Louisiana State University Press, 1979–90.

Showalter, Elaine. *Daughters of Decadence: Women Writers of the Fin de Siècle.* New Brunswick, N.J.: Rutgers University Press, 1993.

Smyth, Ethel. *As Time Went On.* London: Longmans, Green, 1936.

———. *What Happened Next.* New York: Longmans, Green, 1940.

Swinburne, Algernon Charles. *The Poems of Algernon Charles Swinburne.* 6 vols. London: Chatto and Windus, 1904.

Greek Maenads, Victorian Spinsters

YOPIE PRINS

Walter Pater described the Greek spirit as ἱμέρου πόθου πατήρ, "the father of longing and desire"—a phrase quoted from Plato but obliquely signed in Pater's name, as Linda Dowling points out: "Pater, whose own name is veiled in the decent obscurity of the Greek script as *pater*, also knows the longing and desire within Hellenism."[1] Pater is a central figure in Dowling's *Hellenism and Homosexuality in Victorian Oxford*, a book that sets out to analyze "the way Greek studies operated as a 'homosexual code' during the great age of English university reform" (xiii). Dowling focuses in particular on the role "so crucially played by Oxford Hellenism in the modern emergence of homosexuality as a positive social identity" (xvi), and indeed in her account Pater seems to father that identity, as she seeks "to uncover the full homoerotic implicativeness of Pater's writing" (95). I would like to consider some further implications of Greek eros not only as it circulated within Pater's writing and went into circulation to produce homoerotic desire between men, but as it circulated between women as well. While recent critics have emphasized the construction of masculine identities and the mediation of masculine desire in Victorian England through an idealized vision of ancient Greece, the place of women within Victorian Hellenism remains largely unexplored, despite the fact that an increasing number of women were learning Greek in the course of the century. The cultural prestige of Classical studies in nineteenth-century England and the fascination with Greek antiquity in particular created a desire among women to know the language of ancient Greece and, like their male counterparts, they discovered in ancient Greek a new language of desire.[2]

We cannot understand the sexual politics of Victorian Hellenism, then, without also taking into account the entry of women into Greek studies, and especially their increased access to formal education (as opposed to familial access through fathers and brothers, for example). After all, "the great age of English university reform" included not only the revolution of the dons but also the foundation of the women's colleges.[3] Accessible to few, such colleges nevertheless gave the opportunity to an increasing number of middle- and upper-class women to enter the domain of Classical scholarship, previously the inner sanctum of a privileged male elite. Although women were not awarded official degrees at Oxford and Cambridge until well into the next century, and although it was a struggle at first to gain formal admission to lectures and examinations, women were finally able to study ancient Greek within a university setting. The few who did choose this course of study attracted much controversy and publicity, as they embodied contradictory ideas about higher education for Victorian women. A particular anxiety about women assuming the powers and privileges of "Greek learning" is evident in a cartoon from *Punch* in 1876, just after the first women's colleges had been formed at Cambridge University.[4] Entitled "St. Valentine's Day at Girton" (fig. 1), the cartoon depicts two students from Girton College, which was known for its strenuous insistence on women's education in Classical languages. Poring over a Valentine written in Greek, the first one comments, "Charming, isn't it? Gussie must have sent it from Oxford?" The second replies, "Yes, it's out of the *Antigone*— the Love Chorus, you know. How much jollier than those silly English verses fellows used to send!"[5]

Smoking cigarettes and reading Sophocles with apparent ease, these "Girton girls" are the stereotype of the "advanced woman," as Perry Williams points out in her essay on pioneer women students at Cambridge: "The joke turns on the fear that an educated woman will be too much for an ordinary man" (186). Indeed, a woman educated enough to prefer a Valentine in ancient Greek to "those silly English verses fellows used to send" may be less a joke than a threat, especially since the "Love Chorus" in the *Antigone* invokes eros as a force of chaos, beyond control: "Eros undefeated in battle, Eros you destroy all things" (Ἔρως ἀνίκατε μάχαν, Ἔρως ὅς ἐν κτήμασι πίπτεις). The battle of the sexes has been won by the women, it would seem, and there is even a hint that the men may be out of the picture altogether: if the Valentine was sent from Oxford (and surely its charm derives from not knowing for sure) it is now circulating in Cambridge, "at Girton," between two women who share the erotic revelation of reading Greek together. In this moment of intimacy, Greek eros displaces not only "those silly English verses," but also the silly "fellows" who used to send them.

The first generation of women who learned Greek at Cambridge University included Jane Ellen Harrison (1850–1928) and Katherine Bradley (1846–1914). Bradley was one of the earliest students at Newnham College and developed an amateur's enthusiasm for Greek literature that she later shared with her niece, Edith Cooper (1862–1913). They went on to read Classics together at University College in 1878 and became lifelong partners who published poetry under the pseudonym "Michael Field." Although their early collaborations earned critical praise, "Michael Field" lapsed into obscurity once the identities of Bradley and Cooper were revealed to the public. Nevertheless they continued publishing poems and plays as "Michael Field" and have recently

ST. VALENTINE'S DAY AT GIRTON.

First Young Lady (opens Valentine, and reads):—

" 'Ἔρως ἀνίκατε μάχαν,
'Ἔρως, ὃς ἐν κτήμασι πίπτεις,' . . . &c., &c.

CHARMING, ISN'T IT ?   GUSSIE MUST HAVE SENT IT FROM OXFORD ?"

Second Young Lady (overlooking). "YES, IT'S OUT OF THE *ANTIGONE*—THE LOVE-CHORUS, YOU KNOW.   HOW MUCH JOLLIER THAN THOSE SILLY ENGLISH VERSES FELLOWS USED TO SEND !"

Figure 1 St. Valentine's Day at Girton (*Punch*, February 26, 1876)

received attention from critics interested in reconstructing the place of women writers within British aestheticism.[6]

Harrison is better known, in part because of her long-term association with Newnham College: she did the Tripos in Classical Studies from 1874 to 1879 and went on to become an eminent scholar, one of the first women to distinguish herself in the history of British Classical scholarship and influential in developing an anthropological approach to the study of early Greek art and religion. She returned to Newnham in 1898 as Resident Lecturer in Classical Archaeology and continued teaching Classics at Cambridge until 1922; during this time she became interested in the ritual origins of Greek tragedy as well, and played a central role in the circle of scholars known as "the Cambridge Ritualists."[7] Virginia Woolf, one of her great admirers, published Harrison's *Reminiscences of a Student's Life* at Hogarth Press in 1925, and in "A Room of One's Own" Woolf describes "Fernham" College still haunted by the spectral form of J—— H——.

By focusing on these Newnham women—one a poet, the other a scholar— I propose to shift the focus from Hellenism and homosexuality in Victorian Oxford to Hellenism and feminism in Victorian Cambridge. As we change the scene from Oxford to Cambridge, and from the men's colleges to a women's college, we can discern the outlines of a feminine counterdiscourse within the masculine discourses of Victorian Hellenism. Pater's aestheticized and eroticized vision of ancient Greece, formulated within the institutional context of Oxford Hellenism, was reformulated by women associated with Cambridge, who imagined Greece on their own terms and within a female homosocial context. Among many women influenced by Pater in late Victorian England, Michael Field and Jane Ellen Harrison are my two examples; they were fascinated in particular by Dionysus, the archaic god who was also of interest to Pater in his *Greek Studies,* because in the figure of the Greek maenad they found an imaginary alternative to the Victorian spinster. As they transformed the writing of Pater in their own writings, they articulated various forms of feminine desire and contributed to the formation of social identities other than the properly married Victorian woman, or the self-sacrificing and asexual spinster aunt.

In their imaginative identification with Greek maenads, these Victorian spinsters redefined spinsterhood not only in their different styles of writing but also in the lifestyles they chose for themselves. As various critics have argued, the generation of unmarried middle-class women that came of age in the 1870s and 1880s played an important role in the transition from mid-Victorian Old Maid to fin-de-siècle New Woman; during the last three decades of the century, single women were beginning to redefine familial relations and conventional female domesticity.[8] Thus Bradley and Cooper turned the relationship between aunt and niece into an alternative marriage, while Harrison, resolutely refusing to become "Aunt," chose the communal life of a women's college where she cultivated passionate friendships with colleagues and students. By revaluing the role of the aunt we can begin to understand a wider range of sexual dissidence available to Victorian women: insofar as the unmarried aunt occupies an eccentric place both inside and outside the traditional family, she disrupts sexual categories and patterns of lineage within a patrilineal kinship system and introduces the possibility of other kinds of relations between women.[9]

Through the figure of the aunt we can also develop a gendered perspective on the queer genealogy proposed by Eve Sedgwick. In "Tales of the Avunculate," Sedgwick presents the uncle as alternative to "the Name of the Father" in the patriarchal family; under his "queer tutelage" it becomes possible to hold open a space for different sexual identifications. I shall argue that Pater, notwithstanding his name and reputation as the "father" of British aestheticism, proves to be more uncle than father to a generation of wayward daughters. His influence on women writers toward the end of the century demonstrates how the seemingly antiquarian discourses of Hellenism served to create new configurations of sexuality and gender. By reading Greek as "the father of longing and desire," Pater performs the conversion of Classical learning into a queer philology that appealed to women interested in turning Greek eros to their own purposes. Thus, while Pater is not quite the father of feminine desire, his oddly avuncular relation to female aestheticism remains one of the yet untold tales of the avunculate. In telling this tale, however, I do not wish to subsume the aunt into the figure of the uncle.[10] Is there a female counterpart to the avunculate that Sedgwick describes, a non-avuncular "tantulate" perhaps? Is it possible to formulate a "tantular" reading that would allow the figure of the aunt to trouble normative heterosexuality without returning it to the name of the father, or even the uncle whose name is Pater? As I trace Pater's influence on the Hellenism of late Victorian women writers, my argument also emphasizes the asymmetrical positions of the aunt and uncle within that society, in order to call into question, finally, the literary genealogy that has defined British aestheticism on a paternal model. Time, then, for some tales of the tantulate.

<h1 style="text-align:center">I</h1>

"Sexual anarchy began with the odd woman," Elaine Showalter writes, as she chronicles the emergence of new political and sexual categories for unmarried women toward the end of the nineteenth century.[11] In 1862, Francis Power Cobbe had published "What Shall We Do with Our Old Maids?" as a feminist plea for educational and economic reform to encourage greater independence for single women, whose number was, according to the most recent census, rapidly rising. Over the next three decades, the "redundant woman" was recategorized in various ways: a working woman, a suffragette, a single woman living outside the sphere of the family, a woman living with other women, a celibate woman, a mannish woman, a sexually autonomous woman, an "odd" woman not to be paired with a man. This generation of single women resisted traditional spinsterhood even before the "New Woman" of the nineties, so that by the time Eliza Lynn Linton wrote her anti-feminist tirade, "The Wild

Women as Social Insurgents" (1891), the Victorian spinster seemed long out of date. Lamenting that a woman's worth is no longer "reckoned by the flax she spun and the thread she wove," Linton warns against the advent of the Wild Woman: "our Lady of Desire, the masterful *domina* of real life—that loud and dictatorial person, insurgent and something more," who "preaches the 'lesson of liberty' broadened into lawlessness and license" (596). Without saying what "something more" might signify, Linton makes it clear that "unlady-like" and "unwomanly" are terms that have "ceased to be significant"; in her argument the odd woman has become an "odd social phenomenon," defying the laws of gender and producing "other queer inversions" (599).

The queering of the odd woman continues in "The Partisans of the Wild Women" (1892), a sequel to the earlier diatribe of Linton, who now imagines Wild Women consorting with Decadent Men, whose "taste . . . is as queer as their morality" (460). According to Linton, "the truth is simply this—*the un-sexed woman pleases the unsexed man*" (461). "Unladylike," "unwomanly," and now "unsexed," the Wild Woman nevertheless embodies too much sexuality, undomesticated and dangerously out of control. Linton represents the Wild Women as a collective force that exceeds the laws of individual conduct and is gathering momentum: "Let anyone commend to these female runagates quiet-ness, duty, home-staying, and the whole cohort of Wild Women is like an angry beehive which a rough hand has disturbed," Linton writes. Such women "care nothing for home," in contrast to the wives who stay inside, like the pro-verbial busy bees, and "do good work quietly, without tomtoms or cow-horns to call attention to their feats" (463). In a gradual crescendo, the angry buzz of these swarming Wild Women is amplified into the roar of a rushing torrent in "Nearing the Rapids," where they are figured as a disruption of nature that will sweep all of Victorian society over the edge and downward to a swirling maelstrom of sexual anarchy. Of course this idea is produced by a pervasive crisis within Victorian discourses of gender, class, sexuality, race, and empire at the end of the century, as Sally Ledger points out: the fictional New Woman is "a product of, rather than a pioneering voice within, this discursive sphere."[12] Linton's fin-de-siècle hysteria is projected onto the Wild Women, as she de-scribes married women who "stream out" of their houses and into the streets "for the excitement home cannot afford them" (380), and further envisions "the premature initiation of young unmarried women into the knowledge of the mysteries" (385).

This noisy cohort with their tomtoms and cowhorns sounds increasingly like a group of Greek maenads, on their way to unimaginable revels and mysterious rites of initiation. In ancient Greece maenads formed a sacred *thiasos*, a band of women who dressed in animal skins and carried a *thyrsos* twined in ivy to worship Dionysus; dancing to the sound of drums and intoxicated with wine, they became *mainades*, literally, "mad ones." There is historical evidence for the existence of such cults in antiquity, allowing for the temporary reversal of social roles for women as they enacted a ritual of feminine rebellion and gender inversion. Breaking out of the domestic sphere, the maenad crossed the boundary into a domain culturally coded as "natural" and "savage," a place outside the *polis* for the performance of sacrificial rites and ecstatic orgies that would seem to subvert the social order but also sustained it: even while celebrating disorder, maenadic rituals were integrated into the civic ideology and religious life of the Greek cities.[13] But if this ritualized transgression ultimately served as a form of social containment for Greek women, maenadism in Greek myth was associated with more threatening forces of nature, beyond masculine control: a community of women with the power to create and destroy, dedicated not only to song and dance in honor of Dionysus, but to darker acts of destruction like *sparagmos* and *omophagia*, rending apart a sacrificial animal and eating raw flesh. This, at least, is how Euripides represents maenads in the *Bacchae;* the Bacchantes in his tragedy initially nurse wild animals and make the earth stream with wine and milk and honey, but eventually turn against the city of Thebes, tearing its leader from limb to limb in wild frenzy.

As the primary source for speculation about maenadic cults, the *Bacchae* of Euripides attracted a great deal of commentary from Classical scholars, anthropologists, and literary critics toward the end of the nineteenth century.[14] Maenadism appealed powerfully to the imagination of many Victorians, caught up as they were in heated debates about "The Woman Question." Greek maenads seemed the very embodiment of feminine rebellion and unruly female sexuality, denounced by some and celebrated by others. The figure of the maenad appeared with increasing frequency in literature and the visual arts, variously represented as seductive wanton, murderous femme fatale, or raging madwoman, suffering from what Showalter has called the female malady: a madness that is both a symbolic female disorder and a symptom of social disorder in Victorian culture. The Dionysiac abandon of maenads is a recurring theme in paintings by Sir Lawrence Alma-Tadema, for example, who links female sexuality with irrationality and loss of consciousness. In *Autumn: A Vintage Festival* (1873), Alma-Tadema depicts a drunken maenad crowned with ivy and dressed in a leopard skin, eyes half-closed in ecstasy, brandishing a torch that suggests her burning sexuality (fig. 2). Poised on one foot with the other knee lifted, she is in suspended motion, momentarily framed within the painting but also represented as if she is about to move beyond its frame: a mobile figure, and a figure for mobility that cannot be contained. Her pose recalls Greek maenads as they were represented in antiquity, leaping high with their heads thrown back, or rushing forward, thyrsos in hand. In later paintings, Alma-Tadema represented maenads in a wide range of movements and

Figure 2 *Autumn: A Vintage Festival*, by Sir Lawrence Alma-Tadema (1873). Oil on canvas. Reproduced with the kind permission of the City of Birmingham Museums and Art Gallery.

poses: sprawled on the floor, dancing madly, or playing musical instruments, all prompting Ruskin to condemn the "Bacchanalian phrenzy, which M. Alma Tadema seems to hold it his heavenly mission to pourtray" [sic].[15]

Contrary to Ruskin, who preferred his Greeks calm and serene, Walter Pater was more impressed by Greek maenads as a subject "certainly, for art, and a poetry delighting in colour and form," as he writes in his essay "The Bacchanals of Euripides."[16] According to Pater, the inspired enthusiasm of maenads in their "Thiasus" should serve as an inspiration to artists, not only in antiquity but (by implication) in Pater's own time as well: "The imitative arts would draw from it altogether new motives of freedom and energy, of freshness in old forms" (*Greek Studies* 55). The word "motives" has a double meaning that attributes inner energies to outward forms, in keeping with Pater's own aesthetics; he re-motivates an old motif, allowing "altogether new motives of freedom and energy" to be drawn, both literally and figuratively, from the old forms of Greek maenads and transformed into new forms of expression. This aesthetic transformation also motivates Pater's own "imitation" of the *Bacchae*, as he paraphrases the poetry of Euripides in prose form, outlining the plot in order to discover new motives in the tragedy.

Pater describes Greek maenads not unlike Linton's Wild Women, but more enthusiastically, from a poet's perspective:

> Coleridge, in one of his fantastic speculations, refining on the German word for enthusiasm—*Schwärmerei*, swarming, as he says, "like the swarming of bees together"—has explained how the sympathies of mere numbers, as such, the random catching on fire of one here and another there, when people are collected together, generates as if by mere contact, some new and rapturous spirit, not traceable in the individual units of a multitude. Such swarming was the essence of that strange dance of the Bacchic women: literally like winged things, they follow, with motives, we may suppose, never quite made clear even to themselves, their new, strange, romantic god. Himself a woman-like god,—it was on women and feminine souls that his power mainly fell. (*Greek Studies*, 53)

Where Linton hears only the angry buzz of bees disturbed at their beehive, Pater imagines women "like the swarming of bees together," a collective force that creates "some new and rapturous spirit" that has its own strange beauty: their rapture is the expression of an impressionability that is Pater's aesthetic ideal. No doubt the "woman-like god" they worship would be denounced by Linton as an unsexed man, but in Pater's account, Dionysus is the prototype of the decadent aesthete. His Thiasus "is almost exclusively formed of women—of those who experience most directly the influence of things which touch thought through the senses" (54), and although they follow "with motives . . . never quite made clear even to themselves" it becomes clear in the course of the essay what Pater's motivation is for following the twists and turns of their strange dance in his own prose: his rapturous description of maenads is itself a form of rapture, making Pater into an enthusiastic worshipper of Dionysus as well. After all, a Thiasus "almost exclusively formed of women" might include men, and if the power of Dionysus falls "on women and feminine souls," perhaps one of those "feminine souls" is his own.

The blurring of "masculine" and "feminine" qualities allows Pater to assimilate the latter into a redefinition of the former, as James Eli Adams argues: "Pater . . . associates his critical enterprise with icons of gender transgression; more precisely, he emphasizes the construction of a critical subjectivity as a masculine appropriation of traditionally feminine attributes."[17] The maenad's sensuous inspiration is like the passive transparency Pater describes in "Diaphaneitè" (1864) or the aesthetic tact he admires in "Winckelmann" (1867), two earlier essays that also convert "feminine" receptivity into a Hellenized manly ideal; this tendency to aestheticize manhood through Greek enthusiasm is evident in "A Study of Dionysus" (1876) as well.[18] In this essay Pater returns to the origins of Dionysus in primitive Greek religion, beginning with the worship of the vine, tended by female spirits who were "weavers or spinsters, spinning or weaving with the airiest fingers, and subtlest, many-coloured threads" (*Greek Studies,* 4). The progression of Dionysiac worship can be traced in the transformation of the "souls of the individual vine" into "the soul of the whole species, the spirit of fire and dew," personified in Dionysus (5); he becomes a god, worshipped by maenads. Within Pater's anthropological model, this shift from animism to anthropomorphism corresponds to a shift from ritual to myth, which narrates the story of Dionysus in human form. As Dionysus leaves the vineyards and enters Athens, Dionysiac worship is transferred from enthusiastic women to enthusiastic men:

> To this stage of his town-life, that Dionysus of "enthusiasm" already belonged; it was to the Athenians of the town, to urbane young men, sitting together at the banquet, that those expressions of a sudden eloquence came, of the loosened utterance and finer speech, its colour and imagery. Dionysus, then, has entered Athens, to become urbane like them; to walk along the marble streets in frequent procession, in the persons of noble youths. (33–34)

The ritual conception of Dionysus gives way to a mythical conception that is later given poetic form, inspiring "urbane young men" who reconceive the god "to become urbane like them."[19] These Athenian youths take over the role of the maenads and become like the female spirits in the vineyards: the "subtlest, many-coloured threads" spun by those airy spinsters who give life to the vine reappear in their "finer speech, its colour and imagery."

Evolving from half-conscious ritual to conscious myth, Dionysiac religion is finally self-consciously conceived as a symbol by Pater. In the sequence from ritual to mythical to "ethical" conceptions of Dionysus, Pater's essay partakes of the last phase: indeed, the work of the "weavers or spinsters" is now transferred to his own finely woven text as Pater—"through the fine-spun speculations of modern ethnologists and grammarians" (33)—weaves together etymologies, mythologies, historical references, and poetic allusions to create a richly symbolic portrait of Dionysus.[20] Early in the essay he asks his reader to reflect on the making of this symbol; "let him reflect," he writes, "by way of one clearly conceived yet complex symbol," on "all the effect and expression drawn from the imagery of the vine" (2). What makes the symbol both simple and complex is that it expresses itself: the "spirits" literally expressed from the vine are also a figurative expression of spirit. By attending to this figurative logic—just like "the nurses of the vine" who tend to Dionysus in his earliest spiritual form, or the inspired maenads who are the god's later attendants— Pater revives the spirit of Dionysus and asks his reader to do the same. Maenadic enthusiasm is now transferred to the Hellenic enthusiast, who is explicitly addressed as male ("let him reflect") and implicitly identified with the urbane Athenians who recognize Dionysus as one of their own.

This double address—defined by Thaïs Morgan as an "aesthetic minoritizing discourse"—simultaneously appeals to a cultivated reader interested in ancient Greece, and to a minority group that reads Greek with homoerotic or homosexual interests.[21] "A Study of Dionysus" circulated not only among general readers of the *Fortnightly Review,* but within the sexual economy of a male homosocial elite in the Oxford colleges, as various other critics have pointed out.[22] Dionysus defines an alternative masculinity and a form of masculine desire with "modern motives," limned in a portrait of Dionysus by Simeon Solomon, to whom Pater alludes:

> But modern motives are clearer; and in a Bacchus by a young Hebrew painter, in the exhibition of the Royal Academy of 1868, there was a complete and very fascinating realisation of such a motive; the god of the bitterness of wine, "of things too sweet"; the sea-water of the Lesbian grape become somewhat brackish in the cup. Touched by the sentiment of this subtler, melancholy Dionysus, we may ask whether anything similar in feeling is to be actually found in the range of Greek ideas. (*Greek Studies,* 37)

Pater answers his own question in a long excursus on Dionysus Zagreus, an older name for the god in a darker incarnation: the hunter who is himself hunted, torn apart by the women who worship him, self-sacrificed. Glimpsed in Solomon's painting and painted again in words by Pater, this portrait of Dionysus gives us the outlines of the melancholy modern homosexual, as Richard Dellamora has argued in further detail: through the contradictions of the Dionysus myth, Pater expresses the possibility of homosexual desire as well as its ritual sacrifice.[23] Thus Dionysus is not only the source of aesthetic intoxication, but "the god of the bitterness of wine" as well, simultaneously "the expression drawn from the imagery of the vine" and its repression.

While the "modern motives" attributed to Dionysus in the "ethical" phase of his evolution allow Pater to articulate the ethos of male–male desire, he also points to the possibility of reading Dionysus—the god of the "Lesbian grape"—as a figure that mediates desire between women. Both of his essays on Dionysus circulated beyond male circles and within the context of the Victorian "Woman Question," to create an aesthetic minoritizing discourse among women readers as well.[24] Such readers might find themselves implicated in Dionysiac worship at its very origin, in the airy "weavers or spinsters" who nurse the vine (as Pater writes in "A Study of Dionysus") or in the Thiasus of women who "touch thought through the senses" (as Pater writes in "The Bacchanals of Euripides"): a community of women whose sensuous perceptions are not only aestheticized but also potentially eroticized. Pater insists on the central place of women in the early worship of Dionysus, and although in his evolutionary account they are later displaced by Athenian youths and Victorian scholars such as himself, it is also because of this displacement that Pater's maenads remain more mobile than modern enthusiasts. If "modern motives are clearer" for men, who rediscover Dionysus as a "white, graceful, mournful figure, weeping, chastened" (35), it would seem that the "new and rapturous spirit" of maenads who follow Dionysus "with motives . . . never quite made clear even to themselves" (53) introduces an eroticism more freely expressed and less cruelly repressed than the sorrowing Dionysus, precisely because the modern motives of female desire are "never quite made clear." The expression of such motives, without sharp delineation, motivates Victorian spinsters to reclaim Greek maenads for their own purposes: in Pater's Greek essays they discern other forms of Greek eros, not quite within his purview.

II

Katherine Bradley and Edith Cooper, aunt and niece, were related through Katherine's older sister Emma: Katherine had come to live with Emma in 1861 and helped raise Emma's daughter Edith, born in 1862. The sixteen-year age difference between Katherine and Edith, not quite a generation apart, allowed them to play different familial roles: if initially the aunt was like a mother and the niece like a daughter, gradually they became more like sisters, and then more like lovers, and eventually like husband and wife. They considered themselves married, exchanged a vow and "swore / Against the world, to be / Poets and lovers for evermore" ("Prologue," 1893). During her years as a student, Katherine had already dedicated herself to poetry; in 1875, she published a book of verse under the name of "Arran Leigh," leaving her gender ambiguous but placing her poems in the sacred precinct of an inviolable female muse, untouched by men: "Yes, Woman, she whose life doth lie / In virgin haunts of poesie" ("The New Minnesinger," 1875). Under Katherine's tutelage, Edith was initiated into these "virgin haunts" as well. They studied ancient Greek together and made it into their special language of desire: they published poems inspired by the Greek fragments of Sappho, under the pseudonym "Michael Field" in 1889.[25] The poetic collaboration of Bradley and Cooper had already begun the previous decade, however, with their first volume of poetry published under the names of "Arran and Isla Leigh" in 1881. This earlier pseudonym also blurs genders and suggests various possible relationships between the two names: a pair of siblings, a parent and child, a married couple.

The early 1880s were, in fact, their "honeymoon" years. Virginia Blain quotes personal letters from this time between Bradley and Cooper, addressed to "Sweet Wife" and "dear Husband," and when the poetic "progeny" of their marriage did not fare well among critics, Katherine wrote to Edith, "Sweet Wife, the hardships of early married life are beginning: let us bear them together bravely."[26] Blain makes the important point that Bradley and Cooper, "positioned through their relationship aslant to the male line," were "uniquely placed to explore discursive realms beyond the family romance" (240), but it is also and especially *within* their family romance that they discovered other kinds of eros, no matter how unconventional. "We cannot be stifled in drawing room conventionalities," Bradley wrote to Robert Browning, who fondly called them his "two dear Greek women" during visits.[27] To Logan Pearsall Smith these Victorian spinsters seemed like "Bacchic Maenads," thoroughly domestic yet strangely undomesticated, as he recalls visiting them at their home:

> The strangeness of these visits was weirdly heightened by what seemed at first their commonplace character. One received a politely worded invitation to afternoon tea . . . and found in the little house an aunt and niece of pleasantly old-fashioned primness. . . . But this was the maddest of illusions. Never in Cranford was heard talk like their talk when once inspiration fell upon them . . . and as their voices rose and mingled in a kind of chant, the two quietly attired ladies would seem to undergo the most extraordinary transformations; would resume the aspect and airs of . . . the Bacchic Maenads, they really were.[28]

If at first Bradley and Cooper seem like old maids "of pleasantly old-fashioned primness," suddenly they turn into newly inspired beings, whose "mingled" voices intermingle poetry and love.

No doubt Smith's rapturous reminiscence is drawn less from the life of Bradley and Cooper than from their poetry, as their first poetic production under the name "Michael Field" was a drama in verse about a maiden's conversion to Dionysiac worship. Entitled *Callirrhoë: A Drama* and published in 1884, it opens with maenads asleep on the steps of the Temple of Bacchus, in Calydon. Coresus, a new Bacchic priest who leads their entourage, has just arrived to bring tidings to the maids of Calydon about a new revival of his religion; he seeks only "the few, / Who learn it not from custom" but "leap to it adoring" with "the entrancing awe / Of the great mysteries" (9–10). This trance-like, awe-inspired state distinguishes the true maenad from the traditionally pious maiden, as he proclaims: "O ... there / Is the true Maenad! The wide difference / 'Twixt love and love, and oh! the wider room / 'Twixt pieties!" (9). His religion is associated with passions and pieties that demonstrate "the wide difference twixt love and love," without actually naming these different loves. The first Calydonian to be converted is the young maiden Nephele, who appears at the home of Callirrhoë with "crimson vine-leaves" around her feet and "hair unbound" (11–12). She describes how one of the maenads of Coresus "threw her spells on me" and "drew me, in caressing arms" to the maenadic revels:

> And as a bride, half-swooning in the flare
> Of Hymen's torches is borne blindly off,
> I was caught up by the great choric throng,
> And in a daze of wonder found myself
> Whirling the thyrsus ... It may be I swooned. (13)

Nephele is carried "as a bride" to an initiation rite that serves as an alternative to marriage and the revelation of another kind of love: she joins "the great choric throng" of maenads, dancing in ecstasy until she swoons.

If Nephele is a "true Maenad," Callirrhoë seems at first a spinster "trained in the old pieties" (25). Rather than "whirling the thyrsus" outside the city, she is busy twirling the spindle at home, spinning as she sings:

> Ay, twirl the spindle, twirl it round,
> The spindle with the dark wool wound!
> But, maiden, if too well you spin,
> Or twist the threaded purple thin
> With deftest finger, think, oh! think
> Of her whose web of snowy link,
> Deject Arachne, hangs above.
> See that the gods thy spinning love. (11)

Unmarried and still untouched by eros, Callirrhoë is devoted to her father and obedient to the gods. And yet there are moments when she wonders if she is doomed to female domesticity:

I'm tired of spinning! In the viny sweeps
Of sunshine on the hills, if a god lurk,
Deliverer of women from their toil
In household darkness to the broad sweet light,
Do they so ill to flee to him for joy?
"Can it be meant," I often ask myself,
"Callirrhoë, that thou shouldst simply spin,
Be borne of torches to the bridal bed,
Still a babe's hunger, and then simply die,
Or wither at the distaff, who hast felt
A longing for the hills and ecstasy?" (17)

As it turns out, another fate has indeed been spun for her. Coresus falls in love
with Callirrhoë and asks her to follow his god, who will deliver her from servi-
tude and "set / Your limbs free to the rhythm of your soul" (21). This physical
liberation, Coresus promises, will be a religious revelation as well. "Ask yourself," he says to Callirrhoë, "Have you not a deeper need / Than the stale rites
of customary gods can satisfy?" (21).

The new faith he preaches is not only a liberation from religious custom and
filial devotion into a deeper eroticism, but sounds increasingly like a version of
Pater's aestheticism. The domestic life of Callirrhoë pales in comparison to the
"life urbane" of those who follow Bacchus, the god conceived by the lightning
of Zeus and born to Semele:

Seems it so strange
That Semele's sublime audacity
Should be the origin of life urbane?
We must be fools, all art is ecstasy,
All literature expression of intense
Enthusiasm, be beside yourself.
If a god violate your shrinking soul,
Suffer sublimely. (22–23)

The eroticized violence of this Bacchic religion, which originates in the violation of Semele, nevertheless produces ecstasy and enthusiasm: the original inspiration for "all art" and "all literature." Like Pater who discovers a paradigm
for aesthetic response in the receptivity of the maenad, this drama revolves
around the epiphany of a sensuous new aesthetic. But Callirrhoë is terrified by
this vision at first and spurns Coresus, who calls down a curse upon the city
that can only be spared by sacrificing her; out of love for Callirrhoë, however,
he ultimately sacrifices himself instead. Seeing him "suffer sublimely" in accor-
dance with his own credo, Callirrhoë is converted: "I am a Maenad; I must
have love's wine," she exclaims (101), and runs into the woods to join the other
maenads. Now that he appears more god than man, she is prepared to die for
him:

I love him now
With woman's rapture, when the man she loves
Is god for adoration. I am come
Humbly to supplicate I may receive
Initiation in the Bacchic rites,
And die his Maenad. (118–19)

Stabbing herself with "the sacrificial knife" (122), she pours out her lifeblood for Coresus, like a libation of wine.

In the course of events there are other deaths too, sadder and less triumphant than the self-sacrifice of Coresus and Callirrhoë, but nevertheless the tragedy ends in enthusiastic celebration of the new Bacchanalian religion. Michael Field's preface to the play asserts that "the myth of Dionysus is the glorification of enthusiasm," paraphrasing Pater's enthusiastic conception of Dionysiac religion, and suggesting that we read *Callirrhoë* as an initiation rite into the cult of Pater. Much as Pater introduces "A Study of Dionysus" (an essay surely read and admired by Bradley and Cooper) by reflecting on the metaphorical expression of wine, so also Michael Field prefaces *Callirrhoë* with a reflection on the play's central metaphor. "There is nothing lovelier among natural things than a bunch of grapes, a Bacchanalian cluster of rare crimson," the preface asserts; and then again, "there is nothing lovelier among human things than Love with its halo of self-sacrifice" (iv). To combine these two assertions, the preface then adds that "the natural object and the human affection find their harmony in metaphor" and concludes with a poetic invocation that perfectly expresses this metaphor: "Thou art the wine whose drunkenness is all / We can desire, O Love!" The figural progression is as complex as Pater's prose: just as wine is pressed from the grape, so spirit is expressed from the body, and just as love expresses this spirit, so poetry is the ultimate expression of love. But if in Pater's essay the metaphorical reading of Dionysus is directed toward a male reader (Pater, as we recall, asks "him" to reflect on the imagery of the vine), Michael Field's play appeals in particular to female readers by offering a study of Dionysus from the maenad's perspective. *Callirrhoë* is therefore a more feminine "expression" of Pater's metaphor, asking its readers to believe (as Coresus preaches to Callirrhoë) that "all art is ecstasy, / All literature expression of intense enthusiasm," even and especially if the violence of that enthusiasm is embodied by women.

That the play can be read expressively through its own metaphor is clear from the enthusiastic reviews of *Callirrhoë*. One anonymous reviewer in the *Spectator,* despite a "strong prepossession against its subject," is increasingly drawn in—indeed, possessed—by the drama of a woman who learns "the inspiration of a passion that descends from above." After citing a long passage to illustrate Callirrhoë's conversion into a maenad, and further praising the portrait of Nephele as maenad ("the passage, for instance, in which Nephele recounts the intoxication which came over her . . . is full of genius"), the review concludes that "the play seems to express with great power what the emotions can do to fill life with meaning."[29] Here enthusiastic expression (the language of possession, passion, inspiration, intoxication) is transferred from the characters within the play, to the poets who wrote the play, and then to this reviewer of the play, who is now initiating other readers into "intense enthusiasm" as well. Likewise, a review by A. Mary F. Robinson in the *Academy* suggests that "the introduction of Bacchic cult to Calydon" in *Callirrhoë* introduces a new cult to England as well: "Even . . . today, the cult of Dionysus is new-born," she writes enthusiastically. Inspired by the opening scene, Robinson emphasizes that the maenads arrive at a time when "old laws are breaking up; a longing for freedom and mystery is born; tumult is in the air."[30] She sympathizes with the maenads who take over Calydon, not unlike modern-day women who are breaking up old laws and agitating for new freedom. And even the *Saturday Review*, not known for its sympathetic response to Victorian feminism, praises *Callirrhoë* as a drama "animated by inspiration"—"no pallid rehabilitation of the Greek drama, but vital with the spirit of modernism, fruitful of suggestion, brilliant with actuality."[31]

Thus Bradley and Cooper, Victorian spinsters inspired by Pater's Hellenic aestheticism, breathe a modern spirit into Greek maenads. They had long admired Pater, and after finally meeting him in person they wrote, "Wouldn't one give much to surprise the Bacchant in Walter Pater!"[32] But perhaps he would have been as much surprised at what they saw in him, as "the Bacchant" they discover in his writing is surprisingly different from his own vision of the *Bacchae*. While they are interested in reviving the Bacchant in the present, Pater's interest in maenadism is more scholarly and antiquarian; he draws on a knowledge of ancient Greek that is inaccessible to Bradley and Cooper, not only because they lacked philological training but because the very definition of the scholarly conscience, according to Pater in his essay on "Style," is male. Despite her studies in Greek at Newnham College and elsewhere, Bradley in particular was keenly aware of this lack, as she wrote in a journal entry: "There was one sentence of Mr. Pater's which I would not say I could never forgive, because I recognised its justice: but from which I suffered, and which was hard to bear—that in which he speaks of the scholarly conscience as male" (137). Pater's scholarly conscience assumes a long Hellenic tradition carried on by male scholars along a historical continuum that delineates relations between men, and from which women are excluded. The asymmetry between Pater's institutional position and that of Bradley and Cooper introduces a gendered difference in the forms of sexual dissidence available to them: even when they adopt the pseudonym "Michael Field," they are not authorized by the scholarly tradition that allows Pater to be read as the proper name for a masculine style.

While Callirrhoë embodies an aesthetic vision of the past that is associated with Pater, she therefore articulates a different relation to the future. Pater's "aesthetic historicism," as Carolyn Williams has argued, recognizes that the past can only be represented in the present, yet also understands that representation to be a function of the past.[33] Michael Field's *Callirrhoë*, on the other hand, dramatizes how the future depends not only on the reiteration of the past in Pater's terms, but on new inspiration. After her conversion into a maenad, and before the death that will inspire a new Bacchanalian cult in Calydon, Callirrhoë proclaims:

> The Past is what hath been
> Other than now; the Future is a guest
> Comes not to them
> Who will admit no novel influence.
> Such can but iterate themselves. (121)

The very possibility of formulating history as an aesthetic determination is influenced by Pater, yet the particular emphasis on the future also admits new influences that cannot be predetermined. To write such lines, Bradley and Cooper depend not only on Pater's influence but on a "novel influence" that is their own inspiration. "To make the heart a spirit" is the motto of the play, inscribed as its epigraph, and dramatized in a vision of future maenads who "catch up all life . . . / To make sweet passage for their spirit's breath" (119). It is for these future maenads, rather than Coresus, that Callirrhoë sacrifices herself: a true maenad because she remains a spinster.

Later in life, according to Logan Pearsall Smith, Bradley and Cooper abandoned "the cult of Bacchus" and the "Paterian cult of their earlier years"; they converted to Catholicism and adopted the "quiet of their old-maidenly life at Richmond." If at one time "in moments of exaltation they had been heard to express a Dionysiac desire to dance like Maenads, and tear, in their intoxication, young kids from limb to limb," Smith is quick to add that in reality they were "uninebriated ladies."[34] Here Smith deflates his own inflated fiction of "Michael Field"; the projection of maenads into the future by Bradley and Cooper in *Callirrhoë* is projected by Smith into their distant past. In Smith's recollection, the transformation of Victorian spinsters into Greek maenads is a passing phase, a temporary reversal of the domestic order that ultimately allows Bradley and Cooper to be re-domesticated: the transformation of Greek maenads back into Victorian spinsters, the end of an amusing anecdote. But for Bradley and Cooper, the redefinition of Pater's sensuous aestheticism into a form of female eroticism depends not on their literal identification with maenads, but on the mobility of the maenad as a *figure*. In their journals, for example, Edith describes a feverish dream where "vast Bacchanals rush by, Rubenesque, violent. . . . I am Greek, Roman, Barbarian, Catholic, and this multiform life sweeps me toward unconsciousness"; although she feels close to death, "as soon as I am near it, the brilliant swirl of images is round me and I am caught back to life."[35] The "multiform life" of her imagination allows for many forms of identification; indeed she is revived by this "brilliant swirl of images," rushing by like "vast Bacchanals." The sensuous appeal of their "Rubenesque" bodies is "violent," the embodiment of an erotic power that makes Edith feel variously "Greek, Roman, Barbarian, Catholic" in the course of her life with Katherine: such catholicity of feminine sensation made both Bradley and Cooper lifelong maenads according to Pater's ideal, as they aspired "to touch thought through the senses" but without following the dictates of his scholarly conscience.

III

If Bradley and Cooper were influenced by Pater's Hellenism, even while feeling excluded from the scholarly tradition that authorized it, Jane Ellen Harrison leaves no doubt that the scholarly conscience can also be female. Indeed her own sense of style—in her Classical scholarship, and in her life as a Classical scholar—can be understood as a reworking of Pater's legacy from a feminine and increasingly feminist perspective. The Brasenose scholar in his solitary study at Oxford, and the Newnham scholar within her close circle of friends at Cambridge, inhabited different institutions at different historical moments, but both Pater and Harrison developed a style of imaginative scholarly prose ("imaginative prose being the special art of the modern world," as Pater wrote in "Style") in order to articulate a strangely modern vision of archaic Greece. Harrison was known among her contemporaries as "the Scholar-Gypsy of Hellenic Studies,"[36] and although even then her theories about the ritual origins of Greek religion were disputed, and later fell into disrepute, she has been the subject of renewed critical interest in recent years. In re-evaluating Harrison's place within the history of Classical scholarship, most critics tend to emphasize how she was influenced by nineteenth-century anthropology, Classical archaeology, and comparative religion, or how she in turn influenced twentieth-century theories of ritual and myth; however, I want to emphasize that her work merits re-reading within the context of British aestheticism as well.[37]

Harrison visited Pater once and found him to be a "soft, kind cat" who "purred so persuasively that I lost the sense of what he was saying" (*Reminiscences*, 46). Yet she recaptures the sense of what he was saying in another sense, as she recognizes in his writing a desire for sensation that also inspires her own writing. Harrison was an aesthete in her early years as a student, when she decorated her room at Newnham College with Morris wallpaper, embroidered pomegranates on her tennis clothes, and (according to one of her fellow students) wore "a tight-fitting olive-green serge such as used to be supplied to Newnham students . . . in the days of the aesthetic craze . . . with brown hair in a Greek coil at the back."[38] She embraced aestheticism during her years in London as well, where she lectured on Greek art to ladies ("all spinsters, well-born, well-educated, and well off," as she recalls in *Reminiscences*, 51), and when she published *Introductory Studies in Greek Art* in 1885, she was even criticized by a fellow art historian for being too aesthetic. She introduces her *Studies in Greek Art* along the lines of Pater, by asserting that "an impression of the senses" (v) is derived from the contemplation of Greek art and by presenting her own impressions in written form, so that readers "may nurture their soul on the fair sights and pure visions of Ideal art" (vii). Although Peacock argues in her biographical account of Harrison's career that she "actually changed her style" after being criticized for her aestheticism,[39] the transition from art to mythology in Harrison's work is in fact a logical development of her aesthetic principles, and her actual style of writing a further elaboration of them as well.[40] Much as Pater's Hellenism was shaped by the convergence of art historical, literary, and anthropological discourses toward the end of the nineteenth century, so also Harrison increasingly turned to the conceptual models and techniques of other disciplines—such as archaeology and anthropology, as well as sociology and philosophy later on—in order to convey her impressions of ancient Greece even more vividly. And like Pater, she became especially interested in Dionysiac religion as an expression of enthusiasm that she interprets, retrospectively, to be an original aesthetic impulse.

An early version of Harrison's interest in Dionysiac cults is already evident in her brief review in 1894 of *Psyche* by Erwin Rohde, a German scholar whose book about the immortality of the Greek soul is quickly subsumed into Harrison's own discussion of recent British scholarship on the *Bacchae*. The Cambridge Classicist A. W. Verrall (married to Harrison's fellow student at Newnham, Margaret Verrall) is invoked at the beginning of the review for his account of "the problem of the *Bacchae*," but behind Verrall stands Pater's "Study of Dionysus." Harrison moves back from the "rational" Greeks to the "irrationality" of their early religions, and like Pater, she is fascinated with Dionysus Zagreus in particular. He is the god who is "torn to pieces" and worshipped through *ekstasis* and *askesis*. "What a madness it must have seemed!" she exclaims enthusiastically. "To dance till we are dizzy, to toss our heads in ecstasy, may not seem to us the best means of promoting spirituality," she admits, but nevertheless insists that the true spirit of Dionysus is experienced through the senses. The sensuous immediacy of this experience defies the "common sense" of "the thoroughly British Pentheus"; according to Harrison, the women who follow Dionysus have greater access to the truth, even though it is dubbed "dangerous, disreputable, immoral, a peril to hearth and home" ("Rohde's *Psyche*," 165).

Harrison's revisionary Hellenism—a darker, less rational, more primitive vision of the Greeks—is elaborated in *Prolegomena to the Study of Greek Religion*, published in 1903, the first book written after her return to Newnham College as a Lecturer. The first chapter opens with a quotation of "lovely words" from "Mr. Ruskin," who proclaims the "everlasting calm" and "beauty at perfect rest" of the Greeks and believes "there is no dread in their hearts" (*Prolegomena*, 1). Harrison's entire book, however, is dedicated to the dismantling of that Hellenic ideal: like Pater, she prefers the turbulence and tumult of Dionysiac worship over calm contemplation of the Olympic pantheon, and she emphasizes most of all the importance of wine as a source of literal and figurative inspiration. It is "the constant shift from physical to spiritual that is of the essence of the religion of Dionysos," she writes, allowing the "essence" to be expressed in various ways: "the exhilaration of wine," "the physical beauty of a flower," "the sensuous imagery of words," the "strong wine of a new idea," the "magic of another's personality" (453). Here we see how closely Dionysiac worship is linked to metaphorical expression, both in Harrison's account of the ancient religion as a continual process of transformation, and in the movement of her prose through a series of self-transforming figures.

Harrison's chapters on Dionysos are, in fact, the most mobile passages in the book. Harrison originally intended her studies in pre-Olympian religions to focus on the seasonal cycles of Demeter and Persephone, but just as Pater traced these ancient goddesses back to even earlier forces of nature personified in Dionysus, Harrison also found herself drawn to the origins of the Dionysiac Mysteries. She attributed this shift in emphasis to her colleague Gilbert Murray, however, who translated and edited Euripides and was preparing an edition of the *Bacchae* around 1900. As she was conceptualizing her own book at this time, Harrison wrote in a letter to Murray:

> It's rather dreadful, the whole centre of gravity of the book has shifted. It began as a treatise on Keres with a supplementary notice on Dionysus. It is ending as a screed on Dionysus with an introductory talk about Keres. Whose fault is that? *Never, never* again will I ask you to lecture when I am writing a book, a nice sound one too, it was, till last autumn.[41]

This playful banter between colleagues demonstrates the interplay between literary and anthropological reading that characterizes the work of the "Cambridge Ritualists," and indeed the prose of Harrison's *Prolegomena* is interlaced

with verse translations of the *Bacchae* by Murray. She incorporates his translation of the third choral ode into her own argument, for example, in order to
describe the advent of Dionysus from east to west:

> Blessed land of Pierie,
> Dionysus loveth thee,
>   He will come to thee with dancing,
> Come with joy and mystery,
> With the Maenads at his hest
> Winding, winding to the west.[42]

Harrison's idea that Dionysus came from the east, followed by Thracian maenads, is a theory that has since been refuted by Classical scholars, but her emphasis on Dionysus as a foreign god is significant for the purposes of her argument: "Winding, winding to the west," he arrives from Thrace to ancient
Greece, and from ancient Greece to Victorian England. Thus Dionysus is
westernized, even as he is also orientalized.

The vision of Dionysus as exotic foreigner, a feminized immigrant, is part
of his special appeal to women. What distinguishes Harrison's study of Dionysus from Pater and her scholarly contemporaries, in fact, is her increasingly
historical emphasis on the maenads who follow him. She insists they are not
mythical figures but actual women, named "maenads" to represent "a state of
mind and body . . . almost like a cultus-epithet": "Maenads means of course
simply 'mad woman,'" she writes, "and the Maenads are the women-wor-
shippers of Dionysus of whatever race, possessed, maddened or, as the ancients
would say, inspired by his spirit" (388). As women "of whatever race" they
embody a threat to the social order by disordering the categories of race and
gender that produce "proper" womanhood. The subtext here is distinctly Victorian, as Harrison comments wryly, "The chorus in the *Bacchae* call themselves
'swift hounds of raging Madness,' but the title was not one that would appeal
to respectable matrons" (389). Of course the title does appeal to Harrison, who
may be respectably ensconced as a scholar at Cambridge University yet is fascinated with these raging mad wild women. She quotes a passage from the mes-
senger speech from the *Bacchae*, for example, in Murray's translation:

> I have seen the wild white women there, O king,
> Whose fleet limbs darted arrow-like but now
> From Thebes away, and come to tell thee how
> They work strange deeds. (*Prolegomena*, 395)

In a footnote, Harrison adds that Murray's translation of the Greek word for
white (λευκόν) "preserves the twofold connotation of the word, purity and inspired madness" and then adds her own interpretation of the passage: "The
'wild white women' are in a hieratic state of holy madness, hence their miracu-

Figure 3 *Maenad.* Illustration in Harrison's *Prolegomena to the
Study of Greek Religion* (1903), 398.

lous magnetic powers." While purifying the maenads of their barbarism, into
a state of "white" and "holy" inspiration, Harrison emphasizes their disruption
of patriarchal order and gender hierarchies. She delights in quoting Plutarch's
description of Dionysiac orgies, some of which involved "rites of possession
and ecstasy in very barbarous fashion . . . *frightening the men out of their senses,*"
adding her own emphasis. "However much the Macedonian men disliked
these orgies, they were clearly too frightened to put a stop to them," she concludes, because "the women were possessed, magical and dangerous to
handle" (397–98).

Harrison illustrates her imaginary portrait with a figure of "a beautiful raging
maenad" who has all the trappings of Dionysos: a thyrsos in one hand and a
wild leopard as hunting trophy in the other, a fawn-skin draped around the
shoulders, a live snake winding around the head, and hair unbound (fig. 3).[43]
The pose is not unlike the Greek maenad in Alma-Tadema's painting with her
head back and her knee forward, suspended in an ecstatic dance. In Harrison's
illustration, however, the maenad looks more strikingly masculine, and she further insinuates the possibility of gender transgression by comparing the illustration to the scene in the *Bacchae* where Pentheus is dressed like a maenad:

"When Pentheus would counterfeit a Bacchant he is attired just so; he wears the long trailing chiton and over it the dappled fawn-skin, his hair flows loose, in his hand is the thyrsos" (399). The dappled fawn-skin is described in the *Bacchae* with the Greek adjective ποικίλος, a detail that also attracts Pater's attention in "The Bacchanals of Euripides," describing Dionysus in a "long tunic down to the white feet, somewhat womanly, and the fawn-skin, with its rich spots, wrapped about the shoulders" (*Greek Studies*, 59). The adjective ποικίλος has homoerotic associations for Pater and seems to resonate in Harrison's description as well: in Greek it means "dappled," "variegated," or "intricate" and in Victorian England its translation into phrases like "pied beauty" served increasingly as a homosexual code.[44] The intricacy of the image presented by Harrison therefore implies sexual ambiguity as well as a transgression of gender, leading her into a digression on new laws imposed by Solon in fifth-century Athens to regulate "the outgoings of women . . . forbidding by law all disorder and excess." Harrison makes these regulations sound like an Athenian version of the Contagious Diseases Acts in Victorian England, which restricted free movement of women on the streets: "Among these dreary regulations comes the characteristically modern touch that they are not to go out at night 'except in a carriage and with a light before them,'" Harrison concludes, in another wry comment (*Prolegomena*, 400).

Clearly, Harrison's imaginative sympathies are with the maenads, whose historical experience she validates by insisting on the reality of their Dionysiac cults and ritual practices. In her discussion of *omophagia*, Harrison takes Euripides at his word:

> That a feast of raw flesh of some sort was traditionally held to be a part of Bacchic ceremonial is clear from the words Euripides put into the mouth of his Maenads:
>> The joy of the red quick fountains,
>> The blood of the hill-goat torn,
> where the expression in the original, ὠμοφάγον χάριν, 'joy in eating raw flesh,' admits of no doubt. An integral part of this terrible ritual was the tearing asunder of the slain beast, in order, no doubt, to get the flesh as raw as might be, for the blood is the life. (482–83)

Even if the repetition of "no doubt" does not entirely dispel doubt, Harrison makes her explanation of this "terrible ritual" more credible as a form of sacramentalism with Christian overtones, like the sacramental drinking of wine as the blood of life.[45] This metaphorical conversion is appropriate for a god who is himself the expression of that metaphor, according to Pater's logic: the spirit of Dionysus, the god of wine, is thus taken into the body. But another metaphorical conversion is happening as well in Harrison's prose, as she quotes the words "Euripides put into the mouth of his Maenads": these very words produce the joy of eating raw flesh, as they are themselves "red quick fountains" and "blood of the hill-goat torn," taken into the mouth. In Harrison's argument, maenads are therefore given a special capacity to embody language, making their rituals a powerful incarnation of action in the word and the word in action.

These theories about the origins of Dionysiac worship in maenadic cult are further developed in *Themis: A Study of the Social Origins of Greek Religion*, published by Harrison in 1912, along with "An excursus on the ritual forms preserved in Greek tragedy" by Gilbert Murray. Harrison proclaims herself a "disciple" of Nietzsche in the preface to her second edition of *Themis* (viii), but her reading of the darker, Dionysiac side of Greek religion remains less indebted to *The Birth of Tragedy* than it is to the Victorian reception of Euripides. While maenads are not of primary interest to Nietzsche in his account of Dionysus, maenadism is central to Harrison's conception of ritual as a *dromenon*, an action that is "not merely a thing done, but a thing *re*-done, or *pre*-done with magical intent." The *dromenon*, according to Harrison's definition, is "a thing which, like the drama, is collectively performed" and its "basis or kernel is a *thiasos* or *choros*" (*Themis*, xv). The *omophagia* is Harrison's most important example of a *dromenon*, enacted by maenads who therefore give new birth to the god they worship: indeed, in this striking development of Harrison's argument, it turns out that "Dionysos is but his *thiasos* incarnate" (38). Not only do the maenads take his spirit into the body, but he is the very incarnation of their own spirit and thus projected in song: "As Bacchus he is but the incarnate cry of his thiasos, *Iacchus*." She offers an etymology in a footnote to illustrate how "Bacchus" is the proper name that comes from the chant "*Iacchus*," which is itself but a name for the Greek cry "Ϝιϝακχος" (48). In the collective performance of this cry, as a performative utterance, the god is called into being.

Harrison's maenads seem increasingly powerful, then, as her scholarly research moves from an interest in maenads as women who experience ecstasy under the influence of Dionysus (in the 1894 review), to the representation of the maenad as an actively terrifying and transgressive figure during Dionysiac worship (in *Prolegomena*, 1903), to a group of women who are actually responsible for projecting the god they worship (in *Themis*, 1912). Harrison's emphasis on maenadic ritual is often interpreted as part of an argument about matriarchal culture prior to patriarchal mythology, but the maenad also destabilizes the binary opposition of patriarchy and matriarchy, by mobilizing relations between women beyond the maternal role: the power of the thiasos is that it can project and embody multiple relations.[46] The vision of such a community can be understood within the context of Harrison's life at Newnham College, as a place that had in the course of several decades accumulated its own rituals and networks of relationships between women. When Harrison returned to teach at Newnham, she was an impressive figure whose lecture style was always a dramatic performance, like an initiation into the cult of Dionysus, perhaps, with Harrison self-consciously playing the role of the inspired maenad. Already in London she had a reputation for lecturing with a great sense of drama, as "throwing back her head, she burst into a chorus of Euripides in Greek;"[47] at Newnham one of her students in Classics remembered "the time when an unearthly noise filled the room at the end of a lecture," which turned out to be a young man "demonstrating, according to Miss Harrison's instructions, what was meant by a bull-roarer."[48]

In her teaching as in her scholarship, Harrison replayed the rituals of Dionysiac worship in order to initiate others into the expression of a highly aestheticized and eroticized enthusiasm. She performed it in her lectures, and enacted it in her prose:

> I have often wondered why the Olympians, Apollo, Athena, and even Zeus, always vaguely irritated me and why the mystery gods, their shapes and ritual, Demeter, Dionysos, the cosmic Eros, drew and drew me. I see it now. It is just that those mystery gods represent the supreme golden moment achieved by the Greek, and the Greek only, in his incomparable way. The mystery gods are eikonic, caught in lovely human shapes—but they are life-spirits barely held. Dionysos is a human youth, lovely, with curled hair, but in a moment he is a Wild Bull and a Burning Flame. The beauty and the thrill of it! (*Alpha and Omega*, 204–5)

With an ecstatic exclamation at the end of this passage, Harrison recreates the "beauty and thrill" of Dionysus; she too calls the god into being, as a "Wild Bull" or a "Burning Flame." Her enthusiasm was echoed by her students at Newnham, who responded just as enthusiastically; one of them wrote to Harrison that she "stood for all true magic and mystery of the unknown" and had taught "the thrill and passion of intellectual things—the thrill that could be even stronger and more constraining than being in love!"[49] Although critics raged against the "corybantic Hellenism of Miss Harrison"[50] and accused her of debauching young minds,[51] it was the power of her language that entranced her students, an ability to incarnate words that Harrison attributed to Greek maenads but also contributed to the transformation of a traditional Victorian spinster into an untraditionally charismatic figure. Bernard Russell is said to have offered Harrison a bull "on condition she and some of her women friends would guarantee to tear it to pieces."[52]

The tendency to project Harrison into, or out of, her vividly personal writing has become a critical commonplace; but to read Harrison's texts in the strictly psychological terms proposed by her biographer Sandra Peacock ("as studies of ancient religion and as almost autobiographical texts")[53] misses the larger institutional and cultural context in which these texts circulated.[54] Like Pater's homoerotic Hellenism circulating within the walls of Victorian Oxford, the erotic subtext of Harrison's feminized Hellenism is specific to the institution where she lived and wrote, at Victorian Cambridge. In her *Reminiscences of a Student's Life,* Harrison reflected on her choice to live as an unmarried woman in a women's college:

> By what miracle I escaped marriage, I do not know, for all my life long I fell in love. But, on the whole, I am glad. I do not doubt that I lost much, but I am quite sure that I gained more. Marriage, for a woman at least, hampers the two things that made life to me glorious—friendship and learning. . . . Family life has never attracted me. At its best it seems to me rather narrow and selfish; at its worst, a private hell. The role of wife and mother is no easy one; with my head full of other things I might have dismally failed. On the other hand, I have a natural gift for community life. It seems to me sane and civilised and economically right. I like to live spaciously, but rather plainly, in large halls with great spaces and quiet libraries. I like to wake in the morning with the sense of a great, silent garden around me. These things are, or should be, and soon will be, for-bidden to the private family; they are right and good for the community. If I had been rich I should have founded a learned community for women, with vows of consecration and a beautiful rule and habit; as it is, I am content to have lived many years of my life in a college. I think, as civilisa-tion advances, family life will become, if not extinct, at least much modi-fied and curtailed. (*Reminiscences,* 88–89)

As Martha Vicinus has argued, Harrison's independent intellectual life was sustained by Newnham College, where she found an alternative to marriage and familial relations, and an opportunity to "live spaciously" within a female community where other kinds of relationships might have room to grow.[55] In addition to the passionate friendships she developed with male colleagues throughout her scholarly career, she maintained close ties with the women friends who had shared her college days, and she cultivated intense attach-ments to some of the Newnham students she tutored in Greek.

Harrison's deepest relationships were, in fact, mediated by ancient Greek. She began her early studies with a "tragic passion" for Henry Butcher, who coached her in Classics at Cambridge;[56] much later she was engaged to marry R. A. Neill, a Classical philologist at Pembroke who suddenly died. There was also the friendship with her Newnham classmate and fellow Classicist Marga-ret Verrall, who married A. W. Verrall, Professor of Greek at Trinity, and to whom Harrison poured out her heart in letters from London; they collaborated on a book together, *Mythology and Monuments of Ancient Athens* (1890). Her lifelong friendship with Gilbert Murray also involved collaboration through ancient Greek, as she used his translations and interpretations of Euripides in her own work and included his "Excursus" in *Themis;* another member of "The

Cambridge Ritualists" who contributed to *Themis*, and with whom Harrison shared one of her deep intellectual and emotional interests, was Francis Cornford. His wife Frances had been Harrison's student in Greek at Newnham, and when Harrison learned of their engagement, her solution to "the difficulty" of this triangle was to propose "to teach you Greek & for us all three to work together."[57] Toward the end of her life, Hope Mirrlees came to study Greek with Harrison and stayed to become the companion of her final years: a "ghostly daughter," or, at other times, the "younger wife" of Harrison who proclaimed herself "the older wife."[58]

In all such relationships, however defined or ambiguously undefined, Harrison refused the role of the traditional aunt, who was either made subservient to the family or dismissed as dottily eccentric. "Aunt & Uncle have to me always a touch of comedy & even farce about them," Harrison wrote in a letter to Frances Cornford, "You know not what being a real Aunt is. I don't think it is much of a relationship anyhow."[59] For Harrison, family ties were an overdetermined bond that enforced domesticity for women, even when they chose not to marry; to assume the place of the Aunt within this domestic order seemed not only undesirable but a prohibition of other kinds of desire that might be possible for women. As an unmarried woman and a scholar of Greek, Harrison therefore turned to "Greek eros" for the reconfiguration of feminine desire beyond familial relations. To study Greek was to escape the family, as she recounts in a scene from her own youth:

> Some half-century ago a very happy little girl secretly possessed herself of a Greek grammar. A much-adored Aunt [said] in chill, cutting words, "I do not see how Greek grammar is to help little Jane to keep house, when she has a home of her own." A "home of her own" was as near as the essentially decent aunt of those days might get to an address on sex and marriage, but the child understood: she was a little girl, and thereby damned to eternal domesticity; she heard the gates of the Temple of Learning clang as they closed. (*Alpha and Omega*, 117)

Here the girl's love of Greek is presented not only as a desire for knowledge but the source of secret pleasures, forbidden by the "chill, cutting words" of the Aunt. No matter how "much-adored," the role of the "essentially decent aunt of those days" was to maintain domestic order, to teach the girl to "keep house" and thus to damn her to "eternal domesticity." The alternative to such a life is figured in the "Temple of Learning," a glorified place that sounds vaguely Greek and could be unlocked by learning Greek, which therefore becomes a language of and for desire: an access to higher education that is also the revelation of a higher eros, leading the girl out of "a home of her own" and allowing her to grow into a woman with less domesticated desires. This is the woman that Harrison did in fact become, projecting this memory backward from her present perspective as a Greek scholar at Newnham College.

Even more than Harrison's various relationships, mediated by various kinds of desire, she had an eroticized relation to the Greek language itself. Her narrative of the little girl "secretly possessed of a Greek grammar" is included in a 1915 collection of essays entitled *Alpha and Omega*, which already by its very title points to Harrison's personal identification with the letters of the Greek alphabet. In a 1919 pamphlet entitled *Aspects, Aorists, and the Classical Tripos*, Harrison further narrates, in the first person, how "it has happened to me to fall in love with a language." She describes the vivid sensation of learning Greek for the first time, as a revelation of "sudden sense" that is strongly inflected by Pater's aestheticism:

> The sudden sense came over me, the hot-cold shiver of delight, the sense of a language more sensitive than my own to shades of meaning, more delicate in its balance of clauses, in its setting out of the relations of things, more charged with the magic of, well—Intellectual Beauty. (6)

The creation of "shades of meaning" beyond what is straightforwardly meant gives an erotic charge to ancient Greek that Harrison doesn't quite name, not even after the pause of "well—." For what hangs in the balance (or, "in its balance of clauses") is not only "the relations of things," but Harrison's sense of relations between people as well. It is through the "Intellectual Beauty" of the Greek language that Harrison discovers an eros that reconfigures existing relationships and shades into new meanings, beyond anything her own forbidding Aunt would have imagined.

IV

The redefinition of "tantular" relations in Victorian England is a long story, out of which I have drawn but two brief tales, in order to demonstrate how the first generation of women educated at Newnham College used their Greek studies to articulate different forms of feminine desire. It is important not to limit this discussion of Victorian sexual dissidence to a binary opposition between heterosexuality and homosexuality, since such categories were more interestingly mobile at the end of the nineteenth century than they are at the end of our own. As we have seen, the historical place of the Victorian spinster is redefined through the Greek maenad: Bradley and Cooper play out their family romance by mobilizing the maenad as a poetic figure, and Harrison's scholarly interest in maenads allows Greek eros to be mobilized beyond traditional familial relations. The identification of Victorian spinsters with Greek maenads in my argument does not place them "outside" the social order, of course, but demonstrates how the disordering of its internal structure can create the tantalizing possibility of other kinds of relations. Tales of the tantulate might therefore work alongside Eve Sedgwick's tales of the avunculate, "to project into the future a vision of 'family' elastic enough to do justice to the depth and sometimes durability of nonmarital and/or nonprocreative bonds, same-sex bonds, nondyadic bonds, bonds not defined by genitality, 'step'-bonds, adult sibling bonds, nonbiological bonds across generations, etc."[60]

But if, as Sedgwick proposes, "a more elastic, inclusive definition of 'family'" should begin with a theoretical relegitimation of the avunculate, the historical reconstruction of the tantulate should give us another perspective on the avunculate as well. I began by naming Pater as the "father of longing and desire" within the homoerotic discourses of Victorian Hellenism, and in tracing the influence of his Greek essays on women writers I have suggested that they might be read as Pater's wayward daughters. Yet the tendency to read Pater as the "father" of British aestheticism enforces a familial relation, and a literary lineage, that my tales of the tantulate would also call into question: while women writers at the turn of the century are variously aligned with Pater, the path through his writing to their own is never straight. An "avuncular" reading of Pater is complicated by their vexed relation to the cultural genealogy that authorized him, and continues to authorize Pater as a proper name within literary history, while leaving other figures un-named. The mediation of a feminine style through Pater's "queer" philology therefore depends on a reading of masculine style more perverse than even he might have imagined: in the final telling, Pater is neither father nor uncle. To open the discourses of Hellenism and homosexuality to the various possibilities of female homoeroticism—to discover the subtle shades of meaning of ποικίλη in the feminine alongside ποικίλος in the masculine—we will have to find another language for literary kinship as well as other languages for desire.

Notes

1. Dowling, *Hellenism and Homosexuality*, 94.

2. A gradual shift from Latin to Greek in nineteenth-century education reflects the symbolic status and cultural privilege associated with Greek learning in Victorian England, as described by critics such as Jenkyns, *Victorians and Ancient Greece;* Turner, *Greek Heritage in Victorian Britain;* Clarke, *Rediscovering Hellenism;* Dellamora, *Masculine Desire* and "Dorianism"; Dowling, *Hellenism and Homosexuality;* Stray, "Culture and Discipline." On nineteenth-century women learning Greek see Fowler, "On Not Knowing"; current research by Christopher Stray, Edith Hall, and Mary Beard is beginning to document the entry of women into Greek scholarship in further detail.

3. On the changing structure of higher education in late nineteenth-century England and the "revolution of the dons" at Cambridge in particular, see Rothblatt, *Revo-*

lution of the Dons and *Tradition and Change.* On women's entry into Cambridge, see McWilliams-Tullberg, *Women at Cambridge;* Shils and Blacker, *Cambridge Women;* on women's entry into Oxford see Brittain, *Women at Oxford;* Leonardi, *Dangerous by Degrees;* on women at other British universities, see Dyhouse, *No Distinction of Sex?*

4. Although Cambridge was the last of the British universities to award degrees to women, in 1947, it was the first to have women's colleges: Girton College started in 1869 at Hitchin, under the leadership of Emily Davies, and in 1871 Henry Sidgwick and Millicent Garrett Fawcett opened a residential house for women, in the charge of Anne Jemima Clough, as the precursor to Newnham College. A few years later residential halls opened for women at Oxford as well, and full admission was granted to women at University College London in 1878 and Victoria University in 1880.

5. The cartoon is from *Punch* (February 26, 1876) and also reproduced by Williams in "Pioneer Women Students."

6. According to Mary Paley (one of the first students in occupancy at the house opened in 1871 by Sidgwick and Fawcett, and returning as resident lecturer at Newnham Hall in 1875), Katherine Bradley was among the first twenty students at Newnham along with Jane Harrison; see Peacock, *Harrison,* 45. But according to other accounts, Bradley was attending lectures at Cambridge as early as 1868; see Leighton, *Victorian Women Poets: Writing Against the Heart,* 205. In addition to Bradley's sporadic studies at Cambridge (where she did not sit for exams or receive a certificate), her education included private tutoring and studies at the Collège de France, University College, Bristol. For background on "Michael Field," see Sturgeon, *Michael Field;* Sturge Moore, *Works and Days;* and more recently White, "Poets and Lovers"; Laird, "Contradicting Legacies"; Leighton, *Writing Against the Heart,* 202–43; Blain, "Michael Field."

7. For background on Jane Ellen Harrison, see Stewart, *Harrison: A Portrait;* Peacock, *Harrison;* Schlesier, "Harrison"; Lloyd-Jones, "Harrison." See also Calder, *Cambridge Ritualists.*

8. On the transformation of nineteenth-century spinsters into independent women, see e.g. Vicinus, *Independent Women;* Jeffreys, *The Spinster;* Nord, "Neither Pairs Nor Odd"; see also Ledger, *The New Girl.* On further transformations from "old maids to radical spinsters" in the twentieth century, see Doan, *Old Maids.*

9. On maiden aunts in fact and fiction, see Moore, *Cordial Relations;* on queer possibilities of the aunt, see Blain, "Thinking Back"; Lucey, "Balzac's Queer Cousins." I am grateful to Michael Lucey for an early discussion of these ideas.

10. In Sedgwick's discussion of the avunculate, the historical place of the aunt is too easily displaced by the figure of the uncle, as her collocation of "aunts and uncles" tends to obscure a gendered asymmetry of aunt and uncle within a patrilineal kinship system. Thus Sedgwick's rallying cry to "forget the name of the father" has the effect of forgetting the always already improper name of the mother. Indeed in her reading of *The Importance of Being Earnest* the figure of the aunt turns out to be a French "tante," a

slang word that names relations between men but leaves relations between women un-named ("Avunculate," 59).

11. Showalter, *Sexual Anarchy*, 19.

12. Ledger, "New Woman," 25.

13. An early attempt to distinguish between historical and mythical maenads is Rapp, "Die Mänade"; for more recent reconstruction of historical evidence on maenadic cults and current perspectives on their social function, see Bremmer, "Greek Maenad-ism"; Henrichs, "Greek Maenadism"; Zeitlin, "Cultic Models"; Versnel, *Inconsistencies*, 131–50; Obbink, "Dionysus Poured Out."

14. This Victorian interest in the *Bacchae* reflects a critical shift within the nineteenth-century British reception of Greek tragedy, away from Aeschylus and Soph-ocles and toward Euripides. By the turn of the century, an increasing number of edi-tions, commentaries, and translations of Euripides were circulated by British scholars, including Robert Y. Tyrrell (editor of the *Bacchae*, 1892), A. W. Verrall (author of *Eu-ripides the Rationalist*, 1895, and *The Bacchants of Euripides and Other Essays*, 1910), John Edwin Sandys (editor of *The Bacchae of Euripides, with Critical and Explanatory Notes*, 1900), Gilbert Murray (editor and translator of Euripides from 1900 onward, and author of *Euripides and His Age*, 1913), and G. Norwood (author of *The Riddle of the Bacchae*, 1908). On changing views of Euripides in the nineteenth century, see Jen-kyns, *Victorians and Ancient Greece*, 106–11, Dowgun, "Victorian Perceptions of Greek Tragedy"; Henrichs, "Loss of Self"; Michelini, *Euripides and the Tragic Tradition*.

15. Ruskin, quoted in Kestner, *Mythology and Misogyny*, 278. Kestner discusses other Alma-Tadema canvases also depicting Bacchantes, in various poses: in *There He Is!* (1875), a woman dressed in ivy and animal skins leans forward to catch a glimpse of Dionysos; in *After the Dance* (1877), a maenad exhausted from her revels lies asleep; in *The Torch Dance* (1881), a maenad is dancing in a wild frenzy; in *The Women of Amphissa* (1887), maenads are sprawled on marble slabs; in *A Dedication to Bacchus* (1889), mae-nads dance while a girl is initiated into the cult of Dionysus; in *A Bacchante* (1907), maenads are playing cymbals and pipes (Kestner 276–79, 309–10).

16. Pater, *Greek Studies*, 55. "The Bacchanals of Euripides" was written by Pater in 1878, published in *Macmillan's Magazine* in 1889, reprinted as preface to Tyrrell's edi-tion of the *Bacchae* in 1892, and collected in the posthumous publication of Pater's *Greek Studies* in 1895.

17. Adams, *Dandies and Desert Saints*, 156.

18. These essays circulated at different times and in various forms during the last three decades of the nineteenth century. "Diaphaneitè" is Pater's earliest surviving essay, composed in 1864 but not published until 1895 in *Miscellaneous Studies;* "Winckel-mann" was published in 1867 in the *Westminster Review*, and reprinted in 1873 in *Stud-ies in the Renaissance;* "A Study of Dionysus" was published in the *Fortnightly Review* in 1876, and reprinted along with "The Bacchanals of Euripides" in 1895 in *Greek Studies.*

19. These "urbane young men" are like "the delicate people of the city" that Pater mentions later in the essay (35); the adjective "urbane" has the homoerotic associations of the *urbanus vir,* much as Richard Dellamora also points out that the phrase "delicate people of the city" is a euphemism for the *pueri delicati,* boys with adult lovers (*Masculine Desire,* 178).

20. On Pater as "imaginative anthropologist" see Crawford, "Pater's *Renaissance*"; on the figure of the "Interpreter" introduced by Pater in *Greek Studies,* see Carolyn Williams, who analyzes Pater's interpretation of the vine with further emphasis on its "figural maneuvers" (*Transfigured World,* 243).

21. Morgan, "Reimagining Masculinity," 316.

22. In addition to Dellamora, Dowling, Morgan, and Adams already cited, see also the essays collected by Brake and Small in *Pater in the 1990's,* especially Inman and Higgins on Pater's life inside Oxford; on the circulation of Pater's essays outside the academy in carefully selected journals, see Brake in the same volume.

23. Dellamora, *Masculine Desire,* 176–86.

24. In *Masculine Desire,* Dellamora argues that the myth of Dionysus is not only "rehearsal and mask for Pater's particular interest in relations between men within a patriarchal order," but a revaluation of relations between women as well (176); Pater's interest in the myth of Persephone can also be understood as a response to the Woman Question, according to Dellamora. The essay on "Demeter and Persephone" was published in the *Fortnightly Review* in 1876, the same year as "A Study of Dionysus," and both essays were reprinted in *Greek Studies* in 1895. There is a tradition of reading the two myths alongside one another; for a contemporary discussion of cultic models of the feminine in rites of Dionysus and Demeter, see Zeitlin, "Cultic Models." A more detailed study of the influence of Pater's "Demeter and Persephone" on female aestheticism is, for the time being, beyond the scope of my argument.

25. Michael Field's imitations of Sappho in *Long Ago* (London: Bell, 1889) were inspired by a Victorian edition of the Sapphic fragments compiled in Greek and English by Henry Wharton in 1885. On the Sapphic lyrics of Michael Field, see White, "Tiresian Poet"; Prins, "Sappho Doubled" and "A Metaphorical Field"; Reynolds, "I Lived for Art," 295–304.

26. Blain, "Michael Field," 249; on same-sex desire in the poetry of Michael Field, see also Vanita, *Sappho and the Virgin Mary,* 118–35.

27. Sturge Moore, *Works and Days,* 6.

28. Smith, *Reperusals,* 90–91.

29. *Spectator,* 682.

30. Robinson, Review, 395–96.

31. *Saturday Review,* 192.

32. Sturge Moore, *Works and Days,* 120.

33. Williams, *Transfigured World,* 283.

34. Smith, *Reperusals,* 89.

35. Sturge Moore, *Works and Days,* 54.

36. Ackerman, introduction to *Prolegomena,* xiv.

37. For a reassessment of Harrison's place within the history of Classical scholarship and the influence of her work on current theories of ritual and myth, see Ackerman, "Harrison"; Payne, "Modernizing the Ancients"; Henrichs, "Loss of Self"; Versnel, "Sauce for the Goose"; Schlesier, "Prolegomena" and "Mixtures of Masks"; Lloyd-Jones, "Harrison."

38. Peacock, *Harrison,* 41.

39. Ibid., 69.

40. Jessie Stewart jotted in her notes on Harrison's earlier years that "Jane's urge [is] aesthetic not scientific"; Ackerman also notes that Harrison's early writing is "evocative of Pater and the esthetic movement," and that the "desire to see a pattern" is an aesthetic urge that persists throughout all her work (Ackerman, "Harrison," 221–22). Like Peacock, however, Ackerman finally interprets Harrison's turn to the study of religion as a turn away from her earlier aestheticism (223).

41. Quoted by Ackerman in his introduction to *Prolegomena,* xxvii.

42. Harrison, *Prolegomena,* 372; translation by Murray, *Bacchae.*

43. The figure is taken "from the centre of a cylix with white ground at Munich" and was redrawn as an illustration for Harrison, *Prolegomena,* 398.

44. This point about the Greek term ποικίλος, referring to homosexual love in Plato's *Symposium* and recirculated in its various translations as a homosexual code word by Pater and his circle, is made by Crawford in "Pater's *Renaissance*" and further developed by Dowling in "Ruskin's Pied Beauty." Crawford notes Pater's subtle allusion to ποικίλος in describing Dionysus draped in "fawn-skin, with its rich spots" (854).

45. For further discussion of how the sacramental theory proposed by Harrison might be relevant to an understanding of Dionysiac ritual, but as an *inversion* of normal sacrifice, see Obbink, "Dionysus Poured Out."

46. Here I deviate from a feminist reading that would reclaim Harrison in the name of "matriarchy," as if a matriarchal model is the only alternative to patriarchy and the only way to theorize relations between women. Peacock, for example, assumes the centrality of the mother in her biographical reading of Harrison's life and work; a maternal metaphor also informs the reclamation of Harrison as "foremother" for modern lesbian identity in Passman, "Out of the Closet."

47. Peacock, *Harrison,* 62.

48. Phillips, *Newnham Anthology,* 87.

49. Quoted by Vicinus, *Independent Women,* 155.

50. Payne, "Modernizing the Ancients," 187.

51. Stewart, *Harrison: A Portrait,* 88.

52. Quoted by Lloyd-Jones, "Harrison," 39.

53. Peacock, *Harrison,* 184.

54. Thus in her review of Peacock's biography, Mary Beard points out that a recon-

struction of "the intellectual, social and educational background of Victorian Britain would have produced a very different biography" ("Eccentric," 82).

55. Vicinus, *Independent Women*, 152–57.
56. Peacock, *Harrison*, 53.
57. Quoted ibid., 161.
58. Ibid., 112.
59. Ackerman, "Some Letters," 123.
60. Sedgwick, "Avunculate," 71.

References

Ackerman, Robert. Introduction to Harrison, *Prolegomena to the Study of Greek Religion*, xxiii–xxx. Princeton: Princeton University Press, 1991.

———. "Jane Ellen Harrison: the Early Work." *Greek Roman and Byzantine Studies* 13 (1972): 209–30.

———. "Some Letters of the Cambridge Ritualists." *Greek Roman and Byzantine Studies* 12 (1971): 113–36.

Adams, James Eli. *Dandies and Desert Saints: Styles of Victorian Masculinity.* Ithaca: Cornell University Press, 1995.

The Athenaeum. Review of *Callirhoë; Fair Rosamund* (July 5, 1884): 24–25.

Beard, Mary. "An Eccentric Out of Context." *The Times Literary Supplement* (January 27–February 2, 1989): 82.

Blain, Virginia. "'Michael Field, the Two-headed Nightingale': Lesbian Text as Palimpsest." *Women's History Review* 5, no. 2 (1996): 239–57.

———. "Thinking Back through Our Aunts: Harriet Martineau and Tradition in Women's Writing." *Women: A Cultural Review* 1 (1990): 223–39.

Brake, Laurel, and Ian Small, eds. *Pater in the 1990's.* Greensboro: ELT Press, 1991.

Bremmer, Jan. "Greek Maenadism Reconsidered." *Zeitschrift für Papyrologie und Epigraphik* 55 (1984): 267–86.

Brittain, Vera. *The Women at Oxford: a Fragment of History.* New York: Macmillan, 1960.

Calder, William M., ed. *The Cambridge Ritualists Reconsidered.* Atlanta: Scholars Press, 1991.

Carpenter, Thomas H., and Christopher Faraone, eds. *Masks of Dionysus.* Ithaca: Cornell University Press, 1993.

Clarke, G. W., ed. *Rediscovering Hellenism: The Hellenic Inheritance and the English Imagination.* Cambridge: Cambridge University Press, 1989.

Crawford, Robert. "Pater's *Renaissance*, Andrew Lang, and Anthropological Romanticism." *English Literary History* 53, no. 4 (1986): 849–79.

Dellamora, Richard. "Dorianism." In *Apocalyptic Overtures: Sexual Politics and the Sense of an Ending*, 43–64. New Brunswick, N.J.: Rutgers University Press, 1994.

———. *Masculine Desire: The Sexual Politics of Victorian Aestheticism.* Chapel Hill: University of North Carolina Press, 1990.

Doan, Laura. *Old Maids to Radical Spinsters: Unmarried Women in the Twentieth-century Novel.* Urbana: University of Illinois Press, 1991.

Dowgun, Richard. "Some Victorian Perceptions of Greek Tragedy." *Browning Institute Studies* 10 (1982): 71–90.

Dowling, Linda. *Hellenism and Homosexuality in Victorian Oxford.* Ithaca: Cornell University Press, 1994.

———. "Ruskin's Pied Beauty and the Constitution of a 'Homosexual Code.'" *Victorian Newsletter* 75 (1989): 1–8.

Dyhouse, Carol. *No Distinction of Sex? Women in British Universities, 1870–1939.* London: University College of London Press, 1995.

Field, Michael. [Katherine Bradley and Edith Cooper]. *Callirrhoë; Fair Rosamund.* London: George Bell, 1884.

Fowler, Rowena. "'On Not Knowing Greek': The Classics and the Woman of Letters." *Classical Journal* 78, no. 4 (1983): 337–49.

Harrison, Jane Ellen. *Reminiscences of a Student's Life.* London: Hogarth Press, 1925.

———. *Epilegomena to the Study of Greek Religion.* Cambridge: Cambridge University Press, 1921. Reprinted in *Themis,* 1962 edition.

———. *Aspects, Aorists, and the Classical Tripos.* Cambridge: Cambridge University Press, 1919.

———. *Alpha and Omega.* London: Sidgwick and Jackson, 1915.

———. *Themis: A Study of the Social Origins of Greek Religion.* Cambridge: Cambridge University Press, 1912. Rev. 2d ed., 1927. Reprinted with a preface by John C. Wilson. New York: University Books, 1962.

———. *Prolegomena to the Study of Greek Religion.* Cambridge: Cambridge University Press, 1903.

———. "Rohde's *Psyche,* Part II." *The Classical Review* (April 1894): 165–66.

———. *Introductory Studies in Greek Art.* London: T. Fisher Unwin, 1885.

Henrichs, Albert. "Loss of Self, Suffering, Violence: The Modern View of Dionysus from Nietzsche to Girard." *Harvard Studies in Classical Philology* 88 (1984): 205–40.

———. "Greek Maenadism from Olympias to Messalina." *Harvard Studies in Classical Philology* 82 (1978): 121–60.

Hunt, F., ed. *Lessons for Life: The Schooling of Girls and Women, 1850–1950.* Oxford: Oxford University Press, 1987.

Jeffreys, S. *The Spinster and Her Enemies: Feminism and Sexuality, 1880–1930.* London: Pandora, 1985.

Jenkyns, Richard. *The Victorians and Ancient Greece.* Cambridge: Harvard University Press, 1980.

Kestner, Joseph A. *Mythology and Misogyny: The Social Discourse of Nineteenth-century British Classical-subject Painting.* Madison: University of Wisconsin Press, 1989.

Laird, Holly. "Contradictory Legacies: Michael Field and Feminist Restoration." *Victorian Poetry* 33, no. 1 (1995): 111–28.

Ledger, Sally. "The New Woman and the Crisis of Victorianism." In *Cultural Politics at the Fin de Siècle*, ed. Sally Ledger and Scott McCracken, 22–44. Cambridge: Cambridge University Press, 1995.

Leighton, Angela. *Victorian Women Poets: A Critical Reader.* Oxford: Blackwell, 1996.

———. *Victorian Women Poets: Writing Against the Heart.* Charlottesville: University of Virginia Press, 1992.

Leonardi, Susan J. *Dangerous by Degrees: Women at Oxford and the Somerville College Novelists.* New Brunswick, N.J.: Rutgers University Press, 1989.

Linton, Eliza Lynn. "Nearing the Rapids." *The New Review* (March 1894). Reprinted in *Prose by Victorian Women*, ed. Andrea Bloomfield and Sally Mitchell, 377–86. New York: Garland, 1996.

———. "The Partisans of the Wild Women." *The Nineteenth Century* 31 (March 1892): 455–64.

———. "The Wild Women as Social Insurgents." *The Nineteenth Century* 30 (October 1891): 596–605.

Lloyd-Jones, Hugh. "Jane Ellen Harrison." In *Cambridge Women*, ed. Shils and Blacker, 29–71.

Lucey, Michael. "Balzac's Queer Cousins and Their Friends." In *Novel Gazing: Queer Readings in Fiction*, ed. Eve Kosofsky Sedgwick, 167–98. Durham, N.C.: Duke University Press, 1997.

McWilliams-Tullberg, Rita. *Women at Cambridge: A Men's University, Though of a Mixed Type.* London: Victor Gollancz, 1975.

Michelini, Ann Norris. *Euripides and the Tragic Tradition.* Madison: University of Wisconsin Press, 1987.

Mitchell, Sally. *The New Girl: Girls' Culture in England, 1880–1915.* New York: Columbia University Press, 1995.

Moore, Katharine. *Cordial Relations: The Maiden Aunt in Fact and Fiction.* London: Heinemann, 1966.

Morgan, Thaïs E. "Reimagining Masculinity in Victorian Criticism: Swinburne and Pater." *Victorian Studies* 36, no. 3 (1993): 315–32.

Murray, Gilbert. *Euripides and His Age.* Oxford: Oxford University Press, 1913. 2d ed., 1946.

———. *The Bacchae of Euripides, Translated into English Rhyming Verse With Explanatory Notes.* London: George Allen, 1904.

Nord, Deborah Epstein. "'Neither Pairs Nor Odd': Female Community in Late Nineteenth-century London." *Signs: Journal of Women in Culture and Society* 15, no. 4 (1990): 733–54.

Obbink, Dirk. "Dionysus Poured Out: Ancient and Modern Theories of Sacrifice and Cultural Formation." In *Masks of Dionysus*, ed. Carpenter and Faraone, 65–86.

Passman, Tina. "Out of the Closet and into the Field: Matriculture, the Lesbian Perspective, and Feminist Classics." In *Feminist Theory and the Classics,* ed. Nancy Sorkin Rabinowitz and Amy Richlin, 181–208. New York: Routledge, 1993.

Pater, Walter. *Greek Studies: A Series of Lectures.* 1895. Reprint New York: Chelsea House, 1983.

Peacock, Sandra. *Jane Ellen Harrison: The Mask and the Self.* New Haven: Yale University Press, 1988.

Payne, Harry C. "Modernizing the Ancients: The Reconstruction of Ritual Drama 1870–1920." *Proceedings of the American Philosophical Society* 122, no. 3 (1978): 182–92.

Phillips, Ann, ed. *A Newnham Anthology.* Cambridge: Cambridge University Press, 1979.

Prins, Yopie. "A Metaphorical Field: Katherine Bradley and Edith Cooper." *Victorian Poetry* 33 (1995): 129–48.

———. "Sappho Doubled: Michael Field." *Yale Journal of Criticism* 8 (1995): 165–86.

Rapp, A. "Die Mänade in griechischen Cultus, in der Kunst und Poesie." *Rheinisches Museum für Philologie* 27 (1872): 1–22, 562–611.

Reynolds, Margaret. "'I Lived For Art, I Lived for Love': The Woman Poet Sings Sappho's Last Song." In *Critical Reader,* ed. Leighton, 277–306.

Robinson, A. Mary F. Review of *Callirrhoë: Fair Rosamund. The Academy* (June 7, 1884): 395–96.

Rothblatt, Sheldon. *Tradition and Change in English Liberal Education: An Essay in History and Culture.* London: Faber and Faber, 1976.

———. *The Revolution of the Dons: Cambridge and Society in Victorian England.* London: Faber and Faber, 1968.

The Saturday Review. "Some Minor Poets." (August 9, 1884): 192–93.

Schlesier, Renate. "Mixtures of Masks: Maenads as Tragic Models." In *Masks of Dionysus,* ed. Carpenter and Faraone, 89–114.

———. "Jane Ellen Harrison." In *Classical Scholarship: A Biographical Encyclopedia,* ed. W. W. Briggs and W. M. Calder III. New York: Garland, 1990.

———. "Prolegomena to Jane Harrison's Interpretation of Ancient Greek Religion." In *Cambridge Ritualists,* ed. Calder, 185–226.

Sedgwick, Eve. "Tales of the Avunculate: Queer Tutelage in *The Importance of Being Earnest.*" In *Tendencies,* 52–72. Durham: Duke University Press, 1993.

Shils, Edward, and Carmen Blacker, eds. *Cambridge Women: Twelve Portraits.* Cambridge: Cambridge University Press, 1996.

Showalter, Elaine. *Sexual Anarchy: Gender and Culture at the Fin de Siècle.* New York: Viking, 1990.

———. *The Female Malady: Women, Madness and English Culture 1830–1980.* New York: Pantheon, 1985.

Smith, Logan Pearsall. *Reperusals and Recollections.* New York: Harcourt, Brace, 1937.

The Spectator. "A New Poet." (May 24, 1884): 680–82.

Stewart, Jessie G. *Jane Ellen Harrison: A Portrait from Letters.* London: Merlin Press, 1959.

Stray, Christopher A. "Culture and Discipline: Classics and Society in Victorian England." *International Journal of the Classical Tradition* 3, no. 1 (1996): 77–85.

Sturge Moore, T., and D. C. Sturge Moore, eds. *Works and Days: From the Journals of Michael Field.* London: John Murray, 1933.

Sturgeon, Mary. *Michael Field.* New York: Macmillan, 1922.

Turner, Frank M. *The Greek Heritage in Victorian Britain.* New Haven: Yale University Press, 1981.

Vanita, Ruth. *Sappho and the Virgin Mary: Same-Sex Love and the English Literary Imagination.* New York: Columbia University Press, 1996.

Versnel, H. S. *Inconsistencies in Greek and Roman Religion,* vol. 1. Leiden: Brill, 1990.

———. "What's Sauce for the Goose is Sauce for the Gander: Myth and Ritual, Old and New." In *Approaches to Greek Myth,* ed. Lowell Edmunds, 25–90. Baltimore: The Johns Hopkins University Press, 1990.

Vicinus, Martha. *Independent Women: Work and Community for Single Women 1850–1920.* Chicago: University of Chicago Press, 1985.

———. "'One Life to Stand Beside Me': Emotional Conflicts in First-Generation College Women in England." *Feminist Studies* 8, no. 3 (1982): 603–28.

White, Chris. "The Tiresian Poet: Michael Field." In *Critical Reader,* ed. Leighton, 148–61.

———. "'Poets and lovers evermore': The Poetry and Journals of Michael Field." In *Sexual Sameness: Textual Differences in Lesbian and Gay Writing,* ed. Joseph Bristow, 26–43. London: Routledge, 1992.

Williams, Carolyn. *Transfigured World: Walter Pater's Aesthetic Historicism.* Ithaca: Cornell University Press, 1989.

Williams, Perry. "Pioneer Women Students at Cambridge, 1869–81." In *Lessons for Life: The Schooling of Girls and Women, 1850–1950,* ed. Felicity Hunt, 171–217. Oxford: Basil Blackwell, 1987.

Zeitlin, Froma. "Cultic Models of the Female: Rites of Dionysus and Demeter." *Arethusa* 15 (1982): 129–57.

THREE

The Adolescent Boy: Fin-de-Siècle Femme Fatale?

MARTHA VICINUS

Bram Dijkstra in his sweeping survey of fin-de-siècle art argues that women are always dangerous in the fantasies of artists and writers of European high culture.[1] His analysis does include slighting glances at other options, but in the main it confirms what has been too long a critical commonplace, namely that late nineteenth-century Europe was a high point of cultural misogyny. Certainly late nineteenth-century novelists appear to have specialized in portraying unsuccessful marriages or heroes who never marry. Moreover, feminist critics of our own time have largely confirmed Dijkstra's position, by arguing that attacks on women, ranging from such best-sellers as George du Maurier's *Trilby* (1894) to Oscar Wilde's *Salomé* and its many European imitations, were reactions to the very successes of a generation of feminists.[2] Certainly the extraordinary outpouring of vituperation against the "New Woman" novels and novelists seems to confirm this general sense that the 1890s was a high point of gynophobia.[3] Dijkstra's reading of the period, however, is surely simplistic, for it not only denies all agency to women as actors on the cultural stage, but it also ignores the ways in which an artist could problematize the stereotypes of the time. Moreover, his focus on negative images of women either disregards or ignores other powerful cultural images.

As my title indicates, I will argue that the adolescent boy was as troubling for the turn-of-the-century artist as the better-known predatory woman. The continued marginalization of this symbolic figure in literary history points to our own homophobia far more than to contemporary distaste for "the love that dared not speak its name." As Martin Green has pointed out in his study of boys' adventure tales, it was "a striking feature of late Victorian culture that its emotional focus was on boys."[4] Of indeterminate character, this handsome liminal creature could absorb and reflect a variety of sexual desires and emotional needs. He personified a fleeting moment of liberty and of dangerously attractive innocence, making possible fantasies of total contingency and total annihilation. For men, the boy suggested freedom without committing them to action; for women, he represented their frustrated desire for action. But most of all, his presence in fin-de-siècle literature signified the coming of age of the modern gay and lesbian sensibility: his protean nature displayed a double desire—to love a boy and to be a boy.

Throughout Europe the boy became a vessel into which an author—and a reader—could pour his or her anxieties, fantasies, and sexual desires.[5] I will concentrate here, however, on the uses to which well-known Anglo-American homosexual men and women writers put the figure of the boy.[6] The sexual preferences of all the authors mentioned here were accepted and gossiped about by their friends and contemporaries; few were as notorious as Oscar Wilde and Renée Vivien, but all were part of recognized homosexual networks. This essay is an initial effort to trace the ways in which homosexuals of both sexes drew from similar cultural materials to fashion images that recast long-standing stereotypes. The presentation of the extremes of emotional pleasure and social peril was a means of arguing both covertly and overtly the centrality of their love.

Gay and lesbian history has long concentrated on the fin de siècle as a pivotal period during which the longstanding homosexual male culture became a visible part of the mainstream literary world, the modern lesbian identity was delineated, and both the word and the concept "homosexuality" were coined and medicalized.[7] Documentation for this shift has been plentiful, but the focus to date has been on the ways in which a separate subculture defined itself both with and against the new medical paradigms formulated by such well-known sexologists as Richard von Krafft-Ebing, Havelock Ellis, and Sigmund Freud. Remarkably little has been said about the ways in which flourishing homosexual literary circles refashioned common images and character stereotypes in order to confirm its own culture.[8] Medical writers defined only two deviant subjects: the adult effeminate man who sought sexual relations with a young boy, and the mannish woman who desired feminine women. Without repudiating these types, middle-class homosexual writers of both sexes shifted the focus to an idealized adolescent boy. Even though many male homosexuals were not pederasts and most lesbians did not look like boys, he was the defining, free agent who best expressed who they were. We are repeatedly asked to look—and then look again—to see the hidden meaning of the beautiful boy.

Jonathan Dollimore has pointed out that the gay man cannot merge with that which he lacks but must instead create a new sexual paradigm based on similarity. The boy embodied not the Lacanian Other so much as the sexually proximate—the adult viewer's own past, as well as the desired object.[9] For turn-of-the-century writers, he is most attractive as either a fragile, ethereal naif or its opposite, an arrogant, untamed rule-breaker; inevitably the other-worldly boy is discovered to be more knowing than the man, and the boy-adventurer more innocent than he at first appears. All encounters are by definition hazardous and fleeting; violence metaphorically expresses the socially

deviant desire and demonstrates its feared outcome. Death stalks the most lov-
ing of relationships, or the boy commits suicide for reasons known only to the
initiated. Nevertheless, fin-de-siècle homosexual love is made more complete
by the very fact of its transitory and dangerous nature.

Much less has been said about the uses to which lesbian writers have put the
figure of the boy. The most obvious distinction is the shift from the desire for
the boy to being the boy himself. Although lesbians borrowed from gay male
culture in their construction of the boy-as-lesbian-subject, their heroes reverse
or rewrite the conventions of femininity. Lesbians looked to the boy because
he could represent visually their sense of difference from other women. He
represented action without responsibility, a transvestic disguise that permitted
either sexual or emotional aggression or childlike responsiveness. The lesbian
as a character type, as opposed to lesbianism as a temporary premarital aberration, seemed so anomalous that she could only be portrayed in an unnatural
context. Thus, the lesbian-boy, like the adolescent boy in male homosexual
fiction, also inhabited a violent world in which all relations were ephemeral.

An obsession with unrequited love, violence, and death characterizes the
Decadents on both sides of the Channel. The presentation of love as unnatural
and dangerous had its roots in the self-consciously gay writings of Oscar Wilde
(1854–1900) and the young French and English poets who admired him.
These same writers, as well as many others, were fascinated with artificiality,
youthfulness, and moral self-doubt. Decadent images and literary devices were
used as covers for—or representative of—deviant, concealed desires. Masquerade, duplicity, and concealment seem to go hand in hand with violence.

Homosexual writers also reinterpreted common myths, denied or reversed
familiar metaphors, and privileged the mannered, the irrational, and the inexplicable. Often drawing on Classical mythology and biblical stories, they created new plots, settings, and characters. The most obvious positive source for
constituting an alternative homosexual image was Classical literature.[10] The
celebration of pedagogical eros in Greek literature became the cornerstone on
which late nineteenth-century writers could construct a spiritual self-portrait.
Henry Wharton's 1885 translation of Sappho revealed that some of her poems
were explicitly addressed to young women lovers; this edition gave women access to a "Sapphic tradition."[11] In addition to literary precedents, fin-de-siècle
writers refashioned Classical myths and historical figures. Pan, Apollo, Adonis,
Diana, and other figures associated with Nature, youth, and freedom in Greek
mythology were especially popular. They also compared their fictional characters to such well-known boy lovers as Hyacinth, Ganymede, and Antinous,
alerting an inner circle to the implicit sexual message. A reworked classicism
gave same-sex love something more than respectability; it also implied a superior, spiritualized disdain for contemporary materialism and progress.

The leading medical theorists of the time argued that homosexuality was not a choice but a biological necessity—if this were true, then a homosexual writer could associate his or her desire with either a congenital aberration or a mythological figure; in either case, sexuality was not chosen, but intrinsic. Not surprisingly, writers foregrounded the irrational and inexplicable. Since the socially sanctioned cycle of courtship, marriage, and children was irrelevant, much homosexual writing of the time celebrates the sensual moment. Either overtly or covertly, authors signaled a forbidden relationship, a contrary courtship—the biological sameness of the homosexual act. This sameness is made different for men by accentuating the difference in age; for lesbians it is the visual difference encoded in the "boyish" androgyne.[12] By casting the boy as the main figure in their stories of failed regeneration, homosexual writers exaggerated a brief moment of physical perfection as their ideal subject matter. Since the boy inevitably grows up (or, in many of these Decadent plots, dies), the happy, long-term relationship is immaterial.

Men and women whose sexual lives were in opposition to biological reproduction did not defy its hegemony, but rather insisted on a superior option—art. Physical reproduction is replaced with meta-physical and artistic generativity. Indeed, for some writers the permanence of art was the only alternative to the impermanence of a love publicly defined as sterile and transient. In story after story the natural reproductive cycle is thwarted, sidestepped, or intentionally avoided. Nature too is redefined, away from images of fertility toward images of freedom. The cycle of seasonal change, just like the cycle of maturation and marriage, is broken. Yet unlike *Frankenstein* and its many nineteenth-century progeny, the fin-de-siècle homosexual tale did not usurp the divine (and maternal) prerogative of generation but instead celebrated the privileged choice of artistic creativity.[13] In a self-portrait of their persona, Michael Field, the lesbian poets Katherine Bradley and Edith Cooper aptly described the homosexual artist:

> He is a plan, a work of some strange passion
> Life has conceived apart from Time's harsh drill,
> A thing it hides and cherishes to fashion
> At odd bright moments to its secret will.[14]

The Homosexual's Boy

Fin-de-siècle gay male writers wrote within a preexisting homoerotic tradition. They had both literary and cultural models of socially sanctioned homosociality from which to draw. For over a generation, boys' school and adventure stories had demonstrated the civilizing effects of male bonding in single-sex institutions. As Jeffrey Richards has pointed out, "manly love" was encouraged by the study of Classical literature, the anti-heterosexuality edicts of Christianity, and the tenets of British imperialism.[15] Narratives of physical hardship, spiritualized love, and idealistic self-sacrifice all equated youth as the perfect time of life. This idealization of boys in one's own social class may have made it easier to idealize—and use—boys from the lower classes.

The cross-age homoeroticism of the public schools and military was replicated in some of the numerous cross-class descriptions of spunky, virile lads in the slums of London, Berlin, Venice, and other European cities. Seth Koven has described a British version, in which repressed Oxbridge idealists wrote glowingly of the "spirited and manly" "rough lads" with whom they worked in settlement houses and clubs.[16] These obvious projections of spiritualized desire onto the young male body seem characteristic of a barely concealed homosexual desire, but they also point to a particular fascination with earthiness that could easily tip into violence or, as contemporaries called it, "hooliganism." Indeed, "manly love" was a cover for both sexless devotion and a homosexual passion that found an outlet in paying handsome telegraph boys for sexual services.[17] Wilde understood this "rough trade" from his forays among working-class boys and embodied it in his characterization of Sibyl Vane's jealous brother.[18] Frederick Rolfe repaid his English sponsor by sending photographs and writing long descriptions of the boys he had picked up in the slums of Venice. These letters appear to have circulated among the homosexual community in England.[19] Fin-de-siècle men were by no means the first to conflate the spiritual and the earthly in their love.

The focus on the feelings and sensibility of this older protector often distinguishes homosexual from homoerotic fiction. Guiding the boy turns out to be overwhelmingly desirable and dangerous. The privileged creator of art is frequently the chief patron of the boy, establishing art as a tempting alternative to heterosexual reproduction. The most famous artistic rendition of adolescent beauty was Basil Hallward's portrait of his beloved in Oscar Wilde's *The Picture of Dorian Gray* (1890). But Basil is not alone in his desire to form Dorian. Lord Henry Wotton, the man who first seduces Dorian—with a book—is in a childless marriage. Instead, his energy goes into reproducing himself through Dorian. At first he warns Dorian, "To influence a person is to give him one's own soul. He does not think his own natural thoughts, or burn with his natural passions."[20] But soon his erotic attraction is manifest, for he thinks of his words as an arrow, shot to pierce the boy. Wotton plays Dorian like a violin:

> There was something terribly enthralling in the exercise of influence. No other activity was quite like it. To project one's soul into some gracious form, and let it tarry there for a moment; to hear one's own intellec-

tual views echoed back to one with all the added music of passion and youth; to convey one's temperament into another as though it were a subtle fluid or a strange perfume: there was a real joy in that. (Chap. 3, p. 35)

If Basil creates what he hopes will be his most perfect work—a vivid portrait of the thing he loves—Wotton seeks more directly to mold Dorian into an image of himself. Indeed, at one juncture he claims to himself, "To a large extent the lad was his own creation" (chap. 4, p. 57). But "the lad" evades both Basil and Lord Henry to be his own person, becoming a warning to them—and us—of the limits of such self-generation.

Richard Dellamora in his discussion of *The Picture of Dorian Gray* has pointed out that Wilde set a pattern of homosexual writing in which the representation of desire was substituted for desire itself.[21] I find another metonymy is also operative, that of the secret site. Desire is represented not only by the forbidden person, but also by the forbidden place. The plot cannot advance without a hint of the nameless sin or, more positively, an unattainable goal. Dorian hides his sin, represented by the picture, in his old schoolroom, the very place where he was an innocent boy. In time, he kills Basil, disposes of his body, and kills himself in this room. The tutor's room in James's "The Pupil" (1891) remains a much-discussed but never-entered space. However much the pupil and the tutor love each other, they cannot act. The impossibility of fulfillment leaves the room off limits, even though Morgan Moreen "clung to the romantic utility of this when the day, or rather the night, should arrive for their escape."[22] The word "escape" occurs with increasing frequency as the story rushes to the final dénoument—the "boyish joy" of an instant, and then Morgan's death.

In an effort to break the inexorable flow of time, some authors and artists gave their adolescents a mythic status, evoking the mischievous Puck or chthonic Pan, as if to remove them from normal causality. Peter Pan is the most famous example of this figure, but before he is captured by the Irish regiment, Kim also seems able to evade time and place. In "The Story of a Panic" (1902), E. M. Forster portrayed a fifteen-year-old dominated by maiden aunts and officious ministers, who becomes a Pan; only a dark, primitive Italian fisherman understands him. His moments of pure happiness, darting about out of doors, are cut short by the Italian's betrayal; but Gennaro repents and frees the boy. The story ends with Gennaro's sudden death, clasping his bribe, while "there still resounded the shouts and the laughter of the escaping boy."[23]

Both such canonized works as *Kim* and *Peter Pan* and the formulaic boys' adventure tales teeter on the edge of homoerotic violence, while gay texts more openly equate death and violence with the forbidden. Forster's boys are freed from adult destruction by death or magic, but Wilde's darker vision recognized the impossibility of beauty (and innocence) made permanent. Dorian's friendships are "fatal to young men," even though the besotted Basil insists, "Sin is a thing that writes itself across a man's face. It cannot be concealed. . . . Dorian, with your pure, bright, innocent face, and your marvellous untroubled youth— I can't believe anything against you" (chap. 12, pp. 149–50). Exactly what Dorian has done to so many young men is left unnamed, but not unknown; his propensity for violence and sadism has been foreshadowed in his brutal treatment of Sybil. Even if Basil thinks deviant desire cannot be read on Dorian's body, his sexual acts are permanently inscribed on the picture, itself the product of homosexual love.

Death seems to be a means of avoiding the very depravity that marked Dorian's fall into experience. Morgan Moreen, like a latter-day Little Nell, dies just as the sexual consummation he has demanded becomes possible. Alternatively, if one could not escape one's nature, as the sexologists claimed, then one could celebrate its beauty and courage. A. E. Housman turned homosexual suicide into an act of perfect manliness in the plangent verse of *A Shropshire Lad* (1896):

> Oh, soon, and better so than later
>> After long disgrace and scorn,
> You shot dead the household traitor,
>> The soul that should not have been born.[24]

Since love cannot lead to marriage and reproduction, but only "Soul's undone, undoing others . . . to wrong your brothers," better to die "as fits a man." Housman's pessimistic advice, Dorian Gray's striking death, and Morgan's sudden heart attack seem to confirm the implicit self-hatred of the fin-de-siècle homosexual writer. But this is too easy a conclusion. Basil's "splendid portrait" of Dorian's "exquisite youth and beauty" is restored at the end of the novel, as if to commemorate both the creative and destructive elements Wilde found in his own homosexuality. Art remains, though the artist and his subject die. Indeed, the conclusion to Housman's elegy brings us full circle: to honor the boy who killed himself lest he sully others, the narrator brings him a wreath— the poem—"that will not fade." Art memorializes not simply the passing of a temporary moment, boyhood, but also a permanent condition, or in Housman's words, a "soul that should not have been born."

The artist could commemorate the boy, or he could himself be the boy, where the desired object and art become one. Wilde and Housman may have seen their love as doomed, but the sexually polymorphous Aubrey Beardsley found only pleasure in being the boy-artist.[25] The tubercular Beardsley, so commanding in his artistic genius, seems to have identified with self-contained, yet vulnerable, youths, beset by or witness to the raging ferocity of lust around them. His self-portraits exaggerate his youthfulness, portraying him as a sensitive, effeminate naif. Beardsley, unable to act out the full range of his sexual fantasies, cast himself as a passive boy, enmeshed in desire but incapable of execution. In one of his most famous late drawings, he portrays himself as a boy tied to a gigantic phallus, a Pan who cannot play the pipes, either his own or anyone else's. Gazing out at the viewer, he insists that we see the inextricable connection between sex and art not as a personal tragedy, but as a comic necessity. As if to confirm the sexologists' theory that homosexual men and women belonged together in the category of a third sex, his conflation of the artist with the boy leads directly into the lesbian writers' identification with the boy as a marginal sexual subject.

The Lesbian Boy

The extraordinarily varied roles played by the adolescent boy in gay male writing do not characterize lesbian writing of the period. Lesbians were not working within a well-established tradition but were making their own, selecting images from different sources that answered their sense of an unnamed sexual subjectivity. The androgynous boyish heroine, if not an actual boy, was an obvious, even over-determined, choice as a heroine for lesbians. For centuries many women authors had gendered themselves male, both in their use of pseudonyms and in their self-image. On stage, in opera and in the music halls, the boyish male impersonator was a well-established figure. The sexologists, looking around at the numerous unmarried women involved in long-term romantic friendships, identified the "true invert" as a mannish woman.

Identifying oneself as a boy was not simply a matter of taking over male status and freedom. Rather, his liminal sexual position and appearance gave him the necessary combination of familiarity, ambiguity, and distance. For some lesbians the boy was a figure not of adventuresome sexual exploration, but rather of preternatural understanding and spiritual purity. Like male homosexuals, they put themselves in the position of admirers of the boy, pointing to his chaste innocence as representative of a special, lost quality in the modern world. Alternatively, some lesbian writers embraced the figure of the boyish (never girlish) androgyne as representative of their difference from other women. It did not carry the negative connotations of male effeminacy for women, but rather could signify their refusal of heterosexuality. A. J. L. Busst has pointed out that the dominant characteristic of the Decadent androgyne was its identification with the virgin.[26] In a world where virginity was narrowly defined as the absence of heterosexual sex, a purified image of the androgyne could represent a higher form of sexuality. For lesbians such as Renée Vivien, lesbian sex was not merely different from, but better than heterosexuality; this radical message had to be carried by an androgyne, because a boy would have been sullied by the potentiality of male heterosexuality. Other writers, however, found such a figure too unnatural (or too revealing) and chose to cast the sexual outsider as a boy or young man. This "cover" had the additional asset of concealing lesbian desire from the general reader.

At a time when most women writers were dropping the pseudonyms that had characterized an earlier generation, lesbians seemed to flaunt their chosen names. Katherine Harris Bradley (1846–1914) and her partner Edith Emma Cooper (1862–1913) were known by their friends as Michael and Henry; in their correspondence they referred to their joint persona, "Michael Field," as "he."[27] Violet Paget (1856–1935) always wrote under the name Vernon Lee. She and her companion Kit Anstruther-Thomson were both painted by their friend John Singer Sargent as mannish women. Radclyffe Hall, author of *The Well of Loneliness* (1928), was born Marguerite Radclyffe-Hall (1880–1943) but called herself John and dressed in ultra-masculine high fashion. Edith Somerville (1858–1949) and Violet Martin (1862–1915) published jointly under the names E. O. Somerville and Martin Ross. Only Renée Vivien (1877–1909) took a feminine name, but in the process she announced her re-birth into a new life as a French lesbian, rather than remain the prosaic Anglo-American Pauline Tarn; even her name, in spoken French, is indistinguishable from its masculine variant. These self-creations draw attention to the ways in which lesbians conceived of their artistic selves, regardless of their actual appearance, as between the sexes—as mannish women.

One of the most characteristic moves of the turn-of-the-century lesbian writers was to rework familiar mythologies, natural imagery, and Decadent metaphors. Their task was to find ways to express the previously unexpressed, rather than simply avoiding the delineation of heterosexual desire. While others have noted that the early lesbian writers normally chose traditional, even old-fashioned, forms in which to write about their radical subject matter, too little attention has been paid to their use of nonrealistic genres, such as Gothic tales, prose poems, and fantastic fables, genres made popular by their gay male peers. The aestheticism of the Decadents was an attractive option, but it needed to be purged of its misogyny and ennui.[28] As Angela Leighton has pointed out, fin-de-siècle women craved more experience of life and could not afford to pose as weary cynics.[29] A refashioned past, whether Greek or Renaissance—the most popular eras—signaled both learning and an imaginative space where the lesbian imagination might flourish. Exotic settings were also congenial, though "the primitive" was avoided for its connotations with an essentialized, maternal femininity. A fantastic garden, for example, provided the cultivated nature in which the androgynous boy could flourish.

Familiar symbols of femininity, such as the moon, water, and caves, testify to the special powers of women. Michael Field created a lush, teeming world, with Nature at its zenith, as if to celebrate the tactile fullness of the female body. Warm, dark nights in pagan settings are a favorite site for them as well as for other lesbians of the time. On the other hand, Michael Field compare their love to a base metal, as if to underscore not only its durability but also its distance from more traditional images of woman's soft and pliant nature:

> Yea, gold is son of Zeus: no rust
>   Its timeless light can stain;
> The worm that brings man's flesh to dust
>   Assaults its strength in vain:
> More gold than gold the love I sing,
> A hard inviolable thing.[30]

A love "more gold than gold" is impervious to the normal cycle of time and to the possibilities of assault. While gay male writers sought ways to hold forever the passionate moment, Michael Field linked lesbian love to images of pagan immutability.

Snakes—those most polymorphous of traditional symbols—appear repeatedly as positive signs, as if to overturn Eve's sin. Vernon Lee's Prince Alberic willingly kisses a snake, who possesses special powers to aid him. The heroine of Renée Vivien's novel *A Woman Appeared to Me* (1904) describes finding a hermit in the Rockies who warns her that snakes can never be killed but always come back to haunt one. The boyish heroine is herself closely associated with snakes; on one occasion she is described as "glid[ing] over the carpet with a rustle of scales" (32). Both Lee and Vivien see the snake-temptress of Genesis as an embodiment of women's power, for "Dead serpents come to life beneath the gaze of those who love them. The magic eyes of Lilith revive them as moonlight moves stagnant water."[31] Vivien's powerful image reminds the reader of woman as avenger, but recast to emphasize the danger of women's sexual subjectivity even when hidden from the prying eyes of heterosexual society.

Katherine Bradley and Edith Cooper were captivated by the male homosexual culture of the 1890s, even as they remained wary of its misogyny and artificiality. In 1894 they met the artists Charles Ricketts (1866–1931) and Charles Shannon (1863–1937), a sympathetic homosexual couple who shared their commitment to aestheticism and art. They convinced "the Fields" to join them in Richmond, where Ricketts promised to supervise the redecorating of the house he found for them—an offer they only partially endorsed. Edith Cooper wrote in their diary, "They seem fated to befriend our work, and to be associated with us. We are lightly apprehensive; but we cannot reject the only offer of kind-feeling we have had for years."[32] Soon the women were calling

Ricketts "Fay," "Fairyman," and "Painter" and recording his brilliant conversation in their diary. He returned the flattery, calling them "Cher Maître" and "Poet." He also critiqued their poetry and designed and published several of their volumes as part of his Vale Press series. Ricketts especially liked a series of poems they wrote about Italian paintings of fauns, Saint Sebastian, and a shepherd boy—all well-known male homosexual icons. The poem celebrating Giorgione's "A Shepherd-Boy" shows their fascination with the tropes of male homosexuality, including youthful innocence and a bygone golden age:

> The face aglow with southern light,
> Deep, golden sunbrown on the neck;
> Warm eyes, sweet mouth of the softest lips:
>   Yea, though he is not playing,
> His hand a flute Pandean grips,
>   Across one hole a finger laying.[33]

Using a Renaissance painting as their subject matter, they were able to describe in luxuriant detail the erotic attraction of youthful innocence.

On a more literal level, Edith Cooper, short-haired and boyish, knew her attraction to both homosexual men and women; the fifteen-year difference between her and her aunt Katherine also cast her in the role of the young initiate. In recording her delirious fantasies when sick with scarlet fever, Edith compared herself to Antinous, the beautiful boy beloved by the Roman emperor Hadrian. Later, while recovering, she described her desiring self as Mars, and Katherine as Venus.[34] In his condescending memoir of the elderly Fields, Logan Pearsall Smith found such flights of fancy half comic. He emphasized the disjunction between their spinsterish virginity and their wild, imaginative conversation: "The two quietly attired ladies would seem to undergo the most extraordinary transformations; would resume the aspect and airs of the disinherited princesses, the tragic Muses, the priestesses of Apollo, the Pythonesses upon their tripods, the Bacchic Maenads."[35] But Michael Field saw no disjunction between heterosexual chastity and their homosexual nature. When their poetry was spurned by their contemporaries, they retreated behind eccentric old-maidism but continued to write Dionysiac poems addressed to Bacchus, Pan, and Apollo.[36]

The writer who most self-consciously and openly crafted a lesbian literary vision was Renée Vivien.[37] Like Michael Field, she was determined to fashion a positive image of lesbian sexual subjectivity, even if she avoided some of their more overtly sensual descriptions of pagan frolics. Born into a wealthy expatriate family, she spent her short life writing in French a large body of poems, essays, and stories in a Decadent style about lesbian love. *A Woman Appeared to Me* was published with a frontispiece illustration of Leonardo da Vinci's *St.*

John the Baptist, and each chapter began with a brief musical excerpt representative of love or grief. (Both Vivien and Vernon Lee believed that music could
best express the inexpressible; one wrote long descriptions of the emotional
power of music, while the other created literary tone poems.) The novel com-
memorates the 1901 death of Vivien's first love, the pious Violet Shillito, or
Ione, and the end of her passionate love affair with Natalie Clifford Barney, or
Vally. Vivien divides herself into two characters, the narrator, whose "heart
was full of hectic melancholy," and the androgynous, self-contained writer, San
Giovanni. Written as a series of prose poems, each chapter encapsulates a stage
in Vivien's tormented affair with Barney. Ione's illness and death are ignored
under the spell of the charismatic but unfaithful Vally. Eva, who enters the
novel as the affair is ending, offers the narrator the promise of future happiness;
she is a composite of several women with whom Vivien had brief affairs, including Olive Custance, just before she married Lord Alfred Douglas, Oscar
Wilde's boylike lover, in 1902, and Baronne Van Zuylen de Nyevelt, who became Vivien's lover in 1901, after the final break with Barney.[38]

For Vivien all women dabble in same-sex relations, while a few are its representative figures; they must bear the moral and creative burden of fashioning a
new lesbian artistic and literary tradition.[39] Vally and San Giovanni agree that
"To be as different as possible from Nature is the true function of Art" (14).
All experience must be constructed and shaped into art. Vally has an instinctive
love of the artificial; her lips are "long familiar with every verbal artifice," and
she dresses in the costume of a Venetian page or as a Greek shepherd, following
"the music of the invisible pipes of Pan" (9). Mirrors, water, and lakes give
Vivien an opportunity to accentuate the visible sameness, the self-reflexivity,
of lesbian love. Fiction closely reproduces life, for Vivien and Barney both
dressed as pages, one imitating an eighteenth-century courtier and the other a
Hamlet-like nobleman. On other occasions they danced nude and Pan-like in
the woods and staged plays, casting themselves as Greek shepherds and fauns,
figures that also populated the gay male imagination.[40]

San Giovanni resembles the beautiful boy painted by da Vinci and other
Renaissance male artists.[41] Like John the Baptist, she is given prophetic powers, which the other women reverentially heed; Vivien leaves to our imagination who might be the lesbian Saviour. Yet in this over-solemn work, the narrator portrays her better half not only as cool, rational, and contemplative, but
also as mildly comic. San Giovanni admits to dreaming of dressing as a boy in
order to marry her first woman lover, but this is treated as a Romantic aberration rather than as an appropriate response for those outside the bounds of
heterosexual courtship. She soon finds her true métier, for she is discovered "in
flagrante delictu of literary composition," seated on a "worn slab" in a quiet
cemetery, surrounded by "serpents, bats, tombs, solitude" (19). San Giovanni's

roots in the Classical tradition are emphasized by repeatedly calling her an ephebe and having her compose poems about female cults, Sappho, and virginity. Her contemporary subject matter, in a typical Vivien reversal, is the male prostitute, defined as the man who marries for money. Women—within the novel—simply do not marry.

Vivien, like her male contemporaries, naturalizes homosexuality by denaturalizing heterosexuality for those who were—in the language of the day—born inverts. Even though San Giovanni looks like a boy, we are never allowed to forget that she is, instead, an androgyne. Her privileged appearance is underscored by Vally's witticism, "Adolescent boys are beautiful only because they resemble women . . . they are still inferior to women, whom they do not equal either in grace of movement or harmony of form" (7). An "oily" procurer with "the air of a dirty pedlar who offers English tourists the services of untouched young boys" responds by prophesying that the Androgyne will finish her "love-life in the arms of a man," a statement the narrator responds to "in a profoundly shocked tone, 'That would be a crime against nature, sir. I have too much respect for our friend to believe her capable of an abnormal passion'" (8). San Giovanni cuttingly responds, "I neither love nor hate men. . . . They are political adversaries whom I want to injure for the good of the cause. Off the battle-field of ideas, I know them little and am indifferent to them" (8).[42] These witty reversals of expectation echo Wilde's novel while setting a tone of insouciant moral superiority throughout; indeed, "The Charmer of Serpents" echoes Wilde in advising "the ephebe," "Guard against moderation as others guard against excess" (1).

San Giovanni, the Androygyne, is never quite the lesbian boy, however much she plays with this role. But other lesbians cast themselves in their fictions as boys. One of the most interesting lesbian writers of the turn of the century was Vernon Lee, the well-known (and well-connected) art critic and writer of Gothic tales. Unlike Vivien's Androgyne, Lee could not rise above her anger toward condescending men; her bristling intellectuality attracted respect, but few friends.[43] Although American by citizenship, she grew up on the Continent, living with her older half-brother and mother in hotels that bear some resemblance to those inhabited by Morgan Moreen's family during their more successful days. In a series of books and essays she introduced English-speaking readers to Italian art and the psychology of aesthetics. Culture-seeking tourists, such as Henry James's tutor in "The Pupil," took their Baedecker and their Lee when they toured Italy.

In addition to these more weighty works, Lee also wrote ghost stories, which I will argue were her means of describing lesbian desire without facing the public notoriety of Renée Vivien or the critical dismissal of Michael Field. Even though contemporaries recognized her as a lesbian and either accepted or laughed at her intense friendships, the lesbian subtext of much of her writing has been ignored.[44] The greater openness of Vivien has led to her resurrection as a pioneer in lesbian literature, but her near contemporary Lee does not deserve her current neglect.

Like male homosexual writers, Lee frequently used violence and death to represent the destructive nature of same-sex relations. One of the most ruthless boys in any fiction is the villain of her short story "The Wedding Chest," who brutally seizes and disposes of any woman he finds attractive. The illegitimate but high-born Troilo is a "most beautiful youth," with skin "astonishingly white and fair like a woman's," who always seems young, "having no beard, and a face like Hyacinthus or Ganymede, whom Jove stole to be his cup-bearer, on account of his beauty."[45] Lee's heterosexual rake looks more like the object of homosexual desire, as if to underscore his subversion of marriage. Moreover, Troilo is a reminder not of the successful seducer, but of the failed lover who could not keep his light-hearted Cressida. His name and character seem to convey some of Lee's personal anguish (and anger) in regard to the various women who deserted her for marriage. Troilo, the "ferocious and magnanimous" boy, the arch-transgressor, is murdered by Desiderio, the skilled maker of the wedding chest, from whom he had stolen the fair Maddalena. The characters' names indicate their positions in the tragic triangle: the artisan lover who—like Vernon Lee—desires too strongly; the thieving Troilo who—like Vernon Lee—revenges himself upon husbands and fiancés; and fair Maddalena, the unfortunate victim who—like Vernon Lee—never speaks openly of her love.

Prince Alberic, the hero of "Prince Alberic and the Snake Lady," is another of Lee's effeminate heroes, whom she describes as "at once manly and delicate, and full of grace and vigor of movement. His long hair, the color of floss silk, fell in wavy curls, which seemed to imply almost a woman's care and coquetry. His hands, although powerful, were . . . of princely form and whiteness."[46] Alberic is the neglected grandson of the "ever-young" Duke Balthazar, who is bankrupting the Duchy of Luna in order to build a grotto filled with marble animals and a chapel for his sepulchre. The Duke resembles a pantomime dame with his heavy makeup, wigs, and pretensions to youth and gentility; modern readers would recognize him as a camp queen, a figure Lee may indeed have been covertly attacking as a progenitor of false artistic values. The prince spends a lonely childhood, imprisoned in a palace where nothing natural is permitted. He learns about rabbits, herbs, and natural things only through the careful examination of a beautifully wrought tapestry which portrays the tale of his ancestor, Alberic the Blond, and the Snake Lady. A chest with a large crucifix on it covers the lower half of the tapestry; Alberic learns that the beautiful lady has no legs, but a coiling, glittering extremity, only after he has fallen in love with her image. Yet he is so captivated that when the old tapestry is replaced with one depicting Susannah and the Elders (a scene considered more erotically interesting by his grandfather), he slashes it to pieces. His response is one of a series of foreshadowings which predict the tragic conclusion of his love for the Snake Lady.

Alberic is expelled from the artificial, ornate Red Castle and sent to the remote Castle of Shining Waters, where he befriends a common grass snake. He dislikes the richly varied garden surrounding the decaying castle until he recognizes its similarity to his beloved tapestry. But then he ventures beyond the familiar, temporarily forgetting the tapestry. He enters "a tiny little house," where he hears "steps close behind him, and a rustle as of silk." A voice calls him by name, and he goes out to a "very, very deep" well. His experience is redolent with lesbian imagery:

> Alberic, as he bent over, was startled by suddenly seeing what seemed a face filling up part of that shining circle; but he remembered it must be his own reflection, and felt ashamed. So, to give himself courage, he bent down again, and sang his own name to the image. But instead of his own boyish voice, he was answered by wonderful tones, high and deep alternately, running through the notes of a long, long cadence, as he had heard them on holidays at the Ducal Chapel at Luna. (38)

Lee leaves ambiguous whether Alberic has seen himself or someone else reflected in the deep well; the "wonderful tones" responding to his name could be the distorted echo of the well or a magical presence. This mysterious moment culminates with the arrival of "a long, green, glittering thing," the snake with whom his future is enmeshed.

After these events, Alberic spends every evening in the little house or by the well, taught for an hour by his godmother. She also brings him books, horses, and appropriate attire, so that he grows up the very pattern of the perfect prince. Fortunately, the snake never visits at the same time as his godmother, who, like the Duke, hates serpents; Alberic finds it a pity "that so lovely and dear a lady should feel such hatred towards any living creature . . . he loved her too much to dream of thwarting her" (48). For years Alberic lives in an isolated, self-contained idyll of sensual love that needs no sexual consummation. The Oedipal implications of a boy fixated on an erotic mother are irrelevant, for Lee is constructing the ideal lesbian romance. The godmother has created Alberic without reproduction; rather, their relationship is one of reciprocal need. But like the dangerous symbiosis of Lord Henry and Dorian or the tutor and Morgan Moreen, violence is inevitable.

Upon reaching adolescence, the "full-grown and gallant-looking youth" becomes obsessed with the story "he did not know," of his ancester and the Lady

Oriana. At the very edge of defining his own sexual desire, he is "still shy and frightened," for "the greater his craving to know, the greater grew a strange certainty that the knowing would be accompanied by evil" (48). A travelling bard reluctantly reveals to him that "the Fairy Oriana, most miserable of all fairies, [is] condemned for no fault, but by envious powers, to a dreadful fate" (51). Alberic the Blond and Marquis Alberic had both failed to remain faithful for ten years to the Snake Lady, who therefore was still bewitched. This knowledge makes the prince gravely ill, and the local priest warns him against witchcraft. But he rises from his sickbed to follow a nightingale to the well, for "it was, he knew, the hour and place of his fate." Nature pauses, silent, as he kisses the cold snake; so traumatizing is this moment of self-recognition that Alberic falls unconscious:

> When he awoke the moon was still high. The nightingale was singing its loudest. He lay in the grass by the well, and his head rested on the knees of the most beautiful of ladies. She was dressed in cloth of silver which seemed woven of moon mists, and shimmering moonlit green grass. It was his own dear Godmother. (59)

Bathed in moonlight, the preeminent symbol of the feminine, Alberic submits to his fate. Unlike such folk tales as that of the Frog Prince or Beauty and the Beast, a kiss does not free an imprisoned suitor; rather, ten years' fidelity is demanded of the besotted youth.

Lee brings together every explanatory model for the boy's passion: he is fetishistically attached to the tapestry and its narrative; he is a direct descendant in blood and resemblance to the previous two Alberics; he owes all he knows to his beloved godmother. Nature, nurture, and maternal care have all conspired to commit Alberic to an unnatural love. If we interpret Alberic as a lesbian, his attachment to a maternal snake-woman from early childhood mimics what Elaine Marks has defined, in reference to Colette's Claudine series, as the Sapphic school romance: a tomboyish young woman is loved by a motherly older woman.[47] The audacious Colette enjoyed shocking her early twentieth-century French audience, but the puritanical Lee could not imagine the carefree flirtations of Claudine. For her, to desire another woman was to desire torment. The feverish Alberic has a prescient dream in which the Duke and all his marble animals beat him and his pet snake to death. Society will never accept lesbian relations, no matter how pure and selfless.

The tale moves swiftly to its inevitable conclusion. His grandfather discovers that Alberic has "no eyes, let alone a heart, for the fair sex." Desperate for money to complete his art projects, he imprisons his grandson in order to force him to marry a rich tradesman's daughter. On Friday the 13th of August, 1700, in the midst of a thunderstorm, Duke Balthasar "of enlightened mind and delicate taste" visits his stubborn grandson with three advisors. Suddenly "eyeballs starting with terror," he exclaims, "The serpent! the serpent!"

> Alberic threw himself forward. But he was too late. The Jester, with a blow of his harlequin's lath, had crushed the head of the startled creature; and even while he was struggling with him and the Jesuit, the Dwarf had given it two cuts with his Turkish scimitar. . . .
> Alberic had thrown himself on the dead snake, which lay crushed and bleeding on the floor; and he moaned piteously. (71)

The old Duke recovers from his fright, kicks the "mangled head with his ribboned shoe" and laughingly comments, "Who knows . . . whether you were not the Snake Lady?" (71) Alberic refuses "all nourishment" and dies "a fortnight later." His grandfather goes mad, haunted by the rumor that when the prison room was cleaned "the persons employed found in a corner, not the dead grass snake, which they had been ordered to cast into the palace drains, but the body of a woman, naked, and miserably disfigured with blows and saber cuts" (72). The bewitched Snake Lady had finally found a faithful lover, but she was easily destroyed by the prince's enemies, in spite of having survived the infidelity of the two previous Alberics. Yet her magic implicitly remains in Art, for "certain chairs and curtains in the porter's lodge" are made from "the various pieces of an extremely damaged arras, having represented the story of Alberic the Blond and the Snake Lady" (72).

The few critics who have looked at Vernon Lee's stories comment on her obsession with death and with the naked female body.[48] In "The Wedding Chest," Troilo's servants steal the cabinetmaker's daughter Maddalena when she is swimming nude in the Tiber; later her naked, dead body, with her child by her breast, is stuffed into the wedding chest and summarily returned to her father's house by masked servants. Our last image of the Snake Lady is of her dead, naked body. The Freudian Burdett Gardner argues that Lee's preference for artistic perfection, rather than the messiness of actual relations, led her to create idealized, unattainable women. He interprets the Snake Lady as the sexual invert who cannot make a direct appeal "but must 'haunt' the loved one, making use of her supreme gift of language only for one hour each evening at sundown."[49] He concludes that the Snake Lady's teaching of Prince Alberic is reminiscent of Lee's habit of lecturing the women she loved. The story, moreover, was written while Lee was living with Kit Anstruther-Thomson, a woman she was later to describe as "statuesque" with a "virginal expression [that] made one think rather of a very beautiful and modest boy."[50] If we follow Gardner's interpretation, we could see this tale as an example of Lee, the feminine and artistic Snake Lady, who fears to lose her Prince, Kit Anstruther-Thomson.

Vernon Lee, however, may have identified with all the characters in her stories. If she saw herself at times as the victimized Snake Lady, could she not as
easily imagine herself as the destructive, false Duke or the youthful, idealistic
Prince Alberic? She was fiercely loyal to Anstruther-Thomson, though their
relationship and co-authorship was attacked by many erstwhile friends.[51] Lee
may have wished to be an Alberic to her beloved Kit, or she may have feared
that she was the Duke of Luna, tied to the feminine principle and unable to
create true Art. Both Alberic and the villain Troilo are misunderstood, isolated
figures whose passions others consider unnatural. In a revealing diary entry in
1884, Lee examined her relationship with the dead Anne Meyer, a woman for
whom she had had a brief but intense longing. She saw in herself

> a growing desire for artificial ideal beings . . . who can never shift the
> moral light in which we see them, who can never turn round in their
> frames and say "see, we are not what you imagined." . . . Accustomed to
> see everywhere the unreal, accustomed to hanker even for the absolutely
> imaginary as the one and only certainty, I feel as if I had lost nothing or
> but little in the possible loss of the real Mme. Meyer, for does there not
> remain, unchanged and unchangeable, the imagined one? . . . The crea-
> ture born of one's fancy and one's desires, the unreal, one cannot lose. She
> remains and remains to me a certainty.[52]

The dark, morbid Desiderio in "The Wedding Chest" and the unnatural Duke
privilege art over life, creating permanent memorials to death, either to himself, as in the case of the Duke, or to his lost fiancée for Desiderio. The latter
"till his death" preserved "with him always the body of Monna Maddalena in
the wedding chest painted with the Triumph of Love, because he considered
she had died *odore magnae sanctitatis*" (85). The battered chest and the damaged tapestry remain as fragmentary evidence of baffled love.

In some ways, Lee was even more pessimistic than Wilde about homosexual
love, for she could not imagine either a successful work of art or a successful
relationship. Indeed, her biographers assume, following the comments of her
friend, Ethel Smyth, that Lee "refused to face" the fact of her passionate feelings toward women and instead pretended "that to her those friends were
merely *intellectual* necessities."[53] Her tales of frustrated desire, impossible
love—who could be more impossible as a recipient of physical love than a
woman whose lower half is a snake's tail?—seem to confirm this pervasive feeling of defeat. Yet one could argue that Alberic's indifference to eligible women
and loyalty to his godmother demonstrate a faith in an alternative sexual subjectivity for women. The Snake Lady embraces woman's nurturing role, while
biological reproduction is unthinkable. And her "creation," Prince Alberic, is
beautiful in both mind and body.

Although Decadent aesthetics proved to be imaginatively freeing for Vivien and Lee, it was also isolating; in spite of numerous opportunities, neither found a sustaining literary community. Nor could either author accept the light humor of Colette and other French writers, who treated lesbian affairs as simply one more example of the human comedy. Indeed, Vivien's poetry became increasing lugubrious as she moved through anorexia, drugs, and alcohol to Roman Catholicism, before dying in 1909. In 1906 Vernon Lee wrote her friend Maurice Baring, "I can never imagine what I write being read, still less read by anyone in particular."[54] Shorn of the magic of love, Lee looked into the well of her own consciousness and saw only herself. Michael Field, who disliked the Decadents, celebrated their happy love with Sapphic poems published in a deluxe edition of only one hundred copies. But after an initial stir of interest in the late 1880s and early 1890s, nobody read their work, and they grew increasingly eccentric and poetically self-indulgent (they published twenty-seven Elizabethan tragedies, as well as eight volumes of poetry). Serious lesbian writing lacked an audience, although sexual comedy flourished. Only with the publication of *Well of Loneliness* (1928), a realistic novel, and *Orlando* (1928), a fantasy, did the lesbian boy reappear—and live to tell the tale.

Lesbian writers of the fin de siècle disappeared from the literary map, and their current revival is tentative at best. The male tradition, always much stronger, continued, but the horrified public response to the casual homosexuality in Alec Waugh's *Loom of Youth* (1917) signaled a new attitude toward the literary portrayal of boy love.[55] An historical moment in the development of male homosexual and lesbian fiction had passed. The boy could no longer stand, poised between innocence and experience, free to act or to wait. But for a brief period the beautiful boy had rivaled the female vampire as a dangerous object—and subject—of desire. While the fin-de-siècle woman sucked life out of men, the fin-de-siècle boy died lest his love contaminate, and the fin-de-siècle boyish androgyne was ridiculed. Seldom have heterosexual men been so vulnerable, and so well protected, in literature.

Notes

Thanks to Virginia Blain, Barbara Caine, Jonathan Freedman, and Susan Navarette, who provided valuable advice and support. I have especially benefited from Susan Navarette's incomparable knowledge of the 1890s and her generous sharing of references, suggestions, and ideas. Susan Field has been the best of research assistants; this is a small gesture of appreciation. Thanks also to the helpful audiences at the Southeast Nineteenth Century Association conference, the University of New South Wales, and the Humanities Research Centre, Australian National University.

An earlier version of this chapter appeared in the *Journal of the History of Sexuality* 5, no. 1 (1994): 90–114.

1. Bram Dijkstra, *Idols of Perversity: Fantasies of Feminine Evil in Fin-de-Siècle Cultur* (New York: Oxford University Press, 1986).

2. See, for example, Jane Marcus, "Salomé: The Jewish Princess Was a New Woman," *Bulletin of New York Public Library* (autumn 1974): 95–113; Gail Cunningham, *The New Woman and the Victorian Novel* (London: Macmillan, 1978); Patricia Stubbs, *Women and Fiction: Feminism and the Novel, 1880–1920* (Brighton: Harvester, 1979). Rebecca Stott places the femme fatale in the context of imperialism in *The Fabrication of the Late-Victorian "Femme Fatale": The Kiss of Death* (Basingstoke: Macmillan, 1992).

3. For a good sense of the hysteria fomented by some journalists, see James Ashcroft-Noble, "The Fiction of Sexuality," *Contemporary Review* 67 (1895): 490–98; Mrs. B. A. Crackenthorpe, "Sex in Modern Literature," *Nineteenth Century* 36 (1895): 607–16; Hugh E. M. Stutfield, "Tommyrotics," *Blackwood's Magazine* 157 (1895): 833–45; D. F. Hannigan, "Sex in Fiction," *Westminster Review* 143 (1895): 616–25.

4. Martin Green, *Dreams of Adventure, Deeds of Empire* (London: Martin Secker, 1980), 389.

5. The German tradition is especially strong; see the writings of Stefan Georg, Baron Adelswärd-Fersen, Zinaida Gippius, Wilhelm von Gioeden, and slightly later, the negative images of Thomas Mann. These figures are discussed in James W. Jones, *"We of the Third Sex": Literary Representations of Homosexuality in Wilhemine Germany* (New York: Peter Lang, 1990).

6. The fullest treatment of the English idealization of man–boy love is Timothy d'Arch Smith's *Love in Earnest: Some Notes on the Lives and Writings of English "Uranian" Poets from 1889 to 1930* (London: Routledge and Kegan Paul, 1970). His invaluable work makes no attempt to trace the connections between homosexual male poets and lesbian writers.

7. For three different interpretations of the period, see Jeffrey Weeks, *Coming Out* (London: Pluto, 1977); Lillian Faderman, *Surpassing the Love of Men: Romantic Friendship and Love Between Women from the Renaissance to the Present* (New York: William Morrow, 1981); and Eve Kosovsky Sedgwick, *Epistemology of the Closet* (Berkeley and Los Angeles: University of California Press, 1990). A London male homosexual coterie can be traced back to at least the early 1700s, but I am specifically concerned with the central position of homosexuals in the 1890s literary avant garde.

8. For a discussion of the pervasive visibility of the gay male subculture of the 1880s and 1890s, from the perspective of a modern gay man, see Neil Bartlett's *Who Was That Man? A Present for Mr. Oscar Wilde* (London: Serpent's Tail, 1988).

9. Jonathan Dollimore, *Sexual Dissidence* (Oxford: Clarendon, 1991), 33–34, discusses the sexually proximate.

10. Richard Jenkyns in *The Victorians and Ancient Greece* (Oxford: Basil Blackwell, 1980), 280–97, discusses the use of Greek precedents for confusing what he calls "the distinction between sexless devotion and homosexual love."

11. Angela Leighton briefly discusses the importance of Wharton's edition for lesbians in *Victorian Women Poets: Writing against the Heart* (Brighton: Harvester, 1992), 210–11.

12. For a discussion of the importance of difference in current theoretical debates about homosexuality, see Anne Herrmann, "Imitations of Marriage: Crossdressed Couples in Contemporary Lesbian Fiction," *Feminist Studies*, 18, no. 3 (fall 1992): 609–11.

13. I am indebted to Susan Navarette, who discussed the ideas in this paragraph with me.

14. "The Poet," quoted in Mary Sturgeon, *Michael Field* (London: George Harrap, 1922), 24. Sturgeon dates this sonnet from the late 1880s, although it was not published until 1907.

15. Jeffrey Richards, "'Passing the love of women': Manly Love and Victorian Society," in *Manliness and Morality: Middle-class Masculinity in Britain and America, 1800–1940*, ed. J. A. Mangan and James Walvin (New York: St. Martin's, 1987), 102–5.

16. Seth Koven, "From Rough Lads to Hooligans: Boy Life, National Culture and Social Reform," in *Nationalisms and Sexualities*, ed. Andrew Parker, Mary Russo, Doris Sommer, and Patricia Yaeger (New York: Routledge, 1992), 365–91.

17. d'Arch Smith points out the popularity of telegraph boys, who were subject to a high standard of literacy and cleanliness by the General Post Office. See *Love in Earnest*, 29–34.

18. Several critics have argued that Sibyl Vane in *The Picture of Dorian Gray* can be better understood as a masquerading young man. If so, this simply confirms the jealousy of her brother as homoerotic in its intensity—a form of homosexual incest which William Veeder feels characterizes Henry James's relationship with his brother and results in James's numerous portrayals of victimized women, as well as the boy Morgan Moreen in "The Pupil." See his essay "Henry James and the Uses of the Feminine," in *Out of Bounds: Male Writers and Gendered Criticism*, ed. Laura Claridge and Elizabeth Langland (Amherst: University of Massachusetts Press, 1990), 219–51.

19. See his notorious *Venice Letters*, ed. Cecil Woolf (London: Cecil and Amelia Woolf, 1974). These letters by "Baron Corvo" describe in detail his intimacies with boys; they were written to one of his sponsors, Charles Masson Fox, to be shared with other English homosexuals. See Woolf's introduction, p. 12.

20. Oscar Wilde, *The Picture of Dorian Gray*, chap. 2, p. 17. Since there is no standard edition, I also give chapter numbers; I quote from the revised 1891 edition of the novel (reprint, Oxford: Oxford University Press, 1974).

21. Richard Dellamora, "Representation and Homophobia in *The Picture of Dorian Gray*," *Victorian Newsletter* 73 (spring 1988): 29.

22. Henry James, "The Pupil," in *Henry James: Selected Fiction*, ed. Leon Edel (New York: Dutton, 1964), 471.

23. E. M. Forster, "The Story of a Panic," *Collected Short Stories* (London: Sidgwick

and Jackson, 1947), 29. All the English picnickers panic and flee from "the Great God Pan" except the boy Eustace.

24. A. E. Housman, "Shot? So Quick, So Clean an Ending?" reprinted in *Sexual Heretics: Male Homosexuality in English Literature, 1850–1900,* ed. Brian Reade (London: Routledge and Kegan Paul, 1970), 426–27.

25. His unfinished "romantic novel," "Venus and Tannhäuser," plays with a wide range of sexual fantasies. As Tannhäuser, Beardsley passively enjoys all that Venus and her favorite girls and boys provide. It is reprinted in *Aesthetes and Decadents of the 1890's,* ed. Karl Beckson (Chicago: Academy Chicago, rev. ed. 1981), 9–46.

26. A. J. L. Busst, "The Image of the Androgyne in the Nineteenth Century," in *Romantic Mythologies,* ed. Ian Fletcher (London: Routledge and Kegan Paul, 1967), 70. See also pp. 48–52 on the "mentally lascivious woman," best represented for Busst by Rachilde's heroine in *Monsieur Vénus* (1884).

27. Edith Cooper was also known as "Field," but her more common nickname was Henry. See Sturgeon (who refers to Michael Field as "she"), *Michael Field,* 27.

28. For a brief discussion of this, see Elaine Showalter, introduction to *Daughters of Decadence: Women Writers of the "Fin-de-Siècle,"* ed. Elaine Showalter (London: Virago, 1993), xi.

29. See her discussion of the vexed relationship between Michael Field and the leading aesthetes of the 1890s in Leighton, *Victorian Women Poets,* 215–19, 230.

30. Quoted from *Long Ago* (1889) in Sturgeon, *Michael Field,* 12. Leighton argues for their "pagan subtext" and "outdoor aestheticism." See pp. 225, 239, and passim. See also Christine White's discussion of their life-long effort to find a language of love between women, "'Poets and Lovers Evermore: Interpreting Female Love in the Poetry and Journals of Michael Field," in *Sexual Sameness: Textual Differences in Lesbian and Gay Writing,* ed. Joseph Bristow (London: Routledge, 1992), 26–43.

31. Renée Vivien, *A Woman Appeared to Me,* trans. Jeannette H. Foster, intro. Gayle Rubin (Tallahassee, Fla.: Naiad Press, 1976), 62 (originally published as *Une femme m'apparut* [Paris: Alphonse Lemerre, 1904]). See also the only full-length study in English of Vivien, Karla Jay's *The Amazon and the Page: Natalie Clifford Barney and Renée Vivien* (Bloomington: Indiana University Press, 1988).

32. 24 February 1896. Quoted in *Some Letters from Charles Ricketts and Charles Shannon to "Michael Field" (1894–1902),* ed. J. G. Paul Delaney (Edinburgh: The Tragara Press, 1979), 5.

33. *Sight and Song* (London: E. Matthews, 1892), 65. I am indebted to Virginia Blain for drawing my attention to this poem.

34. See the diary entries quoted by Leighton, *Victorian Women Poets,* 213–14.

35. Logan Pearsall Smith, "Michael Field," in *Reperusals and Re-collections* (1937; reprint, Freeport, N.Y.: Books for Libraries, 1968), 91.

36. Leighton, *Victorian Women Poets,* 241–42, discusses their insistence that panthe-

ism without the dangers and pleasures of Eros was false. Their conversion to Roman Catholicism in 1908 dampened but did not destroy their pagan spirits.

37. For Vivien's attempt to create a Lesbos out of time and place in her poetry, see Elise Blankley, "Return to Mytilène: Renée Vivien and the City of Women," in *Women Writers and the City: Essays in Feminist Literary Criticism*, ed. Susan Merrill Squier (Knoxville: University of Tennessee Press, 1984), 45–67.

38. The details about Vivien's life in this paragraph are from Gayle Rubin's introduction to *A Woman Appeared to Me*, xiii.

39. The difficulty of writing from the lesbian subject position is explored in terms of a post-modernist sensibility and Gertrude Stein's concealments and disclosures in her poetry by Penelope J. Engelbrecht, "'Lifting Belly is a Language': The Postmodern Lesbian Subject," *Feminist Studies* 16, no. 1 (spring 1990): 85–114.

40. These events are documented and illustrated in Jean Chalon, *Portrait of a Seductress: The World of Natalie Barney*, trans. Carol Banko (New York: Crown, 1979), and George Wickes, *The Amazon of Letters: The Life and Loves of Natalie Barney* (New York: Putnam, 1976).

41. See James M. Saslow, *Ganymede in the Renaissance* (New Haven: Yale University Press, 1986), for a general survey of Renaissance male same-sex desire. Saslow argues that pederasty was actually not the most common form of homosexual activity, which makes the repeated use of the adolescent boy an even more interesting metaphor for same-sex desire.

42. Vivien's characterization of Petrus the procurer betrays both the casual anti-Semitism of this generation of wealthy lesbians and her dislike of homosexual men. San Giovanni, the moral center of the novel, describes him as "congenitally obscene, like all Levantines. When he leaves, one feels the need to open the windows and shake the hangings" (7).

43. The best-known contemporary account of Lee is in Ethel Smyth's *As Time Went On . . .* (London: Longmans, Green, 1936), 214–15, 243–50.

44. The innuendo and distaste that plagued the uncomfortably intellectual Lee is documented in Peter Gunn's biography, *Vernon Lee/Violet Paget, 1856–1935* (London: Oxford University Press, 1964). See also the more sympathetic treatment of her work by Vineta Colby, *The Singular Anomaly: Women Novelists of the Nineteenth Century* (New York: New York University Press, 1970), 235–304.

45. All quotations of "A Wedding Chest" are from Vernon Lee [Violet Paget], *The Snake Lady and Other Stories*, ed. and intro. Horace Gregory (New York: Grove Press, 1954), 75–85. Originally published in *Pope Jacynth and Other Fantastic Tales* (London: Grant Richards, 1904).

46. Vernon Lee, "Prince Alberic and the Snake Lady," *The Snake Lady*, 42. This story was originally published in *The Yellow Book* 10 (July 1896): 289–344 and reprinted in *Pope Jacynth*.

47. Elaine Marks, "Lesbian Intertextuality," in *Homosexualities and French Literature*, ed. George Stambolian and Elaine Marks (Ithaca: Cornell University Press, 1979), 356–58.

48. Burdett Gardner, *The Lesbian Imagination (Victorian Style): A Psychological and Critical Study of "Vernon Lee"* (New York: Garland, 1987), 306–8, 313–21. This is a reprint of his 1954 Harvard University Ph.D. dissertation. See also Gunn's inappropriate and unfavorable comparison of Lee with Izak Dinesen: "With Vernon Lee's stories of love, often of violent love, we do not feel the same naturalness of experiences. It is partly because of the extremely highly-wrought, contrived, perhaps too intellectual, quality about them. We suspect further that the genesis of these stories comes from unresolved, even unrecognized, tendencies, deeply hidden in the recesses of her own mind" (*Vernon Lee*, 225). He briefly discusses the "theme of feminine nakedness" on p. 227.

49. Gardner, *Lesbian Imagination*, 314.

50. Vernon Lee, introduction to the posthumous papers she collected and published, Clementina Anstruther-Thomson, *Art and Man: Essays and Fragments* (London: John Lane, 1924), 8.

51. See Phyllis Manocchi, "Vernon Lee and Kit Anstruther-Thomson: A Study of Love and Collaboration between Romantic Friends," *Women's Studies* 12 (1986): 129–48.

52. Quoted by Gardner, *Lesbian Imagination*, 311–12. Gardner explains that the excerpt comes from pages "stuffed in an envelope which bears the label in Violet's hand, 'Some (slightly!) autobiographical notes, viz. A.M. in memoriam 1883, . . . preserved from the old notebooks sent to the Cartiena della Lima to make into new paper in March 1920'" (307).

53. Quoted from *What Happened Next* (1940) in Colby, *Singular Anomaly*, 289; italics in the original.

54. Quoted by Colby, *Singular Anomaly*, 293.

55. See Isabel Quigly, *The Heirs of Tom Brown: The English School Story* (London: Chatlo and Windus, 1982), 197–211.

PART TWO

Revisionary Decadence

Victorian Effeminacies

THAÏS E. MORGAN

[handwritten: Ponling → our understanding]

"The main charge I bring against poetry of this kind is its sickliness and *effem-inacy*."[1] 1872: the literary critic Robert Buchanan is inveighing against what he calls the "Fleshly School" of Dante Gabriel Rossetti, Algernon Charles Swinburne, and William Morris because their poetry threatens the very foundations of "true English life" as he understands them.[2] To our ears in the 1990s, this may sound like libel on sexual grounds: "effeminacy" has today become synonymous with male homosexuality. "Effeminacy" is widely interpreted as the visible sign of sexual dissidence, of men who reject the hegemonic norm of hetero-masculinity.[3] As this essay will show, Buchanan's use of the term "effeminacy" verges on and lends itself to the formation of the discourse of sexual dissidence which has informed it since the 1890s.[4] "Effeminacy" in Buchanan's infamous attack on the Fleshly School carries a complex cultural weight. Its main force does not yet depend on the criterion of sexuality which will emerge so strikingly toward the end of the Victorian period. Rather, Buchanan's diatribe seeks to revive the traditional politico-moral ideology of civic masculinity.[5] At the same time, the ambiguous positioning of "effeminacy" in the Fleshly School controversy suggests that this term and concept was undergoing a significant shift at the very point—the early 1870s—at which Buchanan wielded it.

The Fleshly School controversy spanned the last three decades of the nineteenth century. In his detailed study, John Cassidy traces its beginnings to "a mutual antipathy experienced by . . . Buchanan and Swinburne" during the 1860s when they were aspiring poets vying for the favor of the London critics.[6] 1866 saw the publication of both Buchanan's *London Poems* and Swinburne's *Poems and Ballads, Series 1.* The former was well received but the latter was a *succès de scandale.* Buchanan "regarded Swinburne and his friends as poseurs who sought to conquer the literary world by subterfuge . . . rather than by merit and hard work."[7] 1870 saw another contest of publications: Buchanan's *The Book of Orm* and D. G. Rossetti's *Poems.* Whereas Rossetti had insured a favorable reception for his work by arranging for reviews of it by friends in prominent journals, Buchanan had no such coterie to support his efforts. 1871 and 1872 are the best-known years of the Fleshly School controversy. In the first half of 1871, Swinburne published a collection of political poems, *Songs before Sunrise;* Buchanan, not to be outdone, "rushed into print with his hastily conceived and even more hastily written interpretation of the Franco-Prussian War, *Napoleon Fallen.*"[8] In October 1871, Buchanan made another bid for attention: using a pseudonym, he wrote a savage review essay entitled "The Fleshly School of Poetry; Mr. D. G. Rossetti."[9] Early in 1872, Buchanan brought out a book on *The Fleshly School of Poetry and Other Phenomena of the Day,* under his own name, which expanded his attack from Rossetti to Swinburne and Morris—with a snide mention of Simeon Solomon.[10]

The Fleshly School controversy has all the makings of a cultural war. Which side would prevail, the traditional or the oppositional? Volleys were exchanged between Buchanan and Swinburne, Buchanan and William Michael Rossetti, Buchanan and D. G. Rossetti.[11] The stakes were nothing less than dominance over mainstream Victorian discourse in matters moral and aesthetic. An index of the large cultural import of the Fleshly School controversy is the way in which Buchanan was represented by his attorneys at a libel trial against Swinburne in 1876. Reviewing the situation of his initial 1871 essay attacking Rossetti, the prosecution portrayed Buchanan as performing "his *public duty* as a critic and writer" whose mission was "to point out that some of the works . . . were obscene, indecent, and offensive to sound moral and religious taste."[12] His personal animosities toward Swinburne and the Rossetti brothers aside, Buchanan was seeking to be viewed as a central spokesman for "true English life" and its strong defender against that "Fleshly School of verse-writers" who are *"public offenders,* because they are diligently spreading the seeds of disease broadcast wherever they are read and understood."[13] The "effeminacy" in Swinburne's and especially Rossetti's poetry "comes of . . . want of response to the needs and the duties of [their] time."[14] These men have thrust themselves onto the English national stage as *public men* without fulfilling their obligations as such. Instead of upholding the time-honored civic virtues, they "encourage debauchery and [attempt] to demoralise the public."[15]

As Linda Dowling has pointed out, Buchanan's language and ideas in the Fleshly School controversy hark back to the "classical republican discourse" which "had exercised a powerful hold over the English cultural imagination for over two hundred years."[16] In "the long tradition of civic republicanism," the paramount concern is "the ways in which the moral formation of citizens may be effected by the political arrangements and practices of their communities."[17] Much of Buchanan's diatribe depends on an analogy between the individual public man—the soundness of his character and the rightness of his behavior—and the best possible state of society as a whole. This familiar analogy governs thinking about the relation of the citizen to the polity in Plato and Aristotle, Cicero and Quintilian, among other Classical sources. The citizen in question is always a male, and the societal institutions typically function within the structure of a patriarchy.[18] The degree of conformity by its citizens to standards for masculinity is seen by mainstream political thinkers as an index of the welfare and security of the entire state. Thus, in the *Rhetoric*, which establishes criteria for speech by men engaged in the public sphere, Aristotle emphasizes that he who seeks to influence or lead others has an obligation to cultivate those "virtues" "which are most useful to others" in the society.[19] "Self-control is a virtue which disposes men in regard to the pleasures of the body as the law prescribes": by the logic of analogy, if each man's body is well regulated, the larger polity will function well.[20] The reverse is also true: if individuals indulge in "vices of character," such as refusing "to submit to [the] toils" involved in work and military duty owed to the state, or such as partaking in "licentiousness" with women, youths, or slaves which illicitly crosses boundaries of class, gender, or race, then such citizens fail in their role as public men who ought to exemplify the best of society.[21] "The relationship with oneself [is considered to be] isomorphic with the relationship of domination, hierarchy, and authority that one expected, as . . . a free man, to establish over his inferiors."[22]

Clearly, "virtue" comprises both a private practice of managing one's desires and a public discourse in which "law" regulates the male body in the best interests of the polity. The ideal of civic masculinity has three analogous levels: the putative condition of "ethical virility" provides the male citizen with the ability to exercise self-control, resulting in "sexual virility" according to the model of "social virility."[23] The man who fails to meet any area of his obligations is considered "effeminate." This pejorative qualification presupposes a hierarchical gender system: power differentials are translated into and signified by gender terms. The "virile" man stands at the summit of this system. Boys, who are expected to become but are not yet "virile," occupy the next rung. Women, who are assumed to be incapable of rational thought and self-control, two prerequisites for participation in public life, rank below both men and boys.[24] Slaves of either sex are excluded from all aspects of public life. The effeminate poses a problem: as a man he is entitled to the privileges of the dominant order in society, but in comportment he does not conform to the hegemonic norm for masculinity. The *effeminatus* forfeits masculinity and takes on instead what appear to be feminine characteristics: he becomes *ex femina*, neither man nor woman but closer in status to the latter than the former.[25]

Buchanan attacks D. G. Rossetti and Swinburne so vehemently in 1872 because they represent contemporary avatars of the *effeminati* whose presence threatens the most fundamental values of society. Buchanan draws upon a nexus of connections between masculinity and public order. The classical analogy between a man's body and the social body posits *virtus* or manliness and *vis* or power as crucial qualities of each male citizen or *vir*.[26] In turn, each of these concepts refers back to the patriarchal structure of the ideal society in a tight hermeneutic circle. Thus, the *vir* is the adult man responsible for his actions and capable of contributing to the welfare of the state. The latter duty entails marriage: the *vir* must perform as a husband who fulfills his role as procreator. The *vir* must also be a man of character in the sense of having physical as well as moral courage; he must be a 'real man'—"*tulit dolorem ut vir*" ("he bore the pain like a man"), says Cicero, contrasting the masculine man to the *effeminatus* or effeminate man who acts like a woman, lacking self-control.

In sum, the *vir* exemplifies *virtus*, or manliness itself, by striving for excellence in all things. In turn, the *virtus* displayed by the *vir* is what lends his every act and word *vis*, or strength and force. More generally, *vis* undergirds the state: *vis* comprises the power of the individual masculine person and the power of men in groups, like soldiers. At the same time, *vis* connotes moral influence, the effect of a man's *virtus* or virtue on others. In contrast to this network of terms and concepts tying the polity to *vir* or masculinity, the *effeminatus* is the man who has neither *virtus* nor *vis*, neither virtue nor strength, neither self-control nor right to the power of a public man within society.

Buchanan believes that various facets of "effeminacy" as understood within the discourse of civic masculinity are attaining a dangerous prominence in Victorian culture in the early 1870s, and that D. G. Rossetti, Swinburne, Morris, and Solomon are the main disseminators of this threat to British society. *The Fleshly School and Other Phenomena of the Day* is in this sense a patriotic document: Buchanan acts as an alarm to and for his readers. Besides standing squarely on political tradition, Buchanan invests his diatribe with the more recently established authority of Victorian sage discourse. Updating Thomas Carlyle's diagnosis of the condition of England in *Characteristics* (1831), he poses as a "physician" who has come "to put his finger in the true seat of the sore" of "Sensualism" which is currently destroying the nation.[27]

The cultural authority of the sage is not unproblematic, however. As James Adams has argued, the sage ambiguates rather than clarifies genders: "The figure of the priest or prophet has throughout history been associated with a model of masculinity . . . supplementary to or divergent from normative manhood."[28] Carlyle himself represents the fissures developing in Victorian masculinity. On one hand, "It was Carlyle above all who put into circulation a particular conception of manliness as part of a larger vision of bracing conflict and stoically borne suffering in a power-governed universe."[29] He praises the "*wild man*, a man disunited from the fellowship of the world he lives in" but unlikely to be a model citizen as figured by traditional political discourse.[30] In *Heroes and Hero Worship* (1840), Carlyle draws an explicit connection between masculinity, morality, and leadership. "Virtue, *Vir-tus,* manhood, *hero*-hood, is not fair-spoken immaculate regularity."[31] "Manhood" requires a vigilant self-discipline, as both classical political theory and Christian moral teaching prescribe. On the other hand, the very wildness of Carlyle's rhetorical manliness "ostentatiously calls attention to itself," thereby crossing the line between the restraint of virility and the "anxious self-display" associated with effeminacy in a tradition reaching back to Aristotle's *Rhetoric.*[32]

Buchanan's strident accusation of "effeminacy" against the Fleshly School takes on a tone of deepening crisis in this context. Is the "intellectual labor" performed by the Victorian "man of letters" truly manly?[33] A critic and a poet, Buchanan is subject to the same insecurities about masculinity as Carlyle. The "fair-spoken immaculate regularity" of the Victorian lady may be clearly differentiated from the forceful *(vis)* kind of speech characteristic of sage manhood (*"vir-tus"*), but the very virtuousness *(virtus)* of the sage is allied more closely with femininity as constructed by Victorian domestic ideology than with the "*hero*-hood" of masculinity.

The pressure exerted by the rise of the cultural authority of women since the 1840s made differentiation among the manly, the feminine, and the effeminate both increasingly necessary and increasingly difficult. The ideological work required to police the ever-wavering boundaries of gender was a task shared by men and women alike. A few years before Buchanan blasted the effeminacy of "Fleshly" men, the reviewer and social commentator Eliza Lynn Linton had ignited a parallel controversy over the femininity of mid-Victorian women in her article "The Girl of the Period" (1868).[34] Linton seeks to restore what Carlyle called the "fair-spoken immaculate regularity" of womanhood by insisting on absolute difference between masculinity and femininity. Every aspect of the ideal of manliness must have its "essentially womanly" counterpart.[35] Linton reminds her readers of the "relativity" of gender: "the sexes were made for each other," she declares, "but the Girl of the Period does not please men" because "she [acts] against nature" by being "bold in bearing" and "masculine in mind."[36] Linton is looking at Victorian women from what she imagines to be the perspective of Victorian men: "*We* prided ourselves as a nation on *our* women."[37] While conservative domestic ideology receives a boost from her diatribe, Linton's concern for the health of the nation as represented by a proper balance between the womanliness of its women and the manliness of its men also reinforces the heterosexist ideology of civic masculinity. A female sage, she diagnoses the "Girl of the Period" as symptomatic of "the national madness" and advises her readers "to wait patiently" until this disorder of the body politic "has passed, and our women have come back again to the old English ideal."[38]

Buchanan's denunciation of the Fleshly School's effeminacy may be seen as a response to the "Girl of the Period" controversy and also as an attempt to wrest the reins of cultural authority away from influential women writers like Linton. In the opening section of his 1872 pamphlet, Buchanan focuses not on the poets and poetry of the Fleshly School, but on the threat posed to English society by the new visibility of the female body, metonymically signified by "the female Leg" and "its two most formidable rivals—Bosom and Back."[39] In classical political theory, women have no place in the public sphere; they supposedly lack the rationality and self-control which are hallmarks of masculinity. The more overt physical presence of Victorian women in the latest fashions is bemoaned by Linton for betraying "the ideal of womanhood" and by Buchanan for challenging the prerogative of men to dominate the public sphere. The female body, the male body, the "body social" have become sick.[40] For Buchanan, restoration of all these bodies to the health of traditional gender demarcations is his *public* duty as a *man* of letters. Although Buchanan agrees with Linton in discerning signs of disorder among women, by far the greater danger to Victorian society is posed by those men who flout the norms of manhood which undergird "true English life." "There lies the seat of the cancer— there, in the Bohemian fringe of society": there, among those *effeminati* who are currently misleading the public, most conspicuous among them being the "nasty" D. G. Rossetti and the "hysterical" Swinburne.[41]

The second section of *The Fleshly School and Other Phenomena of the Day* widens Buchanan's diagnosis of the ills of Victorian society from London to Europe. Gynephobia is met by xenophobia. Buchanan provides a thumbnail sketch of the history of European poetry. The "dawn" of English poetry with Chaucer held "fair promise," but a "fever-cloud" blew over from Italy, "sucking up all that was most unwholesome" from France on its way. This "miasmic" influence was produced by the courtly love poets, "characterized by affectation, foolishness, and moral blindness." Celebrating their subordination to women, these "singers of the falsetto school" were "peevish men" who promoted effeminacy.[42] The natural superiority of men to women that underpins the order of things was eroded by this foreign literary movement—geographically, morally, and aesthetically incompatible with "true English life." The parallel to the Pre-Raphaelite movement, led by the Italian-named D. G. Rossetti, whose poetry displays "numberless affectations" and whose cohort, Swinburne, celebrates "the smile of harlotry and the shriek of atheism" in a "falsetto," is unmistakable.[43] The effeminacy of the Fleshly School derives from their failure to uphold what Buchanan considers to be the specifically English tradition in literature.[44] To succumb to foreign influences and to place women at the center of concern is to forfeit manhood. Buchanan's hyper-nationalism is compounded by the fact that, as a Scotsman, he feels the need to prove his loyalty to his adopted country by identifying and attacking its cultural enemies.[45]

According to Buchanan, English poetry was headed in the wrong direction due to pernicious influences from abroad until "Wordsworth came, and English literature was saved."[46] The appearance of Wordsworth signaled a return of true manliness to English poetry, but this was not to last long. "In our own day we have had . . . the Spasmodic School," and, currently, "due to a fresh importation of . . . obnoxious matter from France," there is the "Scrofulous School of Literature," inspired by Charles Baudelaire.[47] The poetry of "this dandy of the brothel, this Brummel of the stews" has invaded England with "affected innovations in verse" and "morbid themes."[48] Baudelaire is the mid-nineteenth-century type of the *effeminatus:* "This interesting creature, with his nose sniffing 'distant perfumes,' his carefully-shaven cheeks, and his general air of man-millinery," poses a serious threat to the English nation.[49] Lacking the moral discernment *(virtus)* expected of the true man *(vir)*, the effeminate Baudelaire has introduced "the representation of abnormal types of diseased lust and lustful disease" into poetry, thereby misusing his influence as a public man *(vis)*.[50]

The most conspicuously stricken victim of this foreign contagion is Swinburne, whose "offensive choice of subject," "blasphemy," and "wretched animalism" all derive from Baudelaire, "the godfather as it were of the modern Fleshly School."[51] Already in 1866, Buchanan had greeted the publication of *Poems and Ballads, Series 1* with derision. Swinburne "is quite the Absalom of modern bards,—long-ringleted, flippant-lipped, down-cheeked, amorous lidded."[52] Like Baudelaire, Swinburne is an *effeminatus*. Still, although his poetry is viciously "fleshly" and "blasphemous," Swinburne finally does less damage to British culture than D. G. Rossetti. The "hysterical tone" of Swinburne's "nastiness" "[slays] the animalism," so that the critic's "disgust" eventually "fade[s] away into comic amazement" as he realizes that Swinburne is "only a little mad boy letting off squibs."[53] Swinburne and his poetry are "puerile." In the traditional gender hierarchy presupposed by Buchanan's taunts, the boy or *puer* ranks below the man or *vir* as one who has not yet attained to the responsibility and power of manhood; hence, Swinburne is not really a threat because he is not really a man.

D. G. Rossetti, on the other hand, lays claim to adult manhood and must therefore be held fully accountable for the "meretricious tricks" and "morbid deviations" not only in his own poetry but in that of his followers.[54] Rossetti himself had claimed that his 1870 poems were "perfectly 'mature,'" Buchanan reminds us: "Here is a full-grown man, presumably intelligent and cultivated, putting on record, for other full-grown men to read, the most secret mysteries of sexual connection."[55] Rossetti is effeminate in that he lacks the cardinal qualities of the citizen and public man: self-control in the service of virtue and use of his influence for the common good. Rossetti, "who is formally recognized as the head" of the Fleshly School, presents himself as "a great strong man" or *vir* but in fact he is an *effeminatus* along with Swinburne and Baude-laire.[56] Rossetti is "really dangerous to society" precisely because of this duplic-ity: his poems seem merely sentimental but are actually immoral, "flooded with sensualism from the first line to the last."[57] He appears to be a man but is not.

The main premises of Buchanan's attack on the "effeminacy" of the Fleshly School stem from the ideology of civic masculinity. It is because D. G. Rossetti fails to represent the norms for manhood established in traditional political and moral thought that Buchanan condemns *The House of Life* as "neither po-etic, nor manly, nor even human" but "simply nasty."[58] In the "veritably stupen-dous preponderance of sensuality and sickly animalism" in his poetry, Rossetti shows that he has lost sight of his duty as a public man to uphold the values of British society.[59] Furthermore, his obsession with women and the female body indicates an effeminization of properly masculine emotion: "he regards the feeling for a young woman's person . . . as in itself quite a spiritual sentiment."[60] Rossetti's uxoriousness is a telltale sign of effeminacy according to the ideology of civic masculinity.[61] Buchanan's violent reaction against Rossetti's propin-quity to femininity also displays the gynephobia informing the opening section of his diatribe. Rossetti, by focusing his poetry so intensely on the female "per-son," dislocates the proper hierarchical relation of men to women which orders Victorian society. The effeminate Rossetti is "an emasculated Browning": both poets describe love, but Buchanan finds that Browning's approach remains manly, while Rossetti's shows "nothing virile, nothing tender, nothing com-pletely sane."[62]

Even as Buchanan was attempting to renew the standards of civic masculin-ity, the term and concept of "effeminacy" was undergoing a crucial shift. 1871, the year in which Buchanan published his initial attack, saw the conclusion to the scandalous trial of Ernest Boulton and Frederick Park, "two young men who were arrested in 1870 for dressing as women and subsequently tried for conspiring to commit sodomy."[63] The Woman Question turns into the Man Question as doctors, lawyers, witnesses, and jury try to determine the differ-ence between men and women according to the new terms of bio-medical tax-onomy based on sexuality and the more familiar terms of "manliness"/"woman-liness" based on gender. The pivotal factor is the men's transvestism. Boulton and Park were arrested for transgressing against "public decency": this juridical notion and moral norm is premised on the clear separation of masculinity and femininity. The effeminacy of Boulton and Park—signified by their dressing, gesturing, and speaking like women—confounds the gender distinctions struc-turally necessary to the Victorian status quo. Worse still, they committed this transgression repeatedly *in public:* the indictment emphasizes the transvestites' appearances at "places of public resort" where they did "publicly pretend and hold themselves out . . . to be women."[64] The gender certainty of both men and women in the English public is put into question by this flagrant case of effeminacy.

The Boulton and Park scandal is on Buchanan's mind as he formulates his attack on the Fleshly School in 1871–72. "Sickliness and effeminacy" were spreading from the music halls frequented by men in drag to the hallowed halls of poetry. Cross-dressed men, cross-dressed poems: "public offenders" all![65] As William Cohen astutely observes, however, scandal does double cultural work: "It inculcates an understanding of normative behavior in its audience"; at the same time, "Scandal also provides the opportunity to formulate questions, discuss previously unimagined possibilities, and forge new alliances."[66] The "counterhegemonic potential" of the Boulton and Park trial was realized, for instance, by Simeon Solomon, who collaborated with Swinburne on several "perverse" projects during the 1860s.[67] In letters to Swinburne, who did not attend the trial with him, Solomon describes the delicious spectacle of the queen Boulton cross-dressed as a gentleman: "Bn [*sic*] is very remarkable, he is not quite beautiful but supremely pretty, a perfect figure, manner, and voice."[68]

The uneven reception of Solomon's artwork in the early 1870s suggests the coexistence of at least three discourses on effeminacy. Buchanan speaks for those Victorians who cling to traditional distinctions: when he accuses the Fleshly poets and Solomon of effeminacy, he means that they blur boundaries of gender crucial to the maintenance of things as they have been for a long time. Buchanan divides "English society" into the "kind" that purchases the penny paper, *Day's Doings,* and "another kind" that "goes into ecstasy over Mr. Solomon's pictures. . . . " The former is respectable while the latter is not; it admires falsely "pretty pieces of morality, such as [Solomon's] 'Love dying by the breath of Lust.'"[69] Like Rossetti, Solomon is duplicitous—his art seems beautiful but it represents immoral subjects—, hence effeminate. Buchanan is judging Solomon by the standards of civic masculinity: Solomon errs by *gender deviance.*

Other spokesmen of Victorian culture were remarking with suspicion on Solomon's erotic representation of the male body. Their perspective evinces increasing public awareness of, and homophobia in response to, male–male eroticism and sexuality as highlighted by recent medical discourse and scandals such as that of Boulton and Park. Writing in 1870, the art critic Sidney Colvin warns Solomon against "insufficient manliness" in his choice of subjects and in the "affectation" characteristic of his rendering of male figures.[70] Colvin detects a "sentiment bordering a little on the crapulous" in some of Solomon's images of "the Dionysiac kind" which "carried [such sentiments] about as far as they could go."[71] Similarly, after a visit to Solomon's London studio in 1870, Robert Browning opines that Solomon's pictures are "too affected and effeminate."[72] Later in that year, Browning fulminates against the "effeminacy of his [D. G. Rossetti's] school."[73] Referring to "The Bride, the Bridegroom and the Friend"

(1868), Browning voices "hate" for Solomon's representation of Love "as a lubberly naked young man putting his arms here & his wings there, about a pair of lovers,—a fellow they would kick away, in the reality."[74] Gender deviance—"insufficient manliness"—is beginning to be articulated as *sexual deviance* in such comments. Solomon is judged effeminate by a criterion of gender—"insufficient manliness"—derived from the traditional code of civic masculinity and at the same time by a criterion of sexuality—"crapulous"—in the process of being formed around 1870.

The third discursive current swirling around the term and concept of effeminacy comes from Walter Pater. The very "language of expanded erotic and sensual experience" which Buchanan deplored in the Fleshly School was now available for use as a counter-discourse in which "effeminacy" signifies alternative constructions of masculinity.[75] As Richard Dellamora has noted, Pater singles out Solomon's head of *Bacchus* (1867) and the partly nude figure of *Bacchus* (1868) as exceptional for their representation of ideal male beauty in his 1876 essay, "A Study of Dionysus."[76] It is precisely the "effeminacy" epitomized by Bacchus/Dionysus—"the god . . . 'of things too sweet'; the sea-water of the Lesbian grape become somewhat brackish in the cup"—that Pater celebrates.[77] In such aesthetic minoritizing discourse, "effeminacy" is untied from its moorings in the traditional politico-moral ideology of civic masculinity.[78] "Effeminacy" shifts valence from a negative sign of deficient manhood to a positive sign of perfect masculinity as gender deviance moves into sexual dissidence.

Notes

Special thanks to Julie Codell, Richard Dellamora, and Linda Dowling, who commented on earlier versions of this essay.

1. Robert Buchanan, *The Fleshly School of Poetry and Other Phenomena of the Day* (1872), reprinted in *The Victorian Muse: Selected Criticism and Parody of the Period*, ed. William E. Fredeman, Ira B. Nadel, and John F. Stasny (New York: Garland, 1986), 70 (emphasis added).

2. Ibid., 5.

3. Jonathan Dollimore defines "sexual dissidence" by "conceptions of self, desire, and transgression" in the context of the "dialectic between dominant and subordinate cultures" in *Sexual Dissidence: Augustine to Wilde* (Oxford: Clarendon, 1991), 21.

4. Effeminacy has long been taken as a sign of alternative masculinities, as documented by Michel Foucault in *The History of Sexuality*, vol. 2, *The Use of Pleasure*, trans. Robert Hurley (New York: Pantheon, 1985). However, as Ed Cohen argues, "the 'effeminacy' popularly attributed to the 'aesthetic' or 'decadent' movement had not yet produced an immediate corollary association with sexual relations between men" before

the trials of Oscar Wilde in the 1890s. See *Talk on the Wilde Side: Toward a Genealogy of a Discourse on Male Sexualities* (New York: Routledge, 1993), 136.

5. In her groundbreaking book *Hellenism and Homosexuality in Victorian Oxford* (Ithaca: Cornell University Press, 1994), Linda Dowling discusses the importance of "classical republican theory" for the counter-discourse of Hellenized homosexuality.

6. John A. Cassidy, "Robert Buchanan and the Fleshly Controversy," *PMLA* 67 (1952): 65.

7. Ibid., 69.

8. Ibid., 72.

9. Buchanan's initial attack, "The Fleshly School of Poetry; Mr. D. G. Rossetti," was published in *Contemporary Review* (1871): 334–50.

10. For an account of the reactions to Buchanan's attack on the "Fleshly School of Poetry" during 1871–72 and the several phases of the controversy thereafter, up through the 1890s, see Cassidy, "Buchanan," 78–93.

11. Swinburne threw himself into the fray with several retorts to Buchanan, whereas D. G. Rossetti was much more hesitant. He "composed a pamphlet in answer to Buchanan's charges, but, fearing a charge of libel if it were printed, suppressed it. . . . From the pamphlet he made up a letter called 'The Stealthy School of Criticism,' which he published in the *Athenaeum*" at the end of 1871 (ibid., 77).

12. Quoted by Cassidy, "Buchanan," 86 (emphasis added).

13. Buchanan, *Fleshly School and Other Phenomena*, 33 (emphasis added).

14. Ibid., 84.

15. Ibid., 83. For a comprehensive analysis of the concept of "the public man" since 1870, see Jeff Hearn, *Men in the Public Eye: The Construction and Deconstruction of Public Men and Public Patriarchies* (London: Routledge, 1992).

16. Dowling, *Hellenism and Homosexuality*, xv.

17. Stefan Collini, "The Idea of Character: Private Habits and Public Virtues," in *Public Moralists: Political Thought and Intellectual Life in Britain, 1850–1930* (Oxford: Clarendon, 1991), 95. Although Collini does not directly address "questions of sexual identity and gender construction," he considers the ideal of manliness to be central to Liberalism. See "Manly Fellows: Fawcett, Stephen, and the Liberal Temper," in *Public Moralists*, 171.

18. See Hearn, "Patriarchy, Public Patriarchy, and Related Critiques," in *Men in the Public Eye*, 43–68.

19. Aristotle, *The Art of Rhetoric*, trans. J. H. Freese, Loeb Classical Library 193 (Cambridge: Harvard University Press, 1975), 1.9.1–7.

20. Ibid., 7–15.

21. Ibid., 2.6.7–13. In his cross-cultural study *Manhood in the Making: Cultural Concepts of Masculinity* (New Haven: Yale University Press, 1990), David D. Gilmore finds that men are consistently "expected" "to reproduce sexually, just as they are ex-

horted to produce economically and militarily, and to take on a commanding role in trading and oratory" (105).

22. Foucault, *Use of Pleasure*, 83.

23. Ibid. On the role of "virtue" in the mid-Victorian concept of the public man's "character," see Collini, "Idea of Character": "In both the language of virtue and the language of character there is a similar emphasis on the moral vigour of the citizens as the prime requirement for the health of the body politic" (109).

24. For a detailed historical and rhetorical study of the place of women in the Classical Greek state, see Page duBois, *Sowing the Body: Psychoanalysis and Ancient Representations of Women* (Chicago: University of Chicago Press, 1988). Aristotle makes women's place clear: "Virtues and actions are nobler, when they proceed from those who are naturally worthier, for instance, from a man rather from a woman" (*Rhet.* 1.9.16–23).

25. David M. Halperin argues that "effeminacy" designates *"gender deviance"* but not homosexuality in the texts of ancient Greek and Roman moralists in "Sex before Sexuality: Pederasty, Politics, and Power in Classical Athens," in *Hidden from History: Reclaiming the Gay and Lesbian Past*, ed. Martin Bauml Duberman, Martha Vicinus, and George Chauncey, Jr. (New York: New American Library, 1989), 46 (emphasis in original). "'Soft' [Gk. *malthakoi*, Lat. *molles*] or unmasculine men, far from being a fixed and determinate sexual species, are . . . either men who once experienced an orthodoxly masculine sexual desire in the past or who will eventually experience such a desire in the future. They may well be men with a constitutional tendency to gender-deviance . . . but they are not homosexuals" (47).

26. Dowling analyzes the links among *vir–virtus–virtù* in "Victorian Manhood and the Warrior Ideal," in *Hellenism and Homosexuality*, 32–66.

All definitions of Latin words are taken from *Cassell's New Latin Dictionary*, ed. D. P. Simpson (New York: Funk & Wagnalls, 1968).

27. Buchanan, *Fleshly School and Other Phenomena*, 7. By using "sensualism" synonymously with "animalism," Buchanan shows off his familiarity with current philosophy. "Sensualism" is the doctrine that regards the senses as the source of knowledge, while "animalism" is the doctrine that views man as equivalent to animals. Both terms may carry pejorative connotations: Carlyle urges that "Savage Animalism is nothing, inventive Spiritualism is all" in *Sartor Resartus* (1831). See *The Oxford English Dictionary*, s.vv. "Animalism" and "Sensualism."

28. James Eli Adams, *Dandies and Desert Saints: Styles of Victorian Manhood* (Ithaca: Cornell University Press, 1995), 26.

29. Collini, "Manly Fellows," 187.

30. Quoted in David Riede, "Transgression, Authority, and the Church of Literature in Carlyle," in *Victorian Connections*, ed. Jerome J. McGann (Charlottesville: University Press of Virginia, 1989), 106 (Carlyle's emphasis).

31. Quoted in Adams, *Dandies*, 31 (Carlyle's emphasis).

32. Riede, "Transgression," 114; Adams, *Dandies*, 27. On the strictures against "effeminacy" in public speaking in Aristotle's *Rhetoric*, see my "Mixed Metaphor, Mixed Gender: Swinburne and the Victorian Critics," *The Victorian Newsletter* 73 (1988): 16–19. In light of the evidence and arguments in Dowling, *Hellenism and Homosexuality*, and Adams, *Dandies*, my earlier view that "effeminacy" is tantamount to "homosexuality" in the charges made against Swinburne's poetry by Victorian critics needs to be revised. As the present essay shows, "effeminacy" was not the same as "homosexuality" in the 1860s, when this criticism was written.

33. Adams, *Dandies*, 1.

34. The full text of Eliza Lynn Linton, "The Girl of the Period," is reprinted and useful context given in *Defining Voices*, vol. 1, *The Woman Question: Society and Literature in Britain and America, 1837–1883*, ed. Elizabeth K. Helsinger, Robin L. Sheets, and William Veeder (Chicago: University of Chicago Press, 1983), 103–25.

35. Ibid., 112.

36. Ibid., 112, 108.

37. Ibid., 108 (emphasis added).

38. Ibid., 112.

39. Buchanan, *Fleshly School and Other Phenomena*, 3, 4.

40. Ibid., 5. Catherine Gallagher discusses the female body as metonym for the state of society in "The Body versus the Social Body in the Works of Thomas Malthus and Henry Mayhew," *Representations* 14 (1986): 83–106.

41. Buchanan, *Fleshly School and Other Phenomena*, 7, 37, 36.

42. Ibid., 10.

43. Ibid., 39, 31.

44. In *Nationalism and Sexuality: Respectability and Abnormal Sexuality in Modern Europe* (New York: Howard Fertig, 1985), George L. Mosse argues that the "ideal of manliness was basic both to the self-definition of bourgeois society and to . . . national[ism]" beginning in the early nineteenth century (23). He conflates the several attributes of "manliness" with the specific behavior of "homosexuality," however.

45. Buchanan's animosity toward William Michael Rossetti, which began during an exchange in 1866 regarding Swinburne's *Poems and Ballads, Series 1*, was sparked by xenophobia: "Buchanan saw anything British as basically good and honorable, while that which smacked of the foreign was to be distrusted" (Cassidy, "Buchanan," 69). Buchanan may also have seen himself as a Scots sage. His choice of pseudonym for his initial attack on D. G. Rossetti in 1871, "Thomas Maitland," is the name of a debating opponent in an eighteenth-century Scots treatise on "the peril of men being corrupted by evil influences," an angle "akin to the central thesis of the 'Fleshly School' article" (ibid., 74).

46. Buchanan, *Fleshly School and Other Phenomena*, 14.

47. Ibid., 15.

48. Ibid., 20–21, 19.

49. Ibid., 18.

50. The language of disease running throughout Buchanan's diatribe owes more to what Bruce Haley calls the "moral approach" in Victorian criticism than to the rhetoric of "degeneration" which emerges toward the end of the nineteenth century. See *The Healthy Body and Victorian Culture* (Cambridge: Harvard University Press, 1978). Physiological metaphors were often used to speak of ethical or of spiritual characteristics before such language became invested with racial and class connotations. See, for example, the entry for "morbid"—one of Buchanan's favorite epithets—in *The Oxford English Dictionary*.

51. Buchanan, *Fleshly School and Other Phenomena*, 22, 21.

52. Buchanan, Review of *Poems and Ballads*, *The Atheneum* 48 (1866). Reprinted in *Swinburne: The Critical Heritage*, ed. C. K. Hyder (London: Routledge and Kegan Paul, 1970), 137–38.

53. Buchanan, *Fleshly School and Other Phenomena*, 36.

54. Ibid., 50, 54. William Morris has been infected by "fleshliness," but, fortunately, he "has done some noble work quite outside his ordinary performances" (31).

55. Ibid., 31, 37.

56. Ibid., 31.

57. Ibid., 36, 58.

58. Ibid., 37.

59. Ibid., 67.

60. Ibid., 69.

61. Uxoriousness, or the keeping of company with women generally, is seen as a failure of masculinity in several cultures. "The uxorious Mehinaku man, the homebody or introvert (like his Melanesian counterpart), 'loses part of his claim to masculinity'" (Gilmore, *Manhood*, 92).

62. Buchanan, *Fleshly School and Other Phenomena*, 46, 34.

63. William A. Cohen gives a thorough account and analysis of the Boulton and Park trial in *Sex Scandal: The Private Parts of Victorian Fiction* (Durham, N.C.: Duke University Press, 1996), 73–129. The quotation is on pp. 74–75.

64. Quoted in W. Cohen, *Sex Scandal*, 88. The defense at the Boulton and Park trial dismisses the kind of xenophobic rhetoric that predominates in Buchanan's attack on effeminacy only to reinscribe it: "They libel the morality and character of this country who say that plague exists. . . . The moral atmosphere of England is not yet tainted with the impurities of Continental cities" (quoted ibid., 97).

65. Buchanan, *Fleshly School and Other Phenomena*, 33.

66. W. Cohen, *Sex Scandal*, 4–5.

67. Ibid., 95. For a study of Swinburne's and Solomon's "perverse" collaboration, see my "Perverse Male Bodies: Simeon Solomon and Algernon Charles Swinburne," in *Outlooks: Lesbian and Gay Sexualities and Visual Cultures*, ed. Peter Horne and Reina Lewis (London: Routledge, 1996), 61–85.

68. Quoted in Morgan, "Perverse Male Bodies," 75.

69. Buchanan, *Fleshly School and Other Phenomena,* 38.

70. Sidney Colvin, "Painters of the Present Day: Simeon Solomon," *The Portfolio* 1 (1870): 35.

71. Ibid. Although Colvin's remarks on Solomon are homophobic, his joining in the Fleshly School controversy *against* Buchanan suggests the incoherence of the concept of "effeminacy" in the early 1870s.

72. Robert Browning, *Dearest Isa: Robert Browning's Letters to Isabella Blagden,* ed. Edward C. McAleer (Austin: University of Texas Press, 1951), 330–31.

73. Ibid., 336–37.

74. Ibid.

75. Dowling, *Hellenism and Homosexuality,* 26.

76. Richard Dellamora, *Masculine Desire: The Sexual Politics of Victorian Aestheticism* (Chapel Hill: University of North Carolina Press, 1990), 177–78.

77. Quoted ibid., 177.

78. On aesthetic minoritizing discourse, see my "Reimagining Masculinity in Victorian Art Criticism: Swinburne and Pater," *Victorian Studies* 36 (1993): 315–32.

References

Adams, James Eli. *Dandies and Desert Saints: Styles of Victorian Manhood.* Ithaca: Cornell University Press, 1995.

Aristotle. *The Art of Rhetoric.* Translated by J. H. Freese. Loeb Classical Library 193. Cambridge: Harvard University Press, 1975.

Buchanan, Robert. "The Fleshly School of Poetry; Mr. D. G. Rossetti." *Contemporary Review* (October 1871): 334–50.

———. *The Fleshly School of Poetry and Other Phenomena of the Day.* London: Strahan and Co., 1872. Reprinted in *The Victorian Muse: Selected Criticism and Parody of the Period.* Edited by William E. Fredeman, Ira B. Nadel, and John F. Stasny. New York: Garland, 1986, 1–97.

———. Review of Swinburne, *Poems and Ballads. The Athenaeum* 48 (August 4, 1866): 137–38. Reprinted in *Swinburne: The Critical Heritage.* Edited by C. K. Hyder, 30–34. London: Routledge and Kegan Paul, 1970.

Cassidy, John A. "Robert Buchanan and the Fleshly Controversy." *PMLA* 67 (1952): 65–93.

Cohen, Ed. *Talk on the Wilde Side: Toward a Genealogy of a Discourse on Male Sexualities.* New York: Routledge, 1993.

Cohen, William A. *Sex Scandal: The Private Parts of Victorian Fiction.* Durham, N.C.: Duke University Press, 1996.

Collini, Stefan. *Public Moralists: Political Thought and Intellectual Life in Britain, 1850–1930.* Oxford: Clarendon, 1991.

Colvin, Sidney. "Painters of the Present Day: Simeon Solomon." *Portfolio* 1 (1870): 35.

Dellamora, Richard. *Masculine Desire: The Sexual Politics of Victorian Aestheticism.* Chapel Hill: University of North Carolina Press, 1990.

Dollimore, Jonathan. *Sexual Dissidence: Augustine to Wilde, Freud to Foucault.* Oxford: Clarendon, 1991.

Dowling, Linda. *Hellenism and Homosexuality in Victorian Oxford.* Ithaca: Cornell University Press, 1994.

DuBois, Page. *Sowing the Body: Psychoanalysis and Ancient Representations of Women.* Chicago: University of Chicago Press, 1988.

Foucault, Michel. *The History of Sexuality,* vol. 2, *The Use of Pleasure.* Translated by Robert Hurley. New York: Pantheon, 1985.

Gallagher, Catherine. "The Body versus the Social Body in the Works of Thomas Malthus and Henry Mayhew." *Representations* 14 (1986): 83–106.

Gilmore, David D. *Manhood in the Making: Cultural Concepts of Masculinity.* New Haven: Yale University Press, 1990.

Haley, Bruce. *The Healthy Body and Victorian Culture.* Cambridge: Harvard University Press, 1978.

Halperin, David M. "Sex before Sexuality: Pederasty, Politics, and Power in Classical Athens." In *Hidden from History: Reclaiming the Gay and Lesbian Past.* Edited by Martin Bauml Duberman, Martha Vicinus, and George Chauncey, Jr., 37–53. New York: New American Library, 1989.

Hearn, Jeff. *Men in the Public Eye: The Construction and Deconstruction of Public Men and Public Patriarchies.* Critical Studies on Men and Masculinities 4. London: Routledge, 1992.

Linton, Eliza Lynn. "The Girl of the Period." In *Defining Voices,* vol. 1, *The Woman Question: Society and Literature in Britain and America, 1837–1883.* Edited by Elizabeth K. Helsinger, Robin L. Sheets, and William Veeder, 108–12. Chicago: University of Chicago Press, 1983.

McAleer, Edward C., ed. *Dearest Isa: Robert Browning's Letters to Isabella Blagden.* Austin: University of Texas Press, 1951.

Morgan, Thaïs E. "Mixed Metaphor, Mixed Gender: Swinburne and the Victorian Critics." *The Victorian Newsletter* 73 (1988): 16–19.

———. "Perverse Male Bodies: Simeon Solomon and Algernon Charles Swinburne." In *Outlooks: Lesbian and Gay Sexualities and Visual Cultures.* Edited by Peter Horne and Reina Lewis, 61–85. London: Routledge, 1996.

———. "Reimagining Masculinity in Victorian Art Criticism: Swinburne and Pater." *Victorian Studies* 36 (1993): 315–32.

Mosse, George L. *Nationalism and Sexuality: Respectability and Abnormal Sexuality in Modern Europe.* New York: Howard Fertig, 1985.

Riede, David. "Transgression, Authority, and the Church of Literature in Carlyle." In

Victorian Connections. Edited by Jerome J. McGann, 88–120. Charlottesville: University Press of Virginia, 1989.

Simpson, D. P. *Cassell's New Latin Dictionary.* Rev. ed. New York: Funk & Wagnalls, 1968.

Production, Reproduction, and Pleasure in Victorian Aesthetics and Economics

REGENIA GAGNIER

In a recent article in *ELT* entitled "The Economies of Taste," the British Wilde scholar and cultural theorist Ian Small labeled a school of critics distinctively "American."[1] In contradistinction to the British tendency to emphasize production and producers, these critics had brought to the fore the institutions of the marketplace, the commodification of culture and artists, consumerism, and the psychology of desire for the goods and services of modernity.[2] It is not surprising that this emphasis on markets, commodification, and consumption is more prominent in United States scholarship than in British. As early as the 1840s, John Stuart Mill, Karl Marx, and other observers of the spirit of capitalism anticipated that the United States would go further than Europe in the unrestrained pursuit of markets, and it is a commonplace of political economy that U.S. consumer capitalism had advanced on British industrial capitalism by the end of the nineteenth century. Small is also right to point out that there has been a shift in emphasis in U.S. scholarship away from an aesthetics of production to an aesthetics of consumption. This shift is evidently reconfiguring Victorian studies as a whole, once dominated by figures of industrial revolution and increasingly dominated by figures of speculation, finance, circulation, exchange, and desire in all its modern forms. This drift has entailed a new focus on the late Victorian period. If gender, sexuality, and postcolonial studies have revitalized the whole field of Victorian studies, they have arguably shone with their most brilliance as they have converged with commodity theory on the fin de siècle.

One of the developments of the 1980s that is continuing through the 1990s was what might be called neoliberal scholarship—scholarship that takes for granted that society is about individuals maximizing their self-interest and scholarship that is in itself individualist, sensational, or pleasure-seeking, and expressly commodified. The political critique driving this scholarship identified productivism with masculinist Marxism or heterosexism. Male Leftists had blamed a decline in working-class consciousness on a feminine desire to consume and imitate the decadent leisure class, which betrayal led to universal commodification and massification.[3] Gay critics countered that Marx/Engels were homophobic and/or homoerotic and that their dialectical materialism was modeled on heterosexual gender relations.[4] Feminist critics protested that Marxist productivism had too often relegated women to their reproductive functions and associated them with the Nature that had to be transformed by "Man."[5] In short, the feminist, gay, and multicultural response to this masculine leftism was in defense of desire, especially the desire of the forgotten peoples of modernity for the goods and services of the world (including sexual goods and services). Now although I would maintain that in Marx/Engels the category of "labor" was much more than purely negative, or alienated, but as "species being" could also include the possibility of human creativity itself, and therefore not limited to a putatively "heterosexual" productivism or reproduction, I would also argue that our contemporary defense of desire is as justified as the earlier Marxist defense of the value of "labor." Yet some of the more sensational recent work on what Guy Debord called the society of the spectacle suggests to me that the emphasis on desire has become less a criticism of the limits of productivism, as in Baudrillard's early *Mirror of Production* (1975), where the value of an object was determined less by the labor invested by the producer than by the signification consumed by the buyer, than the concomitant of neoliberal, or market, society itself.[6]

Theoretically, the gender implications of the shift from production to consumption are unstable and potentially volatile. It may be that Marxism and other productivist analytics valued labor at the expense of desire; but inseparable from the centrality of labor was the centrality of the laboring body in social relations. Even if we were to grant a positive role to women-as-consumers in the liberation of desire, late Victorian consumerism in the form of the economics of desire—theorized in marginal utility theory—is precisely known for its formalism and abstraction, qualities that have historically been associated with masculine, abstract, individualism. This means that no gender absolutes can be derived from the shift from production to consumption. It is because neoliberalism, or consumer-driven market policy, is purely formal that it has been able to crow about growth and efficiency while occluding actual social relations. Arguments like Lawrence Birken's, that whereas the labor theory of value made work and property necessary to citizenship, modern mass consumption liberates all alike, are what I mean by neoliberal criticism.[7]

Now surely a criticism that occludes human labor and creativity is as reductive as that which sees people as mere producers and reproducers. Surely people are *both* producers and consumers, workers and wanters, sociable and self-interested, vulnerable to pain but desirous of pleasure, longing for security but also taking pleasure in competition. If we add to these continuums the fact that people may also be idle, apathetic, and unconscious of their motivations, we approach something like the grid of possibilities in modern market society. That is, people do not only identify themselves by what they consume, what they do in their leisure, what constitutes their pleasure—or conversely, by what they do not do, or do not have, in relation to others. They also identify themselves by whether they make nails, automobiles, books, contracts, breakfast, hotel beds, music, babies, or speeches.

The so-called Decadents themselves expressed this range of emotions evoked by modern market society. As early as 1863, Baudelaire had reacted, via his figure of the dandy, against a bourgeois ethos of productivity and domestic reproduction, rejecting masculine virility itself: "The more a man cultivates the arts, the less often he gets an erection."[8] Attacking the socialist-feminist George Sand, he wrote "Only the brute gets really good erections. Fucking is the lyricism of the masses." He himself went on to explore the more voyeuristic pleasures of the *flaneur*. The dandy Barbey formulated the choices to Huysmans between renunciation of worldly goods or total, self-destructive consumption: after *A Rebours* he could only choose between "the foot of the cross or the muzzle of a pistol." *A Rebours* itself proclaimed a weariness of both production and reproduction—Des Esseintes gave himself "a funeral banquet in memory of [his own] virility" and set himself to consuming the exotica of the world.[9] George Moore's hero Mike Fletcher in the novel of that name treated women like cigarettes, consuming and disposing of them in an insatiable search for stimulation:

> More than ever did he seek women, urged by a nervous erithism which he could not explain or control. Married women and young girls came to him from drawing-rooms, actresses from theatres, shopgirls from the streets, and though seemingly all were as unimportant and accidental as the cigarettes he smoked, each was a drop in the ocean of the immense ennui accumulating in his soul.[10]

Oscar Wilde's description of a cigarette also described the perfect commodity: cigarettes, Wilde said, were the perfect type of the perfect pleasure, because they left one unsatisfied.[11] The fin de siècle's basic stances toward the economy—boredom with production but love of comfort, insatiable desire for new sensation, and fear of falling behind the competition—culminated in Max Beerbohm's publication of his *Complete Works* at the age of 24. "I shall write no more," he wrote in the preface of 1896; "Already I feel myself to be a trifle outmoded. I belong to the Beardsley period. Younger men, with months of activity before them . . . have pressed forward since then. *Cedo junioribus*." Beerbohm satirized the duality of aestheticizing/commodifying one's life in *Zuleika Dobson*, in the double images of dandy and female superstar. Real women, like Mrs. (Mary Eliza) Haweis in her *Beautiful Houses* (1881), on the other hand, were packaging the world in moments of taste and connoisseurship and commodifying them for suburban effects. Indeed in political economy it is the comfort of the suburban home, comfort increasingly—or illusorily—accessible to common folks, that won for consumption its status as the essence of modernity.[12]

I could easily multiply examples of late Victorian self-awareness of a shift from production to consumption. But now I want to situate these basic stances toward the economy—the love of comfort, the fear of falling behind the competition, and the insatiable desire for new sensation—in relation to moments in the history of aesthetics and cultural critique. The remainder of this essay will be concerned with the gender valences of broad anthropological models in Victorian aesthetics and economics. These models include conceptions of people as producers or creators; as consumers or creatures of taste and pleasure; of work as alienable or creative; and of works and markets as autonomous or heteronomous. I understand aesthetics as a diverse and often overlapping group of claims made for art and culture, each with particular motivations and specific audiences in a web of social relations. Ethical aesthetics arose with industrialism and was concerned with the creation of self-regulating subjects and autonomous works; aesthetics of production were concerned with producers or creators of work and the conditions of creativity and production; aesthetics of taste or consumption, often with a physiological base, became dominant by the fin de siècle, largely through the dominance of psychology as a discipline in academic institutions; and aesthetics of evaluation, best evoked today under the name of Matthew Arnold, were historically linked with the idea of national cultures and races (remembering the range of meanings these terms encompassed in nineteenth-century Britain).

These aesthetics had a number of points of contact or overlap, but they were often promoted with very different motivations. Mill, like Kant before him, was concerned with the moral good and the creation of the liberal, ethical individual who could be relied on to subjugate individual desires to the social good. The self-styled "political economists of art" (Ruskin's phrase), Marx, Ruskin, and Morris, wanted to provide the conditions for producers whose work would be emotionally, intellectually, and sensuously fulfilling, and whose societies would be judged by their success in cultivating creators and creativity. Aesthetics of taste, deriving from Hume and Burke and merging with associationist psychology after mid-century, distinguished between objects of beauty and then distinguished between those who could and could not distinguish, often claiming that such capacities correlated to physiological or social stages of development. In aesthetics of evaluation, like Arnold's, in which the point was to measure one object against another by standards of "truth" or "seriousness," the "tact" that was thus demonstrated in one's ability to discriminate was less a matter of physiology than status, for Arnoldian evaluation was in the service of locating individuals in relation to class, class in relation to nation or culture, and nation or culture in relation to globe or "civilization." Yet physiology remained in the association of Arnold's ideas of culture with racial types.[13]

Thus some aesthetics were concerned with the human as liberal, ethical individual and others with the human as creator fulfilling her role as producer of the world. Some aesthetics were concerned with the object produced or created, and others with the consumers of objects and their mode of apprehension. Another way I have put this is that some were concerned with productive bodies, whose work could be creative or alienated, while others were concerned with pleasured bodies, whose tastes established their identities. All of these models were inflected by gender typologies and gendered divisions of labor. Granting overlap among these groups, for example, bodies that took pleasure in their labor, much confusion has nonetheless resulted from reifying something called "the Aesthetic" and something monolithic called "value," which reifications have only recently begun to be rectified, primarily through feminist, gay, and postcolonial analytics.[14] The point is to see the tensions or struggles between competing aesthetic models and even within one model alone.

Ethical Aesthetics and the Self-regulating Body

In Kant, the moral good consists in acting autonomously, as one ought, rather than heteronomously, or from desire, emotion, or self-interest. This freedom to act autonomously can only be achieved by reason, but it can be prefigured by feeling, the feeling of freedom from desire or self-interest that we get when we perceive the beautiful object. When we perceive the beautiful object—which in Kant is typically a natural object theoretically accessible to all rather than a work of art, which, Kant says, may give rise to an element of ego or possessiveness—the disjunction between our perception and our concept creates an excess, a free play of imagination, that prefigures moral freedom, or freedom from desire and self-interest. It prefigures the reconciliation between individual and social life that the moral good entails, that is, to act according to duty rather than according to desire or self-interest, or to act in such a way that one's actions embody a universal principle for action.[15] In Kant's *Anthropology*, making a man of taste falls short of making a morally good man, but it prepares him for it by the effort he makes in society to please others.[16] This taste for freedom is thus, notoriously, a form of discipline, a freedom from the selfish desires.

A Kantian judgment of taste is neither simply subjective, relating to the consumer, nor objective, relating to the object. It begins with the harmonious workings of the faculties when a perceiver is confronted with certain objects. At first this aesthetic feeling is subjective and phenomenal. In the disinterested pleasure which comes to me without the element of desire or self-interest, I do not transcend the phenomenal sphere (see "Analytic of Aesthetic Judgment" in *Critique of Judgment*). But Kant insisted, for purposes of the logic of his entire system, that judgments of taste were also objective. When we say that the beautiful object ought to please others also, we bring in rational and objective elements. Recognizing something in us that is common to the species, and something in each member of the species that is not owned but is universal property, we are freed from our former confinedness and limitations (see *ibid.*, "Dialectic of Aesthetic Judgment"). Many people, of course, who are persuaded by Kant's phenomenology of aesthetic feeling—the "free play" of imagination synthesizing perception and concept—are not persuaded by his rationalizing or universalizing of it to make it a symbol of the moral good, or freedom.[17]

Without Kant's metaphysic, John Stuart Mill's aesthetic also functioned as a discipline. In his two major essays on poetry of 1833, Mill distinguishes poetry from mere eloquence by its discipline and autonomy—poetry is: overheard while eloquence is heard; unconscious of listeners while eloquence is directed toward an audience; an end in itself whereas eloquence is a means toward an end; thoughts tinged by feeling whereas in eloquence feelings pour themselves out to other minds; feeling unconscious of being watched whereas eloquence is found in "attitudinizers" showing themselves off before spectators.[18] For Mill, the French—social, vain, and dependent on others—are eloquent but not poetic, subject to law or external constraint but not self-disciplined. The autonomous, disciplined lover of poetry is also distinguished from primitive peoples (or vulgar people in advanced societies) who prefer stories (or novels), as those who prefer "a state of sensibility" are distinguished from those drawn to "mere outward circumstance." Obviously Mill's lover of poetry, even in these early essays, prefigures his lover of liberty in *On Liberty* of 1859, who acts freely without inhibiting the freedom of others.

Because the poet is a disciplined, ethical exemplar, poetry is disciplined feeling, and the lover of poetry is the autonomous, self-disciplined feeler. The poem embodies the process that will educate the readers how to be autonomous (rational, self-reflective) themselves.[19] For Mill, aesthetics partakes of rational self-reflection in the service of progressive individuals. It was clearly Mill's response to democratizing social processes. The essays on poetry were published in 1833, a year after the First Reform Bill, when the pressing concern of idealistic reformers was how to subjugate the masses into responsible citizenship. Now this figure of Kant's moral agent or Mill's reader is an autonomous, self-regulating male, not driven, like Economic Man, by passion or self-interest. To this extent, the ethical aesthetic is a liberal aesthetic and carries with it the masculine appurtenances of liberal autonomy. It should be noted that there is a rich cultural history of masculine autonomy associated with this

repudiation of rhetoric, from the Scottish Enlightenment's stoic, masculine
virtues to Mill's national distinctions between poetry (English) and rhetoric
(French) to Pater's ascetic stylist and Wilde's repudiation of rhetoric in *De Profundis.*

In fiction, an ethical aesthetic and self-regulating bodies may be seen in
Thomas Hardy's *Jude the Obscure* (1895). Ostensibly the story of a working-
class autodidact who attempts unsuccessfully to make the proverbial "better
life" for himself and his family, even naive readers typically sense something
"aesthetic" about *Jude.* It was published in 1895, toward the sunset of late-
Victorian Aestheticism, and it includes a number of tropes familiar to that
declining genre: a Romantic longing for the Beautiful, a Ruskinian appreciation of creativity and the conditions of creation (see below), and themes of taste
and discrimination. It also depicts the proverbial struggle between spirit and
flesh: Jude's youthful attraction to his carnal first wife has disastrous consequences for his subsequent union with a soulmate and equal, the delicate and
intellectual New Woman Sue Bridehead. On Sue's part, first her body and then
her spirit are tortuously subjugated to Victorian marriage laws. The novel as a
whole may be seen, as H. M. Daleski has argued, as Jude and Sue's attempt to
carve out an ethics, an autonomy, of will in the face of necessity. Daleski interprets what might be seen as Sue's cruel virginity as rather an attempt at autonomy or "self-containment."[20] Sue says, regarding her ascesis, that "I never
yielded myself to any lover . . . I have remained as I began," and the constant
references to her epicene nature, her "curious unconsciousness of gender," indicate a technology of the self, if an eccentric one, opposed to her social role as
a woman.[21] Jude's history as the quintessential autodidact, subjecting himself
to study under conditions of severe deprivation, is similar. He studies the Bible
and Classical languages as if individual talent and merit could surmount social
barriers, as if he could make himself. With their final chastisement, their wills
are broken and every attempt at their self-creation has been defeated—Jude's
for education and for meaningful labour, Sue's for female independence, and
their collective dream of unity.

We see a recent treatment of aesthetics as ethics inscribed in the senses or
emotions in the last years of Michel Foucault, from the posthumously published *The Use of Pleasure* (1984) and *The Care of the Self* (1984), volumes two
and three of the *History of Sexuality,* to Foucault's last interviews, in which he
spoke of social practices amounting to ascesis, or self-discipline.[22] Kant's ethics
derived from the systematic relations between the good, the true, and the beautiful; Mill's and Foucault's, respectively, from education and a system of social
practices; but they share an idea of the aesthetic creation of an ethical being.
Two critics strongly influenced by Foucault have emphasized this aesthetic-as-
ethic. In *Outside Literature,* Tony Bennett claims that philosophical aesthetics

has always posited a "universalized valuing subject."[23] He concludes in full
neo-Foucauldian declamatory style that aesthetics "is part of a technology of
person formation whose effects are assessed as positive and productive in serving as a means of normalising the attributes of extended populations as a part
of the more general procedures and apparatuses of government through which,
in Foucault's conception, the attributes of modern citizenries have been shaped
into being" (181). Like Bennett, Ian Hunter sees aesthetics as "the instruments
and objects of a special practice of the self, deployed for essentially ethical purposes. They are the phenomena whose systematically polarized structure is
symptomatic of their systemic use as reflexive instruments of self-problem-
atization and self-modification."[24] This notion of aesthetics as ethics, of self-
regulation in a disciplined society, has been the dominant one among Foucaul-
dians and new historicists, who have focused on bourgeois hegemony, but its

assumptions of constraint, self-restraint, and internal regulation render it inadequate to analyze the hedonics of modern consumer culture. (More on these
hedonics below.) It has been argued elsewhere that Foucault's "aesthetics of the
self" ought to be interpreted not as a technology of the self but as an alternative
to it, as a way that sexual practices or "pleasures" might enable other selves and
new relationships to emerge.[25] Yet whether the "care of the self" or the "use of
pleasure" inclines toward the subjection or liberation of the subject, Foucault's
emphasis remains the ethico-aesthetic production of the self, whose freedom
and autonomy (but not of course its sexual desires) seem characteristic of a
liberal tradition that some feminist critics have found to be idealist and mascu-

line in its freedom and self-control.

The Productive Body

The movement that Ruskin called the political economy of art focused not on
the spectator or consumer but on the producer of the work and conditions of
production: this was Ruskin's aesthetic, Morris's after him, and, of course,
Marx's and generations of Marxists' (although Marxist aesthetics has typically
included a critique of ideology with its critique of production). Contrary to an
aesthetics located in the object (Plato's) or in the perceiver (Kant's or Burke's),
the political economists of art began with the very body of the artist and ended
with a theory of creative production.[26] In *Jude the Obscure*, the builder reads the
buildings at Christminster (i.e., Oxford) as Ruskin "reads" (his own term) the
cathedrals at San Marcos or Amiens:[27] "less as an artist-critic of their forms
than as an artizan and comrade of the dead handicraftsmen whose muscles
had actually executed those forms" (103). These muscles, of course, have been
aestheticized and eroticized, along with their feminine counterpart the reproductive woman, as part of a productivist ethics for a century and a half; if the

model was broadly heterosexual, it was also rooted in the body as firmly as Kant's or Mill's ethico-aesthetic was rooted in the mind. One must not underestimate the extent to which the political economists of art were concerned with ethics and reception ("reading"). Indeed Ruskin is considered the founder of "moral consumption," or the appeal to consumers' social responsibility, and he had affinities with physiological aesthetics in his precise calculations of aesthetic impact on the body, especially on the eye (see the role of "seeing" throughout his work). Yet despite these concerns and affinities, a theory of creative labor motivates the political economists of art; their object was the relations of production and reproduction and the possibilities for human flourishing within them.

We should pause here, in an age of consumer demand, to remark how seriously the nineteenth century from a wide range of perspectives took the labor theory of value, from Ricardo to Marx, Mill, Ruskin, and Hardy. The theory said that the cost of a commodity was the value of the labor power it took to produce it, plus the value of the laborer's wear and tear in production, plus the value of the laborer's family's subsistence, or, as Marx said, the value of laborpower was "the necessaries by means of which the muscles, nerves, bones, and brains of existing laborers are reproduced and new laborers are begotten."[28] Much of the outrage in novels like *Jude*, written well after the theory had been discredited as a theory of price, is against a society that literally undervalues its producers. And Hardy's terms are, like "labor," those of political economy: production, reproduction, and the body whose labor was its defining feature. They are also specifically Malthusian in the body's reproductive capacity. From the beginning Jude is conscious of himself, of his "unnecessary life" (36), as part of Malthus's "surplus population," and his children die "because we are too menny" (356). Correspondingly, Sue's gendered, reproductive labors are what she seeks, hopelessly, to avoid in pursuit of a (bodiless) aesthetic partnership. And reproductive, like productive, labors are, again, embedded in thick social and material relations (see, for example, how bodies are typically marked by gender, race, and class relations).

The impulse to historicize art, to read in art the history of social relations, of course, goes back to Hegel, a student of political economy. Kant's examples in the third *Critique* of the Sublime and Beautiful are drawn from nature, e.g., sublime cataracts and mountains or the beautiful song of a bird. Hegel, on the other hand, made representation central to his aesthetics, deriving the aesthetic impulse from the fact that it was human nature to, as he said, represent ourselves to ourselves. Thus art is an index of its time, its producers, and their conditions of production.[29] At the end of the nineteenth century, in his magisterial *History of Aesthetic* (1892), Bernard Bosanquet saw the culmination of this tradition of philosophical aesthetics in the materialism of Ruskin and

Morris. Insofar as the worker was free in his producing activity, so far would he produce the work of creative humanity. In England, Bosanquet concluded, aesthetic insight had had a remarkable influence on economic theory.[30] The dissolution of romantic art into excessive internality and subjectivity predicted by Hegel would presage the birth of Morris's unalienated worker, whose "art [was] the expression of pleasure in labor," where "pleasure," again, indicates that labor can be creative and fulfilling rather than alienated "toil and trouble."[31] Unlike the monumentally abstract eighteenth-century science of aesthetics, for the Victorians aesthetics was the realm of daily life and its "sense data" or sensuous experience, its pains and pleasures. Bosanquet, for example, was particularly interested in Morris's production in the domestic arts of furniture-making, tapestries, textiles, and carpets.

The Pleasured Body

In contrast was biological or physiological aesthetics, as in Grant Allen's *Physiological Aesthetics* (1877), which, through its position of authority in the academy, rapidly gained dominance over the applied aesthetics of Ruskin and Morris, and in which the cultivation of a distinctive "taste" in the consumption of art replaced concern for its producers. The roots went back to Hume and Burke, who had analyzed the psychological bases of taste. According to Hume, the structure of the mind made some objects naturally inclined to give pleasure or to inspire fear. William Knight in his fin-de-siècle *Philosophy of the Beautiful* (1895) estimated that Burke's influential essay of 1756 had reduced aesthetics to the lowest empirical level, identifying the beautiful with the source of pleasant sensations.[32] In Burkean sensationism, the experience of an elite group of Anglo-Irish takes on the appearance of universalism; the irrational feelings associated with the sublime are given equal place with the sociable feelings associated with the beautiful; and enlightenment or reason is subordinated to mechanism. Burke's very constrained subject—increasingly the subject of political conservatism—is chained to physiology and driven by self-preservation and, to a lesser extent, benevolence. "We submit to what we admire, but we love what submits to us," Burke famously said of our respective reactions to the sublime and the beautiful.[33] We respond naturally to the beautiful in the form of the small, the smooth, the curvilinear, the delicate, and the bright. We admire the sublime in the form of the vast, the rugged, the jagged, the solid and massive, and the dark. Erasmus Darwin perceived the associational basis of the beautiful when he named it a characteristic of Beauty to be an object of Love. We love the smooth, the soft, and the warm because we were once nourished thence. His grandson Charles later theorized the sense of beauty in relation to sexual selection. Many have remarked on the gender implications of Burke's theory.[34] Here I shall explore physiological aesthetics in relation to pleasure and consumption.

Since Hume, biological aesthetics had included custom with physiology in conditioning our response to the beautiful.[35] In the course of the nineteenth century, biological aesthetics merged with established associationist psychology, which gained legitimacy as an academic discipline under Herbert Spencer and Alexander Bain in the century's second half. As it came to dominate economics, psychology, and sociology, it also came to dominate aesthetics, shifting the study from its German roots in ethics or Reason and Victorian roots in production to that of reception, consumption, or individual pleasure. Indeed, for our purposes, the empiricist tradition in aesthetics of Hume and Burke, which is typically opposed to Kantian Reason, is significant for its grounding precisely in sense, in the pleasures of consumption. Bain banished everything but pleasure from aesthetics. Following Bain, in *Physiological Aesthetics* Allen defined the beautiful as that which afforded the maximum of stimulation with the minimum of fatigue or waste, in processes not directly connected with life-serving functions.

Allen wrote, "The aesthetic pleasure is the subjective concomitant of the normal amount of activity, not directly connected with life-serving functions, in the peripheral end-organs of the cerebro-spinal nervous system."[36] Although taste had its source in the brain's hardware, whole societies could cultivate it with Lamarckian consequences. Conditions of leisure give rise to two classes of impulse, play and aesthetic pleasure. In play we exercise our limbs and muscles; in aesthetic pleasure we exercise our eyes and ears—the organs of higher sense as opposed to the more functional senses of taste and smell. In this aesthetic, whose proponents included Spencer as well as Bain, the highest quality or quantity of human pleasure was to be derived from art.[37] Contrary to the expressed goals of social justice and egalitarianism among the political economists of art, the experiencers of this pleasure fall into predictable hierarchies, and here is where aesthetics most heavily draws on a lexicon of civilization and barbarism, or stages of development. With painstaking discussions of the physical origins of aesthetic feelings, Allen ultimately argued that existing likes and dislikes in aesthetic matters were the result of natural selection. From thence it was but a short step to distinguish between stages of aesthetic development, and Aesthetic Man, like Economic Man, was distinguished from others lower in the scale of civilization (whom Allen, following Spencer, Bain, and other associationists interpret, after Burke, as "children" or "savages"). "Bad taste," writes Allen, "is the concomitant of a coarse and indiscriminate nervous organization, an untrained attention, a low emotional nature, and an imperfect intelligence; while good taste is the progressive product of progressing fineness and discrimination in the nerves, educated attention, high and noble emotional constitution, and increasing intellectual faculties" (48). "The common mind," as he put it, "translated the outward impression too rapidly into the reality which it symbolized, interpreting the sensations instead of observing them" (51). Rather than immediately translating the impression into its "real" analogue, on the other hand, the aesthetic mind "dwelled rather upon the actual impression received in all the minuteness of its slightest detail" (51). This, of course, meant that persons of taste dwelt on the representation and their subjective response to it, rather than on any referent it might have in the external world. (The aesthete Walter Pater, as I've argued elsewhere, emphasized this subjective and formalist response in his aesthetic.)[38] Today, institutionalists like Pierre Bourdieu have shown how the tendencies either to "dwell in the referent" or in the representation are distinctive marks of social class.[39]

In an influential article, "The New Hedonism," Grant Allen, the author of *Physiological Aesthetics* and by then publicist of the New Woman, specifically opposed the New Hedonism, or the philosophy of pleasure and pain, to the Old Asceticism, which he associated with the work ethic and self-restraint, specifically targeting the productivist tradition represented by Carlyle.[40] "Self-development," he proclaimed, "is greater than self-sacrifice" (382). Yet although Allen's interest is in pleasure, feeling, and sensation, these are inextricably linked with sexual reproduction, and the document is specifically an argument in favour of sex: "Now there is one test case which marks the difference between the hedonistic and ascetic conception of life better than any other. I am not going to shirk it. . . . From beginning to end, there is no feeling of our nature against which asceticism has made so dead a set as the sexual instinct" (383–84). In lists comparable to those of *Physiological Aesthetics*, Allen argues that from the beautiful song of the bird to the pleasing physical properties of animals, flowers, and fruits, "every lovely object in organic nature owes its loveliness direct to sexual selection" (385). He goes on to attribute all our "higher emotions"—"our sense of duty, parental responsibility, paternal and maternal love, domestic affections . . . pathos and fidelity, in one word, the soul itself in embryo" (387)—to "the instinct of sex." Thus the reproductive body returns at the fin de siècle to haunt the consuming or pleasured body, in direct evolutionary descent: the highest pleasures derive from the most basic instinct to reproduce. Throughout the 1890s Allen's heterosexual aesthetic, with its beautiful body of sexual selection, was in cultural dialectic, both implicit and explicit, with other, perverse aesthetics. In some cases, as I wrote some years ago, art for art's sake was allied with a defense of sex for sex's sake, or nonreproductive sex.[41] In other cases, the aesthetic was not beautiful at all, but sublime and terrible, and its body was often abject, repulsive. We have come to call this Other body the "Gothic" body.[42]

Physiological aesthetics—aesthetics that calculated immediate pleasure—was pervasive in the fin de siècle. Not just in Pater's *Renaissance,* in which he wrote that our object was "to get as many pulsations as possible into the given time,"[43] but also in Vernon Lee's "psychological aesthetics." (Physiological and psychological were used interchangeably.) Based on her reading of Allen, Lee experimented on the sensitive body of her lesbian lover, Clementina Anstruther-Thomson, which aesthetic experiments compromised the ethical aesthetics Lee had inherited from Ruskin and the missionary aesthetics the aristocratic Anstruther-Thomson had inherited from a tradition of women's philanthropy.[44]

In fiction, we could choose from many examples but shall stay with Hardy's *Jude the Obscure,* exquisitely divided between two incompatible aesthetics, one productivist, deriving from Ruskinian principles of work and creativity, and one physiological, discriminatory, an aesthetics of taste. The first espouses a labor theory of value, as in Jude's esteem for his craft and his belief that his educational labors will result in class mobility, and the other espouses a standard of taste, best illustrated in the contrast between Arabella and Sue. In Sue Bridehead—small, delicate, and bright—we perceive the beautiful who naturally evokes Jude's benevolent response. Uncommonly sensitive to the sufferings of birds (34), pigs (36), rabbits (234), and women (289), Jude and Sue's heightened "sensitivity" (305) is manifested not only in sympathy toward vulnerability but also in their mutual recoil from vulgarity. Jude, of course, castigates himself for his innate and vicious attraction to women and spirits. Yet he cannot help his aesthetic sense feeling violated when Arabella reveals a hairpiece on their wedding night: he felt a sudden distaste for her, "a feeling of sickness" (79). He regrets their marriage, "based upon a temporary feeling which had no necessary connection with affinities that alone render a life-long comradeship tolerable" (90). He shares those affinities with Sue, who is "light and slight, of the type dubbed elegant" (109) and variously described as "uncarnate" (207), a "disembodied phantom hardly flesh at all" (265, 413), and "a phantasmal bodiless creature" (279). The cruelty that Sue's bodilessness entails for her husbands is forgiven by Jude's agonized "all that's best and noblest in me loves you, and your freedom from everything that's gross has elevated me" (285). Sue demands this sublimation and continually condemns the carnal Arabella (Matter to Sue's Reason) as "low," "coarse," and "vulgar" (285, 287, 290). Indeed, we might understand Arabella as instinctively acting upon Hume's famous dictum that "Reason is and ought only to be the slave of the passions, and can never pretend to any other office than to serve and obey them," in which a minimal reason relates means to ends but makes no claims concerning the rightness of ends.[45] Jude's communal feeling as a stonemason can no more

be reconciled with these hierarchical tastes as an aesthete than his feeling for
the laborer can be reconciled with his chastisement of the body. One aesthetic
is productivist, the other is discriminatory and ascetic.

The example of *Jude* takes us full circle, for of course *Jude the Obscure* is
about desire: the desire to be free of one's class, one's gender, one's marriage
and reproductive function. It is about the desire to live aesthetically the life of
rich and varied sensations that Jude associates with the mental life and material
beauty of Oxford. But unlike Jude, Hardy is not an idealist but a realist, and
his novel is ultimately an anti-aesthetic, showing how social institutions oppose
the aesthetic life. Yet with hindsight we recall that just as *Jude* was revealed to
the world, to cause the scandal that its demands on behalf of women and working people brought down on Hardy (such that he blamed it for his final turn
from fiction to poetry), just then "labor" activists with their productivist ethics
and sexual dissidents with their pleasures were meeting in the social networks
of Edward Carpenter, Olive Schreiner, Gertrude Dix, Eleanor Marx, and Amy
Levy, to name just a few.[46]

And the desire for the good things of the world persists and is exacerbated
in our own time. When political theorists say, as they are wont to do today,
that economic liberalism is the total subordination of the economy and politics
to "culture," they are defining "culture" for our time as the desires, needs, and
tastes of individuals: the end of history in consumer culture. Economists today
have a principle that "tastes are exogenous." This means that the construction
of taste is external to their models; that they no longer ask why people buy
what they buy or do not buy what they do not. The principle is often extended
further, to an aesthetic laissez-faire, claiming that it is of no concern what others like, that it is an intrusion on people's liberty to speculate on the rightness—
or even the origins—of their tastes. Revealed preference theory ensured that
the only "preferences" revealed were those revealed by consumption patterns,
whether or not such so-called preferences were determined by financial constraint or even coercion. Yet as economists have abandoned inquiry into the
complexity of choice and preference, cultural critics have become more sophis-
ticated at analyzing precisely that. The leveling of high and low culture in the
broader conception of culture that characterizes most literature and culture de-
partments has resulted in superb research on why people have the tastes they
have. And at no time in history has the construction of taste been more significant.

The sociologist J. Urry describes contemporary global culture as images, language, and information flowing through "scapes" of geographically dispersed
agents and technologies.[47] This cultural flow gives rise to a cosmopolitan civil
society that "precipitates new modes of personal and collective self-fashioning
as individualization and cultural formations are . . . combined and recombined"

(64). Urry insists that it is important to see how heavily *culturalized* the flows are, how much global *cultures* have to do with global constructions of preferences of taste: "Increasingly economies are economies of signs. . . . This has implications for the occupations structure and hence for the increasingly culturally constructed preferences of taste" (65). It is precisely this cultural construction of taste that is the province of critics of culture.

But as we study what statistical price lists and microeconomics cannot tell us, that is, as we study the construction of taste, we must remember that people are not only consumers. We are both workers and wanters, born of labor and desire. Although there has been a shift in emphasis from production to consumption, and the dominant tendency within rich nations today is to think more of individuals than social groups and more of desire than scarcity, there is more to be said about the relationship between production and consumption in both economics and aesthetics. An aesthetics and economics of pleasure became salient in ideological terms at the fin de siècle, having competed with ethical, political economic, and evaluative models. It was doubtless Anglo-American society in the 1980s, with its construction of society as individuals maximizing their self-interest and pursuing happiness, which sensitized us to this development and which leads to our emphasis on consumption and excess rather than production or self-regulation. Yet the record of competing models is worth keeping if we want less reductive accounts of market society.

This essay has concentrated on a plurality of aesthetics in Victorian Britain as a way to critique reified notions of "the Aesthetic," indicating some of the gendered tensions between them. It is clear that in nineteenth-century Britain, aesthetic agendas were related to economic agendas in which key elements were the artist as creative or alienated producer, the man of taste or the critic as consumer, and the work as autonomous ("value") or commodified ("price"). If economics in the nineteenth century defined itself as the domain for the provision for the needs and desires of the people, aesthetics was in its most inclusive sense the apprehension and expression of the people's needs and desires at the level of sense, feeling, and emotion. It follows that economic and aesthetic models of production, consumption, taste, and the rest may be seen in their fullest interrelations, including the gender implications of such models.

Notes

1. Ian Small, "The Economies of Taste: Literary Markets and Literary Value in the Late Nineteenth Century," *English Literature in Transition* 39, no. 1 (1996): 7–18.

2. Small used my work in *Idylls of the Marketplace* and more recently on the histories of economics and aesthetics, but he might have used any number of recent works on commodification, largely but not exclusively from the United States: Andrew Miller's

book *Novels behind Glass,* Anne McClintock's work on commodity racism, Rita Felski's on feminine modernity as the erotics and aesthetics of the commodity; Kathy Psomiades's work on how the duality of femininity permitted Aestheticism to both acknowledge and repress art's status as commodity; and Laurel Brake's work on the periodicals market. Writing on Wilde, Richard Dellamora has recently used Bataille to talk about "nonproductive expenditure." In *The Ruling Passion,* Christopher Lane has focused on exchange as a motive for empire, which would be nothing new except that he means exchange of sexual desire among men rather than goods. Talia Schaffer has shown how the respective commodifications of "interior design" versus "home decoration" in the fin de siècle were gendered. And so forth. Regenia Gagnier, *Idylls of the Marketplace: Oscar Wilde and the Victorian Public* (Stanford: Stanford University Press, 1986); Andrew H. Miller, *Novels behind Glass: Commodity Culture and Victorian Narrative* (Cambridge: Cambridge University Press, 1995); Anne McClintock, *Imperial Leather: Race, Gender, and Sexuality in the Colonial Contest* (New York: Routledge, 1995); Rita Felski, *The Gender of Modernity* (Cambridge: Harvard University Press, 1995); Kathy Alexis Psomiades, *Beauty's Body: Femininity and Representation in British Aesthetics* (Stanford: Stanford University Press, 1997); Laurel Brake, *Subjugated Knowledges: Journalism, Gender, and Literature in the Nineteenth Century* (London: Macmillan, 1994); Richard Dellamora, "Wildean Economics," Paper presented at CUNY Graduate Center, May 1995; Christopher Lane, *The Ruling Passion: British Colonial Allegory and the Paradox of Homosexual Desire* (Durham, N.C.: Duke University Press, 1995); Talia Schaffer, "The Women's World of British Aestheticism," Ph.D. dissertation, Cornell University (1995), esp. chap. 1, "The Home is the Proper Sphere for the Man: Inventing Interior Design, 1870–1910."

3. These charges are addressed in Felski, *Gender of Modernity;* Carolyn Kay Steedman, *Landscape for a Good Woman* (New Brunswick, N.J.: Rutgers University Press, 1987); and Pamela Fox, *Class Fictions: Shame and Resistance in the British Working-Class Novel, 1890–1945* (Durham, N.C.: Duke University Press, 1994).

4. See Andrew Parker, "Unthinking Sex: Marx, Engels, and the Scene of Writing," in *Fear of a Queer Planet,* ed. Michael Warner (Minneapolis: University of Minnesota Press, 1993), 19–41; and Andrew Hewitt, "Coitus Interruptus: Fascism and the Deaths of History," in *Postmodern Apocalypse,* ed. Richard Dellamora (Philadelphia: University of Pennsylvania Press, 1995), 17–40.

5. See Donna Haraway, *Simians, Cyborgs, and Women* (New York: Routledge, 1991), chap. 7, "'Gender' for a Marxist Dictionary," p. 127.

6. See my summary of Baudrillard's *Mirror of Production* (St. Louis: Telos, 1975) in *Idylls,* 9–10. See also Guy Debord, *Society of the Spectacle* (New York: Zone, 1994).

7. Lawrence Birken, *Consuming Desires: Sexual Science and the Emergence of a Culture of Abundance, 1871–1914* (Ithaca: Cornell University Press, 1988).

8. See *The Painter of Modern Life and Other Essays,* trans. and ed. Jonathan Mayne

(London: Phaidon, 1966), 28–29, and *My Heart Laid Bare and Other Prose Writings* (London: Soho, 1986), 175–210, 213.

9. *Against Nature* (Harmondsworth: Penguin, 1982), 27.

10. George Moore, *Mike Fletcher* (1889; New York: Garland, 1977).

11. *The Picture of Dorian Gray*, in *The Portable Oscar Wilde*, ed. Richard Aldington (Harmondsworth: Penguin, 1978), chap. 6, p. 228.

12. See, for example, Peter J. Taylor, "What's Modern about the Modern World-System? Introducing Ordinary Modernity through World Hegemony," *Review of International Political Economy* 3, no. 2 (Summer 1996): 260–86.

13. See Robert Young, *Colonial Desire: Hybridity in Theory, Culture and Race* (London: Routledge, 1995), 55–89.

14. Probably the best known recent reification of "The Aesthetic" is Terry Eagleton's in *The Ideology of the Aesthetic* (Oxford: Blackwell, 1990); for a similar treatment of "Value," see Steven Connor, *Theory and Cultural Value* (Oxford: Blackwell, 1992). For an alternative approach see Martha Woodmansee, *The Author, Art, and the Market* (New York: Columbia University Press, 1994).

15. Immanuel Kant, *Critique of Judgment*, trans. Werner S. Pluhar (Indianapolis: Hackett, 1987).

16. Immanuel Kant, *Anthropology from a Pragmatic Point of View*, trans. Mary J. Gregor (The Hague: Nijhoff, 1974), 111–12.

17. See especially Pierre Bourdieu, *Distinction: A Critique of the Judgment of Taste* (Cambridge: Harvard University Press, 1988); Stanley Fish, *Doing What Comes Naturally* (Durham, N.C.: Duke University Press, 1989); and Barbara Herrnstein Smith, *Contingencies of Value: Alternative Perspectives for Critical Theory* (Cambridge: Harvard University Press, 1988).

18. "What is Poetry?" and "The Two Kinds of Poetry," in *The Collected Works of John Stuart Mill*, ed. John M. Robson, vol. 1 (Toronto: University of Toronto Press, 1963), 341–53, 354–65.

19. For a detailed analysis of Mill's aesthetic and of its compatibility with Mill's larger views in *On Liberty*, see Kenneth Brewer, *"Lost in a Book: Aesthetic Absorption 1820–1880,"* Ph.D. dissertation, Stanford University, 1998, chapter 3, "The Absorption of John Stuart Mill," 41–57.

20. H. M. Daleski, *Thomas Hardy and the Paradoxes of Love* (New York: Columbia University Press, 1997).

21. Thomas Hardy, *Jude the Obscure* (1895; London: Macmillan, 1974), 169. All further references to *Jude* will be in the text.

22. "On the Genealogy of Ethics," in *The Foucault Reader*, ed. Paul Rabinow (New York: Pantheon, 1984), 340–73.

23. Tony Bennett, *Outside Literature* (New York: Routledge, 1990), part 3, pp. 117–92.

24. Ian Hunter, "Cultural Studies and Aesthetics," in *Cultural Studies*, ed. Lawrence Grossberg et al. (New York: Routledge, 1992), 356.

25. See Dellamora, "Wildean Economics."

26. See Ruskin, *The Political Economy of Art* (1857), in *Unto This Last and Other Essays* (London: Dent, 1932), 1–106.

27. See Ruskin, "The Nature of Gothic," in a later edition of *Unto This Last and Other Writings*, ed. Clive Wilmer (London: Penguin, 1985), 77–110, and *The Bible of Amiens* in *On Reading Ruskin*, trans. and ed. Jean Autret et al. (New Haven: Yale University Press, 1987).

28. Karl Marx, *Capital*, trans. Samuel Moore and Edward Avcling, ed. Fredrich Engels (New York: International Publishers, 1967), 572.

29. G. W. F. Hegel, *Hegel's Aesthetics: Lectures on Fine Art*, trans. T. M. Knox (Oxford: Oxford University Press, 1975).

30. Bosanquet meant, of course, *critical* economic theory, as in Ruskin's critique of political economy *Unto This Last* or Morris's socialism.

31. Bernard Bosanquet, *History of Aesthetic* (London: George Allen and Unwin, 1892), 441–71. The definition of art as "the expression of Man's pleasure in his labour" is Morris's in his Introduction to the Kelmscott "Nature of Gothic."

32. William Knight, *Philosophy of the Beautiful* (London: Murray, 1895).

33. Edmund Burke, *A Philosophical Enquiry into the Origin of our Ideas of the Sublime and the Beautiful*, ed. James T. Boulton (Notre Dame, Ind.: University of Notre Dame Press, 1986), 113.

34. See, for example, Peter de Bolla, *The Discourse of the Sublime: Readings in History, Aesthetics, and the Subject* (Oxford: Blackwell, 1989), 56–58; Terry Eagleton, "Aesthetics and Politics in Edmund Burke," *Irish Literature and Culture*, ed. Michael Keneally (Gerards Cross: Colin Smythe, 1992), 25–34; Barbara Charlesworth Gelpi, "'Verses with a Good Deal about Sucking': Percy Bysshe Shelley and Christina Rossetti," in *Influence and Resistance in Nineteenth-Century English Poetry*, ed. G. Kim Blank and Margot K. Louis (New York: St. Martin's, 1993), 150–65; Mary Poovey, "Aesthetics and Political Economy in the Eighteenth Century: The Place of Gender in the Social Constitution of Knowledge" in *Aesthetics and Ideology*, ed. George Levine, (New Brunswick, N.J.: Rutgers University Press, 1994), 79–105.

35. David Hume, "Of the Standard of Taste," in *Essays Moral, Political and Literary*, ed. Eugene F. Miller (Indianapolis: Liberty, 1963), 226–52.

36. Grant Allen, *Physiological Aesthetics* (London: Henry S. King, 1877), 34. Further page references will be in the text.

37. See Spencer, "Use and Beauty" (1852), reprinted in *Essays Scientific, Political, and Speculative*, vol. 1, pp. 433–37 (London: Williams and Norgate, 1883); and Alexander Bain, *The Emotions and the Will* (New York: Appleton, 1888), esp. chap. 14, "The Aesthetic Emotions," 225–63.

38. Regenia Gagnier, "On the Insatiability of Human Wants: Economic and Aesthetic Man," *Victorian Studies* 36, no. 2 (winter 1993): 125–54; "Is Market Society the *Fin* of History?" in *Cultural Politics at the fin de siècle,* ed. Sally Ledger and Scott McCracken (Cambridge: Cambridge University Press, 1995), 290–310.

39. Bourdieu, *Distinction.*

40. *Fortnightly Review* (March 1894), 377–92.

41. Gagnier, *Idylls of the Marketplace,* chap. 4, pp. 137–76.

42. See Kelly Hurley, *The Gothic Body: Sexuality, Materialism, and Degeneration at the Fin De Siècle* (Cambridge: Cambridge University Press, 1996).

43. Walter Pater, *Selected Writings,* ed. Harold Bloom (New York: Signet, 1974), 17.

44. See Diana Maltz, "Engaging 'Delicate Brains': Vernon Lee, Kit Anstruther-Thomson and Psychological Aesthetics," in *Women and British Aestheticism, 1860–1934,* ed. Talia Schaffer and Kathy Alexis Psomiades (Charlottesville: University Press of Virginia, forthcoming).

45. David Hume, *Treatise of Human Nature* (Harmondsworth: Penguin, 1969), 415.

46. See Sally Ledger, *The New Woman: Fiction and Feminism at the Fin de Siècle* (Manchester: Manchester University Press, 1997), esp. 35–61.

47. J. Urry, "Is the Global a New Space of Analysis?" *Review of International Political Economy* 3, no. 2 (summer 1996): 61–66.

SIX

"Men of My Own Sex": Genius, Sexuality, and George Du Maurier's Artists

DENNIS DENISOFF

"These inspired epicenes, these gifted epileptoids, these anæmic little self-satisfied nincompoops"; "rickety, unwholesome geniuses, whose genius (such as it was) had allied itself to madness"; "little misshapen troglodytes with foul minds and perverted passions":[1] it is understandable if these lines from George Du Maurier's *Martian* (1897) lead one to assume that the popular illustrator and novelist was not especially fond of the male dandy-aesthetes to which he refers. As Regenia Gagnier has demonstrated, their flagrant self-advertising and talent for reading the risqué interests and decorous limitations of their middle-class audience irritated many members of Victorian society.[2] Du Maurier's work reveals, however, that the dandy-aesthetes attained such high cultural cachet at the end of the century not simply because they could work their audience, but because they positioned their persona at the center of a power struggle over the sexualization of the ideal type of artist. *Trilby*'s author was involved in this struggle as well; as part of a community of men growing increasingly uncomfortable with their own perceived slide away from the sphere of "real" artists toward the realm of insincere, hack writers and illustrators, Du Maurier explores in his work the matrix of economic, aesthetic, sexual, and ethical ideologies in which this process was situated.

At first glance, Du Maurier appears to have attempted to reinforce his own cultural authority by demonizing the dandy-aesthetes. Ironically, however, his cartoons helped make their persona so popular that it became an even greater threat to the heteronormative, masculine image of the artist on which he preferred to model himself. The complex vacillations in his cartoons and last two novels, *Trilby* and *The Martian*, reflect less one individual's antagonism than a broader cultural instability regarding sexual identities. In this regard, it is *Trilby* that most adroitly reveals the at times strained but not always combative interaction among identity traits. Although frequently reinforcing heterosexual/homosexual and masculine/feminine binary paradigms, *Trilby* has each central male character display diverse traits based on sexuality, gender performance, ethnicity, genius, and artistic genre, each of which carries a different, fluctuating weight within the character's identity. In this novel, Du Maurier suggests that conventional men such as himself, who have an investment in the arts, should base their decision on how much to tolerate and to encourage another male artist's transgressivity not simply on the form or degree of any one of these traits, but on their unique combination in relation to the person's immediate cultural context.

The Anti-Dandy Humor of Du Maurier's Cartoons

Du Maurier himself took part in both the bohemian and the commercial societies which his oeuvre at times criticizes. In recollections and biographies of the author, the descriptions of his studies at the atelier Gleyre in Paris from 1856 to 1857 focus no more on painting than on the male artists' carousing and pranks. Henry Silver records Du Maurier reminiscing about "[James] Whistler and his vie de Boheme in Paris, and of the nude model fingering his fair friend while the students made hobby horses of their chairs . . . d. M. tells of students drinking champagne at a sou a bottle."[3] However, as Du Maurier's close friend Thomas Armstrong points out, "We were none of us real Bohemians, for we had those behind us in England who would have come to our help if we had been in dire necessity."[4] Du Maurier's Parisian year of homosocial bonding was sanctioned by a traditional coming-of-age narrative which, encouraged by the young artist's sudden partial blindness, led to a return to the conventions and values with which he was raised. Back in London, Du Maurier shared a flat with Whistler, took part in Arthur Lewis's bachelor parties, and held a peripheral position in the "St. John's Wood Clique" of male artists. He also became friends with the Ionide and Prinsep families, the latter being well known for having invited G. F. Watts to dinner in 1850 and letting him stay for 20 years. For the most part, however, Du Maurier remained on the fringes of the Victorian art world; one gets a sense of his conservatism when he describes his first few years back in London as "a clear, honest, wholesome, innocent, intellectual, and most industrious British bohemia."[5] He also began to voice jealousy toward artists, such as Frederic Leighton, who he felt were attaining fame too easily or directing too much of their attention to potential patrons. In 1893, after Val Prinsep, a painter whom Du Maurier appears to have admired as much for his looks as for his talent, had not visited Du Maurier's home for roughly 20 years, the latter implied that his friend's absence was an act of snobbery.[6]

Punch, for whom Du Maurier worked most of his adult life, offered him an alternative male arts community with which to identify. The initials carved into the staff table, the closed-door meetings and suppers, and the recorded bits of witty conversation all suggest a close-knit men's club, a group that Mark Lemon, a member of the staff, describes as "one of the most extraordinary literary brotherhoods the world has seen."[7] One historian fondly imagines their weekly meetings, emphasizing that the staff members "secure to *Punch* that quality of tradition and healthy sense of prestige which strengthen [the magazine] against every assault, whether of man or of Time himself. . . . The tenderness of the Staff for the honour, good name, and pre-eminence of *Punch* is delightful and touching to behold."[8] Du Maurier suggests not only the pride and self-respect of the *Punch* staff, but also indirectly its elitism, when, in *The Martian*, he has the narrator flatter a community of commercial illustrators as "admirable in industry and talent, thorough artists and very good fellows all round" (335), while the novel's hero discredits those writers whom he has not seen at any of the clubs to which he belongs (390). Du Maurier's jealousy of and impatience with poseurs is the flip side of his sense of privileged responsibility for ensuring that an ethical and sexual regulation be placed on his society's notion of an ideal artist.[9]

Defending those in the field of journalism who were proud of their cultural influence and the responsibility it entailed, Du Maurier's *Punch* cartoons reflect the position, frequently voiced by literary reviewers of the time, that the dandy-aesthetes who claimed to be artists or connoisseurs were in fact vulgar, self-promoting shams who not only lacked innate talent and the skills arising from strenuous practice, but also enacted an elitist, bachelor lifestyle that threatened to supersede an emergent heterosexual identity. Although Du Maurier's cartoons conveyed, as Gary Schmidgall puts it, a "profoundly conservative reaction" to the dandy-aesthetes, it is enlightening to differentiate among the concerns embodied in Du Maurier's critique, as well as the tensions among the diverse forms of "deviancy" with which the persona was associated.[10] In the ironically titled 1878 cartoon "A Rising Genius" (fig. 1), Du Maurier has a "fashionable scribbler" assert the pretentious claim, "I never read Books—I *write* them!"[11] The scribbler's physiognomy functions as a cipher that confirms an interpretation of him as insincere and superficial. Positioned amidst a current of virile swells in the act of courting women, the speaker, like most of *Punch*'s early dandy-aesthetes, has longish, unkempt hair, heavy-lidded eyes, a small figure, and curved hips.[12] These characters usually stand with their arms gently bent toward their hips, while their bodies perform something of a whip-lash curve. The stance and grooming, seen as both feminine and bohemian, contrast with the "masculine" pose of the other men in the drawing, who tend toward straight lines and sharp angles.[13] Not only are acts of display gendered in this cartoon, but those that are gendered female are marked as *conscious* performance while those gendered male are inscribed with an *inherent* stability that transcends cultural change. While men's effeminacy had been read by this time as signaling sexual deviancy, and even homosexuality explicitly, the correlation was still ambiguous for many.[14] The dandy-aesthete's effeminate performance in this cartoon signals more generally his unhealthy fastidiousness re-

A RISING GENIUS.

Young Lady (in course of conversation). "You've read PENDENNIS, of course?"
Fashionable Scribbler (who is, however, quite unknown to fame). "A—PENDENNIS! AH!—LET ME SEE! THAT'S THACKERAY'S, ISN'T IT? No, I've not. The fact is, I never read Books—I write them!'

Figure 1 A Rising Genius (*Punch*, May 11, 1878)

garding surface image, in contrast to the assumedly direct, masculine self-image of the gentlemanly swells. The "scribbler's" implied attention to form over substance reflects not simply his lack of knowledge regarding respected authors such as Thackeray, but his distance from any inherent artistic talent. True genius is more subtly apparent, Du Maurier would have us believe, because it is signified unintentionally.

Pierre Bourdieu discusses the self-awareness inherent in an approach such as Du Maurier's. Arguing that taste is a learned quality, Bourdieu notes that elitist groups such as the "academic aristocracy" are essentialist, but that the "same essentialism requires them to impose on themselves what their essence imposes on them—noblesse oblige—to ask of themselves what no one else could ask, to 'live up' to their own essence."[15] The act of "living up" emphasizes the performance actually required of any community wishing to argue that their social value is innately obvious—that it is, paradoxically, *not* in need of performance. In "A Rising Genius," Du Maurier suggests essentialism by establishing a community of swells performing masculinity that basically outnumbers the competition. The cartoonist's anxious self-valuation arises from the same concern that James Eli Adams has put forward as central to Thomas Carlyle's efforts to justify the worth of the man of letters without suggesting that he felt it needed justification: "How does one attach a normative masculinity to a vocation that inheres less in action than in a mode of being—or, more precisely, that makes being itself a mode of action?"[16] In Du Maurier's view, artistic legitimacy should be viewed as the result of genius brought to the fore through strenuous training. By commodifying the persona of the artist and art connoisseur, the dandy-aesthete threatened to refute the assumption that society valued and rewarded artists based primarily on their genius and skill. This is the message of a Du Maurier cartoon published in the autumn of 1880, in which a female dandy-aesthete voices her desire to "live up to" a teapot,[17] an echo of Oscar Wilde's comment, made while still at Oxford, that he found it "harder and harder every day to live up to [his] blue china."[18] Du Maurier attempts to undermine the woman's claim to refined taste by having her direct it at an object that he felt it was obvious did not deserve such attention. Ironically, he challenges the woman's elitism with the same stroke that implies his own sense of superiority over those members of the bourgeoisie who were making art criticism a popular pastime by supporting the revolution in domestic taste. The ultimate twist is that performance and packaging were already the principal, if unacknowledged, means by which people like Du Maurier were able to legitimize their own discriminating taste to the general public. As Bourdieu puts it, the cultural elitists struggle to "live up" to their own essence (something which is as manufactured as a teapot), and the dandy-aesthete's self-commodification threatened to expose the artifice of an identity that Du Maurier wished to believe was the result of essential qualities and years of hard work.[19]

By the late nineteenth century, British society had reached a new peak in its ability to take in and reproduce cultural trends and icons, a talent that some interpreted more anxiously as a loss of resistence. Attributing this development in part to the enhanced reach of the print media, Roger Henkle concludes that, by the 1880s, "The English were absorbing and reprocessing ideas, events, and modes of behavior with a rapidity that could not have been possible even twenty years earlier."[20] The success with which the risqué version of the male dandy-aesthete in particular had been absorbed into mainstream culture is suggested by both the rapid multiplication of dandified ladies' men and feminized husbands within the pages of *Punch*, and their transformation into effeminate art connoisseurs uninterested in heterosexual dalliance. During the 1870s, Du Maurier frequently presents his dandy-aesthetes as married. This positioning of the characters within the family unit could be seen as the textual manifestation of anxieties arising from the infiltration of aesthetics into domestic values. And yet, this representation of a threat to a familiar lifestyle

NINCOMPOOPIANA.

(*Surfeited with excess of "cultchah," Prigsby and his Friends are now going in for extreme simplicity.*)

Prigsby. "I CONSIDAH THE WORDS OF '*LITTLE BOPEEP*' FRESHAH, LOVELIAH, AND MORE SUBTILE THAN ANYTHING SHELLEY EVAH WROTE!" [*Recites them*

Muffington. "QUITE SO. AND SCHUBERT NEVAH COMPOSED ANYTHING QUITE SO PRECIOUS AS THE *TUNE!*" [*Tries to hum it*

Chorus. "HOW SUPREME!"

Figure 2 Nincompoopiana (*Punch*, December 20, 1879)

would have also enhanced audience awareness of people's interests in alternatives. The cartoons encourage readers to consider the degree to which Aestheticism and commodity culture caused the devaluation of heteronormative family roles, as Du Maurier implies, and the degree to which the movement's popularity was itself due to various individuals' growing unwillingness to sustain the normative personas. While dandy-aesthetes threatened to make the artist and heteronormative male mutually exclusive, men like Du Maurier wished to identify with both.

Du Maurier's 1879 drawing for his "Nincompoopiana" series (fig. 2)[21] appeared less than two years after "A Rising Genius" (fig. 1). Unlike the earlier cartoon, with its isolated "scribbler" circumscribed by images of angular masculinity, "Nincompoopiana" offers Du Maurier's first representation of an all-male community of dandy-aesthetes, a sign that such gatherings had become common among certain segments of society. The cartoonist continues to challenge the dandy-aesthetes' claims to membership in the creative aristocracy by having a cluster of them listen in apparent rapture to the self-righteous author Prigsby lecture on "Little Bo Peep"'s superiority over the works of Percy Shelley. A bust of Antinous, the Emperor Hadrian's male lover, hovers in the background, fusing Aestheticism to sexual nonconformity, a relation also implicated by the men's physical features and stances. Some of Prigsby's admirers sit in the familiar pose of the dandy-aesthete while others exaggerate it by twisting one leg around the other and tucking their hands into their hair or between their thighs.

Retaining the heavy eyelids, full lips, and vacant expressions of Du Maurier's earlier caricatures, the men also sport the large body and clean-shaven face of Wilde, who, having recently moved to London, had taken no time in making himself known as Aestheticism's main product and promoter.[22] Du Maurier's antagonism toward what he viewed as the dandy-aesthetes' vulgar self-advertisement did not keep the last two decades of the century from seeing an increase in the number of such individuals along with their literary coteries and precious publications. Nor did Du Maurier ever fully relinquish his influence on the image. Shifting from cartoons to the novel, his representation of a broader spectrum of artistic types shows a desire on his part to delineate more precisely what he did and did not admire in the persona. In *Trilby*, Du Maurier splits the dandy-aesthete, embodying certain idealized artistic traits within the sensitive English gentleman, while imposing less desirable components onto a Jewish genius.

Trilby's Spectrum of Genius

In contrast to his earlier cartoons' inscription of ethical deviancy onto a feminized and homosexualized male body, Du Maurier's novel *Trilby* (1894) presents such unconventionality as a sign of possible creative genius. The author still denigrates artistic egoism and self-commodification, but in this text he does so through an anti-Semitic depiction of the mesmerizing musician Svengali. Despite the fact that, by the late nineteenth century, West European Jews were physically indistinguishable from other West Europeans, the Jewish stereotype fulfilled a position of alterity necessary to naturalize the Aryan, heterosexual male.[23] Du Maurier allows no ambiguity regarding Svengali's alterity; he defines his origins as distant Eastern Europe, refers to him as a "dazzling specimen" of the race (50), depicts him with an oily, pointed, beard and "bold, black, beady Jew's eyes" (49), and offers a stream of other negative stereotypes.[24] The caricature was a common one in late-Victorian England, where an assumed physical difference between Jews and gentiles made the Jewish man a surrogate for all men considered to be threateningly abnormal. Du Maurier's novel also combines ethnic and sexual normativity with economic stability by sustaining the common association of Jews with avarice. In the eyes of *Trilby*'s narrator, the mesmerist is the epitome of greed: "Svengali walking up and down the earth seeking whom he might cheat, betray, exploit, borrow money from, make brutal fun of, bully if he dared, cringe to if he must—man, woman, child, or dog—was about as bad as they make 'em" (47). According to Sander Gilman, this greed signals an inability to produce or to appreciate anything of transcendent value, with the Jew taking money as a substitute for love and beauty.[25] Du Maurier's self-promoting, Aestheticist fakes are therefore connected to the anti-Semitic stereotype not only through suggestions of sexual and ethnic deviancy, but also through commercial greed and all-consuming egotism. The mutual field of apparent flaws—what Judith Halberstam describes, in her study of gothic horror, as a "technology of monstrosity"—made the late-Victorian dandy-aesthete and the Jew virtually interchangeable stereotypes signifying cultural degeneracy.[26]

Addressing Bram Stoker's *Dracula*, Halberstam argues that, within the context of the novel, the eponymous character is "otherness itself, a distilled version of all others produced by and within fictional texts, sexual science, and psychopathology."[27] A similar definition can be given of Svengali, with the qualification that Du Maurier (and Stoker, for that matter) does not have the villain signify pure alterity for all people; the ubiquitous potential infiltration of the self by otherness—in this case, the verging monstrosity of the creative genius—problematizes any explicit polarity.[28] The representation of Svengali as a serious threat is validated precisely by the norm's dependence on the Other for its own naturalization. In *Trilby*, Du Maurier uses this fluidity of signification to create a spectrum of genius that ranges from the ideal artist—which he associates with painting and *tinges* with ethnicity, sexual unconventionality, and a penchant for music—to the threatening commercialist—which he associates with music and saturates with Jewishness and extreme narcissism. Contrary to the usual critical interpretation of Little Billee as a prude and Svengali as a demon, Du Maurier actually conjoins the two men by positioning them at different points on a spectrum of genius. The spectrum is imbued throughout by ethnicity, sexual unconventionality, and musicality, but only its negative end is tainted by concerns with fame, money, and self-advertising.

Suggesting the dangerous fluidity of artistic genius around which Du Maurier's moral message is constructed, *Trilby*'s narrator comments that the talent of the main hero, the painter Little Billee, is in part due to his "faint suggestion of some possible very remote Jewish ancestor—[his] tinge of that strong, sturdy, irrepressible, indomitable, indelible blood which is of such priceless value in diluted homœpathic doses" (8). In fact, the narrator observes, most of us have "at least a minimum of that precious fluid." Svengali's Jewish blood, however, is apparently far less diluted, coming as it does from Eastern Europe; in contrast to Little Billee's quaint, clean, and gentlemanly Englishness, Svengali is depicted as bringing a threatening foreignness to the Left Bank.

A similar tinge of nonnormative traits is apparent in the hero's sexual proclivities. 1894 was, in Brian Reade's words, a "golden year for homosexuals in England,"[29] and thus a potentially explosive time for Du Maurier to be affiliating himself with Aestheticism's supporters, since the sexual deviancy that he had helped attach to this community had, for many, become a fact rather than a slur.[30] Seemingly undeterred by this development, Du Maurier complicates the gender and sexuality of his hero. In the very first description of Little Billee, the author emphasizes the young man's effeminacy: "Little Billee was small and slender, about twenty or twenty-one, and had a straight white forehead veined with blue, large dark blue eyes, delicate, regular features, and coal-black hair. He was also very graceful and well built, with very small hands and feet, and much better dressed than his friends" (7). The narrator also mentions Little Billee's "almost girlish purity," as well as his "affectionate disposition, his lively and caressing ways" (10). Nina Auerbach argues that, in Du Maurier's writing and drawing, "the women are free, mobile, and flexible, and the men appear by nature corseted and strangulated."[31] Notably, Little Billee is one of the few characters who does not fit either gender category as Auerbach describes them. In a drawing of him that Du Maurier did for the first edition of *Trilby*, the hero hunches his short, slight frame forward over his crossed legs, and rests his hands demurely on his knee. Auerbach, who analyzes this particular picture, is correct in pointing out that Du Maurier usually depicts men as stiff and restrained, but here and elsewhere Little Billee problematizes conventional gender performance by exhibiting the looseness, but not the freedom, of most of Du Maurier's female characters.

The hero's own greatest fetish is the boyish Trilby's feet, although they are not his sole erotic attraction. The narrator says of the hero, "Little Greek that he was, he worshipped the athlete" (204), such as his friend Taffy, "the huge naked Briton" "who was like unto the gods of Olympus!" (54, 204). Leonée Ormond suggests that Taffy, while never becoming a talented artist, combines Du Maurier's gentlemanly and physical male ideals—the former having been found in Thomas Armstrong (who studied at Gleyre's studio with Du Maurier) and the latter in the tall, brawny Val Prinsep (who studied at Gleyre's after Du Maurier left).[32] The author had apparently hoped that Prinsep would marry his sister but had to settle for Taffy marrying Little Billee's. In *Trilby*, Du Maurier never hesitates to mention Taffy's physical qualities, frequently describing the character in hyper-masculinizing, phallic language, as one who "lung[es] his full spread with a [fencing] foil, in all the splendour of his long, lithe, youthful strength" (38) and "tower[s] cool and erect, foil in hand" (43); Taffy is "a towering figure of righteous Herculean wrath" (55) who performs acts of physical strength and dexterity among a group of male fans, while Little Billee generally stands back in demure admiration (see 67, 78, 107, 134). Ensuring that the erotic potential of such "Greek" appreciation is not lost on his readers, Du Maurier also presents an otherwise unnecessary discussion of a slim, sixteen-year-old Greek who goes by a nickname because his real name is "much too lovely for the Quartier Latin, and reminded one too much of the Isles of Greece—where burning Sappho loved and sang" (108–9), Greek and Latin both being languages, we are informed, that are "highly improper . . . in which pagan bards who should have known better have sung the filthy loves of their gods and goddesses" (41). Little Billee also finds pleasure in studying "London life at its lower den—the eastest end of all" (180), "wherever he could meet his kind, high or low" (184): "He liked to feel the warm contact of his fellow-man at either shoulder and at his back" (184). Du Maurier attempts to contain his hero's worship for the male body and same-sex cameraderie, how-ever, through aesthetics: "I think," muses the narrator, "all this genial caressing love of his kind, this depth and breadth of human sympathy, are patent in all his work" (184). We are often informed that Little Billee views the world through a "quick, prehensile, aesthetic eye" (17), and it is this trait that gives him the license to linger over Taffy's luscious limbs. Little Billee's art and aes-thetic temperament apparently save his taking of erotic pleasure in other men from being read as subversive.

The use of aesthetics to sanction the eroticism of a character's interests was also adopted as a strategy by the dandy-aesthetes. The Aestheticist claim to purely artistic appreciation devoid of ethical or political interests made the erotic element of appreciation less direct a threat to conventional Victorian morality and enhanced the opportunity for same-sex and other less accepted forms of erotic admiration. When Queensberry's defense questioned Wilde on a passage from *Dorian Gray* in which Basil Hallward describes his feelings for Dorian, Wilde is said to have explained its homoeroticism by stating: "I think it is the most perfect description possible of what an artist would feel on meet-ing a beautiful personality that he felt in some way or other was necessary to his art and life." "You think that is a moral kind of feeling for one man to have toward another?" persisted the defense. "I say," replied Wilde, "it is the feeling of an artist toward a beautiful personality."[33] Similarly, when Wilde was asked in court to explain the love letter/prose poem that he had written for Douglas "apart from art," Wilde—apparently always the aesthete—replied that he could not do so.[34] In these instances, Wilde's image as a dandy-aesthete—whether sincere or not—maintained a discursive incommensurability that pro-tected him, to a degree, from discussing his homosexual attraction in tradi-tional moral or juridical terms.

Wilde's novel precedes Du Maurier's in using the space of sexual maneuver-ability created by a person's claim to a purely aesthetic appreciation of the hu-man body. As Ed Cohen has pointed out, *Dorian Gray* never overtly refers to same-sex eroticism, but Basil's portrait of Dorian functions as an object of mediation for male–male desire.[35] In a similarly triangulated sense, Wilde presents Aestheticism itself as a mediator of attraction and influence between men.[36] Early in his novel, Lord Henry's Aestheticist monologue infiltrates Dorian's mind: "The few words that Basil's friend had said to him—words spoken by chance, no doubt, and with wilful paradox in them—had touched some secret chord that had never been touched before."[37] Lord Henry, having watched the young man's resulting sexual-aesthetic awakening, echoes Pater in arguing that the aesthete is not simply somebody who views life as art, but somebody who can develop this viewpoint in others, particularly those who are already inclined toward such a change (55). For Lord Henry, a discriminating temperament does not erase erotic attraction but includes it in its shameless, all-encompassing revision of the way a person sees the world and identifies oneself. Du Maurier presents Little Billee, despite his own conservatism, as having just such a temperament.

In his discussion of "moral sexlessness" in "Winckelmann," Pater holds that "Greek sensuousness . . . does not fever the conscience: it is shameless and childlike."[38] Similarly, Du Maurier's narrator describes Trilby as "equally unconscious of self with her clothes on or without! . . . she was absolutely without that kind of shame" (77). He goes on to offer his own description of "moral sexlessness": "All beauty is sexless in the eyes of the artist at his work—the beauty of man, the beauty of woman, the heavenly beauty of the child" (78). The narrator then proclaims the superiority of men's beauty over that of women, who simply lack "proper physical training" (78). Here we see what Richard Kelly has described as Du Maurier's ideal of an unattainable beauty, a "curious amalgam of machismo . . . and of aesthetic sensibility as represented in the conclusion of Walter Pater's *The Renaissance*."[39] Following Pater's association of aesthetic temperament with shameless sensory pleasure and male beauty, Du Maurier portrays Little Billee as a polite, middle-class, but nevertheless sexually unconventional genius. And yet, the fact that the extensive descriptions of Little Billee's admiration for Taffy's body are given by the narrator, and not the hero at all, challenges Du Maurier's suggestion that the homoeroticism is entirely an incidental byproduct of the hero's innately aesthetic eye. This transposition of the hero's tastes onto the narrator is a reflection not of the author's desire to use a coded discourse to address a homosexual readership, but of his attempt to situate innate artistic talent within a heterosexual identity that he could call his own, a type of genius absent from Svengali's calculating approach to the beauty of others.[40]

Svengali represents the distant end of the spectrum of genius—shallow, self-centered commercialism. With his scraggly, black hair, mischievous, heavy-lidded eyes, svelte body, and comparatively foppish sartorial inclinations, this man is Du Maurier's *Punch* dandy-aesthete taken to a derogatory extreme. A comparison of figures 1 and 2 with another cartoonist's caricature of the antagonist in "The Marvellous Feat of Tree-ilby Svengalivanised!" (fig. 3)—a spoof of Herbert Beerbohm Tree's 1895 stage performance as Svengali—makes it apparent that the 1878 "Rising Genius" tends more toward Svengali than toward Wilde.[41] Du Maurier presents Svengali, like the "scribbler," as an extreme narcissist: "He had but one virtue—his love of his art; or, rather, his love of himself as a master of his art—*the* master" (46). Svengali personifies both the egocentric poser ("I, and nobody else—I—Svengali—I—I—*I!*" [27]) and the greedy usurper of other people's identities, reflecting Du Maurier's fear that the dandy-aesthete was both making a claim to the normative identity of the artist and challenging the authority of the burgeoning identity of the heterosexual male. Suggesting the broader cultural reading of the dandy-aesthete as a double-edged threat, the same accusation of simultaneous insincerity and dangerous attraction was, if the newspaper records of the case can be depended on for basic facts, made against Wilde in court. Much as certain dandy-aesthetes seemed to have lured Victorians into a culture of conspicuous consumption defined by chinamania, lilies, and male–male attraction, Svengali's mesmeric powers permitted him to take over the will of others. In contrast to Little Billee's and Du Maurier's principal association with the visual arts, the author chooses music to signal this extreme of insatiable consumption.

Du Maurier's novel focuses on two male artists' attraction to the eponymous heroine. The painter's first great work is a drawing of Trilby's left foot, while the musician uses hypnotism to make music through the tone-deaf heroine's perfectly formed mouth.[42] In the novel's most powerful manifestation of artistic misogyny, Trilby's disengendered voice functions for Little Billee and Svengali as a transit point for erotic interaction couched in a discourse of artistic appreciation. At the same time, Trilby's beauty emphasizes a polymorphous realm of desire that Little Billee finds both attractive and repulsive, rewarding and debilitating. Early in the novel, we are informed of the hero's weakness for the musical voice: "He had for the singing woman an absolute worship. He was especially thrall to the contralto—the deep low voice that breaks and changes in the middle and soars all at once into a magnified angelic boy treble. It pierced through his ears to his heart, and stirred his very vitals" (49). Svengali's conversion of Trilby into a musical instrument of his will reverberates in the effect that her singing has on Little Billee: "Her voice was so immense in its softness, richness, freshness, that it seemed to be pouring itself out from all round; . . . the seduction, the novelty of it, the strangely sympathetic quality! . . . Little Billee had lost all control over himself. . . . He believed himself to be fast asleep and in a dream, and was trying his utmost not to wake; for a great happiness was his" (242–43). Trilby begins her performance in the lowest fe-

Mr. Tree Svengalivanting. "You must learn to love me!"

Figure 3 The Marvellous Feat of Tree-ilby Svengalivanised! (*Punch*, November 16, 1895)

male range and Little Billee's appreciative climax occurs when the voice reaches
the highest male range. Du Maurier emphasizes the gender ambiguities implicated in his hero's appreciation by noting that Trilby's voice "might almost have
belonged to any sex" (14), making one feel "instinctively that it was a real pity she
wasn't a boy, she would have made such a jolly one" (16). In addition to her
voice, Trilby sports other masculine qualities that the male characters find
attractive. Apparently "too tall for her sex" (103) and on occasion wearing a
French infantry soldier's overcoat and "male" slippers (14), she is complimented for being "as upright and straight and honourable as a man" (104). In
the narrator's opinion, she "would have made a singularly handsome boy" (16).
Du Maurier makes it clear that the male artist's admiration of gender ambiguity precedes Svengali's hypnotism. Nor is this attraction exclusively Little Billee's, since it is demonstrated by a number of male characters.

Little Billee's polysexual, musical admiration was not especially unique in
late-Victorian society. The contralto was greatly respected and its overlap with
the boy treble was established. Discussing what she calls "homovocality"—a
combination in a female opera singer of vocal technique, theatricality, and attitude that suggests a principal attention to her female audience—Terry Castle
notes that the contralto was most likely to become a homoerotic icon for
women because so many of her roles would be performed *en travesti*—that is,
in drag as a man.[43] With the decline in the castrato's popularity and numbers
in the late eighteenth century, opera's male heroes were increasingly played by
contraltos. As Margaret Reynolds argues, in eighteenth-century opera, aural
abilities actually superseded gender-identification when choosing performers:
"Everyone knew that opera was sound and spectacle, and they discounted all
other considerations. If anyone thought at all about the gender absurdities they
witnessed, the audience enjoyed the play of innuendo and suggestion."[44] This
phenomenon, however, fostered anxieties as the Victorian drive to classify sexuality intensified. Reynolds, Philip Brett, and others argue that music's lack
of specific meaning has resulted in its not being easily coopted in support of
heterosexist conventions.[45] Historically, this has made it both a symbol of complete self-sacrifice to aesthetic pleasure and a threat of moral and sexual ambiguity or deviance. To many of Du Maurier's readers, Trilby, who herself spends
a period of time disguised as a man (296), would have suggested a contralto
performing *en travesti*. Reflecting a recognition among Trilby's late-Victorian
fans of her unique combination of gender traits, one of the earliest spoofs of
Du Maurier's novel—Charles Williamson's 1894 play *Twillbe*—had a man
play the role of the heroine. The artist John Sloan, who could sing falsetto,
performed in comic drag, including false breasts and feet.[46] Sloan thereby emphasizes a view of both Trilby's gender and her beauty (her feet being Little
Billee's first source of inspiration) as constructs, shifting the tinge of deviancy

that Du Maurier felt genius required even further into the dangerously dissident end of the spectrum.

Du Maurier's correlation of music with uncontrollable attraction also has
literary precursors that position it within a specifically same-sex male discourse
of aesthetic sympathy—a discourse indebted to Pater's famous argument, in
The Renaissance, that all art *"constantly aspires toward the condition of music."*[47]
According to Pater, music is the ideal art form because it disempowers the
understanding's ability to distinguish content from "spirit," and it is this inca-
pacitation that, in later works by other authors, appears as the evocation of an
erotically tinged, amoral sympathy.[48] The most overt example is the mutual
male–male seduction of a musician and audience member in the pornographic
novel *Teleny,* which first began circulating privately in 1890 and was published
three years later. The eponymous hero, whose telepathic abilities come from
his "gypsy" blood (an alterity akin to Svengali and Little Billee's Jewish blood),
is inspired during his public piano recital by the dandiacal Camille Des Grieux,
a "sympathetic listener." Teleny's performance leads Camille to sexual orgasm
and then leaves him, like Little Billee, "powerless to applaud; . . . dumb, mo-
tionless, nerveless, exhausted."[49] Lord Henry's influence on Dorian's identity—which would not have been lost on Du Maurier—is similarly described
as a musical arousal of sympathy, the touching of "some secret cord . . . vibrat-
ing and throbbing to curious pulses" (29–30). For Lord Henry, talking to Dorian feels like "playing upon an exquisite violin. He answered to every touch
and thrill of the bow. . . . There was something terribly enthralling in the exercise of influence. No other activity was like it. To project one's soul into some
gracious form, and let it tarry there for a moment; to hear one's own intellectual
views echoed back to one with all the added music of passion and youth" (41).
Lord Henry's transformation of Dorian into "a real work of art" (55) parallels
Svengali's conversion of Trilby into a vehicle for his own musical genius. The
male–male co-dependency is more apparent when one recognizes that Little
Billee's "strange sympathy" and orgasmic reaction is as much a result of Svengali's skills as Trilby's voice, which has quite the opposite effect on her audience
without the hypnotist's influence.

Du Maurier plays with his readers' notions of music as threateningly amor-
phous when he depicts Little Billee, in accord with his diluted drops of Jewish
blood and moderate sexual unconventionality, as having a soft spot for that
particular group of singing voices seen to transgress sexual boundaries. Although a gender-based sexual binary is apparent, Du Maurier's depiction remains what might be more precisely described as hermaphroditic—with both
genders constantly resurfacing in the heroine's image—even as this sexual ambiguity is itself filtered through a lens of visual and aural aesthetic attraction
that reduces the significance of gender in the broader context of pleasure. Little

Billee and Svengali's sexual-aesthetic admiration for Trilby demarcates her body as a site of erotic possibilities for the men where her attractive femaleness is persistently rendered necessary yet secondary to the potential reconfiguration of the woman as male. In combination with their diverse forms of transgressivity—sexual, aesthetic, ethnic, and so on—the men's admiration functions to signify their artistic potential. Although this aesthetic devotion points to an anxiety regarding the celebration of artistic catharsis as a corollary for the pleasures of an inchoate sexual identity, the difference between Little Billee and Svengali, with regard to this particular trait, is the *degree* of their transgressivity. Little Billee's use of Trilby as both object and vehicle of desire is deemed acceptable because it is commingled with a romantic attraction that keeps the artist from following Svengali in allowing his genius to overwhelm other value systems.

The Neo-Priapists and *The Martian*'s Sardonic Vision

The hetero hero of Du Maurier's *Martian* is the out-of-this-world gorgeous Barty Josselin, who surpasses even Taffy's physical beauty and gentlemanliness. He even proves to be a genius of a writer. Accommodating Du Maurier's affiliations with the *Punch* club and men like Prinsep, the narrator of the novel, Robert Maurice, confidently acknowledges that, although "woman meant much for him," Barty "loved best to forgather with those of his own sex" (297). It was therefore, perhaps, inevitable that Barty would come in contact with those other admirers of male beauty—the dandy-aesthetes: "They made much of him, painted him, wrote music and verses about him, raved about his Greekness, his beauty, his yellow hair, and his voice and what not, as if he had been a woman. He even stood that, he admired them so!" (336). Robert is pleased to report, however, that the mutual admiration is only temporary; like Barty, the narrator is "fond of men's society; but at least I like them to be unmistakably men of my own sex, manly men, and clean" (336). The hero's affiliation with the "neo-priapists" (336), like Little Billee's and Du Maurier's stints in Bohemia, is read by Robert as a temporary digression with no long-term implications.

The Martian is a diluted version of Du Maurier's earlier effort in *Trilby* to correlate sexual ambiguity and artistic genius. With this last novel, the author joined the wave of artists and journalists who, in the final few years of the century, anxiously proclaimed their distance from anything associated with homosexual culture. As with his participation in the construction of the dandy-aesthete persona, Du Maurier's shift in attitude reflects broader concerns regarding the formative artistic identity with which he wished to self-identify. Richard Dellamora has shown that the general homophobia with which Britain brought in the new century resulted from a complex interweaving of sexual scandals and sociopolitical developments which involved homosexuality, women's rights, the thriving, sensationalist press, and enhanced tensions between Liberals and Whigs.[50] For Du Maurier, a major element in this cultural crisis was the popularity of *Trilby*—a phenomenon to which his own death has been attributed.

The story of the overwhelming success of Du Maurier's novel and related commodities is well known. There were gallery shows of *Trilby* paintings, photographs, and drawings. Both the town in Florida and the hat design named after the heroine still exist today.[51] Du Maurier even played into the momentum somewhat when, in *The Martian*, he has Barty writes the best-seller *Berthe aux grands Pieds*. "Trilbymania" products also include various parodies, such as Williamson's *Twillbe*, Edgar Smith's *Trilby: A Burlesque*, William Muskerry's *Thrillby: A Shocker in One Scene and Several Spasms*, and Charles Puerner's *Thrilby*, complete with the villain "Spaghetti." Herbert Beerbohm-Tree's production of Paul Potter's dramatic version of the novel turned out to be his biggest financial success to date. Jules Zanger attributes the success of the production in part to the fact that the drama addressed itself to rising popular anti-Semitic fears and prejudices (33).[52] Du Maurier's Svengali, however, also personifies the greed, elitism, and quest for fame that he had associated with the dandy-aesthete. *Punch*'s popularization of the persona as sporting signs of sexual deviancy, combined with the active, late-Victorian homosexual culture and the notoriety of the Wilde trials, would have led many playgoers to see Svengali—whom Tree played as a dandiacal Satan—as the "High Priest of the Decadents," the term used by the *National Observer* to describe the convicted Wilde.[53] Conflating the image of the dandy-aesthete and the homosexual, the lawyer Edward Carson, in his attack on Wilde, proclaimed, "I do not profess to be an artist; and when I hear you give evidence, I am glad I am not."[54] Appearing at the same moment that Aestheticism and an identity based on same-sex erotic attraction converged in Wilde's public persona to create a human target out of what *News of the World* called "the aesthetic cult, in the nasty form,"[55] *Trilby* became, regardless of the author's intentions, a potent compendium of Victorian anxieties regarding the influence of the dandy-aesthete. Du Maurier's next novel, *The Martian*, comes across as the author's anxious attempt to clarify his own position within the late-Victorian field of art and literature.

Du Maurier did not see his success as the result of genius: "this 'boom' rather distresses me when I reflect that Thackeray never had a 'boom'. And I hold that a 'boom' means nothing as a sign of literary excellence, nothing but money."[56] He told a reporter that his next novel would be called *Soured by Success*, and Barty's first novel is appropriately titled *Sardonyx*. Like Du Maurier, Barty is uncomfortable with his own fame and refers disparagingly to commercial writers, "the grubs of Grub Street, who sometimes manage to squirt a drop from their slime-bags on to the swiftly-passing boots that scorn to squash them" (390). He saves most of his criticism, however, for the "second-rate" decadents, "those unpleasant little anthropoids with the sexless little muse and the dirty little Eros" (390), "little misshapen troglodytes with foul minds and perverted passions, or self-advertising little mountebanks with enlarged and diseased vanities; creatures who would stand in a pillory sooner than not be stared at or talked about at all," "these inspired epicenes, these gifted epileptoids, these anæmic little self-satisfied nincompoops" (335–36). The term "nincompoops" evokes Du Maurier's popular "Nincompoopiana" cartoon series that was far less bilious in its critique of dandy-aesthete communities. The reference to the pillory, meanwhile, brings to mind Wilde's famous courtroom speech in which he argued that "the love that dare not speak its name . . . is beautiful, it is fine, it is the noblest form of affection. . . . The world mocks at it and sometimes puts one in the pillory for it."[57] Du Maurier's foaming rant suggests the author's anxiety, like that of so many other self-identified heterosexual artists and journalists, over being associated with the dandy-aesthetes; "One got a bad name," he warns, "by being friends with such nondescripts" (336). Having previously criticized these artists for their weak work and financial motivations, he now fears that he will be included amongst them. "How encouraging it is to think," remarks this discriminating consumer of *The Martian*, soon after his primal name-calling, that "there are no such people now, and that the breed has been thoroughly stamped out!" (337). "Who ever hears of decadents nowadays?" (390). His effort in *Trilby* to suggest a positive relation between unconventional sexuality and artistic genius is here sacrificed to the aim of countering a fear that *Trilby*'s popularity would convert Du Maurier himself into an image of the commercial sham that he had been critiquing for decades. However, his attempt to stabilize a self-identity as the admirable artist by eradicating the commercially and sexually threatening dandy-aesthete only emphasizes the fact that the latter persona had itself become an identity with which he would always be associated.

Notes

The research and writing of this chapter was supported by a postdoctoral fellowship at Princeton University from the Social Sciences and Humanities Research Council of Canada. For their comments and input on earlier versions of this work, I would like to thank Richard Dellamora, Jason Haslam, Michael M. Holmes, Elaine Showalter, and the anonymous readers of this collection.

1. George Du Maurier, *The Martian* (1897; London: Harper, 1898), 336, 335, 336. Further quotations from this book will be referenced in the text.

2. Regenia Gagnier, *Idylls of the Marketplace: Oscar Wilde and the Victorian Public* (Stanford: Stanford University Press, 1986).

3. Quoted in Leonée Ormond, *George Du Maurier* (Pittsburgh: University of Pittsburgh Press, 1969), 42.

4. Thomas Armstrong, *Thomas Armstrong C.B., A Memoir*, ed. L. M. Lamont (London: M. Secker, 1912), 121.

5. Quoted in Derek Pepys Whiteley, *George du Maurier: His Life and Work* (London: Art and Technics, 1948), 23.

6. Ormond, *Du Maurier*, 114, 231.

7. Quoted in T. Martin Wood, *George Du Maurier: The Satirist of the Victorians* (London: Chatto and Windus, 1913), 167.

8. M. H. Spielmann, *The History of "Punch"* (London: Cassell, 1895), 65, 83.

9. R. G. G. Price notes the misogynistic influence that this all-male society had on *Punch*'s representation of women; see his *A History of Punch* (London: Collins, 1957).

10. Gary Schmidgall, *The Stranger Wilde: Interpreting Oscar* (New York: Dutton, 1994), 56.

11. George Du Maurier, "A Rising Genius," *Punch* (May 11, 1878): 210.

12. M. H. Spielmann, *History*, records an episode in which the *Punch* inner circle jokingly set up a collection so that Charles H. Bennett, who sported the long hair of an artist, could, in their words, "have his damn hair cut and rejoin the assembly of the brethren" (77).

13. Du Maurier was not the only cartoonist to adopt this marginalizing discourse of the body, as is proven by the pictures in the issues of May 30, 1874: 232 and September 21, 1878: 122. For a discussion of the complex significations of male effeminacy prior to the 1890s, see Thaïs Morgan's contribution to this collection and James Eli Adams's *Dandies and Desert Saints: Styles of Victorian Masculinity* (Ithaca: Cornell University Press, 1995). For a historical survey of nineteenth-century West European masculinity's developments, see Peter Stearns's *Be a Man! Males in Modern Society* (New York: Holmes and Meier, 1991).

14. For a contemporary explicit correlation of the dandy-aesthete with same-sex male desire, see Charles Edward Hutchinson's privately published pamphlet *Boy Worship* (1880).

15. Pierre Bourdieu, *Distinction: A Social Critique of the Judgement of Taste*, trans. Richard Nice (Cambridge: Harvard University Press, 1984), 24.

16. Adams, *Dandies and Desert Saints*, 34. Du Maurier's cartoons reflect a strategy in line with Carlyle's decision, as analyzed by Adams, to attack the dandy as a means of ascribing heroism to men of letters such as himself who lacked outward signs of productive labor.

17. George Du Maurier, "The Six-Mark Tea-Pot," *Punch* (30 October 1880): 293. For a discussion of Du Maurier's representation of the aesthetic woman in this cartoon, see Kathy Psomiades, *Beauty's Body: Femininity and Representation in British Aestheticism* (Stanford: Stanford University Press, 1997), 154–55.

18. Richard Ellmann, *Oscar Wilde* (1987; London: Penguin, 1988), 43. Richard Kelly points out that chinamania did not begin with Wilde, but with Swinburne and Rossetti, who were rival collectors (Richard Kelly, *George Du Maurier* [Boston: Twayne, 1983], 34). It is illuminating to note, however, that, through *Punch* (and Du Maurier in particular), it is a Wildean character that takes possession of the fad. That Wilde was seen as *the* dandy-aesthete of the last two decades of the nineteenth century is apparent not only from *Punch* spoofs of Aestheticism, which focused heavily on Wilde, but also from various Aestheticist parodies including those by Mary Humphrey Ward, *Robert Elsmere* (1888; Lincoln: University of Nebraska Press, 1967), 396; Robert Hichens, *The Green Carnation* (1894; New York: Dover, 1970), passim; and G. S. Street, *Autobiography of a Boy: Passages Selected by His Friend G. S. Street* (London: Lane, 1894), passim.

19. While people such as Wilde argued that taste was a construct that reinforced certain sociopolitical agendas, they did not necessarily disown the predominant Victorian belief in substantive values. Gagnier discusses this issue in both *Idylls of the Marketplace* and "Is Market Society the Fin of History?" in *Cultural Politics at the Fin de Siècle*, ed. Sally Ledger and Scott McCracken (Cambridge: Cambridge University Press, 1995), 290–310.

20. Roger B. Henkle, *Comedy and Culture: England 1820–1900* (Princeton: Princeton University Press, 1980), 322. Henckle's analysis adds a new dimension to some twentieth-century theorists' descriptions of Victorian literary production as a process of addiction and degeneracy; see Q. D. Leavis, *Fiction and the Reading Public* (London: Chatto and Windus, 1939), 152; Richard D. Altick, *The English Common Reader: A Social History of the Mass Reading Public 1800–1900* (Chicago: University of Chicago Press, 1957), 364; and R. V. Cox, "The Reviews and Magazines," *The New Pelican Guide to English Literature: 6. From Dickens to Hardy* (London: Penguin, 1982), 196. Echoing certain Victorian concerns, these scholars depict the commercially aware authors as seductive opiate-mongers that leave their buyers drugged, addicted, and stupider than when they entered the den. One of the most astute analyses of the Victorian publishing industry and the commodification of aesthetics and Aestheticism is Laurel Brake's *Subjugated Knowledge: Journalism, Gender and Literature in the Nineteenth Century* (New York: New York University Press, 1994).

21. George Du Maurier, "Nincompoopiana," *Punch* (December 20, 1879): 282.

22. Richard Ellmann, *Wilde*, describes Wilde as having briskly cultivated "the art of self-advertisement" after he moved to the city (78), and Henckle concludes that Wilde's contemporaries saw him as "a strange new product of the intensified media orientation and fashion consciousness" (322). Wilde's entry into Du Maurier's cartoons is gradual—here an echo of his discussion of blue china, there his clean-shaven contrast to

earlier dandy-aesthetes, and so on—a process that reflects not only the infiltration of the persona of the dandy-aesthete into Victorian notions of the artist, but also the gradual recognition of an inchoate homosexual identity.

23. See Sander Gilman, *The Jew's Body* (New York: Routledge, 1991), passim; and *Freud, Race, and Gender* (Princeton: Princeton University Press, 1993), 49–52.

24. George Du Maurier, *Trilby* (1894; London: Dent, 1994), 49, 50. Further quotations from this book will be referenced in the text.

25. Gilman, *Jews' Body*, 124.

26. Judith Halberstam, *Skin Shows: Gothic Horror and the Technology of Monsters* (Durham, N.C.: Duke University Press, 1995).

27. Halberstam, *Skin Shows*, 88.

28. Talia Schaffer analyzes the mutual infiltration of Dracula and Jonathan Harker in her essay "'A Wilde Desire Took Me': The Homoerotic History of *Dracula*," *English Literary History* 61 (1994): 381–425.

29. Brian Reade, ed., *Sexual Heretics: Male Homosexuality in English Literature from 1850 to 1900* (London: Routledge and Kegan Paul, 1970), 53.

30. Robert Hichens's *The Green Carnation* is one of numerous texts from the 1890s that expose the reality to which Du Maurier's cartoons so often allude. Completed by the early summer of 1894 and published anonymously in September, Hichens's novel parodies the relationship between Oscar Wilde and Alfred Douglas. In April of 1894, Douglas had written a telegram in response to his father Lord Queensberry's attack on his and Wilde's romance with the line "What a funny little man you are" (quoted in Ellmann, *Wilde*, 394). Revealing just how public their relationship was, we find *The Green Carnation*'s Reggie Hastings (the character modeled on Douglas) using that exact line in a letter to his own father (2). *The Green Carnation* had a wide audience that included Queensberry, ensuring that anybody who thought, or hoped, that the relationship of these two well-known men was secret now knew otherwise.

31. Nina Auerbach, "Magi and Maidens: The Romance of the Victorian Freud," *Critical Inquiry* 8 (1981): 289.

32. Ormond, *Du Maurier*, 454.

33. *Daily Telegraph*, quoted in Ed Cohen, *Talk on the Wilde Side: Toward a Genealogy of a Discourse on Male Sexualities* (New York: Routledge, 1992), 162.

34. Quoted in H. Montgomery Hyde, *The Trials of Oscar Wilde* (London: William Hodge, 1948), 115.

35. Cohen, 75–77.

36. For a discussion of nineteenth-century mediated male–male desire, see Eve Kosofsky Sedgwick, *Between Men: English Literature and Male Homosocial Desire* (New York: Columbia University Press, 1985).

37. Oscar Wilde, *The Complete Works of Oscar Wilde* (New York: Harper and Row, 1989): 29–30. Future quotations from this book will be referenced in the text.

38. Walter Pater, *The Renaissance* (1873; Cleveland: Meridian, 1967), 211.

39. Kelly, *Du Maurier,* 141–42.

40. Jonathan Grossman argues that Du Maurier's heroine functions to sanction the narrator's reminiscences regarding the same-sex encounters experienced by the young English men in the novel "without threatening a (current) heterosexual identity," in "The Mythic Svengali: Anti-Aestheticism in *Trilby,*" *Studies in the Novel* 28 (winter 1996): 531. However, the heroine's unconventionality in both her relation with men and her physiological and sexual attributes—coupled with the sheer volume of homoerotic experiences in the novel—problematizes such a binary reading.

41. "The Marvellous Feat of Tree-ilby Svengalivanized," *Punch* (November 16, 1895): 232.

42. For an insightful and entertaining analysis of Trilby's famous foot and mouth in relation to spectacle and cultural politics, see Mary Russo's analysis of the novel in *The Female Grotesque: Risk, Excess and Modernity* (New York: Routledge, 1994).

43. Terry Castle, *The Apparitional Lesbian: Female Homosexuality and Modern Culture* (New York: Columbia University Press, 1993), 228–29.

44. Margaret Reynolds, "Ruggiero's Deceptions, Cherubino's Distractions," in *En Travesti: Women, Gender Subversion, Opera,* ed. Corinne E. Blackmer and Patricia Juliana Smith (New York: Columbia University Press, 1995), 136–37.

45. Philip Brett, "Musicality, Essentialism, and the Closet," in *Queering the Pitch: The New Gay and Lesbian Musicology,* ed. Philip Brett, Elizabeth Wood, and Gary C. Thomas (New York: Routledge, 1994), 9–26. Other insightful analyses of the operatic voice in relation to same-sex desire include Terry Castle's discussion in *The Apparitional Lesbian;* Wayne Kostenbaum, *The Queen's Throat: Opera, Homosexuality, and the Mystery of Desire* (New York: Poseidon, 1993); and Elizabeth Wood, "Sapphonics," in *Queering the Pitch,* 27–66. See also the essays in *The Work of Opera: Genre, Nationhood, and Sexual Difference,* ed. Richard Dellamora and Daniel Fischlin (New York: Columbia University Press, 1997).

46. Avis Berman, "George Du Maurier's *Trilby* Whipped Up a Worldwide Storm," *Smithsonian* 24, no. 9 (December 1993): 124.

47. Pater, *Renaissance,* 129.

48. In "Arnold, Winckelmann, and Pater," in *Masculine Desire: The Sexual Politics of Victorian Aestheticism* (Chapel Hill: University of North Carolina Press, 1990), 102–16, Richard Dellamora offers a sensitive analysis of the relation between sympathy, aesthetics, and sexuality that reverberates in later Victorian literature.

49. *Teleny; or, The Reverse of the Medal: A Physiological Romance* (1893; London: GM Press, 1986), 31.

50. Dellamora, *Masculine Desire,* 193–217. For a broader discussion of gender issues in Victorian journalism, see Brake, *Subjugated Knowledge.*

51. See Berman, "Worldwide Storm," and Edward Purcell, "Trilby and Trilby-Mania, The Beginning of the Bestseller System," *Journal of Popular Culture* 11 (summer 1977): 62–76.

52. Jules Zanger, "A Sympathetic Vibration: Dracula and the Jews," *English Literature in Transition* 34 (1991): 33–44.

53. Quoted in Brian Roberts, *The Mad Bad Line: The Family of Lord Alfred Douglas* (London: Hamish Hamilton, 1981), 228.

54. Quoted in Hyde, *Trials*, 133.

55. Quoted in Ellmann, *Wilde*, 450.

56. Quoted in Robert H. Sherard, "The Author of 'Trilby'." *McClure's Magazine* 4, no. 5 (April 1895): 399–400.

57. Quoted in Ellmann, *Wilde*, 435.

"Desire Without Limit": Dissident Confession in Oscar Wilde's *De Profundis*

OLIVER S. BUCKTON

What might be termed the confessional significance of Wilde's writing—in particular, the ways in which it can be read as revealing the "secret" of his sexuality—has become one of the central preoccupations of recent criticism dealing with his work. In particular, *The Picture of Dorian Gray, The Importance of Being Earnest,* and *De Profundis* (the title only posthumously attributed to the letter he wrote to Lord Alfred Douglas from Reading Gaol) have come under exhaustive scrutiny for the clues they might provide about the relationship between Wilde's aesthetic and sexual practices.[1] In order to interrogate some of the critical assumptions currently circulating about Wilde's sexuality, my essay takes as its starting point Jonathan Dollimore's important insight that Wilde was able to perceive the ideological effects and limits of his society, and that his work as a whole "recognizes the priority of the social and the cultural in determining not only public meaning but 'private' or subjective desire."[2]

With this emphasis on the specific cultural and historical conditions of Wilde's art, Dollimore departs from Richard Ellmann's biographical conclusion that Wilde "belongs to our world more than to Victoria's."[3] Wilde's writing, stylistically and thematically, certainly anticipates many aspects of modernist writing; but his aesthetic preoccupations as well as his moral sensibility locate him firmly in the Victorian era. The wish-fulfillment of claiming Wilde for contemporary agendas of sexual and textual politics is precisely what my own essay seeks to challenge. However, this is not to say that any reading can offer us the "truth" of Wilde's identity. The claim to "unmask" Wilde in this way only perpetuates the fiction of a "real" self underlying the performance, or appearance of selfhood, and so reinforces the high valuation of "sincerity" that Wilde's work sought to dismantle. As Dollimore observes, "Wilde's transgressive aesthetic is the reverse: insincerity, inauthenticity, and unnaturalness become the liberating attributes of decentred identity and desire."[4]

The 1895 trial proceedings which resulted in Wilde's imprisonment for two years with hard labor for his sexual transgressions have taught us to read Wilde's works for signs of his sexual "nature" and can be seen to inform even those readings that decry the damaging effects of prison on Wilde's life and work. My reading of Wilde's prison letter to Douglas examines its development of a counterdiscourse with which to challenge the hegemony of the public construction of Wilde as sexual pervert and corruptor-of-youth. Wilde, in the sexual and aesthetic crisis brought on by his conviction and imprisonment for homosexual offenses (or "gross indecency with another male person," as the 1885 legislation termed it), projected onto the figure of his erstwhile lover, Lord Alfred Douglas, those characteristics that he believed were responsible for the tragedy that had befallen him. That the crisis was in part an aesthetic one is indicated by his declaration that "everything about my tragedy has been hideous, mean, repellant, lacking in style."[5] Hence, this essay will treat Douglas—or "Bosie"—as a literary creation of Wilde's, rather than as an actual historical person.

Douglas's chief flaw, according to Wilde, is his refusal to accept his share of responsibility for the disaster that befell Wilde: "That from beginning to end you were the responsible person, that it was through you, for you, and by you that I was there, never for one instant dawned upon you" (*DP*, 448). Indeed, Douglas's uncanny ability to remain free of blame links him with other characters created by Wilde who evade punishment for their transgressions: in the comic vein of *Earnest*, Jack and Algy succeed in protecting their social privilege despite their various misdemeanors; and in a tragic mode, Dorian Gray long defers the crisis resulting from his clandestine transgressions and fateful wish. If the figure of Douglas resembles Dorian more than Algy, this is because it was the former character to whom Wilde attributed the insidious power to destroy the life of an artist; and it was from the position of the ruined artist that Wilde wrote his prison letter to Douglas.

From "Epistola" to "De Profundis"

Wilde wrote the letter on prison notepaper between January and March of 1897, shortly before his release from Reading Gaol. He somewhat frivolously titled the letter, in a parody of the papal decree, "Epistola: in carcere et vinculis." Following Wilde's death in 1900, Robert Ross published excerpts from the work in 1905 that gave no indication of the fact that they were taken from a letter to Douglas. Indeed, Ross's preface to the 1905 edition strongly hinted that the excerpts were taken from a letter to himself.[6] The excerpts from the letter selected by Ross for publication were intended to portray Wilde's spiritual crisis and conversion and were published with the explicit purpose of rehabilitating Wilde's reputation with the British public. The gambit succeeded, as the majority of critics found in the expurgated edition of 1905 a new moral seriousness, remorse, and sincerity, suggesting that Wilde had seen the error of his "perverse" ways. As one critic wrote, "The book is beautiful in all its misery, and worth a million of the dishonest self-revelations of the men who write about their souls as if their bodies were mere pillow-cases." Of the early reviewers, only G. B. Shaw argued on behalf of "the *comedic* view of *De Profundis*."[7]

While William T. Stead wrote Ross to offer his "thanks for having permitted us to see the man as he really was," E. V. Lucas complained that the mood of *De Profundis* "is not sorrow but its dexterously constructed counterfeit," and argued that Wilde's "artifice was too much for him; his poses were too insistent—had become too much a part of the man—to be abandoned."[8] Apparently, Lucas had missed one of the central tenets of Wilde's aesthetic creed: that the "mask" or "pose" is not distinct from the "real man," but that social behavior, indeed human personality itself, is a series of masks without any consistent or unified identity (or face) existing underneath. Lucas's criticism refuses to consider that the difference between the "genuine emotion" of sorrow and its "counterfeit" might be impossible to fix with any certainty. Indeed, if to express an emotion is immediately to place it under suspicion of insincerity, then a literary confession such as Wilde's is certain to appear counterfeit.

And yet, Lucas's attack on *De Profundis* is more revealing than Stead's praise of it. Lucas's claim that Wilde is constructing another pose in his letter at least avoids the delusion that we have, through the mediation of the confessional text, attained access to "the man as he really was." George Street's review of *De Profundis* observed that "people who heartily admire [Wilde's] style, so limpid and graceful, so brilliant in its unforced elegance and adornment, think that here the use of it is a token of insincerity. Surely, rather, its absence would have been. It had grown into his nature; he could not write differently without an effort."[9] This remark transforms one of Wilde's central dicta—"Truth is entirely and absolutely a matter of style"—into something radically different, and paradoxically un-Wildean: style, in Street's view, has become a matter of *nature*.[10] Lucas offers a similar concept of style as a kind of natural development when he claims that Wilde's poses "had become too much a part of the man to be abandoned."

This critical distortion of Wilde's anti-essentialist position on the importance of style is related to the fact that Wilde's "nature"—specifically, his sexual nature—was being constituted and defined during his trials. Indeed, Wilde's sexual nature was discursively constructed on the basis of his literary style as much as, or more than, the evidence of his sexual acts. Jonathan Dollimore, in an important reading of what he calls Wilde's "transgressive aesthetic," draws attention to the "perceived connections between Wilde's aesthetic transgression and his sexual transgression" and stresses the relationship between these transgressions and the "nature" or identity that was conceived of and represented as lying behind it. At the period of Wilde's trials, according to Dollimore, "Society now regarded homosexuality as rooted in a person's identity; this sin might pervade all aspects of an individual's being, and its expression might become correspondingly the more insidious and subversive."[11] To view Wilde's style as inhering in or straightforwardly revealing his nature is to undercut his protest against essentialist conceptions of the self. According to Dollimore, however, "Wilde confirmed and exploited this connection between discursive and sexual perversion," for example in a famous statement from the prison letter: "What the paradox was to me in the sphere of thought, perversity became to me in the sphere of passion" (*DP*, 466). Wilde's prison letter emerges from the crucible, brought to a white heat during his trials, in which his sexual "nature" and his literary "style" had been welded into a single, "indissociable" transgression.

Hence, the very (re)naming of the prison letter as "De Profundis" served to announce its confessional account of a spiritual crisis, and to mask over its dissident elements. Wilde, renouncing both the traditional forms of Victorian autobiography and the fixities of sexual identity, used the prison letter to exploit the fluidity of roles and theatrical self-presentation that he had mastered as a dramatist. Although this was an ostensibly private letter—in the words of Regenia Gagnier "the only work he wrote without an audience"—*De Profundis,* in common with a number of classic autobiographical texts, is in fact addressed to a highly specific audience: the only reader, in fact, by whom Wilde felt his confession would be understood.[12]

The Lure of Appetite

Unlike the classical autobiographer, who often chastens his prior self for immoderate, or misdirected, appetites, Wilde attacks the younger Bosie not only for his own excessive sensuality, but for having brought out Wilde's. Saint Augustine, for example, provides an account of his sexual lust as a young man in order to criticize his rebellion against, and celebrate his ultimate acceptance of, the higher love for God. An even stronger influence on Wilde's confessional writing, however, is the autobiographical poetry of Wordsworth, such as the *Prelude,* in which the poet writes critically, if somewhat generally, of his youthful self "that my delights (such as they were) were sought insatiably" and describes himself as having been

> often greedy in the chase,
> And roamed from hill to hill, from rock to rock,
> Still craving combinations of new forms,
> New pleasure, wider empire for the sight.[13]

Here it is the "insatiable" quality of desire, rather than the object of the desire itself that is rendered problematic.

Though Wilde, like Augustine and Wordsworth, dramatizes the shamed recollection of his earlier self-indulgences as a painful but necessary duty, the tone in the letter is blatantly elegiac, allowing him to surround himself, imaginatively, with the material luxuries now beyond his reach: "The Savoy dinners—the clear turtle-soup, the luscious ortolans wrapped in their crinkled Sicilian vine-leaves, the heavy amber-coloured, indeed almost amber-scented champagne—Dagonet 1880, I think was your favourite wine?—all have still to be paid for" (*DP*, 507). The last note of financial responsibility returns Wilde—and the reader—to the traumatic reality of incarceration and bankruptcy, yet the tone of the passage remains strongly invested in recapturing the very pleasures it apparently renounces. Wilde writes self-reproachfully that by indulging Bosie's desires, "I . . . let myself be lured into the imperfect world of coarse uncompleted passions, of appetite without distinction, desire without limit, and formless greed" (*DP*, 463).

The representation of a dangerously excessive appetite also links Wilde's prison letter to *The Importance of Being Earnest*, his final play. In both cases, appetite is mocked as gluttony, while uncontrolled consumption is portrayed as a vice that undermines the moral integrity of the subject. Wilde's parody of Augustinian, and Wordsworthian, ideals of an austere, disciplined maturity, which is shown as having emerged from a dissolute, self-indulgent youth, appears in *Earnest* as Algy is on the point of being arrested for debt: in the original four-act version of the play a horrified Miss Prism remarks, "£762 for eating! How grossly materialistic! There can be little good in any young man who eats so much and so often," to which Dr Chasuble promptly adds, "It certainly is a painful proof of the disgraceful luxury of the age. We are far away from Wordsworth's plain living and high thinking."[14] The same quotation from Wordsworth's "Sonnet written in London, 1802" is used by Wilde in his letter to Bosie, to protest the cost of his lover's excessive appetite for expensive food and wine:

> My ordinary expenses with you for an ordinary day in London—for luncheon, dinner, supper, amusements, hansoms and the rest of it—ranged from £12 to £20, and the week's expenses were naturally in proportion and ranged from £80 to £130. For our three months at Goring my expenses (rent of course included) were £1340. Step by step with the Bankruptcy Receiver I had to go over every item of my life. It was horrible. '*Plain living and high thinking*' was, of course, an ideal you could not at that time have appreciated, but such extravagance was a disgrace to both of us. (*DP*, 428)

Wilde's past life is here reduced to a column of debts. The agonizing process of going over "every item of my life" prefigures the approach he adopts in his retrospective letter to Bosie, where he reminds his lover of the numerous expenses incurred on his behalf, that contributed to Wilde's ruin: "There was not a glass of champagne you drank, not a rich dish you ate of in all those years, that did not feed your Hate and make it fat" (*DP,* 445).

And yet, Wilde's echo from his play tends to recall a note of humor to the otherwise grim account of Bosie's extravagant appetite that undercuts the seriousness of his accusation. The irony is, of course, that "Plain living and high thinking" was the most unlikely ideal to be associated with Wilde himself: rather than hypocritically claiming this presumed virtue as his own "ideal," Wilde sabotages the ideal itself by invoking the absurd context of the suppressed scene from his play. Wilde's distrust of "appetite" and its destructive effects in his prison letter seems, on the surface, uncharacteristic and even disingenuous. For he has, at least in recent years, become identified with a "transgressive aesthetic" that sought, precisely, the disintegration—or, alternatively, the multiplication—of the self through the destabilizing and subversive force of desire. Dollimore, for example, presents Wilde as one whose "concept of the individual is crucially different from that sense of the concept which signifies the private, experientially self-sufficient, autonomous, bourgeois subject," and argues that his "Deviant desire reacts against, disrupts, and displaces from within: rather than seeking to escape the repressive ordering of sexuality, Wilde reinscribes himself within and relentlessly inverts the binaries upon which that ordering depends."[15]

Oddly, however, Dollimore does not recognize this transgressive force in Wilde's prison letter: indeed, rather than extending to *De Profundis* his shrewd account of Wilde's practice of subverting aesthetic and moral codes "from within," Dollimore describes the letter as "a conscious renunciation by Wilde of his transgressive aesthetic." Arguing that Wilde, in *De Profundis,* "repositions himself as the authentic, sincere subject which before he had subverted," Dollimore characterizes the letter as "tragic" in its portrayal of the "defeat of the marginal and the oppositional which only ideological domination can effect; a renunciation which is experienced as voluntary and self-confirming but which is in truth a self-defeat and a self-denial massively coerced through the imposition, by the dominant, of incarceration and suffering and their 'natural' medium, confession."[16]

I maintain that *De Profundis* powerfully demonstrates Wilde's resistance rather than capitulation to those coercive pressures of ideology with which he was confronted. The prison letter destabilizes the confessional integrity of the individual (sexual) subject by splitting its characteristics between Wilde himself and the figure of "Bosie," thereby revealing the autobiographical critique of a "past self" as an ideological fiction, while also making manifest the desiring intersubjectivity of "author" and "reader." Rather than positing a gulf between his present and past selves—the purported object of the autobiography being, as in the *Prelude,* to bridge this gulf—Wilde constructs an opposition between himself and Bosie that the letter initially seeks to maintain and totalize, attributing to the latter figure the youthful appetites and "perversions" from which the suffering Wilde must distance himself. And yet, the letter is itself the means of rhetorically undoing that opposition, by ultimately recalling the rejected figure of Bosie to form a dual subjectivity founded on shared desires, remembered pleasures, and textual reciprocity.

Face to Face: Wilde's Specular Confession

The initially radical division between self and other in *De Profundis* can be explained in part by the very crisis of Wilde's life that resulted in his imprisonment and that motivated him to write the letter. In one of the most powerful passages, Wilde describes the tormenting monotony of prison existence and suggests that the letter has grown out of the enforced remembering that his isolation brings:

> With us time itself does not progress. It revolves. It seems to circle round one centre of pain. The paralysing immobility of a life, every circumstance of which is regulated after an unchangeable pattern, so that we eat and drink and walk and lie down and pray, or kneel at least for prayer, according to the inflexible laws of an iron formula. (*DP*, 457)

That the experience of this horrifying stasis—contrasted with which the "external forces" of change appear all the more attractive—is of central importance to Wilde's act of remembering and writing is affirmed by his advice to Bosie: "Remember this, and you will be able to understand a little of why I am writing to you, and in this manner" (*DP*, 458). As Regenia Gagnier writes, Wilde's "self in his letter is a self constructed in a particular imaginative act of resistance against insanity and against the material matrix of prison space and time, that is, confined, segmented space and timelessness."[17]

The figure of "Bosie" becomes more than an individual lover or reader, more even than the embodiment of all the mistakes that Wilde believed he had made: he comes to represent all the malevolent forces that had brought Wilde into disgrace. Indeed, behind Douglas's reckless behavior, Wilde detects a greater, more abstract malignity, "as if you yourself [Douglas] had been merely a puppet worked by some secret and unseen hand to bring terrible events to a terrible issue" (*DP*, 443). Wilde creates in Bosie the demonic, compulsive consumer whose ultimate achievement was to orchestrate the public cannibalizing of Wilde himself. Hence, points in the narrative that Gagnier describes as "hopelessly confused," such as Wilde's statement that "I blame myself for the entire ethical degradation I allowed you to bring on me" (*DP*, 429), become intelligible as part of Wilde's subversion of the confessional mode. Gagnier finds in this sentence a "crazy syntactical subordination of subject and object,"

but in fact Wilde invokes the conventional "mea culpa" of confessional remorse, only immediately to displace the cause of his "ethical degradation" on
to Bosie himself.[18]

Motivated not by a desire for deeper self-knowledge or even self-reproach,
but by the genre-induced need for distance from his past, Wilde's letter springs
into being as an assault on another's identity, rather than as a revelation of his
own: as he writes to Bosie, "You must read this letter right through, though
each word may become to you as the fire or knife of the surgeon that makes
the delicate flesh burn or bleed" (*DP*, 425). The confessional force of Wilde's
narrative emerges not at the points where it reveals his secrets, but at those
where it demonstrates the impossibility of doing so, or where it obscures
Wilde's failings with Bosie's defects. Drawing attention to the presence of a
scandalous secret, shared by himself and Bosie, Wilde defers the disclosure of
that secret while inviting the reader or audience to speculate as to its nature. If
Wilde writes out of a desire for revenge against Bosie, then the inner springs
of this revenge will remain concealed. It is as though, as Marion Shaw has
remarked of late-Victorian confessional narratives, "The secret itself is nothing, or at least not anything that the mind can be brought 'to set to paper';
what is important is the journey to the secret, the act of confession itself."[19]

The rhetorical effect of the letter is, moreover, to demonstrate the absence
of any "secret" behind the mask of style. Wilde's subversive textual practice
suggests that regardless of how "sincere" the confession might appear, the self
it claims to unveil is a stylistic construct. Hence, the statements that would
seem to indicate an authentic, "truthful" basis for his confession must be examined carefully for their self-deconstructing irony. To better comprehend the
subversive autobiographical resonances of Wilde's letter, we might turn to Paul
de Man's account of prosopopoeia—"the fiction of an apostrophe to an absent,
deceased, or voiceless entity, which posits the possibility of the latter's reply
and confers upon it the power of speech."[20] By treating the autobiographical
address as a rhetorical fiction, de Man evacuates the confessional "self" of its
essentialist content. *De Profundis* is, self-evidently, an address to an absent person: indeed, Bosie is not only absent, but also apparently voiceless. Wilde begins his letter by reproaching Bosie for his long silence:

> After long and fruitless waiting I have determined to write to you myself,
> as much for your sake as for mine, as I would not like to think that I
> had passed through two long years of imprisonment without ever having
> received a single line from you. (*DP*, 423–24)

Had Wilde not needed to recreate Bosie's voice, and face, in the void of prison,
his own letter would not have been written. Gagnier claims that Bosie's "remembered image recreated for him [Wilde] the world outside"; but it would

be equally valid to say that Wilde reconstructs images from the world outside so as to render intelligible and "memorable" Bosie's face and voice.[21]

Yet the letter is not merely a way of filling the silence; it is also an attempt to prompt a reply. When, toward the end of his letter, Wilde announces his expectation of a reply—"As regards your letter to me in answer to this, it may be as long or as short as you choose" (*DP*, 510)—the reader is struck by the implausibility of the idea that Bosie would be inclined to reply to it. The letter here enacts the *fantasy* of the possibility of Bosie's reply, but this fantasy is already doomed to futility: not because of Bosie's failure to read the letter, nor even because of the material restrictions placed on Wilde's correspondence; but because the figure of prosopopoeia attempts to mask the *illusion* of the other's presence and power of reply. By inscribing within his letter the anticipated response of a reader, Wilde abandons the autonomy of his narrative as confessional statement and reveals its dependence on a rhetorical figure.

The fictional devices of Wilde's apostrophe are perhaps most apparent in the proliferation of detail regarding his relationship with Bosie. Wilde is of course not simply reciting the facts of his relationship with Bosie: he is presenting a counterdiscourse by constructing an account of the relationship that differs materially from the "version [that] has now actually passed into serious history [and] is quoted, believed, and chronicled" (*DP*, 456). Wilde's account of the traducement he had suffered during his trials is accompanied by a mockery of the official tableau:

> At the end, I was of course arrested and your father became the hero of the hour: more indeed than the hero of the hour merely: your family now ranks, strangely enough, with the Immortals: for with that grotesqueness of effect that is as it were a Gothic element in history, and makes Clio the least serious of all the Muses, your father will always live among the kind pure-minded parents of Sunday-school literature, your place is with the Infant Samuel, and in the lowest mire of Malebolge I sit between Gilles de Retz and the Marquis de Sade. (*DP*, 430–31)

An important function of this counterdiscourse is the displacement of guilt onto those to whom it partly belongs. Yet in its attempt to produce in Bosie a consciousness of responsibility for the consequences of their shared pleasures, *De Profundis* reaches an impasse: as a literary figure for the displacement of guilt and desire, "Bosie" is incapable of possessing or expressing the conscience Wilde seeks to awaken. Wilde, attempting to provoke a response from Bosie, actually accuses Bosie of committing the acts for which Wilde himself had been punished:

> The sins of another were being placed to my account. Had I so chosen, I could on either trial have saved myself at his expense, not from shame

indeed but from imprisonment. Had I cared to show that the Crown witnesses . . . had been carefully coached by your father and his solicitors . . .
in the absolute transference, deliberate, plotted, and rehearsed, of the actions and doings of someone else on to me, I could have had each one of
them dismissed from the box by the Judge. (*DP,* 452)

There can be little doubt, from the details the passage provides of Queensberry's involvement in the scandal, that the "someone else" alluded to by Wilde
is Bosie himself. Yet why, in a text that does not hesitate elsewhere to direct
abuse at its target, does this passage avoid naming the person described as
"such an enemy as no man ever had" (*DP,* 452)? The attempt to answer this
question will lead us to the central, specular relationship with the reader that
disrupts the confessional structure of *De Profundis.*

Wilde presents his narrative as a mirror in which Bosie will be confronted
with his own hideous visage. In one crucial passage, Wilde reminds Bosie that

I could have held up a mirror to you, and shown you such an image of
yourself that you would not have recognised it as your own till you found
it mimicking back your gestures of horror, and then you would have
known whose shape it was, and hated it and yourself for ever. (*DP,* 452)

Wilde's letter here performs the same mirroring function that it allegorizes.
Indeed, the rhetorical effect of the passage is to establish a specular relationship
between author and reader, Wilde and Bosie, mediated by the "mirror" of the
letter itself. As the letter's constructed reader, "Bosie" is both the abjected
"other" and the necessary, inverse reflection of Wilde's originative claim as "author."

Hence, the subjectivity of Wilde constitutes itself not autonomously, by asserting a prior self-presence which his narrative merely reproduces; but rhetorically and secondarily, by addressing the absent "Bosie" as the necessary counterpart to his authorial persona. In this sense, the letter's emphasis on Bosie's
immoderate appetites is not simply an illustration of Wilde's condemnation of
his lover's character, but a strategically necessary part of Wilde's self-portrayal:
Bosie's role as an obsessive "consumer" seems to secure his derivative position
as reader of Wilde's text as well. This leaves Wilde free to occupy the more
elevated position of the creative originator of texts, the author. However, the
specular effect produced by the letter-as-mirror should remind us that Wilde
can only recognize "himself"—that is, his precarious position as author, which
the letter attempts to stabilize—in the mirror "image" of Bosie, his imaginary
reader.

This specular relationship between Wilde and Bosie, author and reader, suggests the constitution of an autobiographical subject through lack rather than
(self-)presence, interdependence rather than autonomy, and self-dissolution

rather than unity. De Man describes this rhetorical constitution of subjectivity as "the autobiographical moment," which "happens as an alignment between the two subjects involved in the process of reading in which they determine each other by mutual reflexive substitution." The "self" of the autobiographer, although he "declares himself the subject of his understanding," is in fact the outcome of a textual displacement, in which author and reader "both depend on a substitutive exchange that constitutes the subject."[22] The letter, that is, initially attempts to put Bosie in his place by bringing him "face to face" with his own monstrous image; but the destabilizing effect of the text/mirror between Wilde and Bosie serves to remind us of the substitutive, imaginary structure of this confrontation.

The specular, complementary relation between Wilde and Bosie—who emerge as the two "selves" or functions necessary for the constitution of a single, textual subject—recurs in another striking formulation: "I have had to look at my past face to face. Look at your past face to face" (*DP,* 508). "You" and "I" here fall into substitutive alignment with "face to face": the hierarchical relation between author and reader is displaced by a complete equivalence of two faces, looking at each other, reflecting (on) each other's "past," before linking to form a single, sutured subject. Wilde's assertion of a moral and temporal priority over Bosie—having already achieved, through the suffering caused by his imprisonment, the moral insight that Bosie must strive for—is undermined by the symmetry of the rhetorical figure. Though Wilde begins the letter by emphasizing his radical difference from Bosie, asserting that "from the very first there was too wide a gap between us" (*DP,* 425), by the end of the letter this "gap" has been rhetorically closed by the assertion of a shared subjectivity. Bosie's textual role as the counterpart of Wilde is by no means a harmonious one, however: Wilde writes with apparent remorse that "it was only in the mire that we met" (*DP,* 432). For Wilde, the textual interdependency between himself and Bosie, which the letter foregrounds, is a source of distress, implying the dissolution of his "Individualism"—the quality in himself that he considers most "Christlike"—and a reminder of their sexual intimacy, concerning which he has come to feel ambivalent, referring to sex as the "terribly fascinating . . . topic around which your talk invariably centered" (*DP,* 432).

The shadowy figure of guilt evoked by Wilde's language is not "another" at all, but the inverted projection of his own "face," a (self-)image on which he depends for authorial self-recognition. If prosopopoeia is that mode of writing "by which one's name . . . is made as intelligible and memorable as a face," then the uncertainty about the "name" that is thus rendered memorable (or, indeed, whether the "name" and the "face" will match up at all) is endemic to the confession. As the textual figure—the cluster of images and tropes— necessary for the letter's apostrophic fiction, "Bosie" is also the object of abjection needed to sustain the text's antitheses between innocence and guilt, creation and consumption, loyalty and betrayal, originality and imitation, on which the narrative logic depends. And yet, the abjected figure of "Bosie," which occupies the subordinate position in every dichotomy, frequently threatens to usurp Wilde's role (and rule) as "author." Wilde's godlike power to create and destroy "character"—a literary prerogative taken from him during the trials, and which the letter is anxious to reclaim—is repeatedly ambushed by his own *bête noir*, a Caliban-like figure of unbridled appetite—"You had no motives in life. You had appetites merely" (*DP*, 425)—threatening to consume the very narrative from which the author has banished him.

Indeed, the dialectic between author and reader is founded on an explicit struggle for control. The role of "Bosie," initially consigned to the debased status of "passive" consumer, is transformed into a nefariously active one, whose appetitive nature manifests a stronger will than Wilde can invoke as creator. When Bosie is accused of being "the true author of the hideous tragedy" (*DP*, 448), it serves to expose the entirely strategic nature of Wilde's later claim to "authorship" of his own downfall, by attempting to find in his ruin a paradoxical form of self-assertion, or even self-creation: "Nobody, great or small, can be ruined except by his own hand" (*DP*, 465). If, overall, Wilde seeks to displace responsibility for the tragedy onto Bosie, his sole authorship of the letter, as of all his texts, is something that he jealously guards. Bosie's conspicuous failure to write—not only his long "silence" as a correspondent, but his incompetence as a translator of Wilde's work, as where Wilde reproaches him for "the schoolboy faults of your attempted translation of *Salomé*" (*DP*, 432)—makes Wilde's literary successes all the more distinctive and triumphant. Indeed, the contrast between Wilde's "artistic life" and Bosie's "sterile and uncreative" (*DP*, 426) influence is one of the hinges on which the narrative of selfhood in the letter depends.

Wilde depicts Bosie's textual incompetence as a symptom of the unrestrained desire of which Bosie is the victim: for example, his callous failure to write to Wilde in prison follows on the heels of his indiscreet publication and circulation of Wilde's own letters. As Wayne Koestenbaum has argued, *De Profundis* "warns that tragedies come from misreading, miswriting, or mishandling letters," and Douglas emerges as the sinister agent of all these disruptive actions.[23] In particular, Wilde's enraged indictment of the use made of a "charming letter" he wrote Douglas defines his view of the epistolary text as a dangerous and unstable object:

> Every construction but the right one is put on it: . . . I produce the original letter myself in Court to show what it really is: it is denounced by your father's Counsel as a revolting and insidious attempt to corrupt Innocence:

ultimately it forms part of a criminal charge: . . . I go to prison for it at last. That is the result of writing you a charming letter. (*DP,* 441)

Bosie's chief infringement here is of textual propriety: a private letter should not be "published." Disputing the prosecution's claim that he "corrupted" the innocence of young men, Wilde responds by protesting against a more significant corruption, that of his own writing. His attempt to reclaim the meaning of his letter, "to show what it really is," founders nonetheless on the court's greater interpretive authority.

Douglas's epistolary irresponsibility—which culminates in the "silence" that Wilde's letter seeks to fill—emerges elsewhere in the narrative as the source of Wilde's greatest anguish. Wilde's most aggrieved protest is connected to his horror that the entire British public has been able to "read" him, in the press coverage of his trials, as though he were an "open postcard" (*DP,* 446) rather than a private letter. The agonizing loss of privacy, the absence of a "mask" with which to construct and control his public persona, is most vividly dramatized in the famous description of Wilde's purgatory on the platform at Clapham Junction:

> Of all possible objects I was the most grotesque. When people saw me they laughed. Each train as it came up swelled the audience. Nothing could exceed their amusement. That was of course before they knew who I was. As soon as they had been informed, they laughed still more. For half an hour I stood there in the grey November rain surrounded by a jeering mob. For a year after that was done to me I wept every day at the same hour and for the same space of time. (*DP,* 491)

Wilde's account of his repugnance at being on display "for the world to look at" is directly related to this lack of control over his public image, his inability to compose his face and body in a guise that would keep the observer at an awed distance. The possession of himself as a unique subject drains away and is consumed by the encroaching consciousness of the crowd, whose activity and growth is proportional to Wilde's stasis and disappearance: it is as though Wilde is turned into a statue, a monument of disgrace, by the objectifying gaze of the hostile mob. Among that crowd, in Wilde's imagination, is Bosie, who seized the "opportunities" of publicly humiliating Wilde even after his imprisonment.

Wilde's attempt to reclaim agency in his letter—not only by dramatically reenacting what had happened to him at Clapham Junction, but also by weeping at precisely the same time every day—actually underscores his passivity, his reactive role in responding to events and crises that have been "authored" by "someone else." Paradoxically, the letter's determination to displace the "sins" with which he had become identified onto "another," diminishes his own role in the confession, creating a fascinating mystery around the "someone else"—who, we can only presume, is Bosie—that gradually transcends his own role. Complaining that he has been removed from the public stage through Bosie's agency, Wilde bizarrely repeats this same process in his letter, whereby Bosie's "subjectivity" becomes more compelling and influential than his own. The reversal of roles between author and reader exemplifies a pattern of substitutive specularity between Wilde and Bosie that reinforces their complementary relation, despite the letter's repeated portrayal of a stark moral and intellectual contrast. For example, Wilde's frequent attribution to Bosie of "the supreme vice [of] shallowness" (*DP*, 425), seeks to banish Bosie to the realm of insignificance, and to establish his own depth by contrast. Describing his relationship with Bosie as "intellectually degrading to me" (*DP*, 427), Wilde again identifies Bosie with a stage of his past that he has left behind. Likewise, Wilde constructs a cautionary figure, "he who does not know himself," and writes that "I was such a one too long. You have been such a one too long" (*DP*, 425).

The letter's attempt to establish and totalize an antithesis between Wilde and Bosie—the latter being the figure of errant desire associated with the author's disavowed past—founders on the substitutive specularity of the letter itself. When Wilde advises Bosie, for example, that "you will let the reading of this terrible letter—for such I know it is—prove to you as important a crisis and turning-point of your life as the writing of it is to me" (*DP*, 448), the effect is not to differentiate between the "writing" and "reading" functions of the text—to distinguish the creative, morally purposeful author from the sterile, indolent consumer—but to connect them by invoking the autobiographical figure of the "turning point." The letter is represented as having exactly the same effect on each of them: hence their distinct roles are collapsed into a shared subjectivity, dramatized by their mutual substitution in the text. The classic confessional claims to self-delineation and individual enlightenment are dismantled by the textual reciprocity of dual selves.

Conclusion: "No name at all"

Douglas's violation of Wilde's textual secrecy is compounded by his promiscuous dissemination of Wilde's letters which are represented, like the painting in *Dorian Gray*, as the receptacle of a vital and dangerous secret.

> You had left my letters lying about for blackmailing companions to steal, for hotel servants to pilfer, for housemaids to sell. That was simply your careless want of appreciation of what I had written to you. But that you should seriously propose to publish selections from the balance was almost incredible to me. (*DP*, 453–54)

Stripped of his "secret," Wilde is thereby deprived of his most effective mask. The violence of the letter, then, functions multivalently as the defender of Wilde's secret, the accuser of Bosie for breaking the contract with Wilde, and the punitive dismantler of Wilde's "identity" to a standardized sign, "no name at all . . . , merely the figure and letter of a little cell in a long gallery" (*DP*, 454), devoid of all individual "style."

With its reiterated statements of horror at an unsought, and deeply humiliating, public exposure, Wilde's letter reveals a strategic resistance to and subversion of the conventional confessional narrative. Far from being a repressive or externally enforced concealment of a shameful truth, the "secret" is for Wilde the soil of complex experience and disciplined desire, in which the seed of what he called "individuality" might flourish. Culminating in the recognition that "secrets are always smaller than their manifestations" (*DP*, 506), Wilde's letter relentlessly traces this growth of a shared secret into a manifestation the effects of which were at once personal, cultural, and multifariously textual. As the climactic cultural manifestation of his secret, his trials and conviction inaugurated a series of events over which Wilde had lost control. The prison letter seeks to reclaim control of his secret, and to reinscribe it in a narrative of his own construction. Hence, far from being a work in which Wilde repents of his crimes and confesses his guilty secret, the letter is a celebration of the power of secrecy to free desire from the banal or violent invasions of public scrutiny.

Though Wilde's letter denounces Bosie as the "other" from which the confessional subject must establish a safe distance, it is crucial that this denunciation is rhetorically undone by the mediation of the letter and its inscription of the reader as necessary counterpart. This implied reader of *De Profundis*, whatever else he might be, is free: and the letter seeks to punish him for this undeserved freedom, which has been secured at Wilde's expense. Asserting that Bosie belongs to "a race, marriage with whom is horrible, friendship fatal, and that lays violent hands either on its own life or on the lives of others" (*DP*, 440), Wilde conceives of his letter as a form of justified self-defense. Yet he also depicts, with graphic relish, the pain that his letter will inflict on his reader. Hoping that his unflattering portrayal of Douglas "will wound your vanity to the quick," Wilde advises him to "read the letter over and over again till it kills your vanity" (*DP*, 424). The language suggests a therapeutic purpose of moral rejuvenation, as though the letter were destroying a diseased organ; but to kill Bosie's vanity, founded on the beauty of his face, is not only to kill Bosie himself, but to eradicate the specular duality he forms with Wilde. If, in the careless hands of Bosie, the letter produces a series of random explosions, Wilde methodically transforms it into an instrument of disfiguring, defacing, and suicidal violence. By so doing, he deconstructs the singularity of the autobio-graphical subject and dissents from the power of confession to determine the guilt and marginality of those in whose voices it claims to speak.

Notes

A longer version of this chapter appears in Oliver S. Buckton, *Secret Selves: Confession and Same-Sex Desire in Victorian Autobiography,* © 1998 by The University of North Carolina Press. Used by permission of the publisher.

1. For recent examples of criticism of these writings that focuses on Wilde's sexual-ity, see Ed Cohen, *Talk on the Wilde Side: Toward a Genealogy of a Discourse on Male Sexualities* (New York: Routledge, 1993) and "Writing Gone Wilde: Homoerotic De-sire in the Closet of Representation," *PMLA* 102 (1987): 801–13; Christopher Craft, "Alias Bunbury: Desire and Termination in *The Importance of Being Earnest*," *Represen-tations* 31 (summer 1990): 19–46; Richard Dellamora, *Masculine Desire: The Sexual Pol-itics of Victorian Aestheticism* (Chapel Hill: University of North Carolina Press, 1990), esp. chap. 10; Jonathan Dollimore, "Different Desires: Subjectivity and Transgression in Wilde and Gide," *Genders* 2 (summer 1988): 24–41; and *Sexual Dissidence: Augustine to Wilde, Freud to Foucault* (Oxford: Clarendon, 1991); Lee Edelman, *Homographesis: Essays in Gay Literary and Cultural Theory* (New York: Routledge, 1994), esp. chap. 1; and Wayne Koestenbaum, "Wilde's Hard Labor and the Birth of Gay Reading," in *Engendering Men: The Question of Male Feminist Criticism,* ed. Joseph A. Boone and Michael Cadden (New York: Routledge, 1990), 176–89.

2. Jonathan Dollimore, *Sexual Dissidence: Augustine to Wilde, Freud to Foucault* (Ox-ford: Clarendon, 1991), 11.

3. Richard Ellmann, *Oscar Wilde* (New York: Knopf, 1988), 589.

4. Dollimore, *Sexual Dissidence,* 14.

5. *The Letters of Oscar Wilde,* ed. Rupert Hart-Davis (New York: Harcourt, 1962), 490. Further references to this edition of the letter known as *De Profundis* will be cited parenthetically as *DP* in the text.

6. H. Montgomery Hyde has traced the history of the letter in terms of the rivalry between Ross and Douglas for the affection of Wilde during his lifetime, and for the association with his name after his death. See Hyde, "The Riddle of De Profundis: Who Owns the Manuscript?" *The Antigonish Review* 54 (summer 1983): 107–27, esp. 111–19.

7. *Oscar Wilde: The Critical Heritage* ed. Karl Beckson (London: Routledge and Kegal Paul, 1974), 257–58, 244 (original emphasis). As Shaw went on to claim, "There is pain in it, inconvenience, annoyance, but no real tragedy: all comedy."

8. Beckson, *Critical Heritage,* 242, 245.

9. Ibid., 253.

10. Oscar Wilde, *The Artist as Critic: Critical Writings of Oscar Wilde,* ed. Richard Ellmann (Chicago: University of Chicago Press, 1969), 305.

11. Dollimore, "Different Desires," 34.

12. Regenia Gagnier, *Idylls of the Marketplace: Oscar Wilde and the Victorian Public* (Stanford: Stanford University Press, 1986), 180. In this context, I am dissatisfied with Wayne Koestenbaum's hasty move "to generalize from Bosie's position to the stance of post-Wilde gay readers" ("Wilde's Hard Labor," 178): not because I believe that Wilde attempts to exclude other readers, but because the specific series of displacements I trace depends on his construction of "Bosie" as his alter ego, and hence "Bosie's position" is the central preoccupation of the letter as an autobiographical narrative.

13. William Wordsworth, *The Prelude: A Parallel Text,* ed. J. C. Maxwell (Harmondsworth: Penguin, 1971), 1805–6 version, 11.186–87, 190–94. In the 1850 version of the poem, Wordsworth modifies the tone slightly, by omitting the line containing "greedy in the chase."

14. Oscar Wilde, *The Importance of Being Earnest: A Trivial Comedy for Serious People in Four Acts as Originally Written by Oscar Wilde,* ed. Sarah Dickson (New York: New York Public Library, 1956), 77.

15. Dollimore, "Different Desires," 28, 31.

16. Ibid., 40 n. 58.

17. Regenia Gagnier, "*De Profundis* as *Epistola: in Carcere et Vinculis:* a Materialist Reading of Oscar Wilde's Autobiography," *Criticism* 26, no. 4 (fall 1984): 335. Gagnier goes on to argue more specifically that Wilde's letter "was an indirect response to the uselessness of prison labor" (338).

18. Ibid., 342.

19. Marion Shaw, "'To Tell the Truth of Sex': Confession and Abjection in Late Victorian Writing," in *Rewriting the Victorians: Theory, History and the Politics of Gender,* ed. Linda M. Shires (New York: Routledge, 1992), 95–96.

20. Paul de Man, "Autobiography as De-Facement," in *The Rhetoric of Romanticism* (New York: Columbia University Press, 1985), 75–76.

21. Gagnier, "*De Profundis,*" 342.

22. De Man, "Autobiography," 70, 72.

23. Koestenbaum, "Wilde's Hard Labor," 178.

PART THREE

Dissident Aesthetics

The Elusive Queerness of Henry James's "Queer Comrade": Reading Gabriel Nash of *The Tragic Muse*

ERIC HARALSON

> The scene will be in London . . . in a very different *monde;*
> considerably the "Aesthetic." . . . It won't be improper;
> strange to say, considering the elements.
> —Henry James, *Letters* (1888)

> Was Gabriel Nash vice? Was Mrs. Dallow virtue?
> —William Dean Howells, review of *The Tragic Muse*

By common consent, from early reviews to recent criticism, Gabriel Nash is the "Oscar Wilde figure" of *The Tragic Muse,* Henry James's 1890 novel about artistic vocation and the fate of art in a debased and debasing material world.[1] The work centers on the development of two young aspirants, Miriam Rooth, who conquers the London stage by exercising the "unscrupulous . . . wanton" willpower of the born artist, and Nicholas Dormer, who violates "innumerable vows and pledges" of family tradition by renouncing a career in Parliament for one in portrait-painting.[2] Gabriel Nash is the book's blithe spirit, championing Paterian sensation over bourgeois banality, awakening Nick Dormer to the life of art, and analyzing the plight of the artist in a vulgar, commercialized modernity with all of James's own fervor but none of his despair. As the closest approximation to the "Wildean aesthete" in James's fiction,[3] Nash will repay study, particularly since that stereotype would soon fuse with another—the homosexual—through an intricate process of cultural articulation and social regulation. *The Tragic Muse* bears the markings not only of an author with deeply mixed feelings about male–male desire, including his own, but also (and therefore) of its provenance midway between the Criminal Law Amendment Act of 1885, featuring Henry Labouchère's infamous rider penalizing "gross indecency," and the 1895 trials that invoked this statute to *re*figure the "Oscar Wilde figure" forever.

Of necessity, that is, the British and American reviewers who saw James's whimsical "apostle of being" and "artistic epicureanism" as "a clever sketch of Oscar Wilde" could *not* have meant the same thing that Richard Ellmann,

Regenia Gagnier, and Joseph Litvak mean in positing Nash to be a "veiled portrait of Wilde himself."[4] As Alan Sinfield observes, we run the risk of viewing Wilde—or even the less vivid John Addington Symonds, another referent for James—as "always-already queer," when only the pressure of 1895 would convert the "vaguely disconcerting nexus of effeminacy, . . . idleness, immorality, luxury, insouciance, decadence and aestheticism" of the previous two decades into the currency of "an unspeakable of the Oscar Wilde sort."[5] It is perhaps for this reason that reviews of *The Tragic Muse* mainly applauded the author's skill in rendering the "flitting . . . metaphysical person" of Gabriel Nash or, at the worst, deplored "the inanities indulged in by this modern type of humanity" and sympathized with an Anglo-American public "struggling to grasp" his doctrines (*CR*, 224, 227, 238). Apparently no one perceived the behavior of "Nick's queer comrade," in the novel's phrase, as signifying precisely *that* queerness (*TM*, 44).

And yet, as Philip Horne points out, "queer" had a restless life of its own in Victorian usage, being "powerful *because* it is multiple and ambiguous," and Nash's queerness may actually have gained salience for being inchoate—a source not of coherent suspicion but of nagging irresolution that *prevented* suspicion from cohering.[6] In a way that suggestively mirrors the response of Nick's family and fiancée—the "high, executive" dowager Lady Agnes Dormer, two sheltered sisters, and the ambitious young widow Julia Dallow (*TM*, 31)—the novel's first readers confessed to obscure misgivings about Nash, calling him "an unsolved problem," wishing him away as "a superfluous figure altogether," or deprecating his "nebulous, unreliable" moral bearings (*CR*, 226, 232, 240). Tacitly, they agreed with Lady Agnes that her son should be "making sure of his seat" in Parliament by marrying Julia, who controls the borough of Harsh, rather than pursuing his "nast[y] hankerings" after art or opening his studio— "that unnatural spot," as one sister puts it—to Gabriel Nash (*TM*, 54, 364, 367). Without sharing Julia Dallow's outright revulsion toward "that horrid man," reviewers clearly sided with her on the duty of Victorian masculinity to engage in productive labor ("Pray, isn't a gentleman to do anything, to be anything?") as against Nash's credo of sublime inutility—his "career" of feeling, his perverse lexicon à la Wilde ("failure" is "having something to show"; "actions" are "all the things I don't do"), and his sole impetus, as one reader noted, to "lounge and gratify his sense of the beautiful" (*TM*, 26, 27, 79, 123, 303; *CR*, 233). Lost on such critics was James's extensive satire on the "ordered void" of philistine England, for not unlike the Dormer women, they seemed distracted by a prevision of "mysterious depths of contamination" beneath Nash's aestheticism and of *other* inversions that his "twaddle of the underworld" might condone (*TM*, 26, 325, 385). In a word, wasn't there something fishy—and below the waist, no less—about this self-described "merman wandering free" (*TM*, 117)?

If the queerness of "Nick's queer comrade" was before the letter, then, it was nonetheless always all-ready for what Lynda Zwinger playfully calls "the sexuality Henry James's sex would have had had he had any."[7] In fact, the dismissive irony that issues from both Dormer and the narrator, yet catches "exactly the tone of Mr. Gabriel Nash," provides the clue to James's own worry for "contamination," which led him not merely to make light of the "settled equilibrium" of normative structures under critique—marriage, the patriarchal family, standards of gentlemanly endeavor—but also to protest too much against Nash's substantiality as a social or even a corporeal presence. How could Nash possibly pose a threat to "a much more positive quantity" like Julia Dallow when his own trademark was just his "unclassified condition, the lack of all position as a name in well-kept books"? How could he have *any* sexuality to bother about when he was as "transient" as "vapour or murmuring wind or shifting light" (*TM*, 52, 70, 347, 505)? As Christopher Lane has seen, *The Tragic Muse* found James at cross purposes, mobilizing his aesthete as a fundamental affront to the heterosexualized order of things while counterplotting an "erasure of homosexual meaning" in which Nash "never embodies *more* than a fantasy."[8] By the same token, this studiously cultivated ethereality contained implicit—if impossible—advice for men of "the Oscar Wilde sort" as a new decade of surveillance and punishment dawned: go in for manner, and try not to matter.

* * *

Peace be to you on Henry James. If you like his work
the man himself is nothing in it one way or the other.
—Flannery O'Connor, *The Habit of Being*

As the *Manchester Guardian* suggested in designating Nash a "shadowy, fantastic [figure] whose rank in the writer's estimation it is hard to fix" (*CR*, 225), the character's elusiveness stands in some definite yet occluded relation to James's elusiveness. For a proper approach to the novel, we must leave Nash momentarily in suspense—his natural state, in any case—while attempting to gauge the author's more general stance toward both the fact of homosexual existence and the evolving discursive regime that surrounded it.

It might be said that for James in the broad period before 1895, homosexuality occupied the space of both "the real" and "the romantic" in his well-known distinction between the modes of cognitive purchase underwriting the Anglo-American novel: "The real represents . . . the things we cannot possibly *not* know, sooner or later, in one way or another. . . . The romantic stands . . . for the things . . . that reach us only through the beautiful circuit and subterfuge of our thought and our desire."[9] On the one hand, James could not *not* have known a great deal about English sexual politics, for he was acquainted with all the principal actors in the sordid drama that unfolded with the criminal code revision of 1885: Labouchère, whose aggressive politics James discussed with his sister Alice and whose journalistic exposés struck him as rudely "star-[ing] one in the face"; Lord Rosebery, one of the "Snob Queers" reviled by the Marquess of Queensberry en route to his confrontation with Wilde; George Curzon, who would humiliate Wilde for publishing *The Picture of Dorian Gray;* W. E. Henley, whose review deemed *Dorian Gray* fit for only "outlawed noblemen and perverted telegraph boys"; Frank Lockwood, the Solicitor-General whose zealous prosecution turned the tide against Wilde and who inspired one of James's late stories; "the atrocious Alfred D[ouglas]," as James came to regard Wilde's companion; and finally Robert Ross, another of Wilde's intimates, who remained a special friend of the American author.[10] Not least, of course, there was Oscar Wilde himself, familiar to James as society phenom, potential rival, and antipodal creature since 1882.[11]

This extraordinary commerce with cultural arbiters from the highest ranks of government, journalism, and the arts, coupled with James's omnivorous "craving for gossip" (as Edmund Gosse termed it), gives warrant to Wendy Graham's claim that the writer who began *The Tragic Muse* in 1887–88 was "fully attuned to the regulatory strain" impinging on British sexual dissidence.[12] At the same time, it is worth querying the texture of that attunement, espe-cially given the inflationary temptation to recast James as having run with "a fast European circle of gay men," in the casual words of a recent biographer.[13] Here Sinfield's warning against anachronistic misconstruction seems even more crucial than with Wilde, for James's manner of engagement with the social and personal fact of same-sex passion (by no means a rare one) was fur-tive and intermittent at best, constantly vacillating between detection and de-flection, flirtation and flight. Litvak's apt impression of James as both "prepared for the Wildean solicitation" of *Dorian Gray* and prepared against it—and of *The Tragic Muse* as "intertextual foreplay" under layers of vagueness—indicates an authorial mind in which "the real" of homosexuality registered by circuit and subterfuge indeed.[14]

Moreover, as an outsider to English life wanting to stay well in, whatever James *expressed* about homosexuality underwent intense public conditioning and was governed by dictates of genteel decorum as much as by fear of legal sanction—or better, was subject to a "voluntary" code of conduct increasingly reinforced by threat of law and withering scandal. It was completely character-istic of James, for instance, to resort to clubby humor when thanking Gosse for passing on a copy of the underground treatise *A Problem in Modern Ethics* (1891)—to call Symonds's plea for the acceptance of homosexuality "a queer place to plant the standard of duty"(!), to imagine the "capital sport" that would ensue were he to attract "a band of the emulous," and to sign off: "Yours—if I may safely say so!—ever, H. J." (*L*, 3:398). By 1895, with the first trial of "the wretched O. W." under way, the joke had suddenly turned grave, and James, returning yet another batch of Symonds's writings to Gosse, found himself reaching for the plain brown wrapper: "These are days in which one's modesty is, in every direction, much exposed, and one should be thankful for every veil that one can hastily snatch up" (*L*, 4:12). As my examples suggest, James's psychic posture can only be half understood by watching his coy game with Wilde, which must be placed alongside his more regular—if equally complex—interactions with men of his own more cautious constitution. As we shall see by tracing this triangle with Symonds and Gosse back to its beginnings, James's care for what men might "safely say" to one another and his penchant for snatching up veils originated well before *The Tragic Muse*.

* * *

> It is only the man himself who knows (and he knows very indistinctly) with what forces he has to measure himself . . . [and how to solve] the problem of correlating his dominant passion with the facts of existence.
> —John Addington Symonds, *Memoirs*

It is popular to cite "The Author of 'Beltraffio'" (1884) as an important node in the growth of James's art-theory and gender politics, and specifically—following the notebook "germ"—as a melodrama of "hysterical aestheticism" grounded in Symonds's domestic troubles (*N*, 57). In Jonathan Freedman's summary, James amplified hearsay from Gosse into "a tale of . . . horror in which a mother lets her child die rather than grow up with a homosexual father."[15] From our perspective, there can be no question that Mark Ambient— or Symonds, as freely translated into the author of an "aesthetic war-cry" on behalf of "the gospel of art"[16]—connotes "a homosexual father." But interestingly, James himself did not notice this connection—or did not acknowledge it—until Gosse brought it to his attention. In fact, their virtual collaboration in composing and then reading the story demonstrates how fiction could serve as a vehicle for gradually confessing—or all but confessing—to a common knowledge that neither man could fully admit to himself.

Pace biographer Fred Kaplan, that is, the notebook's term for Symonds's works—"hyperaesthetic"—did *not* function for James as "a polite synonym for homoerotic," and the proposition that he knew of Symonds's "divided life" years before "The Author of 'Beltraffio'" simplifies both the elaborate epistemology of such men and the delicate folkways of Victorian homosociality.[17] Symonds "had the tendencies confusedly" (in Forster's phrase),[18] and what he called his "tyrannous emotion, curbed and suppressed for the most part" (*Memoirs*, 24) was on view neither in his bearing—"a mild, cultured man, with the Oxford perfume," as James recorded him (*L*, 2:102)—nor in his published writings, which on the contrary stressed the "well-deserved discredit" attaching to "Platonic love."[19] True, Symonds had sounded Gosse on his "sympathy with the beauty of men," sending him verses on Greek love in testimony to the "root of Calamus within our souls"; yet he had also warned adamantly against the morbid inference that he supported "perverted sexual passion" as a present-day practice. Reticent and conflicted about the "obstinate twist" of "instinctive abnormality" in his own nature, Gosse had cause to take Symonds at his word—or at least, absent an opening from James, to keep speculation to himself.[20]

In the same vein, although Symonds had described the privately printed *A Problem in Greek Ethics* (1883) to James's boyhood friend from Boston, Thomas Sergeant Perry, he again underscored his strictly "philosophical interest" in "that unmentionable custom wh[ich] perplexes every student of Plato," and the two American writers restricted their gossip to the poor health that beset Symonds's family (*Letters* 2:896, 934).[21] As for James's own overture to the ailing Englishman in Davos in 1884—professing to share Symonds's "unspeakably tender" feeling for Italy and urging that "victims of a common passion should sometimes exchange a look"—the ulterior motive that such diction *seems* to betray is ruled out by its very suggestiveness: if he had meant it, he would not have said it (*L*, 3:29–31).[22] Perhaps it is also symptomatic that James's "handtouch," as Symonds called it, went unreturned.

Not surprisingly, then, James's preparatory notes for "The Author of 'Beltraffio'" say nothing about Symonds's homosexuality but instead project a study of his uncongenial and "very typical" modern marriage, in which *religion* serves as the arena of contest. In a move more subtly rehearsed in *The Tragic Muse*, the notebook finds James planning to deploy a woman—Symonds's "Calvinistic wife" Catherine—as the voice of societal antagonism toward art, thus making the couple's domestic tension emblematize a cultural economy in which aestheticism is "aggravated, made extravagant and perverse" by the persistent censure of (particularly female) "rigid moralist[s]." Like the oppressed Symonds, that is, but unlike the resolutely unmarried James, Mark Ambient would be "impregnated—even to *morbidness*—with the spirit of Italy, the love of beauty" (*N*, 57; emphasis added). Still, his "godless ideas" would be secular rather than sexual in kind—with his "absence of Christian hopes" for an afterlife triggering his wife's sacrifice of their son—and Ambient's unconventionality was not, in any case, to manifest itself in actual deviance: he would remain "perfectly decent in life" (*N*, 57–58).

Yet godless ideas, like queer ones, have a force of their own. When James addressed himself to the story proper, his germinal intuition of the hostility between the love of art and earthly pleasure, on one hand, and the duty to marriage and paternity, on the other, sprouted unexpected meanings. Ambient turns out to be not merely "decent" but driven to self-censorship by "an extreme dread of scandal"; "strange oppositions" in his "faded and fatigued countenance" appear to reflect an "active past" in which oriental adventures figure prominently; and even his loyal sister characterizes a certain strand in his thinking—with telltale hesitancy—as "well, really—rather queer!" Most acutely, his wife Beatrice—as Catherine Symonds is ironically renamed—fears that some "subtle poison," communicated by physical intimacy, will destroy the moral fiber of their boy, whose pet-name "Dolcino" shows the father's contagion already at work ("AB," 323, 306, 329).[22] By means of a narrative strategy that would become a staple for him, James gestured vaguely but ominously toward "blanks" in Ambient's history and self-construction that were left for the reader to fill in (*FW,* 1188).

Or *partial* blanks, more accurately. For the tale introduces a character unforeseen in the notebook, an American dilettante now *reliving* his youthful pilgrimage to Ambient's country home in Surrey—the visit that had culminated in Dolcino's demise. It is this narrator, rather than Ambient, who provides the best index to James's self-distancing from "hyper-aesthetic" men and his muffled recognition of the way in which beauty worship might shade into homosexuality, thus compromising his own "unspeakably tender" passions. As he does *not* do with Gabriel Nash, James openly condescends to the narrator's "little game of new sensations" in England, his habit of seeing nearly everything—but especially the "languid and angelic" Dolcino—in a precious Pre-Raphaelite frame ("AB" 303, 342). Just as James's reviews of the 1870s routinely scolded an array of British and continental "advocates of 'art for art'" for polishing their style as if morality were something extrinsic or optional—"a coloured fluid kept in a big-labelled bottle in some mysterious intellectual closet"—he taxes his narrator for idolizing Ambient's "effort to arrive at a [perfect] surface," a shallow artistry of "purest distillation[s]" (*FW,* 157; "AB," 332).

But as I have indicated, the story's prime value as a precursor to *The Tragic Muse* lies in its strong suggestion—strongly disciplined—that this cult of perfervid aestheticism constitutes a hotbed of dangerous male bonding. The narrator emerges as patently infatuated with Ambient ("my heart beat very fast as I saw his handsome face"); he relishes his exemption from procreative obligations ("children are terrible critics"); and he reinvests any paternal impulse he may have had in "nurs[ing]" Ambient's manuscripts and battening on Dolcino's "enchanting little countenance" ("AB," 305, 325, 327, 340). In fact, the narrator inadvertently reveals that it was his own advent in Ambient's private sphere—and his bald display of adoration for the older artist—that precipitated the family tragedy. Furnished with hard proof of where her husband's impossible, godless ideas could lead, Beatrice had acted to "prevent Mark from ever [again] touching" the boy, putting him safely beyond reach of the narrator in the process: "So I never touched Dolcino" ("AB," 329, 345).[24]

Thus by every implication of his being—to borrow a phrase for Olive Chancellor of *The Bostonians* (1886), another queer figure under wraps[25]—Ambient signifies "a homosexual father," just as his relation to his disciple reads as queer tutelage and Dolcino as a "victim to . . . the heavy pressure" generated by the trio's head-on collision with heteronormativity (*N*, 57–58). Yet when Gosse complimented the author of "The Author of 'Beltraffio'" for hitting upon Symonds's secret, James affected a naïveté worthy of the tale's narrator: "Perhaps I *have* divined the innermost cause of J. A. S.'s discomfort—but I don't think I seize . . . exactly the allusion you refer to. I am therefore devoured with curiosity as to this further revelation. Even a postcard (in covert words) would relieve the suspense of the perhaps-already-too-indiscreet—H. J."[26] As is clear from the shuttling rhetoric and the request for covert words, James had no real need of further revelation but was instead, like Gosse, searching for a breach in the "don't ask, don't tell" policy of Victorian manhood through which to whisper, and thereby verify, the fact of male–male desire, that innermost of causes. Like Symonds himself, they found themselves bound by a schizophrenic method of disclosure and disclaimer, collaborating against the enforcements of tacitness whereby the "open secret," in D. A. Miller's concept, served "to conceal the knowledge of the knowledge" of homosexuality—to keep it for the time, in Gosse's gothic image, "buried alive and conscious, but deprived of speech."[27]

Even at this early stage, then, James's devouring curiosity was powerfully checked by "the devouring *publicity*" of modern life, best exemplified by Labouchère's brand of journalism (*N*, 82, 84). "Showing one's self" to learn "the truth that turns one inside out" was all well and good for actresses like Miriam Rooth, but the writer who would imagine her battled against both the inhibitions of his antebellum upbringing and the social constraints of Englishness, which combined to prevent one hand from knowing what the other did—or again, from admitting to such knowledge (*TM*, 110). Eventually James would relax his own "rigid moralist" side in self-ironic fictions—offering a youth at Yale who "richly suppose[s] himself to be reacting against Puritanism," an American in Paris confronting his "ascetic suspicion of . . . beauty."[28] But in the phase before *The Tragic Muse*, he mistrusted the "brilliant chiaroscuro of costume and posture" in authors like Swinburne,[29] saw in Huysmans "all the signs of complete decadence—elaborate & incurable rot," and sustained a need *not* to see how his vocabulary for aestheticism drifted into both the vitriolic journalese of "mock-hysterical aesthetes" and the evolving medical discourse of homosexual "morbidity" that Symonds would denounce as "ludicrously in error"—

"more humane, but . . . not less false, than that of sin or vice."[30] Ambivalent to begin with, and pushed toward "vigor and decisiveness" and "absolute straight- ness in style" (in brother William's manly phrases),[31] James still had to wait for Gabriel Nash to instruct him that in a world of homogeneous heterosexual men, "affectation" is "always the charge against a personal manner: if you have any at all people think you have too much" (*L*, 4:384; *TM*, 120). Unfortunately, that lesson came just as a stylish personal manner was becoming grounds for heightened suspicion, as well as for a new scope of criminal prosecution.

*   *   *

> Divided I was, I recall, between the dread and the glory
> of being . . . greeted, "Well, Stiffy—!" as a penalty of
> the least attempt at personal adornment.
> —Henry James, *A Small Boy and Others*

In keeping with the new need for greater circumspection, the ontology of Gabriel Nash is markedly insubstantial and paradoxical. Throughout much of the novel he is—like Wilde's Bunbury—"somewhere else at present,"[32] with conjecture placing him in locales that smack of exotic sensualism (Samarcand, Granada, Cashmere) while defying close inspection. Even his own reports of his travels have an air of fantastic remoteness: "His Sicily might have been the Sicily of *The Winter's Tale.*" As for Nash's descents on London, not even Nick Dormer has "detected the process" of "his means, his profession, his belong- ings" or the address of his dwelling, since all correspondence is directed to a fictitious club, "the Anonymous, in some improbable square" (*TM*, 21, 263, 501, 505, 516).

Further, the very terms in which Dormer praises Nash's distinction—he does not "shade off" into other men but remains "neat as an outline cut out of paper"—imply that he maintains the barest minimum of presence in the social text. He is the fragrant "solitary blossom" without the "worldly branch" or the "dangling accidents and conditions" that secure most men in English public and domestic life; yet if this means "you know what you've got hold of" in Nash, as Nick contends, it also means that you never have hold of it for long. The diplomat Peter Sherringham—Julia Dallow's brother, who is also Dor- mer's cousin—comes closer to the truth in his impression that "you never knew where to 'have' Gabriel Nash," for his status as a "solid, sociable fact" is always provisional and qualified by his serene refusal to matter, his being "ready to preside with a smile even at a discussion of his own admissibility" (*TM*, 53, 60, 375, 509).

What bears emphasizing is the evidence that Nash, for all his conventional laziness, must *labor* to resist being located in the interlocking grid of class, professional, and behavioral markers of Victorian masculinity. Nash is unconditional and immaterial—"nothing but a mind," as one reviewer complained (*CR*, 240)—because he assiduously acts to avoid embodiments that fall subject to political specification ("I've no *état civil*") and thus to both public vulnerability and state regulation. One should not be fooled, in other words, when he advertises his "little system" of comportment as unprecedented "candour"—as "being just the same to every one"—for it is actually *the* manner par excellence. Like Miriam Rooth, who is "protected and alienated" from Sherringham's unwanted advances by her stage costume, Nash carries his theatricality to such an extreme of consistency as to be all impersonal surface, no available depth (*TM*, 27, 116, 118, 463). Rather startlingly, James seems not only to have discerned a point in what he once considered Wilde's "pointless nomadism"[33] but also to have revalued Wilde's dandyism, while conveniently assigning his disdain for its "repulsive and fatuous" side to Mrs. Dallow (*TM*, 115; *L*, 3:372).

For apart from his angelic "facial radiance," Gabriel's chief means of seeming "positive and pervasive" while having a "baffling effect" on gender taxonomy is his chatter—a persiflage that holds the floor by its "conspicuous and aggressive perfection" and its "mellifluous," almost orphic musicality (*TM*, 20–21, 41, 263, 510). Sinfield's reading of Victorian dandies as shrewdly hiding-in-plain-sight—"they *passed* . . . not by playing down what we call camp . . . but by manifesting it exuberantly"—applies as well to the proleptically queer Nash, with the caveat that *his* flamboyance is strictly vocal and gestural, and his effeminacy expressed more in personal qualities—"a lady . . . in tact and sympathy," as Miriam calls him—than in physical adornment (*TM*, 273).[34] It is as if, in a move meant to be at once sanitizing and saving, James has shorn the dandy of disagreeable coiffure (Nash has "a mere reminiscence of hair") and divested him of inculpatory dress—"I can't afford the uniform (I believe you get it best somewhere in South Audley Street)"—while carefully leaving him only a "great deal of manner" and Wilde's tuneful "mezzo voice" (*TM*, 20, 21, 385–86).[35]

Yet the countervailing burden of the novel is that, in the emerging regulatory climate, one literally could not be careful enough. "The historical positing of the category of 'the homosexual,'" Lee Edelman writes, "textualize[d] male identity as such, subjecting it to the alienating requirement that it be 'read,' and threatening . . . to strip 'masculinity' of its privileged status as the self-authenticating paradigm of the natural." Though not "the gay man" so much as the gay manqué of *The Tragic Muse*, Nash is sufficiently different to challenge the masculinity of others to "*perform* its self-evidence" and, perhaps more disconcertingly, sufficiently normal to frustrate efforts to pinpoint his variation: "fair and fat" and lacking the "loose, faded uniform" of the *Punch*-style aesthete, he signifies "immediately as a gentleman" and thus perversely compounds his effect of deconstructive aggravation (*TM,* 20, 385).[36]

Indeed what the novel most unequivocally conveys—despite its chary fashioning of Nash—is contempt for the "unmemorable men" of the English political-professional class, with their fatal "want of imagination." Treated to a near view of not only Rosebery, but John Bright, Charles Dilke, and the "dreary incubus" Gladstone, James set British statesmen down as "very measurable creatures" with "not a grain of . . . inspiration," while the body politic en masse was "grossly materialistic," in need of "blood-letting"; even England's standard man of culture (Gosse excepted) struck him as "dense and puerile," a being "whose central fire doesn't reach . . . to his extremities" (*L,* 2:100–1; 3:53, 105, 146, 210, 219). *The Tragic Muse* imports these invidious judgments from James's correspondence, but more crucially, it penetrates to the unspeakable doubt at the core of "successful" Victorian manhood: what if the construct of the (re)productive gentleman is just that, a construct manufactured in performance and therefore liable to inauthenticity, to sudden rupture and self-emptying, perhaps even to inversion of parts? As James Eli Adams writes, in discussing Pater's interventions in the quest for socially authoritative "masculine charisma": "The discipline of the aspiring gentleman . . . depend[ed] on a fundamentally theatrical strategy of self-presentation," which was, however, "emphatically repudiated" when it veered into dandyism and other suspect gender styles.[37]

This worry for the integrity of one's self-projection notably visits Peter Sherringham, upon discovering that his rival for Miriam's hand—the actor Basil Dashwood—is "straight-featured," not bohemian, with an "imperturbable 'good form'" that almost surpasses his own: "[Dashwood] looked remarkably like a gentleman, . . . carry[ing] this appearance . . . to a point that was almost a negation of its spirit." Pressed on one side by the need to differentiate his own appearance from Dashwood's uncanny simulation—a facade, as Nina Auerbach remarks, for the "shrewd professional acumen of the untalented"[38]—Sherringham also becomes embroiled with Nash, whose hovering about the London stage calls into question the diplomat's kindred enthusiasms. These masculine mirrorings, and especially the queasy self-estrangement they induce in Sherringham, are quite calculated on James's part. It *inheres* in the psychic texture of Victorian gentlemanliness that a "man of emotions controlled by training," with a steadfast "eye upon Downing Street," should find the irresponsible aesthete an object of "baleful fascination," and theatergoing a necessary "corrective to . . . the humiliation [and] bewilderment" of bureaucratic life. Like Ford Madox Ford, who saw how the British colonizer "takes refuge in . . . official optimism" so as not to be "move[d] . . . beyond bearing,"[39] James uses

Sherringham to dissect the typical "Englishman's habit of not being effusive," his combined envy and fear of Nash-like "volatility," and his regrettable "absence of a little undulation" in both character and hair (*TM*, 38, 148, 226, 326, 341, 389, 392).

But James launches a wholesale critique of normative maleness in all its (dis)-guises and venues. Political masculinity is represented not only by the "grotesquely limited" Mr. Macgeorge, whom Julia invokes to whet Nick's jealousy and Parliamentary zeal, but also by Sir Nicholas Dormer, a mediocrity turned household saint by a timely death. Men of the idle aristocracy find their exemplar in Percival Dormer, known for "the infallibility of his rifle" and his frequently indulged "consolation of killing something," while the provincial connoisseur is satirized in the late George Dallow, "too fat and with a congenital thickness of speech" and a "tiresome insistence upon purity and homogeneity" in art (*TM*, 162, 254, 485). Worse still, the wealthy bachelor Charles Carteret, former adviser to Dormer Senior, simultaneously inscribes homosocial power and, in John Carlos Rowe's terms, "epitomizes the deeply repressed homosexual panic at the heart of English patriarchy."[40] "Espousing nothing more reproductive than Sir Nicholas's views" and engendering "nothing but an amiable little family of eccentricities," Carteret proposes to fund Nick's future if he will concede that the pencil and brush are "not the weapons of a gentleman" and conform to type: in short, replicate his father, and then himself in a son (*TM*, 62, 359).

But what to do with young men who are not keen on the fray, or on wielding a manly weapon? It is not clear how Nick is "going to be like papa," as his sister says, when "there is no one like your father," as Lady Agnes counters, but it is perfectly clear that their maneuverings—in collusion with Carteret, Julia, and the "strenuous shade" of Sir Nicholas himself—register a prodigious investment in the outcome of Dormer's masculinity (*TM*, 32, 65). As Richard Dellamora has shown, this kind of anxious campaign to cut Nick's ties to his aesthetic friend from Oxford and install him as politico-paterfamilias instances a growing demand, as England verged on imperial decline, that "gentlemen" distinguish themselves from "effete and ineffectual" nomads like Nash, with their undecided sexing.[41] Not surprisingly, Nash stands nearly alone at the other end of this tug-of-war, trying both to subvert the new vocabularies of medico-juridical censure—it is Dormer who shows "grossness of immorality" for entertaining Carteret's "depraved tastes"—and to thwart Julia's attempt to erect Nick as the proper (heterosexual) English gentleman (*TM*, 265, 127).

As many readers have noticed, the novel is rife with phallic allusiveness, starting with Dormer's parliamentary designation as Julia's "member":[42] she "wants Nick to stand," wants to "bring him in for Harsh," her "nasty little place," a notoriously "tight squeeze" for Liberal candidates; evidently politics, not art, is the realm of easy virtue, for although Dormer remains Julia's top choice, "she'll go over for her man . . . the fellow that stands, whoever he is" (*TM,* 35–36, 166–67). Yet wordplay of this sort, if nominally more ribald in James's case, seems equally liable to Geoffrey Harpham's stricture on reading Conrad's scatological prose. In the writings of both men, sexuality tends to get "sublated . . . and rerouted . . . into stylistic deformations," or passages in which sexual signifiers gambol beyond authorial control in "the chaotic domain of secondary meanings."[43] One cannot assume, in short, that the campy-critical punning of *The Tragic Muse* is any more conscious than were the "homosexual" ramifications of Mark Ambient's "hysterical aestheticism"; rather, it is just this relative latency or autonomy of narrative effects that claims our attention as a biographical and cultural symptom.

As with "The Author of 'Beltraffio,'" this later text, too, gives off mixed and muted signals, in spite of (if not because of) James's greater aplomb on the verbal surface. On the one side, the (homo)sexualized overtones of Nash's vow to extricate Dormer from a political marriage to Julia—"Baleful woman! . . . I'll pull you out!"—*seem* to resonate further in the pointed joke that Gabriel is "never another man" in heteroromantic contests; in the cryptic hint that his "bloom" is guarded because it is "morbid, as if he had been universally inoculated"; and in Nick's surmise that "if a sore spot remained" in Nash's sensibilities "the hand of a woman would be sure to touch it." Yet again the novel contains its own drift, discreetly keeping the mutual attraction between the two friends "not quite sexual"[44] and ridiculing the popular belief that men like Nash repair to "dusky, untidy" dens for dusky, untidy deeds—indeed, that "the comic press . . . [is] restrained by decorum from touching upon the worst of their aberrations" (*TM,* 104, 127, 372, 505).

But if *The Tragic Muse* proliferates in inadvertent, excessive, and finally conflicting meanings—in itself a token of the complex social dynamics it engages—James's conclusion is pat enough, anticipating an insight from (of all people) Wilde's Algy Moncrieff: "in married life three is company and two is none" (*Earnest,* 260). For the novel adumbrates both Nick's eventual "recapture" for heteronormativity and the assimilation of his aberrant "weapons" into the precincts of gentility—all in fulfillment of Nash's prophecy: "Mrs. Dallow will swallow your profession if you'll swallow hers, . . . and every one, beginning with your wife, will forget there is anything queer about you." Dormer's new line of portrait-painting provides not only the axis along which this seizure will occur (as his "perpetual sitter," Julia will dominate his vision) but also the means of Nash's expulsion from the text—both that of the novel and that of "normal" society. Posing for his old friend, Nash feels "infinitely examined and handled," fixed by Nick's "certainty of eye" from a position of "almost insolent vantage"; tellingly, this conversion from ironic observer to scrutinized object robs Nash of his strategic banter and composure (he becomes "silent, restless, gloomy, dim"), prompting his last resort of "melt[ing] back" into "the ambient air." As if this forced evacuation (or evaporation) were not enough, James emphasizes Nash's resistance to representation—to cultural surveillance, and the regulation that follows in its train—in the fantasy that his image is "gradually fading from the canvas" (*TM*, 259, 507–8, 510–11, 515–16).

As for the man who is left with only this fading canvas, the ending suggests that Nick's concerted program of disavowal—"it represented Gabriel Nash . . . but it doesn't represent . . . anything now"—and rationalization—"Even if [Nash's designs] were perfectly devilish, my good sense has been a match for them"—fails of its aim, proving instead Miriam Rooth's argument: "a demon that's kept under is a shabby little demon." Provoked to "unreasoning resentment" by the reproach of Nash's portrait, Nick isolates and punishes it—"jamm[ing] it into its corner, with its face against the wall"—in order to get on with his marriage and his tepid career in art (*TM*, 412, 515, 518). The overt meaning of this violent act—that Dormer recognizes how his achievements will fall short of Nash's dreams for him—should not mask the fact that it gestures toward more painful losses as well. If Sara Blair is right that "the novel's ambivalence about the forms of otherness with which it identifies" terminates when it "ambivalently contracts" in a finale of conservative marital comedy,[45] one *particular* form of otherness—male–male desire—seems decisive in this retrenchment.

*　*　*

"You can't have been a fable—otherwise you would have
had a moral. . . . I'm not sure you won't have had one."
—Nick Dormer to Gabriel Nash, *The Tragic Muse*

In a loose analogy to Oscar Wilde's shifting iconography in England's sociopolitical narrative, Gabriel Nash marks the spot in English fiction that would one day yield such characters as E. M. Forster's Risley, with his Stracheyesque flourishes and "unmanly superlatives" (*Maurice*, 31), and Evelyn Waugh's Anthony Blanche, with his reappropriative riffs on the discourse of "degeneracy" and the "obscure and less easily classified libido" of homosexual panic.[46] In Nash, that is, James sketched a proto-gay character but smudged those lineaments that were most personally offensive to him and most susceptible to the "complicated, ingenious machinery" of law and order that would soon enmesh Wilde. As part of this delicate balancing between homophobic and homophilic impulses, James toyed with the hope that Style itself—one's "rendering of the text," as Nash calls it—might constitute a world elsewhere, removed from the risks of both normative and innovative masculinities, as well as an all-purpose defense against society's new instrumentalities for probing one's "much exposed" modesty (*TM*, 27, 120).

As James would write to Gosse on the eve of the Wilde trials, Pater had successfully negotiated with publicity by cultivating "the mask without the face"—"there isn't in his total superficies a tiny point of vantage for the newspaper to flap its wings on"—but then Pater had been "negative & faintly-grey."[47] Symonds had erred on the other side, as James came to feel in that same anxious season, evincing a "need of taking the public into his *intimissima* confidence" that was "almost insane."[48] For in this era of "skewed scales and judicial wig," with the "vicious-looking switch" waving in the air—James's metaphor for criticism, but borrowed from quite another punitive regime—the best tactic for queer comrades was to keep the body of their text private by keeping it lively and elusive, "conspicuously . . . draped" in the "amplitude of costume" that is style (*EL*, 1232). In a word, it was only *as* a figure that an "Oscar Wilde figure" stood any real chance of survival.

Yet James's fable contains another moral, more fundamental if less obvious even to the author himself. In the character of Gabriel Nash, *The Tragic Muse* presents a mere "photograph of the ghost" of homosexuality, to adapt Dormer's phrase for his own picture of the aesthete. Nonetheless, that ghost promises to haunt modern culture in ceaseless "disruptive return[s]" from its exile at the "constitutive outside" of the heterosexual domain (*TM*, 509).[49] What else are we to make of Nash's final speech, uttered in that queerly seductive voice and in accents of "unusual seriousness": "I dare say I'm eternal" (*TM*, 511)?

Notes

Thanks to David McWhirter for including an early version of this piece on the Modern Language Association panel "Henry James and Queer Theory" (1995). Thanks also to Joseph Bristow for his help with the essay.

1. See Regenia Gagnier, *Idylls of the Marketplace: Oscar Wilde and the Victorian Public* (Stanford: Stanford University Press, 1986), 103; Richard Ellmann, *Oscar Wilde* (New York: Knopf, 1988), 179; Jonathan Freedman, *Professions of Taste: Henry James, British Aestheticism, and Commodity Culture* (Stanford: Stanford University Press, 1990), 183.

2. Henry James, *The Tragic Muse* (1890; Harmondsworth: Penguin, 1978 [text following the first ed.]), 240, 298. All subsequent references are cited parenthetically as *TM*.

3. David McWhirter, "Restaging the Hurt: Henry James and the Artist as Masochist," *Texas Studies in Literature and Language* 33, no. 4 (Winter 1991): 466.

4. *Henry James: The Contemporary Reviews*, ed. Kevin J. Hayes (Cambridge: Cam-

bridge University Press, 1996), 221, 224, 238 [hereafter cited as *CR*]; Joseph Litvak, *Caught in the Act: Theatricality in the Nineteenth-century English Novel* (Berkeley and Los Angeles: University of California Press, 1992), 276.

5. Alan Sinfield, *The Wilde Century: Effeminacy, Oscar Wilde and the Queer Moment* (New York: Columbia University Press, 1994), 2–3; the latter phrase, of course, is from E. M. Forster's *Maurice* (New York: Norton, 1971), 159. In scouring *The Tragic Muse* and Gabriel Nash for signs of homosexual discourse or representation of queer experience, it is useful to heed Sinfield's comment on *Dorian Gray:* while "the whole book is pervaded with queerness," the "queer image refuses to cohere—refuses to meet our expectation that there will be a character in the twentieth-century Wildean image" (100–1). Joseph Bristow likewise cites "the notorious invisibility—and yet unwavering implication—of same-sex desire" in Wilde's contemporaneous work; "'A complex multiform creature': Wilde's sexual identities," *The Cambridge Companion to Oscar Wilde*, ed. Peter Raby (Cambridge University Press, 1997), 204.

6. Philip Horne, "Henry James: The master and the 'queer affair' of 'The Pupil,'" *Critical Quarterly* 37, no. 3 (Autumn 1995), 81.

7. Lynda Zwinger, "Bodies That Don't Matter: The Queering of 'Henry James,'" *Modern Fiction Studies* 41, nos. 3–4 (Fall-Winter 1995), 658. Zwinger warns against reductive readings of the fiction as the "repository of James's own unacted sex acts"; instead, it "anatomizes the key structures of sexuality per se—how it is constructed, policed, exchanged, perpetuated" and gravitates toward stress points at which the hetero-norm of the bourgeois Anglo-Saxon family (e.g., the Dormers) is "vulnerable to deviation and perversion" (667).

8. Christopher Lane, "The Impossibility of Seduction in James's *Roderick Hudson* and *The Tragic Muse*," *American Literature* 68, no. 4 (December 1996), 750, 755. More broadly, Sara Blair argues that the novel's exploration of self-renovative opportunities in modern cosmopolitanism brings on an "involuntary movement of defense" and that its subversive energies are "ultimately redirected, so as to protect James's project of culture-building against both provincial Anglo-Saxonism and incursion by more virulently transgressive forces," among them "decadents, anarchists, homosexuals, aliens and Jews"; see *Henry James and the Writing of Race and Nation* (Cambridge: Cambridge University Press, 1996), 134.

9. Henry James, *Literary Criticism: French Writers, Other European Writers, The Prefaces to the New York Edition,* ed. Leon Edel (New York: Library of America, 1984), 1062–63 [hereafter cited as *FW*].

10. *The Diary of Alice James,* ed. Leon Edel (New York: Dodd, Mead, 1964), 98–99; *The Notebooks of Henry James,* ed. F. O. Matthiessen and Kenneth B. Murdock (New York: George Braziller, 1955), 84, 265 [hereafter cited as *N*]. On the criminal law amendments, Rosebery, Curzon, Henley, and Lockwood, see Richard Dellamora, *Masculine Desire: The Sexual Politics of Victorian Aestheticism* (Chapel Hill: University of North Carolina Press, 1990), chap. 10; and Ed Cohen, *Talk on the Wilde Side: Toward*

a Genealogy of a Discourse on Male Sexualities (New York: Routledge, 1993); on James's friendship with Ross, see Ann Thwaite, *Edmund Gosse: A Literary Landscape, 1849–1928* (Chicago: University of Chicago Press, 1984), 358–63. Also before *The Tragic Muse,* James knew socially Count Robert de Montesquiou, of Huysmans and Proust fame, and the "little infantile Lord Ronald Gower—not so handsome as his name," who would have an affair with James's beloved Morton Fullerton; Henry James, *Letters,* 4 vols., ed. Leon Edel (Cambridge: Harvard University Press, 1974–84), 2:99, 102; 3:93; 4:731 [hereafter cited as *L*].

11. See Ellmann, *Wilde,* 178–79, and Freedman, *Professions of Taste,* chap. 4.

12. Evan Charteris, *The Life and Letters of Sir Edmund Gosse* (London: Heinemann, 1931), 178; Wendy Graham, "Henry James's Subterranean Blues: A Rereading of *The Princess Casamassima,*" *Modern Fiction Studies* 40, no. 1 (Spring 1994), 53.

13. Sheldon M. Novick, whose *Henry James: The Young Master* (New York: Random House, 1996) stirred controversy by positing a youthful affair between James and Oliver Wendell Holmes, views Nash as "the passive, manipulative" "villain" of *The Tragic Muse.* Novick has since back-pedaled from his biographical speculation, calling it "no more than an interpretation" (James Family List, 12/19/96, 8/28/96).

14. Litvak, *Caught in the Act,* 274.

15. Freedman, *Professions of Taste,* 172.

16. Henry James, "The Author of 'Beltraffio,'" in *The Complete Tales of Henry James,* vol. 5, ed. Leon Edel (Philadelphia: Lippincott), 303 [hereafter cited as "AB"]. Edel's text is taken from *Stories Revived* (London, 1885) and thus substantially follows the original form in *English Illustrated Magazine* (June–July 1884). As Phyllis Grosskurth observes, "Many people have the vague but mistaken impression that [Symonds] was associated with the aesthetes of the *fin de siècle* . . . an association . . . [that] would have been an anathema to him" (introduction to *The Memoirs of John Addington Symonds* [London: Hutchinson, 1984], 13 [hereafter cited as *Memoirs*]). When Wilde sent him *Dorian Gray,* Symonds found it engaging but "unwholesome" and feared that its "morbid & perfumed manner of treating such psychological subjects" would "confirm the prejudices of the vulgar" (*The Letters of John Addington Symonds,* ed. Herbert M. Schueller and Robert L. Peters, vols. 2, 3 [Detroit: Wayne State University Press, 1968–69], 3:477–78 [hereafter cited as *Letters*]).

17. Fred Kaplan, *Henry James: The Imagination of Genius* (New York: Morrow, 1992), 301–2. As Symonds's memoirs make clear, his visit to London in February 1877 (when he met James) was accounted for by his Renaissance lectures at the Royal Institution, and not even his doctor suspected him of passing an afternoon with a "splendid naked piece of manhood" in a brothel near the Regent's Park Barracks. That Symonds was in the midst of a homophobically charged campaign for the Oxford chair in poetry would have made a further cause for secrecy; see *Memoirs,* 254–56, and Dellamora, *Masculine Desire,* 158–64. On the James–Symonds relation, see also Wendy Graham, "Henry James's Thwarted Love," *Genders* 20 (Fall 1994): 66–95.

18. E. M. Forster, *Commonplace Book,* ed. Philip Gardner (Stanford: Stanford University Press, 1985), 224.

19. Quoted in Dellamora, *Masculine Desire,* 157.

20. Thwaite, *Edmund Gosse,* 182, 322; Dellamora, *Masculine Desire,* 23.

21. See Virginia Harlow, *Thomas Sergeant Perry: A Biography* (Durham, N.C.: Duke University Press, 1950), 313. In March 1888, Symonds consulted Perry on the history of *paiderastia* in preparation for *A Problem in Modern Ethics* (1891), another work he vowed to keep "in obscurity" (*Letters,* 3:302). I have found no evidence that Perry ever received *Greek Ethics* or *Modern Ethics,* but again the hazy operations of the Victorian men's lending library militate against certainty. It seems vital to understanding the tensions involved in confidential communication that not even Gosse saw *Greek Ethics* until the end of 1889 (eight years after its printing), and that (contra Edel) Gosse did not share *Modern Ethics* with James until January 1893, two years after he had seen Symonds's proofs (*Letters,* 3:436); see Edel, *Henry James: A Life* (New York: Harper and Row, 1985), 438.

22. In his compelling brief for the value of "erotic [reader] response" to the "sentimentally attaching power" of literature, *Closet Writing/Gay Reading: The Case of Melville's "Pierre"* (Chicago: University of Chicago Press, 1993), James Creech interprets James's feeler to Symonds as "textual cruising," irresistible even to a man so "frightened [and] vulnerable"; but it is unclear why "we must read" an 1884 letter as if it were informed by an emotional state and a political climate that would not fully obtain until the Wilde trials, a decade later (see pp. 44, 51, 96–97).

23. As Symonds had only daughters, the fact that his fictional counterpart has only a son reveals James's dramatic intuition at work: patriarchal culture has more at stake, and more anxiously, in the proper molding of Dolcino. James's sense of the gothic intensity of this social interest is underlined here by the conjunction of "poison" and the character-name Beatrice, borrowed from Hawthorne's "Rappaccini's Daughter."

24. James's belated recognitions show also in his suggestive revisions; the narrator's matter-of-fact "So I never touched Dolcino" becomes "So I never laid a longing hand on Dolcino"; the simple *"Beltraffio"* ("AB," 355) becomes "the black 'Beltraffio,'" a much more dangerous manual of alterity; and Beatrice's "long, slender hands" ("AB," 311), which intervene so destructively in this quarrel over an emergent masculinity, become the "slightly too osseous hands" of death itself; for these later variants, see Henry James, *Stories of Writers and Artists,* ed. F. O. Matthiessen (New York: New Directions, 1903), 86, 94, 58.

25. See Terry Castle, *The Apparitional Lesbian: Female Homosexuality and Modern Culture* (New York: Columbia University Press, 1993), chap. 7.

26. *Selected Letters of Henry James to Edmund Gosse, 1882–1915: A Literary Friendship,* ed. Rayburn S. Moore (Baton Rouge: Louisiana State University Press, 1988), 32.

27. D. A. Miller, *The Novel and the Police* (Berkeley and Los Angeles: University of California Press, 1988), 205–6; Thwaite, *Edmund Gosse,* 320.

28. Henry James, "The Pupil," in *Tales of Henry James*, ed. Christof Wegelin (New York: Norton, 1984), 192; *The Ambassadors*, ed. S. P. Rosenbaum (New York: Norton, 1964), 118.

29. Henry James, *Literary Criticism: Essays on Literature, American Writers, English Writers*, ed. Leon Edel (New York: Library of America, 1984), 1283 [hereafter cited as *EL*].

30. Harlow, *Perry*, 317; Ellmann, *Wilde*, 156; *Letters*, 3: 710.

31. Because affinities between James and Wilde have been harder to see than differences (not least by the two artists themselves), it helps to invoke a contemporary critic like the New England tastemaker T. W. Higginson, who complained in 1879 that James (unlike Howells) failed to represent the "vigorous and breezy natural man" and who reviewed Wilde's 1882 *Poems* under the title "Unmanly Manhood"; see "Henry James, Jr.," in *The Question of Henry James: A Collection of Critical Essays*, ed. F. W. Dupee (London: Allan Wingate, 1957), 21; and Sinfield, *Wilde Century*, 3–4.

32. Oscar Wilde, *The Importance of Being Earnest*, in *Plays* (Harmondsworth: Penguin, 1974), 303 [hereafter cited as *Earnest*].

33. Thus Ellmann, *Wilde*, 179.

34. Sinfield, *Wilde Century*, 3.

35. Ellmann, *Wilde*, 38.

36. Lee Edelman, *Homographesis: Essays in Gay Literary and Cultural Theory* (New York: Routledge, 1994), 12.

37. James Eli Adams, *Dandies and Desert Saints: Styles of Victorian Masculinity* (Ithaca: Cornell University Press, 1995), 192, 186.

38. Nina Auerbach, *Communities of Women: An Idea in Fiction* (Cambridge: Harvard University Press, 1978), 133.

39. Ford Madox Ford, *The Spirit of the People* (1907), excerpted in *Writing Englishness, 1900–1950: An Introductory Sourcebook on National Identity*, ed. Judy Giles and Tim Middleton (London: Routledge, 1995), 46.

40. John Carlos Rowe, "Racial, Sexual, and Aesthetic Politics in *The Tragic Muse*," chap. 4 of *The Other Henry James* (Durham, N.C.: Duke University Press, 1998), 94.

41. Dellamora, *Masculine Desire*, 199.

42. McWhirter, "Restaging the Hurt," 465.

43. Geoffrey Galt Harpham, *One of Us: The Mastery of Joseph Conrad* (Chicago: University of Chicago Press, 1996), 176–80.

44. Rowe, "Racial, Sexual," 92.

45. Blair, *Henry James*, 155.

46. Evelyn Waugh, *Brideshead Revisited* (Boston: Little, Brown, 1945). Like Nash, Blanche points to the mutually constitutive relation between sexual normativity and national-cultural loyalty, resisting "attempt[s] . . . to make an Englishman of him" and becoming "a nomad of no nationality." More concertedly than James, and without Forster's animus toward the "effeminate" aesthete, Waugh criticizes men who exorcise

same-sex passion by scapegoating gays and who reproduce "cretinous, porcine sons" for the further (de)generation of the race (46–50). On Forster, see Joseph Bristow, *Effeminate England: Homoerotic Writing after 1885* (New York: Columbia University Press, 1995), 55–99.

47. Moore, *Selected Letters*, 120.

48. Kaplan, *James*, 403–4.

49. Judith Butler, *Bodies That Matter: On the Discursive Limits of "Sex"* (New York: Routledge, 1993), 9–10.

NINE

George Santayana and the Beauty of Friendship

CHRISTOPHER LANE

> There is a mystery [to the] union of one whole man
> with another whole man. . . .
> —George Santayana, "Friendships," *Soliloquies in England and Later
> Soliloquies,* 56

> It's a popular error to suppose that Puritanism
> has anything to do with purity.
> —Santayana, *The Last Puritan,* 13

George Santayana was not the first writer or philosopher to reflect on the sexual constituents of aesthetics and creativity. An elaborate history of this reflection would return us—via Arnold, Pater, Ruskin, Newman, and Carlyle, to name only the most obvious Victorian aestheticians—to Aristotle's *Poetics* and Plato's *Symposium.*[1] Santayana's literary and philosophical work is notable, however, for highlighting sexuality's turbulent relationship with aesthetics. Despite his immense intellectual effort to the contrary, Santayana displays for us a profound conceptual difficulty about desire and eroticism that not only influenced late-Victorian debates about aesthetics and sexuality, but anticipated Freud's earliest discussions of creativity and sublimation.[2] In his recent study *George Santayana: A Biography,* John McCormick confirms this reading: "Santayana applied certain findings of recent psychology to aesthetics, a novel and even startling procedure in 1896, particularly in his suggestion that sex and aesthetics are allied. . . . Santayana's argument derived in part from Stendhal's *De l'amour,* but it also anticipated Freudian theory."[3]

Santayana's lectures on aesthetics, given at Harvard at the cusp of the last century and published in 1896 under the title *The Sense of Beauty,* also partially bridge a transatlantic gap among scholars and writers in Boston, Oxford, and London. Writing to Thomas Munro from Rome on December 13, 1928, for example, Santayana insisted retrospectively that he was

> not very much later than Ruskin, Pater, Swinburne, and Matthew Arnold:
> our atmosphere was that of poets and persons touched with religious en-
> thusiasm or religious sadness. Beauty (which mustn't be mentioned now)
> was then a living presence, or an aching absence, day and night: history

was always singing in our ears: and not even psychology or the analysis of works of art could take away from art its human implications. It was the great memorial to us, the great revelation, of what the soul had lived on, and had lived with, in her better days.[4]

"But now," Santayana laments, "analysis and psychology seem to stand alone: there is no spiritual interest, no spiritual need. The mind, in this direction, has been *desiccated*" (239; original emphasis). Elaborating on Santayana's inadvertent contribution to this psychic "desiccat[ion]," I offer here a reading of the impact—both violent and strangely conducive—of sexuality on Santayana's life and theories of artistic pleasure. Departing from standard approaches to Santayana's work claiming that he successfully transvalued sexuality into art or, related, that sexuality was basically irrelevant to his philosophy and life,[5] I contend that for Santayana the relations among art, desire, and object-choice ironically became troubled, even antagonistic, when he sought in art a redemptive and desexualizing power. Santayana occasionally sexualized beauty and creativity, but what interests me more is the conceptual labor informing his aesthetic theory—a type of philosophical overreach deriving in part from Santayana's desire to bridge the work of such diverse influences as Plato, Keats, Schopenhauer, Lotze, Emerson, William James, and Pater. One effect of this overreach, I suggest, is a fascinating oscillation between passion and asceticism, which fosters in *The Last Puritan* (1935) what Mario Van de Weyer, Santayana's friend, calls "Puritanism Self-condemned."[6] Santayana concurs, somewhat tautologically: "Puritanism is a natural reaction against nature" (11).[7] Building on these and related suggestions in Santayana's love sonnets and *The Sense of Beauty*, I think it is appropriate—if slightly anachronistic—to consider these works an inadvertent contribution to late Victorian accounts of sexual desire.

Santayana's precise willingness to conflate persons and things assists our interpretive aims; he frequently sees people as works of art and art as the study of people. Santayana certainly does not consider art and life homologous, but as susceptible to the influence of comparable passions.[8] In *Persons and Places* (1944), he argues that similitude between persons and things arises when the subject binds itself too closely to an object, an argument building on related claims in Plato's *Phaedrus* and Arthur Schopenhauer's *World as Will and Idea* (1818). Santayana remarks, "To possess things and persons in idea is the only pure good to be got out of them; to possess them physically or legally is a burden and a snare. . . . A perfect love is founded on despair."[9] Underscoring this burden's psychic implications, *The Sense of Beauty* argues that "the human mind is a turbulent commonwealth."[10]

In claiming that Santayana's philosophy assisted contemporaneous theories of art and sexuality, I want to distinguish the type of generic, object-less love and pleasure recurring in his work from what is often called "self-love" or "narcissism." I take this distinction from Santayana himself, who argued: "The *perfect* lover must renounce pursuit and the hope of possession. His person and life must, in his own eyes, fall altogether out of the picture. . . . It is therefore psychologically not only possible but normal for the passion of love to be self-forgetful, and to live on in the very act of sacrifice and personal despair. So transformed, the great passion becomes worship" (*Persons* 428–29; original emphasis).

How close is this argument to suggestions of self-annihilation and even of passion's ability to destroy us? After all, while Santayana tries to distance his argument about passion from Stendhal's accounts of *"l'amour-physique"* and *"l'amour de vanité"*—terms that Santayana rejects as "obviously imperfect and impure" (428)—he nonetheless wants to conceptualize a type of "passion of love, sublimated, [that] does not become bloodless, or free from bodily trepidation" (429). The fundamental *difficulty* he attributes to sexual desire is thus distinct from the relative calm he finds in creativity and oblation: "Falling in love is often fatal and involuntary," he warns,

> although it can sometimes be headed off; but then reason and duty come in, in a strong soul, to suppress or sacrifice the passion. But what is reason or duty? Either another passion—the passion for harmony and integrity in the soul—or social conventions, expediencies, and taboos. Against everything of the latter kind a transcendental free spirit rebels; and there I see the secret of tragic strength being often mixed with an extraordinary fatalistic weakness. (473)

Let us consider the implications of this "extraordinary . . . weakness," asking too how the ensuing psychic hemorrhage affects Santayana's ideas of beauty, particularly beauty in another person—and even in another man. *The Sense of Beauty* aims, in McCormick's words, "to define aesthetics and to explain its naturalistic base in psychology" (123); it strives initially to distinguish object love from love of people, arguing that "sex is not the *only* object of sexual passion" (*Sense* 40; emphasis added). Here Santayana implies and withholds a claim—which Socrates and Phaedrus debate extensively in Plato's *Phaedrus*, and which Freud, Santayana's contemporary, later refined—that oblation, narcissism, and creativity all obtain from "sexual passion."[11] It may shock Santayana scholars to link the apparently asexual philosopher with Plato *and* Freud, but Santayana tells us clearly in 1896 that "passion . . . overflows and visibly floods those neighbouring regions which it had always secretly watered" (*Sense* 40).[12] And all three thinkers concur, in Santayana's words, that "halfway between vital and social functions, lies the sexual instinct" (37). In Freud's work, however, this "halfway" point is not sexuality detached from an object, but a modified form of homosexuality he calls "sensuous" same-sex attachments. In

Group Psychology and the Analysis of the Ego (1921), Freud claims that the "emotional tie" is the "successor to a completely 'sensual' object-tie with the person in question or rather with that person's prototype (or *imago*),"[13] and the "person in question" for Freud—given his focus here and elsewhere on masculine identification—is invariably male.

Although Santayana did not formulate the same claim unequivocally, his work on beauty represents subjects, society, and sexuality as similarly fraught with problems of "connexion" (*Sense* 37). Ostensibly, these are connections between men and women in which beauty seems to bind an otherwise fraught social and psychic gap. Later in *The Sense of Beauty*, however, the distinction initially sought between persons and things shifts to one between procreation and sexual beauty, and here things get complicated. "Beauty," Santayana writes, "borrows warmth . . . precisely from the waste, from the radiation of the sexual passion" (38). Here he differs slightly from Freud, who tried initially to give sublimated drives a type of purity untarnished by psychic waste—untarnished, that is, by the homoerotic factor making sublimation possible;[14] like Santayana's, Freud's conception of sublimation failed entirely in this regard.[15] Santayana's notion that beauty emerges from a depletion or *wasting* of desire nonetheless points up his complicated relation to late-nineteenth-century arguments about passion and asceticism, and this tension is the fundamental interest of my essay.[16]

McCormick notes that toward the end of 1887, when Santayana (then twenty-four) was in Berlin studying the philosophy of Rudolf Hermann Lotze, he wrote William Morton Fullerton, a friend from Harvard and an "exquisite rakehell, probably both homo- and heterosexual, . . . [later] the lover of the Ranee of Sarawak and of Edith Wharton, among others" (37), asking: "What is one to do with one's amatory instincts?" Santayana expatiates at length on this problem, claiming that after

> a boy lives to his twelfth or fifteenth year . . . in a state of mental innocence, . . . he grows more and more uncomfortable, his imagination is more and more occupied with obscene things. Every scrap of medical or other knowledge he hears on the subject he remembers. Some day he tries experiments with some girl, or with some other boy. This is, I say, supposing he has not been corrupted intentionally and taken to whorehouses in his boyhood as some are, or fallen a victim to paiderastia, as is the lot of others. But in some way or other, sooner or later, the boy gets his first experience in the art of love. Now, I say, what is a man to do about it? It is no use saying that he should be an angel, because he isn't. Even if he holds himself in, and only wet dreams violate his virginity, he is not an angel because angels don't have wet dreams. He must choose among the following:

Amatory attitudes
1. Wet dreams and the fidgets.
2. Mastibation [*sic*, written in Boston dialect].
3. Paiderastia.
4. Whoring.
5. Seductions or a mistress.
6. Matrimony.

I don't put a mistress as a separate heading because it really comes under 4, 5, or 6, as the case may be. A man who takes a mistress from among prostitutes, shares her with others, and leaves her soon, is practically whoring. A man whose mistress is supposed to be respectable is practically seducing her. A man who lives openly with his mistress and moves in her sphere is practically married. Now I see fearful objections to every one of these six amatory attitudes. 1 and 6 have the merit of being virtuous, but it is their only one. 2 has nothing in its favor. The discussion is therefore confined to 3, 4, and 5. 4 has the disadvantage of ruining the health. 5 has the disadvantage of scenes and bad social complications—children, husbands at law, etc. One hardly wants to spend one's youth in acting French dramas. 3 has therefore been often preferred by impartial judges, like the ancients and orientals, yet *our prejudices against it are so strong that it hardly comes under the possibilities for us.* What shall we do? Oh matrimony, truly thou art an inevitable evil!

As you perceive, I do not consider sentimental love at all in my pros and cons. It is only a disturbing force, as far as the true amatory instincts are concerned. Of course it has the same origin, but just as insanity may spring from religion, so sentimental love may spring from the sexual instinct. The latter, however, being intermittent, which religion is not, the insanity produced is temporary. Here is a serious letter for you: now answer it like a man and a Christian (in the better sense of the word, which is "a fellow such as I approve of"). (Quoted in McCormick 70–71; emphasis added)

McCormick adds, "No answer from Fullerton to Santayana's unusual letter survives. Homosexuality is absent from the list of amatory attitudes, an irony of omission, perhaps" (71). He refers here to the fact that in 1887 Benjamin Jowett suspended Santayana's close friend and perhaps subsequent lover, John Francis Stanley, second Earl Russell (Bertrand Russell's older brother), from Balliol College, Oxford, because "a scandalous letter of Russell's had come to light" acknowledging that Lionel Johnson (Santayana's and Russell's mutual friend) "had spent a night in R[ussell]'s room" (quoted 65). Refusing to admit that he and Johnson had spent a night together, Russell later belabored his "innocence" so extensively in his autobiography that even Santayana, reading Russell's patently absurd claim—"I was entirely possessed by that white virginal flame of innocence which I think is even stronger in adolescent boys than in girls"—acknowledged, in a "private" aside to himself, "This is true as regards Lionel Johnson and Russell, but it is a lie if applied to R. in his general habits—a cheeky lie, when so many of his readers know the facts" (quoted in McCormick 65). Yet while Santayana's October 20, 1929, letter to Russell overall is quite revealing of the two men's intimacy, in *Persons and Places* Santayana speaks only elliptically of Russell's "petty vices, which gave him infinite trouble and no pleasure" (309). In an interesting aside, however, he does admit that "what damned [Russell] was not the things of which he was accused . . . , but his own perverse way of *wasting* his opportunities" (309; emphasis added). In other words—and with embarrassing practical and conceptual consequences—the ideal of sublimation again surfaced as a failed imperative.

Santayana's letter to Fullerton and subsequent remarks about Russell aid us greatly in determining his own critical relation to sexual drives. Many other examples illustrate this relative crisis. When recalling the poet A. E. Housman in 1929, Santayana remarked to Daniel Cory, his friend and confidant: "I suppose Housman was really what people nowadays call 'homosexual.'" According to Cory, Santayana added, "as if he were primarily speaking to himself: 'I think I must have been that way in my Harvard days—although I was unconscious of it at the time.'"[17] Much later, on August 17, 1945, Santayana wrote Cyril Clemens, claiming that when dining with Housman many years earlier, the poet "was amiably silent. However, I had meantime read *The Shropshire Lad,* and *Last Poems,* and now *More Poems,* always with tears. There is not much else than tears in them, but they are perfect of their kind" (quoted in McCormick 118). Responding to this and similar preoccupations, McCormick notes of Santayana's 1929 conversation with Cory,

> Santayana may have consciously misled the young man who might become his Boswell; or Cory, always at pains to present his subject in the best light, may have edited Santayana's words. It is hardly credible that a man of Santayana's education, urbanity, and circle of acquaintance could have remained unconscious of his own tendencies until sixty-five. He knew enough Greek to gather that not all love in Plato's circle was Platonic; he knew Tacitus on the later Roman emperors; and he lived through Oscar Wilde's trial[s] in 1895, his imprisonment and exile. Nor could the house guest of Howard Sturgis at Windsor and the classmate and friend of William Fullerton be unaware of homosexuality as a word or as a fact of many men's lives. (51)

To repeat: "What is one to do with one's amatory instincts?" (quoted in McCormick 70). Nine years after asking Fullerton this question, Santayana engaged it philosophically in *The Sense of Beauty* when, to quote a line from one of his 1896 "sublimated love sonnets," he tried to explain why "[t]he spirit [must] purge away its proper dross."[18] The "purge" wasn't always successful;

indeed, it remained something of an ongoing disturbance in Santayana's literary and philosophical work. Many years later, in *Realms of Being* (1927–38), Santayana therefore avowed that "carnal pleasures . . . , which are but welcome pains, draw the spirit inwards into primal darkness and indistinction."[19] Despite his subsequent claims about the mind's "desiccat[ion]," Santayana represents the unconscious here not as a benign influence, but as a cause of internal havoc: "The chained dogs below keep on barking in their kennels."[20]

Numerous cultural and philosophical influences converge in these statements. In striving to illuminate the affective, even erotic hinge between subjects and groups, however, Santayana and his contemporaries turned more often to Plato than to Marx and Engels. In August 1896, Santayana wrote Conrad Slade from Oxford, noting, "My idea is to go on with my writing, but at the same time to see something of people, and if possible to read a little Plato, and see what the aesthetic religious and philosophical atmosphere in England is now-a-days" (*Letters* 45). The following year, he wrote Guy Murchie from Cambridge, England, noting, "I am now at work on an exposition and defence of Plato's bad treatment of poets, whom, as you may know, he banished from his republic as trivial and demoralizing persons"; he added that he would teach a course primarily on Plato when he returned to Harvard (57, 56). To make sense of Santayana's work on object-choice and creativity, we must therefore briefly revisit Plato's arguments about love and desire.[21]

In the *Symposium*, Plato has Diotima tell Socrates that love arises as a power "between [the] divine and mortal" (202E). Diotima adds that love's power lies in "[i]nterpreting and transporting human things to the gods and divine things to men; entreaties and sacrifices from below, and ordinances and requitals from above: being *midway* (ἐυ μέσω) between, it makes each to supplement the other, so that the whole is combined in one" (202E; emphasis added).[22] By representing love as a go-between, transporting (διαπορθμεῦον—literally, "carrying across") "entreaties and sacrifices" from men to gods, and "ordinances and requitals" from gods to men, Plato uses Diotima to suggest not that love rescinds—or leaves behind—the erotic, but just the reverse: Love exists in addition to the erotic, she insists, arguing later that previous and "lesser" loves should be "used as steps" (ὥσπερ ἐπαναβαθμοῖς χρώμενον; 211C) to attaining a greater—and still physical—form of love.[23] Thus it would be wrong to claim that love and the erotic are mutually exclusive in Plato's philosophy.

By reproducing this argument alongside Diotima's related claim that "procreation in the beautiful" (τόκος ἐν καλῷ, 206C; or, as other translations put it, "giving birth in beauty" and "begetting on a beautiful thing by means of both the body and the soul") is more alluring than biological procreation, Santayana molded Plato's aesthetic arguments to late-Victorian Hellenistic conceptions of art and masculine beauty. For this reason, however, Santayana's conception of love and beauty is not devoid of tension. Indeed, in reproducing Diotima's depiction of love as a *dynamic* intermediary between "gods . . . and men," Santayana grasps that love rarely forms a stable "supplement" between gods and men, such that "the whole is combined in one" (202E). He finds instead that love arises as a volatile excess, pushing the lover *(erastēs) beyond* the beloved *(erōmenos)* in ways that point up both parties' mutual deficiencies.

Although I will later analyze Santayana's 1896 sonnets in some detail, it seems useful to illustrate two examples of his poetry's affective turbulence. In Sonnet XVI, Santayana tells us,

> A thousand beauties that have never been
> Haunt me with hope and tempt me to pursue;
> The gods, methinks, dwell just behind the blue;
> The satyrs at my coming fled the green.
> The flitting shadows of the grove between
> The dryads' eyes were winking, and I knew
> The wings of sacred Eros as he flew
> And left me to the love of things not seen.
> 'T is a sad love, like an eternal prayer,
> And knows no keen delight, no faint surcease. (98)

Perhaps the first thing we note in this poem is that beauty is not singular. That Santayana invokes a thousand haunting beauties here suggests that no single vision of beauty—and thus desire for a single object—is possible. To put this slightly differently, Santayana's poetic vision engages part objects—imagoes— that surface as recollections belying immediacy and reciprocity; their distorting character *removes* Santayana and his reader from immediate contact with the beloved.

This sonnet counters in tone and substance a number of Santayana's related poems in which his faith in a redemptive deity is strongly pronounced. Whereas in Sonnet XVI the poet likens "sacred Eros" to "an eternal prayer, / [that] knows no keen delight, no faint surcease," in Sonnet XVIII he seems to withdraw this Hellenistic pronouncement: "My angel is come back," he now declares, "Oh, trust in God, and banish rash despair, / That, feigning evil, is itself the curse!" (98, 99). Before we attain this "trust in God," however, we read an ever bleaker, more ironic account of beauty's ability to ensnare the *erō-menos:*

> O subtle Beauty, sweet persuasive worth
> That didst the love of being first inspire,
> We do thee homage both in death and birth.
> Thirsting for thee, we die in thy great dearth,
> Or borrow breath of infinite desire
> To chase thine image through the haunted earth. (99)

If "Beauty" in this sonnet represents the cause of desire (it "didst the love of being first inspire"), it doesn't appease desire but exacerbates it, generating a craving precisely from its failure properly to materialize or impose limits on the poet's erotic demands ("we die in thy great dearth"). In despair, the poet finds himself taunted by a vision whose perfection is unrealizable. Refusing to question the validity or degree of idealization informing this vision, he has no option but "To chase thine image through the haunted earth." In this and similar sonnets, as I shall show, Santayana's conception of desire and beauty does indeed corroborate McCormick's claims that he "applied certain findings of recent psychology to aesthetics" (124).

That Santayana's aesthetic vision oscillates between Victorian and "modern" conceptions of art and beauty may derive from his dissatisfaction with the traditional—or phenomenological—school of aesthetics. As Kailash Chandra Baral claims, this school aimed at "discriminating the aesthetic from the moral and cognitive dimensions of human experience."[24] Yet Santayana also was ill at ease with the "so-called modern school" of aesthetics, which, Baral argues, "put emphasis on [the] psychological interpretation of beauty."[25] In *The Sense of Beauty,* Santayana argues that our understanding of beauty "must be nothing less than the exposition of the origin, place, and elements of beauty as an object of human experience," and he elaborates: "We must learn from [this definition], as far as possible, why, when, and how beauty appears, what conditions an object must fulfill to be beautiful, what elements of our nature make us sensible of beauty, and what the relation is between the constitution of the object and the excitement of our susceptibility" (11).

We are clearly some distance here from Arnold's famous dictum that we "see the object as in itself it really is,"[26] a demand that generally bored Santayana, whose curiosity about "the relation . . . between the constitution of the object and the excitement of our susceptibility" is more amenable to Freud's contemporaneous interest in making clear the role of fantasy in defining external meaning and events (*Sense* 11). In 1897, the year after Santayana gave his lectures on beauty, Freud revised his theory of seduction, placing greater emphasis on the internal apprehension of sexual meaning. Santayana, however, would not, and could not, follow Freud in pursuing the implications of this conceptual reorientation. Some of this resistance is attributable to Santayana's limited (and generally desexualized) conception of the unconscious. *The Sense of Beauty* remains precisely that—an endeavor to locate beauty's "sense," its cognitive dimension. Yet as we'll see, Santayana's perspective on beauty differs only slightly from what Freud would later consider a type of cognitive *disorder,* in which the *object* is understood to elicit fantasy and cause desire.

The gap emerging here between the object and the subject's fantasy of it arises in Santayana's reflections on beauty as the turbulent sensations an object can evoke in its viewer or lover. In his section on "Aesthetic and Physical Plea-sure," Santayana calls these sensations "a complication" (23), immediately after noting the "imagination['s ability to] invade . . . the sober and practical domain of morals" (23).[27] Partly for this reason, he rejects Arnold's and others' faith in the object's immanent beauty as "radically absurd and contradictory" (*Sense* 29), insisting instead that beauty is a "value . . . which affects our senses and which we consequently perceive" (29). At the same time, Santayana acknowl-edges that the subject's sensations about an object, which are "compacted of all the impressions, feelings, and memories, [and] which offer themselves for association, . . . fall within the vortex of the amalgamating imagination" (29).

Here and elsewhere, we see Santayana grappling with the vagaries of fantasy in his wish to theorize not only beauty but the aesthetic basis of sexual attrac-tion. And it's here that *The Sense of Beauty* appears to suffer its greatest (and most interesting) conceptual problem. Santayana introduces aesthetics to bio-logical accounts of sex attraction to illustrate how fantasy pushes us beyond biology and how our interest in objects arises as a compromised choice. The logical result of this argument is an emphasis on heterosexuality's *noninevita-bility;* in enhancing biological attraction, beauty paradoxically projects it into a different ontological register. Thus we read in *The Sense of Beauty,* "The attrac-tion of sex could not become efficient unless the senses were first attracted. The eye must be fascinated and the ear charmed by the object which nature intends should be pursued" (38). Two paragraphs earlier, we see Santayana pushing to improve the "precision" of biology's influence on human procreation to ensure that a man can quickly find "the one female best fitted to bear [his] offspring . . . , leaving *his* energy and attention free at all other times to exercise the other faculties of his nature" (38; emphasis added).

What precisely is Santayana trying to formulate here? Without aesthetics, he declares, "there is a great deal of groping and waste; and the force and con-stancy of the [procreative] instinct must make up for its lack of precision" (38)—an idea echoed in Sonnet XIII: "Why this inane curiosity to grope / In the dim dust for gems' unmeaning ray?" (*Poems* 97). In the next paragraph of *The Sense of Beauty,* Santayana states that if we could somehow perfect biology, the procreative instinct, "like all those perfectly adjusted, would tend to be-come unconscious" (38). And he then reveals the basis of his thesis: "It is *pre-cisely from the waste,* from the radiation of the sexual passion, that beauty bor-rows warmth" (38; emphasis added). Santayana has already told us that the aesthetic, while necessary for perfecting human procreation, ultimately is su-perfluous to it. Put another way, he tells us that the aesthetic is not reducible to sex attraction for reproductive ends; it is instead contingent on what *escapes* this economy as "waste"—that is, as the beauty and passion informing poetry. In ways that Freud would formulate more succinctly twenty-five years later, in

Group Psychology, Santayana theorized for beauty in 1896 what many decadent artists and writers in Europe and Britain struggled to convey in their fiction and poetry: a profound rapport among creativity, beauty, and same-sex desire. Of course, Victorian Hellenists had advanced similar claims nearly five decades before Santayana; his role was to aid the Hellenists' *philosophical* claims, providing theoretical weight to their "spiritual procreancy" precisely when their related emphasis on male love was attacked and legally challenged in Britain.[28]

Santayana represents objects as "organiz[ing]" and "classif[ying] the diffused experiences of life"; they "frame . . . the world . . . out of [a] chaos of impressions" (*Sense* 29). Objects give us a reprieve from formlessness and anxiety, and so are susceptible to idealization, a condition, as we'll see below, on which Santayana frequently elaborates. When the subject invests a specific object with erotic longing, however, the object acquires a different type of "power," combining in the subject "exquisiteness and breathlessness with awe" (37). And by exacerbating the subject's demand still further, the object and the "dumb and powerful [sex] instinct" it elicits "join . . . to possession the keenest pleasure, to rivalry the fiercest rage, and to solitude an eternal melancholy" (39); one might call these passions the vicissitudes of the transference.

Our discussion could widen immeasurably at this point, highlighting parallels with Walter Pater's related discussion of subjectivity and diffusion in *The Renaissance: Studies in Art and Poetry* (1873, revised 1893).[29] We could also enumerate links between Santayana and William James (a mentor he didn't entirely admire) on the issue of autonomy and subjective defenses.[30] To avoid oversimplifying these complex and nonidentical antecedents, however, I want to limit my argument to two claims. First, Santayana's discussion—in *The Sense of Beauty,* his sonnets, and other texts—of the subject's internal ambivalence about love and longing modifies the prevalent claim in Santayana studies that his interests were as ascetic as the philosophy he seemed consistently to espouse.[31] Second (and related), Santayana's misogynistic reduction of women to procreation (the flip side of his and his characters' chaste idealization of them) by inference leaves aesthetics and sexuality—the "surplus" constituency of everyday life—entirely to men.

In light of Santayana's extensive meditations on sex attraction in *The Sense of Beauty* and elsewhere—as well as our discussion of Santayana's erotic passions and McCormick's speculation that in 1896 Santayana may have had "an intense physical affair" with the second Earl Russell (119), Joseph Epstein's impatient response to McCormick's suggestion that Santayana may have had a "homosexual temperament" seems wrong.[32] Insisting that "homosexual temperament" is itself an "unfortunate phrase," Epstein writes that any attention to Santayana's erotic interests is "the sheerest twaddle," for it involves a type of speculation "worthy of Barbara Walters."[33] Such chastening reminders about the intentional fallacy and potential abuses of psychobiography may be useful. But Epstein's point, phrased as *incredulity* about same-sex attraction, not only taints homoeroticism with a type of shame that Santayana never simply endorsed in his writing, but ignores in his philosophy, fiction, and poetry Santayana's profound meditation on the vagaries and psychic complexity of *every* erotic object's "turbulent" impact on the subject.

Let us therefore consider in greater detail how Santayana's philosophy informs his poetry. The importance—and difficulty—of such consideration is suggested by a letter Santayana wrote Henry Ward Abbot on January 16, 1924, calling his "sublimated love sonnets" "an evasion of experience, on the presumption . . . that experience would be a ghastly failure" (*Letters* 208). Such "evasion" and dread of failure did not prevent Santayana from reflecting on love and desire, but no doubt contributed to his difficulty in candidly representing this desire. Thus William G. Holzberger, editor of *The Complete Poems of George Santayana*, wisely notes that the "quest to determine whether a real woman, loved by the poet, generated the Lady of the Sonnets may prove futile in light of an aspect of Santayana's personality ['a tendency toward homosexuality'] that became public recently and that had long been suspected" (52). Santayana partly corroborates this reading: "The lady of the sonnets, far from being the one you absurdly mention [Cory's edition doesn't enlighten us here], is a myth, a symbol: certainly she stands for Somebody, not always for the same Somebody, and generally for a hint or suggestion drawn from reality rather than for any specific passion; but the enthusiasm is speculative, not erotic" (*Letters* 208).

Such admissions relieve us of one interpretive dilemma concerning attribution and the type of authority we might invest in biography. But the problem doesn't end here. Santayana's sonnets are such an insistent account of "prolonged sexual conflict," in McCormick's words (49), that we might gently dispute Santayana's claim that

> love has never made me long unhappy, nor sexual impulse uncomfortable: on the contrary in the comparatively manageable form in which they have visited me, they have been *great fun*, because they have given me an interest in people and (by a natural extension of emotion) in things, places, and stories, such as religion, *which otherwise would have failed me altogether.* (208; final emphasis added)

Engaging these remarkable admissions—particularly the subsequent claim that a "golden light of diffused erotic feeling fall[s] upon . . . the world"—I suggest that Santayana doesn't sustain simple assumptions of homosexual latency or stable object-choice. Instead, he makes clear a related—and perhaps conceptually more interesting—issue: an inability to desexualize aesthetics and creativity. Here I am reengaging my earlier thesis that Santayana's effort to *limit* desire generated a type of philosophical overreach in his work: The effort to absorb only partially congruent theories of desire and beauty exacerbated his loss of control over these elements.

Between 1885 and 1904, Santayana regularly contributed poetry to the *Harvard Monthly,* publishing a collection of these poems in 1894 as *Sonnets and Other Verses.* Holzberger notes that while Sonnets I–XX were written between 1882 and 1893, Sonnets XXI–L were written exclusively in 1895, the year Oscar Wilde was convicted for "gross indecency" and sentenced to two years' imprisonment with hard labor in Reading Gaol (720–22). In 1896, Santayana was on leave in Cambridge, England, and may have had a sexual affair with the second Earl Russell. Of course, we need accept neither McCormick's suggestion here—nor the mounting evidence that Santayana, aged twenty, had already written a number of passionate sonnets for Ward Thoron, then seventeen, and Warwick Potter, then roughly twenty-one—to observe a fascinating tension in Santayana's poetry.[34] This tension arises as an identificatory conflict between Christianity—which enhances Santayana's interest in repose, contemplation, and serenity—and Hellenism—which usually generates in his poetry greater unrest than satisfaction. In the opening sonnet, for instance, particularly its third and fourth lines, we see Santayana torn between Christian and Classical precepts:

> I sought on earth a garden of delight,
> Or island altar to the Sea and Air,
> Where gentle music were accounted prayer,
> And reason, veiled, performed the happy rite.
> My sad youth worshipped at the piteous height
> Where God vouchsafed the death of man to share;
> His love made mortal sorrow light to bear,
> But his deep wounds put joy to shamèd flight.
> And though his arms, outstretched upon the tree,
> Were beautiful, and pleaded my embrace,
> My sins were loth to look upon his face.
> So came I down from Golgotha to thee,
> Eternal Mother; let the sun and sea
> Heal me, and keep me in thy dwelling-place. (91)

One effect of this poetic turbulence is that Christ, who incarnates in "deep wounds" the love that God "vouchsafe[s]" in line six, begins to acquire an erotic significance for the poet. We are told that "his arms . . . / Were beautiful, and pleaded my embrace." In "c[oming] down from Golgotha," the mount on which Christ was crucified,[35] we see the poet—despite his longing to recover Eden—turn not to Christ or God but, out of shame, to "Eternal Mother," perhaps an invocation of Nature gesturing to a more pagan conception of beauty and desire.[36]

In Sonnet II, this brief turn from Christianity, granting Santayana space to advance pagan and Classical motifs, recurs with more insistence than confidence. The transition seems the result of a deliberate *pursuit* of temptation rather than an inadvertent effect of his shame before Christ:

> Slow and reluctant was the long descent,
> With many farewell pious looks behind,
> And dumb misgivings where the path might wind,
> And questionings of nature, as I went.
> The greener branches that above me bent,
> The broadening valleys, quieted my mind,
> To the fair reasons of the Spring inclined
> And to the Summer's tender argument.
> But sometimes, as revolving night descended,
> And in my childish heart the new song ended,
> I lay down, full of longing, on the steep;
> And, haunting still the lonely way I wended,
> Into my dreams the ancient sorrow blended,
> And with these holy echoes charmed my sleep. (91)

To what does the poet descend here? While his "slow and reluctant" task resembles Christ's coming to Earth and Orpheus's descent into Hades to rescue Eurydice, Santayana's "dumb misgivings" are more tentative than Christ's and Orpheus's, and they entail besides—"With many farewell pious looks behind"—"questionings of nature." Such questioning recalls the phrase "*against* nature," used in Santayana's day to represent sodomy as "the sin so horrible that it must not be mentioned among Christians (*peccatum illud horribile, inter Christianos non nominandum*)." Highlighting an awkward affiliation to Christian *and* Classical precepts, the poet concludes: "Into my dreams the ancient sorrow blended, / And with these holy echoes charmed my sleep." These and other lines demonstrate that the poet's conflict isn't solved: He remains "full of longing," haunted by a desire perhaps exacerbated by his earlier "descent," possibly an allusion to sodomy. Certainly, the "dumb misgivings" and "questionings of nature" persist in his sleep, "haunting still the lonely way I wended," as if the final "blend[ing]" of "longing" and "ancient sorrow" can "charm" the poet's sleep only because longing itself is tolerable as a wish informing dreams.

With this turbulent and only partial transition between Christian and Classical precepts, Santayana advances a related proposition—that love, in failing to identify God as its exclusive object, pushes the lover toward narcissism or abjection. In the poetic schema of Santayana's sonnets, the object is often denounced as cruel and inaccessible. By emphasizing this outcome in Sonnet VI,

Santayana argues that love engenders blindness and self-deceit—that the inspiration it generates isn't altruistic, as the lover wants to believe, but entirely self-serving. (This is so even if, as in Sonnet VII, the poet uses love to attempt to disband his identity and to forget himself. "I would I might forget that I am I" [94], he writes, but the very expression of the wish makes the result impossible and the statement a tautology.) Further, by abandoning the claim that love generates wisdom, Santayana urges us in Sonnet VI to refuse love's snares:

> Love not as do the flesh-imprisoned men
> Whose dreams are of a bitter bought caress,
> Or even of a maiden's tenderness
> Whom they love only that she loves again.
> For it is but thyself thou lovest then,
> Or what thy thoughts would glory to possess; (93)

The voice we read here arguably is the Santayana contemporary readers know best—the poet and philosopher bound upon an ascetic course, wisely rejecting the snares of passion and deliberately choosing solitude and skepticism over the folly of infatuation. Doubtless, this is the poetic and philosophical voice Santayana preferred, capturing a strength he struggled privately to maintain. Yet it's not the only voice we hear in his poetry. In Sonnet XXIV, to be sure, this disenchantment and self-questioning seem more pronounced, the poet's persona striving to expose a certain fraudulence in his belief that marriage will make him happy. However, if the drive toward solitude in these poems smothers an impulse to connect, the very urgency of desire radically undermines his anticipation of serene autonomy:

> Although I decked a chamber for my bride,
> And found a moonlit garden for the tryst
> Wherein all flowers looked happy as we kissed,
> Hath the deep heart of me been satisfied?
> The chasm 'twixt our spirits yawns as wide
> Though our lips meet, and clasp thee as I list,
> The something perfect that I love is missed,
> And my warm worship freezes into pride.
> But why—O waywardness of nature!—why
> Seek farther in the world? I had my choice,
> And we said we were happy, you and I.
> Why in the forest should I hear a cry,
> Or in the sea an unavailing voice,
> Or feel a pang to look upon the sky? (106)

The "chasm" invoked in line 5 bears heavily on my immediate argument about Santayana's work as well as my wider thesis, elaborated elsewhere, about propinquity and asymmetry in the Victorian era.[37] If, as the poet ruefully insists, this "chasm 'twixt our spirits yawns as wide / *Though* our lips meet, and clasp thee as I list," the yearning bid for completion that Santayana announces ("The something perfect that I love is missed") may exist not only despite physical intimacy, but crucially *because* of it. Perhaps for this reason, oblation seems to lapse in these sonnets into sterility, even boredom: "And my warm worship freezes into pride." Pride about what? Acknowledging, perhaps, that such "worship" leans on nothing more than a rigid idea of the beloved's perfection.

Resembling key moments in *The Sense of Beauty*, Santayana's frustration with oblation here seems not only to question object-choice (and thus the inevitability of heterosexuality), but to clear a path for the expression of another kind of love. In Sonnet XIV, Santayana writes of wanting to protect "my nature's shell . . . / Where now, perchance, some new-born Eros flies" (97). In Sonnet XXXI, too, he ruminates in detail on the affective states informing brotherhood, friendship, love, and religious worship:

> A brother's love, but that I chose thee out
> From all the world, not by the chance of birth,
> But in the risen splendour of thy worth,
> Which, like the sun, put all my stars to rout.
> A lover's love, but that it bred no doubt
> Of love returned, no heats of flood and dearth,
> But, asking nothing, found in all the earth
> The consolation of a heart devout.
> A votary's love, though with no pale and wild
> Imaginations did I stretch the might
> Of a sweet friendship and a mortal light.
> Thus in my love all loves are reconciled
> That purest be, and in my prayer the right
> Of brother, lover, friend, and eremite. (110)

Endorsing these claims, McCormick tells us that Santayana's "prolonged sexual conflict . . . dates from early in his Harvard career, when he met Ward Thoron, seventeen, and thus three years younger than he was. The intimacy of the two young men produced the 'Sonnet' which Santayana later indicated was 'Ward's' and dated as 1884 or 1885" (49):

> Pale friends you wish us ever to remain:
> The thriftless seasons no new hope must bring
> To tempt our thoughts on more adventurous wing?
> Must we the pulses of a heart restrain
> Or rob the prelude of its sweet refrain,—
> That subtle music each entrancèd spring
> Hath heard anew its captive lovers sing
> And in the buzz of summer lost again?

I have been guileless long: angels and you
And beauty in my dreams together played.
The sunshine and your smile my heaven made
Laden with some great joy that I half knew.
That holy happiness did mortal prove;
A wind blew, and dim worship flamed to love. (*Poems* 396)

"Angels and you / And beauty in my dreams together played": These words again combine Christian and Classical motifs, blending the ethereal with the corporeal (McCormick 50). Indeed, frustration with the ethereal seems to inspire this sonnet, the poet longing for a reciprocal passion that will invigorate the relationship with lust: "The thriftless seasons no new hope must bring / To tempt our thoughts on more adventurous wing?" From this perspective, "pale friends" implies weakness and lack of resolve, perhaps even cowardice in refusing to undertake this "adventure." Considering this material, there *is* some justification for arguing that when Santayana writes, in Sonnet XXXII, "Be mine, be mine in God and in the grave, / Since naught but chance and the insensate wave / Divides us, and the wagging tongue of men" (110), he is representing social disapproval, or homophobia, as the sole hindrance to same-sex passion.

However, if Santayana's ambivalence about desire renders heterosexuality noninevitable, as I've argued in this essay, it also preempts a purely gay-affirmative reading.[38] Put another way, that Santayana aspires to an autonomy *releasing* him from the burden of objects makes it difficult to see how his involvement with another man could entirely resolve this conflict. Indeed, if we bear in mind Santayana's elaborate meditation on *internal* resistances to love and desire, it is near impossible to argue convincingly that he is representing only Victorian society's hostility toward same-sex love. Instead, Santayana gives us a powerful account of the extremities of longing. In Sonnet XXIII, for example, he asks:

But is this love, that in my hollow breast
Gnaws like a silent poison, till I faint?
Is this the vision that the haggard saint
Fed with his vigils, till he found his rest?
Is this the hope that piloted thy quest,
Knight of the Grail, and kept thy heart from taint?
Is this the heaven, poets, that ye paint?
Oh, then, how like damnation to be blest!
This is not love: it is that worser thing—
Hunger for love, while love is yet to learn.
Thy peace is gone, my soul; thou long must yearn.
Long is thy winter's pilgrimage, till spring

And late home-coming; long ere thou return
To where the seraphs covet not, and burn. (106)

"This is not love: it is that worser thing— / Hunger for love": Santayana returns us here to the idea that desire depletes, rather than enhances, identity—
that pursuing beauty leads the lover not toward the "whole," as Diotima contends in the *Symposium* (202E) and Santayana urges in Sonnet VI ("Love but
the formless and eternal Whole"; *Poems* 93), but toward his own ontological
unraveling. Santayana returns us, in other words, to the idea that desire is the
very element fostering a "waywardness of nature" (Sonnet XXIV; 106). Searching for love and beauty, the poet finds neither when, intimate with his beloved,
he logically should find both: "The chasm 'twixt our spirits yawns as wide /
Though our lips meet, and clasp thee as I list, / The something perfect that I
love is missed" (106).

Santayana's complex relationship to the sublime and the unconscious means
ultimately and counterintuitively that his account of love and desire is
neither hopeless nor idealistic. His poetry offers instead the perspective of a
"chasm . . . yawn[ing]" between two lovers, which elicits desire without simply
enabling its fulfillment. The result is turbulent and compelling, helping us
push aside fantasy in order to grasp the remarkable, even productive obsti-
nacy of a lover's will. As Santayana wrote Ward Thoron in one untitled verse
(1887):

> At last, dear Ward, I take a rhyming quill;
> From its cleft point there springs an inky rill
> Whose twisted stream, with intersecting flow,
> Shall trace the ways my feet and fancies go
>
> .   .   .   .
> The world is wide: it is not flesh and bone
> And sun, and moon, and thunderbolt alone;
> It is imagination swift and high
> Creating in a dream its earth and sky.
> Why then gape idly at external laws
> When we ourselves have faculty to cause?
> Build rather on your nature, when you can,
> And bid the human spirit rule the man,
> Nay, not the man, but all the world as well,
> Till man be god of heaven and of hell.
> Come, mad ambition, come, divine conceit,
> That bringest nature down at fancy's feet,
> Alone creative, capable alone
> Of giving mind the sceptre, man the throne.
> Build us more pyramids and minsters still
> On thine own regal cornerstone: *I will!* (192–93)

Notes

I thank Donald Whitfield for assisting me with references and translations from the Greek, and Richard Dellamora, Jason Friedman, William G. Holzberger, and William Halloran for their invaluable comments on an earlier draft. A longer version of this essay appears in my book *The Burdens of Intimacy: Psychoanalysis and Victorian Masculinity*, © 1999 by the University of Chicago. All rights reserved.

1. Aristotle, *Poetics*, trans. Richard Jenko (Indianapolis: Hackett, 1987); Plato, *Symposium*, trans. W. R. M. Lamb, Loeb Classical Library (1925; Cambridge: Harvard University Press, 1991). Subsequent references to the latter work appear in parentheses in main text.

2. See Freud, "Creative Writers and Day-Dreaming" (1907; 1908), *The Standard Edition of the Complete Psychological Works of Sigmund Freud*, ed. and trans. James Strachey (London: Hogarth, 1954–73), 9:143–53 and *Leonardo da Vinci and a Memory of His Childhood* (1910), *Standard Edition* 11:63–137. For an overview of Freud's arguments, see H. W. Loewald, *Sublimation: Inquiries into Theoretical Psychoanalysis* (New Haven: Yale University Press, 1990); and for more specific readings, see Leo Bersani, "Erotic Assumptions: Narcissism and Sublimation in Freud," *The Culture of Redemption* (Cambridge: Harvard University Press, 1990), 29–46; *The Freudian Body: Psychoanalysis and Art* (New York: Columbia University Press, 1986); and Jean Laplanche, "To Situate Sublimation," trans. Richard Miller, *October* 28 (1984): 7–26. This essay owes much to the work of Laplanche and especially Bersani.

3. John McCormick, *George Santayana: A Biography* (New York: Knopf, 1987), 124. Subsequent references to this superb biography appear in parentheses in main text.

4. Santayana, *The Letters of George Santayana*, ed. and intro. Daniel Cory (New York: Scribner's, 1955), 238–39. Subsequent references appear in parentheses in main text.

5. See Joseph Epstein, "George Santayana and the Consolations of Philosophy," *The New Criterion* 5, no. 10 (June 1987): 15–27, and Joel Porte, "Santayana's Masquerade," *Raritan* 7, no. 2 (1987): 129–42.

6. Santayana, *The Last Puritan: A Memoir in the Form of a Novel* (London: Constable, 1935), 11. Subsequent references appear in parentheses in main text.

7. Both Van de Weyer and Santayana appear in propria persona at the beginning and end of *The Last Puritan*.

8. Thus Willard E. Arnett, engaging what Santayana calls "a life of reason": "Vital animal desires and impulses . . . , combined with peculiarly human needs and characteristics in their relation to the environment, are the foundation of all the goods man can pursue. . . . However, Santayana also observes that not all men love or seek harmony, because its achievement demands the sacrifice of vital passions and interests which some are not willing to make" (*Santayana and the Sense of Beauty* [Bloomington: Indiana University Press, 1955], 4–5).

9. Santayana, *Persons and Places: Fragments of Autobiography* (1944), ed. William G. Holzberger and Herman J. Saatkamp, Jr. (Cambridge: MIT Press, 1986), 428. Subsequent references appear in parentheses in main text. This line invokes and significantly transforms Santayana's earlier claim in Sonnet XXXIII (1895): "A perfect love is *nourished* by despair" (*The Complete Poems of George Santayana: A Critical Edition,* ed. and intro. William G. Holzberger [Lewisburg, Pa.: Bucknell University Press, 1979], 33; emphasis added). Subsequent references to *The Complete Poems* also appear in parentheses in main text.

10. Santayana, *The Sense of Beauty: Being the Outline of Aesthetic Theory* (1896; New York: Dover, 1955), 22. Subsequent references appear in parentheses in main text.

11. See Freud, *Three Essays on the Theory of Sexuality* (1905), *Standard Edition* 7:217–19; Plato, *Euthyphro, Apology, Crito, Phaedo, Phaedrus,* trans. Harold North Fowler, Loeb Classical Library (1914; Cambridge: Harvard University Press, 1995).

12. "All that seems certain," Freud writes in *Civilization and Its Discontents* (1929, revised 1930), "is [beauty's] derivation from the field of sexual feeling. The love of beauty seems a perfect example of an impulse inhibited in its aim. 'Beauty' and 'attraction [*Reiz*]' are original attributes of the sexual object" (*Standard Edition* 21: 83). Notes Freud's translator, James Strachey: "The German '*Reiz*' means 'stimulus' as well as 'charm' or 'attraction'" (83n.).

13. Freud, *Group Psychology and the Analysis of the Ego* (1921), *Standard Edition* 18: 138.

14. Freud, *Three Essays,* 178; *Group Psychology,* 138. Arnett overlooks most of Santayana's conceptual difficulties when arguing, "The sexual instinct [according to Santayana] is fundamental; because man is incessantly responsive to and solicitous concerning the opposite sex, he is also sensitive to other and various aspects of the world about him, and is capable of feeling tenderness and concern for all things. It is due to the sexual instinct, Santayana suggests, that a great part of man's aesthetic feeling is sentimental rather than perceptive and mathematical" (*Santayana and the Sense of Beauty,* 32–33). Jerome Ashmore is more accurate when summarizing the object's "indeterminacy" in Santayana's work (see *Santayana, Art, and Aesthetics* [Cleveland: Western Reserve University Press, 1966], 17). However, like Arnett, he attributes a coherence to Santayana's conception of passion, pleasure, and desire (10); related claims surface in Irving Singer, *Santayana's Aesthetics: A Critical Introduction* (Cambridge: Harvard University Press, 1957), 44, and M. M. Kirkwood, *Santayana: Saint of the Imagination* (Toronto: University of Toronto Press, 1961), 78. For an overview of these texts and their impact on Santayana studies, see Frederick W. Conner, "'To Dream with One Eye Open': The Wit, Wisdom, and Present Standing of George Santayana," *Soundings* 74, 1–2 (1991): 159–78, and Timothy L. S. Sprigge, *Santayana: An Examination of His Philosophy* (New York: Routledge, 1974, 1995). Finally, for useful engagements with Santayana's politics, see A. L. Rowse, "Santayana: A Prophet of Our Time," *Contemporary Review* 260, no. 1517 (June 1992): 320–23 and Kenneth S.

Lynn, "Santayana and the Genteel Tradition," *Commentary* 73, no. 5 (May 1982): 81–84.

15. See James Strachey's introduction to Freud's *Papers on Metapsychology* (1915), *Standard Edition* 14: 106. And for an excellent account of this failure, see Bersani, "Erotic Assumptions."

16. I summarize some of these arguments in "'Thoughts for the Times on War and Death': Militarism and Its Discontents," *Literature & Psychology* 41, no. 3 (1995): 1–12, and *The Ruling Passion: British Colonial Allegory and the Paradox of Homosexual Desire* (Durham, N.C.: Duke University Press, 1995); see also Geoffrey Galt Harpham's fine study *The Ascetic Imperative in Culture and Criticism* (Chicago: University of Chicago Press, 1987).

17. Daniel Cory, *Santayana: The Later Years: A Portrait with Letters* (New York: Braziller, 1963), 40.

18. Santayana, *Complete Poems*, 95.

19. Santayana, *Realms of Being* (1927–38; New York: Scribner's, 1942), 706.

20. Ibid., 689.

21. Santayana's most elaborate account of Platonism is *Platonism and the Spiritual Life* (New York: Scribner's, 1927), but see also his earlier study *Scepticism and Animal Faith: Introduction to a System of Philosophy* (New York: Scribner's, 1923), esp. 225–26, and "Apologia pro mente sua," in *The Philosophy of George Santayana*, ed. Paul Arthur Schilpp (New York: Tudor Publishing, 1940), esp. 542–49.

22. In a longer version of this essay, published in my book *The Burdens of Intimacy: Psychoanalysis and Victorian Masculinity* (Chicago: University of Chicago Press, 1999), I show how Diotima's speech influences the way Oliver Alden, Santayana's protagonist in *The Last Puritan*, defines his own passions on pp. 527–28 and 695. In the interests of concision, the version published here can stress only the aesthetic and philosophical tensions anticipating Santayana's "memoir in the form of a novel." I have also cut several endnotes that represent Santayana's interest in "literary psychology" and the unconscious.

23. I am indebted to Gregory Vlastos's invaluable reading of love and friendship in Aristotle's *Rhetoric* and Plato's *Republic, Lysis,* and *Symposium* ("The Individual as an Object of Love in Plato," in his *Platonic Studies* [Princeton: Princeton University Press, 1973, 1981], esp. 31–34).

24. Kailash Chandra Baral, "George Santayana and the Sense of Beauty," *Punjab University Research Bulletin* 19, no. 1 (1988): 59. See McCormick on Santayana's related critique of Hegel and Josiah Royce (*Biography*, 91–93), and Henry Wenkart on Santayana's aesthetic understanding of "experience" ("Santayana on Beauty," *Analecta Husserliana* 12, *The Philosophical Reflection of Man in Literature*, ed. Anna-Teresa Tymieniecka [Dordrecht: Reidel, 1982], 323–25).

25. Baral, "Sense of Beauty," 59.

26. Matthew Arnold, "The Function of Criticism at the Present Time" (1864), in

The Collected Prose Works of Matthew Arnold, vol. 3, ed. R. H. Super (Ann Arbor: University of Michigan Press, 1962), 258.

27. For a useful elaboration, see Frank Lentricchia, "Philosophers of Modernism at Harvard circa 1900," *South Atlantic Quarterly* 89 (1990): 790–92.

28. See Linda Dowling, *Hellenism and Homosexuality in Victorian Oxford* (Ithaca: Cornell University Press, 1994), pp. 67–103; Richard Dellamora, *Masculine Desire: The Sexual Politics of Victorian Aestheticism* (Chapel Hill: University of North Carolina Press, 1990), 33, 169–71, 196–99; also David J. DeLaura, *Hebrew and Hellene in Victorian England: Newman, Arnold, and Pater* (Austin: University of Texas Press, 1969), 171–81; Richard Jenkyns, *The Victorians and Ancient Greece* (Cambridge: Harvard University Press, 1980), esp. 140–53.

29. See Walter Pater, *The Renaissance: Studies in Art and Poetry* (1873, 1893), ed. Donald L. Hill (Berkeley and Los Angeles: University of California Press, 1980), 455.

30. See Santayana, "Apologia pro mente sua," in *Philosophy,* 499, 503; Lisa Ruddick, "Fluid Symbols in American Modernism: William James, Gertrude Stein, George Santayana, and Wallace Stevens," in *Allegory, Myth, and Symbol,* ed. Morton W. Bloomfield (Cambridge: Harvard University Press, 1981), 335.

31. Ross Posnock writes of "Santayana's fastidious, immaculate asexuality," his excellent essay demonstrating that such fastidiousness ultimately could not veil Santayana's own internal sexual tensions ("Genteel Androgyny: Santayana, Henry James, Howard Sturgis," *Raritan* 10, no. 3 [1991]: 61–62). And McCormick writes: "There can be no doubt that Santayana was the subject of a prolonged sexual conflict, one which challenges the accepted wisdom that he was cold, detached, and somehow lacking in humanity, a view that he himself did so much to affirm" (*Biography,* 49).

32. For additional elaboration on Santayana's homophilic attachments in Boston and England, see Posnock "Genteel Androgyny," 58–62, 67–70; Anthony Woodward, *Living in the Eternal: A Study of George Santayana* (Nashville: Vanderbilt University Press, 1988), 11–12; Andrew Holleran, "(Artificial) Marble," *Ground Zero* (New York: Plume, 1988), 101–12; and Douglass Shand-Tucci's excellent study, *Boston Bohemia, 1881–1900: Ralph Adams Cram: Life and Architecture* (Amherst: University of Massachusetts Press, 1995), 168–250.

33. Epstein, "Consolations of Philosophy," 18.

34. See McCormick, *Biography,* 49, and Robert K. Martin, *The Homosexual Tradition in American Poetry* (Austin: University of Texas Press, 1979), 108–14. Santayana's four elegiac sonnets "To W. P." appear in *The Complete Poems,* 125–26. The poet writes: "But yet I treasure in my memory / Your gift of charity, and young heart's ease, / And the dear honour of your amity" (126). Holzberger explains that Potter, among Harvard's class of 1893, "became Santayana's constant companion" while Santayana was an instructor in philosophy at that school and the organizer of regular "poetry bees" (41), and he continues: "Recalling the friendship almost fifty years later, Santayana writes that he came to think of him 'as a younger brother and as a part of myself.' Warwick

Potter graduated with his class, and later that summer, together with his brother Robert, went for an ocean cruise aboard a yacht owned by a wealthy friend [Edgar Scott]. In October of 1893, in the harbor of Brest, Warwick, who had been terribly seasick, contracted cholera and died. The sudden death of this young friend had a powerful effect on Santayana and contributed to the influences that were bringing about the spiritual crisis he would later call his *metanoia*" (41; see also 613).

35. According to Matthew 27:33–34, "Golgotha" means "The Place of the Skull."

36. Santayana makes clear his thoughts on paganism and desire in "The Dissolution of Paganism" and "The Poetry of Barbarism," both in *Interpretations of Poetry and Religion* (New York: Scribner's, 1900), 49–75 and 166–216 respectively. See also McCormick, *Biography*, 84 and 133.

37. See Lane, *Burdens of Intimacy*, 1–43.

38. See Martin, *Homosexual Tradition*, 108–14.

Ten Percent: Poetry and Pathology

ROBERT SULCER, JR.

"I delight in fine pictures—I long to be able to paint such. I strive and strive, and can't produce what I want. That is pain to me, and always *will* be pain, until my faculties lose their keenness, like aged eyes. Then there are many other things I long for"—here Philip hesitated a little, and then said—"things that other men have, and that will always be denied me. . . . I think of too many things—sow all sorts of seeds, and get no great harvest from any one of them. I'm cursed with susceptibility in every direction, and effective faculty in none. . . . I flutter all ways, and fly in none."
—Philip, in George Eliot's *The Mill on the Floss*

Even in childhood I was mad about men in uniform. . . . Passing through the railway station, I saw, with that inward eye that is the curse of solitude, my sister squatting by the ticket office to play with a baby bear that a sailor had on a lead. He stood for a while watching my sister and I watched him.
—Quentin Crisp, *The Naked Civil Servant*

"with that inward eye that is the curse of solitude"

The passages above demonstrate a complex web of identities, genres, and institutions revealing my central concern in this essay—the concurrent emergence at the fin de siècle of male homosexual identity and literary study. Quentin Crisp, in some ways the kind of gay man looming over this project, joins these concerns with his somewhat self-loathing sentence about queer self-discovery. I quote his passage because, long an admirer of Wordsworth's "The Daffodils," I've wondered in the last few years if what we ask students to do in literary analysis—and in the institution of English studies underwriting such a disciplinary practice—is to see things with that "inward eye / Which is the bliss of solitude," a skill seemingly predicated upon privileging a "different" and therefore elite vision, as opposed to a democratic one. Crisp says that his awareness of his identity as a homosexual attends precisely the moment that he recognized an inner self—"that inward eye that is the curse of solitude." This gay self-consciousness, pathologically represented as a "curse," he then links to a certain kind of "literary" and "sensitive" response to a text—the same inward eye not only of desire but of analysis—precisely the kind of analysis expected in the interpretation of texts undertaken by criticism within English studies.

Mediating these two discourses of pathology and "sensitive" reception is Philip from *The Mill on the Floss,* the prototypical nineteenth-century aesthete, one informed by the discipline of sexology: bored, lethargic, suffering from ennui. Ever nervous, frail, and aesthetic—all Victorian euphemisms for the emergent homosexual—Philip thinks excessively but is unable to do; he is too weak to will his intentions into rhetorical action. The primary characteristic of the late-Victorian, Wildean aesthete, such a construction is also the one given by the nascent discourse of sexology, which called the homosexual into discourse as it constructed him as an object of analysis. Finally, sexology grows with the homosexual and is influenced by the homosexual subject of it (witness the sexological work of Carl Ulrichs and of Symonds), and the discipline of sexology, itself encouraging the "close reading" of the deviant body by the professional, crystallizes all the concerns we have seen into one powerful and overdetermined figure: a nervous, overtly critical invert whose experience of the closet, the sexually "pathological," and the "perverse" enables him, in sexological fashion, rigorously and professionally to read signs, to find in them the "meaning" that the "masses" cannot. In this sense, the figure embodies the layered etiologies of homosexuality, sexology, and literary study. So I want to ask, provisionally, if you have to be queer (or queer-identified) to do English studies, which raises another question: Is English studies queer?[1]

Tights, Cassocks, and Gowns

John Addington Symonds (1840–1893) embodies these shifts from acts to identity and from public to private, interpretive culture. The career of Symonds, a minor Victorian man of letters, may be divided into two phases: his academic years, during which he wrote scholarly works on poetry and Classical culture; and the years following his botched candidacy in 1877 for the Oxford Professorship of Poetry, during which he was effectively outed, and after which he became interested in sexology and wrote polemical literature on behalf of homosexual liberation. *A Problem in Modern Ethics,* printed privately in 1891, belongs to this later phase. "Addressed," according to its title page, "Especially to Medical Psychologists and Jurists," the essay deploys the language of pathology for literature, literary criticism, and homosexual expression. Throughout his work, Symonds argues that homosexuals, or "Urnings," the term he borrows from Karl Ulrichs' sexological work, abound throughout culture, including its highest and most literary echelons.[2] Affecting a scholarly, objective tone throughout, he writes an academic essay with a certain Modernist and New Critical reserve. Symonds attempts a reverse historiography in which he calls on ancient Greece and other such eras to demonstrate the universality and cultural legitimacy of homosexuality, and his survey of many literatures—anthropological, scientific, polemical—culminates in the "imaginative," in which he offers a proto-queer reading of Whitman. The invisibility of homosexuality and Symonds' own queerness authorize him as a scholar to unearth the homoerotic, and detective-like metaphors and images of queer criticism surface and resurface throughout the work as he attempts to unveil the seemingly heterosexual as homosexual. Symonds' is a methodical reading practice with homosexuality as its object and its method.

Generally an essay legitimating the homosexual by demonstrating his centrality in all Western cultural projects, as well as his superiority to heterosexuals in all things artistic, *Modern Ethics* attempts to articulate a theory and strategy for homosexual liberation:

> Are people, sound in body, vigorous in mind, wholesome in habit, capable of generous affections, good servants of the state, trustworthy in all the ordinary relations of life, to be condemned at law as criminals because they cannot feel sexually as the majority feel, because they find some satisfaction for their inborn want in ways which the majority dislike?[3]

It is just this attempt to naturalize and therefore legitimate and liberate homosexuality, furthermore, which underwrites his critical authority; to show that homosexuality is "natural" and therefore universal, one must reveal where it is hidden and has passed as straight and "natural." Indeed the need to construct a queer self invested with academic and cultural capital motivates the hermeneutic effort itself. Symonds therefore assumes the depth model, the job of the critic to uncover—the strategy of mimetic criticism, as well as the primary hermeneutic maneuver of most queer criticism.

From the beginning, Symonds' essay configures the homosexual as a reader, one able to locate the value of texts and of bodies. A number of times in the essay Symonds invites a reading of the homosexual and invokes a proximity between the homosexual and interpretation itself. He constructs the queer body, for example, as a cipher through which truth can be ascertained, especially in the courts and through the identification of symptoms of disease ("If a criminal act be proved . . ." [25]), and affects an evasively Whitmanesque style avoiding the essay's topic until the third page: "In the bivouac of the Keltish warriors, lying wrapped in wolves' skins round their camp-fires; upon the sands of Arabia" (2). The Whitmanian use of prepositional phrases seductively to undress the very subjects from whom he attempts to distance himself academically and anthropologically tells much about the later mingling of poetry, criticism, body, and profession in the Whitman section, "Literature: Imaginative." In the fourth part of the argument, as he addresses "Vulgar Errors," Symonds, discussing the "inborn" (11) nature of the homosexual, finds, in a universalizing move, the homosexual to be everywhere, and it is precisely

Symonds' homosexuality and his interest in the place of biography in textual
analysis that authorize him to embark on a reading practice unearthing the
homosexual, locating his minority presence at the same time that he says, to
adopt gay-lib parlance, that "we are everywhere":

> The vulgar expect to discover the objects of their outraged animosity in
> the scum of humanity. But these may be met with every day in drawing-
> rooms, law-courts, banks, universities, mess-rooms; on the bench, the
> throne, the chair of the professor; under the blouse of the workman, the
> cassock of the priest, the epaulettes of the officer, the smock-frock of the
> ploughman, the wig of the barrister, the mantle of the peer, the costume of
> the actor, the tights of the athlete, the gown of the academician. (11–12)

Thus Symonds, in an unrepresentatively large number of academic examples, wants to say that homosexuals are like everyone else, yet seeks out, by
uncovering physical evidence, their essential, here nearly genital difference; in
a detective-like, formalist method, he hermeneutically and campily feels up the
garments of his textual tricks. And in a move that throughout sexological research connects the homosexual's sensitivity with his sexual sensitivity, Symonds here moves from architectural and more general sites of power (draw-
ing-rooms, law-courts, universities) to sites that link the homosexual's body
with institutional power and the body politic (the bench, throne, chair, cassock,
wig, gown). Especially important for the later trajectory of my argument, Symonds links the site of the anus—then as now a metonym for the homosexual
man—with the site of cultural power, choosing as vehicles for the connection
precisely the places where homosexuals *sit* to make their decisions (the bench,
the throne, the chair). He thus heralds a later textual strategy in the essay—
joining the queer sensitivity of the anus with the sensitivity in cultural matters
that the culturally privileged homosexual wields.

Throughout the essay, then, the need to authorize oneself professionally and
queerly—that is, the need to boost one's cultural capital while also legitimating
one's sexuality—coincides with the rigorous practice of close reading, of her-
meneutics itself, a hermeneutic practice which is, moreover, sexological. Symonds invokes Whitman as a way to both incarnate and codify the queer body
and a disciplinary practice at the same time. One reads the (queer) body as one
reads a text, and the homosexual, master of both textual reading and the queer
body, becomes the professional negotiating the two, constructing himself and
constructed even as he reads and constructs the text of his sexual identity. But
the analytic gaze is paradoxically evaluative, too, for in naturalizing and normalizing homosexuality, he also oversteps his detached boundaries and suggests that homosexuals are at the very center of culture, sensitive, artistic. And
it is precisely a result of their pathology that they are thus inclined. When

Symonds quotes the physician Paul Moreau, for example, he says that "the union of unrestrained debauchery and ferocity with great mental gifts strikes him [Moreau] as a note of disease" (31) and thereby rehearses a very long association between art and mental illness, one at the heart of the private versus the public (the artist's intense inner vision, born of pathology, versus the needs of the mundane polis). Such concerns culminated at the fin de siècle with the publication of Max Nordau's *Degeneration* (1892), in which pathological degeneracy underwrites the artistic vogue of the day, decadence, with its priests of unrestrained art and love, such as Oscar Wilde. As "*a morbid deviation from an original type*," the fin-de-siècle degenerate in the language of Nordau's analysis suffers from the same problem that the emergent homosexual does—the deviation or falling from—pathologizing of—a norm.[4] Indeed the language many sexologists and psychiatrists use to define the late nineteenth-century homosexual, "invert," participates in just this hierarchy of value that suggests that the same-sex–identified subject reverses the sexual norm.[5]

The coupling of homosexuality and interpretive ability was common in sexology and other late-Victorian discourses of sexuality. Edward Carpenter, Symonds' contemporary, who was a tireless social advocate and led a much more "out" existence, portrays this notion of the Urning's ability to link and mediate cultures:

> And in truth it seems the most natural thing in the world that just as the ordinary sex-love has a special function in the propagation of the race, so the other love should have its special function in social and heroic work, and in the generation—not of bodily children—but of those children of the mind, the philosophical ideals which transform our lives and those of society.[6]

Indeed this intermediary status authorizes homosexuals as "interpreters of men and women to each other" (190). And although Carpenter's polemic inveighs against views of the homosexual as "abnormal and morbid," he nevertheless pathologizes the homosexual in aesthetic terms—as if words like "Urning" were not enough—for he praises his "defects, if such exist, in the direction of subtlety, evasiveness, timidity, vanity, etc."[7] The emphasis on subtlety in particular stresses not only the aestheticized homosexual but also an academic and critical turn toward the subtle, the nuanced, the queer. Thus ironically it is precisely the Urning's minoritized difference from the culture s/he interprets that allows him/her to universalize, to become a link between all cultures. (Carpenter discusses both men and women "Urnings.") This negotiation of minoritizing and universalizing ideas of the homosexual launches a queer disciplinary practice, for, as Carpenter argues for the need to understand the Urning, he makes his appeal through the discourse of science, reason, and objectivity, as "the best attitude we can adopt is one of sincere and dispassionate observation of facts" (186). Yet however much the homosexual in such a scenario is not morbid, he is nevertheless constructed as a pathological deviation from the "norm," a higher, rarefied specimen whose sensitivity is reflected in his interests no less than in his ganglia, as Carpenter quotes Ulrichs again: "The nerve system of many an Urning is the finest and most complicated musical instrument in the service of the interior personality that can be imagined" (198). Indeed it is the homosexual's critical, artistic ability that positions him as the very figure of interpretation: "A certain freemasonry of the secrets of the two sexes . . . may well favour their function as reconcilers and interpreters" (200). Increasingly sensitive as he is, then, the Urning is able to practice evaluative reading that is "objective" but nevertheless discriminates in a canonizing move, of course, to favor the best and brightest in culture, increasingly becoming, such an argument concludes, the male homosexual.[8]

As Symonds and Carpenter begin to forge a recognizable cultural type, a distinctly literate and literary homosexual critic, they resist the Victorian university's concept of literary value. The late-Victorian period in England witnessed a divisive debate at Oxford and Cambridge, for example, over whether vernacular English literature should be a university subject, a debate best crystallized in John Churton Collins' vehement demand for the teaching of the subject within a broad liberal arts tradition in his *The Study of English Literature: A Plea for Its Recognition and Organization at the Universities* (1891). This polemic reveals the larger culture's linking of the study of art and literature with normalcy rather than degeneracy. Inveighing against philological pedagogies that demanded rote reproduction of publication dates, authors' surnames, and word-counting, Collins insists that in a class on *Paradise Lost*, "what a teacher has to explain is how and why the poem could have been produced only by an Englishman."[9] A need to consolidate national identity aggrandized Anglo-Saxon language and literature as an increasingly powerful and explanatory category for claiming racial and national privilege. With the mid-Victorian career of David Masson as professor of English literature at University College (London) and various Scottish universities, literature became a way of constructing a healthy national identity, distinguishing what was generative about the Anglo-Saxon race from what was degenerative in other races. With a racist pedagogy centered on counting the number of Anglo-Saxon words in texts, praising the racial purity of those with the highest percentage (Chaucer good, Spenser bad), Masson reveals that much of the Victorian proliferation of English studies within universities stemmed from a Nordau-like fear of cultural and literary degeneration.[10] By placing the pathologized homosexual at the very center of culture as a uniquely sensitive, subtle, and interpretive being, Symonds and Carpenter strategically resist the associa-

tion of canonical literature with generative imperial health, insisting instead
that literature inheres precisely in the pathological, the perverse, the *"morbid
deviation from an original type,"* the queer.

One in Ten: Sexuality and Canonicity

A Problem in Modern Ethics is the ideal text within which to link the dual emergence of homosexual identity and literary study, itself an attempt to "close read"
the author's "corpus." The text acts as an interdisciplinary amalgam—by turns
literary criticism, armchair sexology, and queer polemic. A peculiarly sexological form of literary criticism, the essay is a polemical attempt to justify homosexuality through the evidence of several discourses and disciplines, from psychology to literature, but one which relies on literary metaphors of canonicity
and on sexological metaphors of pathology to argue alternately that the homosexual is normal and special, but in all cases deserving of his/her rights. It is
perhaps telling, then, aside from mere pre-scientific tendencies of nomencla-
ture, that Symonds categorizes each of the arguments from the disciplines he
invokes as "Literature" ("Literature: Pornographic and Descriptive; Literature:
Medico-Forensic; Literature: Medico-Psychological; Literature: Historical
and Anthropological; Literature: Polemical; Literature: Idealistic"), in only the
last of which does he treat imaginative literature. Thus the text's interdisciplinary structure itself suggests Symonds' mingling of sexology and literature, with
a problematic assumption that literature, precisely because it imagines other,
coded worlds and possibilities, is an inherently progressive space.

Though what concerns us most directly is the last chapter, in which Symonds sexologically reads Whitman, he prefaces that chapter with many more
"scientific" chapters that lay the theoretical groundwork he invokes in the last.
Indeed his purpose throughout the essay seems to be to authorize himself
through a distant detachment whose critical purchase is close reading, consistent with his tendency to out the homosexual through exegesis, lifting up
gowns, cassocks, and the like to do so. Symonds never really outs himself,
largely assuming a clinical and critical tone, choosing "hosts" such as medical
authorities and first-hand accounts of inverts to make his case and thus professionalizing himself in the masked and opaque way that any reader does—dis-
placing, in closeted fashion, his/her interpretive energies onto the text and saying, as does the New Critic, that it's not s/he who finds something; it's just
there. Though he admits he is not himself a sexologist or scientist, Symonds
quotes such figures with authority, but not nearly so often as he does firsthand
accounts of "inverts." In a professionalizing and classist move consistent with
the construction of the homosexual as private, unmentionable, critical, and
professional, Symonds enlists professionalism in the service of antihomopho-

bic critique when he writes of one study that it does not grow out of the personal experience of an invert and that the author "writes with excusable animosity. We see at once that he is neither a philosopher by nature, nor a man of science, but *only a citizen,* endowed with the normal citizen's antipathy for passions alien to his own" (21; emphasis added). Constructed by sexological and legal discourses as a minority—and therefore as unable to participate productively in majority-rule democracy—constructed outside of language and within the closet ("the love that dare not speak its name"), yet invested with elite academic capital, the homosexual, deprived of the "state," works furtively from his much more hospitable, vague, and veiled world of "culture." As David Evans suggests in a critique of liberal-humanist constructions of justice and citizenship, the category of citizenship, so resonant with the polis, democracy, and the public "man of letters," may be inappropriate to the category of the homosexual, who is ever interpellated along a private/public axis. He quotes B. S. Turner's *Citizenship and Capitalism:* "If 'Citizenship involves . . . social membership and participation in society as a whole,' sexual citizenship involves partial, private, and primarily leisure and lifestyle membership."[11] Consistent with this private sphere of influence is the written, privately published and subculturally disseminated (as is the case with this essay), and "professional" scholarship embodied here by Symonds.

Symonds most succinctly shores up his "authority" on matters of the closet through both personal and "scientific" evidence. In a deft rhetorical move, he ends his medical chapter with the first-hand account of an invert from one of the case studies of the German sexologist, Richard Krafft-Ebing. Relating a common and still quite contemporary story of shame, loneliness, and suicide, the anonymous invert says, also in a subtly deft way, that

> It is only one who has some approximate notion of the mental and moral sufferings, of the anxieties and perturbations, to which an Urning is exposed, who knows the never-ending hypocrisies and concealments he must practice in order to cloak his indwelling inclination . . . it is only such a one, I say, who is able properly to wonder at the comparative rarity of mental aberrations and nervous ailments among this class of Urnings. (74)

Though he won't directly say that he is so qualified to speak, the Urning's emphatic "I say" suggests that a queer such as himself is the one qualified to speak, to uncover the queer textual body, to understand the concealments and the cloaking. Symonds himself carefully supports this notion that it's a wonder all homosexuals aren't nelly nerve bundles, saying "This is powerfully and temperately written" (74). Still he distances himself as a reader of the personal testimony of an "informant," and by so doing he not only professionalizes the queer as an object of study but also depersonalizes him by abnegating any personal identification he might have with his subject matter. And although one might say that the medical chapter approaches a counterdiscourse refuting medical and homophobic testimony, Symonds channels the invert's language into the professional by saying, in the last paragraph of the chapter, that all he can conclude from the invert's testimony is that we should focus the medical study of homosexuals on embryology, on a lack of correlation between sexual instincts and sexual organs, rather than on mental pathology or the innately differential nervous system of the homosexual.

In an alternately universalizing and minoritizing section on anthropology, Symonds thoroughly essentializes the queer body and establishes its psychophysiological connections to the literary. He uncovers a link between anal receptivity and the impressionistic receptivity of the passive critic, the analyzer rather than the producer/writer. Discussing the anthropological work of Paolo Mantegazza, which postulates that homosexuality results from a misdirection of male sexual energy from the penis to the anus, Symonds notes that one type of sodomite in Mantegazza's system is "psychical, . . . 'specific to intelligent men, cultivated, and frequently neurotic,' but which he [Mantegazza] does not attempt to elucidate, though he calls it 'not a vice, but a passion.'" (82). Indeed this representation is that of the sensitive, critical homosexual who, having failed to shore up his phallic identity and retreating to the anus, in the words of Philip from *The Mill on the Floss*, "flits and flies," but cannot be decisive. His perversion is an emotional passion rather than a physical act, and we therefore see familiar, dual representations of the homosexual: at one pole, hypersexual; at another, anti-sexual, such an ennuyé that he can barely move, much less fuck. This notion of the receptive, non-producing critic, so central to the shift from public man of letters/orator to the aesthete/critic, is underwritten by a passive anal identity; the critic's reception of impressions, in Symonds' and Mantegazza's account, is inextricably linked to his anal reception of other things. Such a construction also participates in the sexological chiasm Carpenter undertakes in his characterization of the invert: a more or less strategic vacating of the sexual and other energies of the body through ennui and a transference of that energy to the mind and the critical capacity. The homosexual is all mind, no body; all anus, no phallus.

In linking two kinds of passivity, anal and intellectual, Symonds demonstrates that the shift in male–male relations from sodomy or an agent of specific acts to homosexuality or an inner sense of identity still gets mapped onto the anus; the queer's self-consciousness inheres in the psychic construction of the anus. Ed Cohen discusses the hermeneutic imperative within discourses of sodomy, as the late-eighteenth century's Edward Coke establishes that there must be proof for sodomy, the *penetratio*, a proof that "induc[ed] the body to testify against itself" and that then was used as a symbol of warning in public execution, the body still signifying.[12] As the anus functions in the West as a peculiarly hermeneutic fetish, to receive anally is to receive critically. So if the homosexual man of letters cannot now produce (either in a phallic, heterosexual and ejaculatory sense or in the sense of creative and oratorical energy), he can receive; he can criticize and he can be fucked, in an economy that renders the two activities part of the same passive self-consciousness.

If the homosexual is bolstered, as Carpenter puts it, by an infinitely complex nerve system stringed finer than an instrument, and by an ability to receive sense impressions passively, literary critical anal(ysis) becomes the mental seat, as it were, of such reception. If indeed, as in Symonds' formulation, the extremely sensitive contours of the anus help to construct the notion of the homosexual, who presumably, in such an economy, enjoys anal stimulation, as a uniquely sensitive being with respect to other matters of reception—of art and literature—it becomes just this anal sensitivity, this awareness of excessive and rarefied feeling, that enables him to find the special in literature, the defamiliarization or pathologized ten percent that inculcates recognition in the queer reader.

Situated as an alternately central and marginal cultural figure—interpreting but distant from the culture he comes from—the homosexual in this configuration walks slippery terrain. Symonds' idea of homosexuals as just plain folks, for example, is ironically mediated through a discourse of the special, minority status of the homosexual. Ironically, Whitman, the pre-identity professor of homoeroticism and the subject of much of Symonds' essay, relying more on a discourse of acts, suffused his vision of American culture with male–male desire in a universalizing move—one which saw the homosexual as the very embodiment of the state and civic rhetoric, rather than its private, elitist challenge.[13] For the universalizing Whitman to be the Ur-text of a pathologizing and minoritizing argument is consistent with Symonds' alternate use of sexology and pathology on the one hand and his undercutting of them on the other. Paradoxically, again, the universal nature of the homosexual, as Carpenter has articulated it, his social and essentially rhetorical ability to link cultures, sets him apart and therefore distinguishes him, pathologizing and minoritizing him even as he attempts to universalize. Symonds says that Whitman's "love of comrades" is the very type of the universal, a social glue, for "He regards it [the love of comrades] essentially as a social and political virtue. This human emotion is destined to cement society and to tender commonwealths inviolable" (*Modern Ethics*, 121). Yet Symonds ironically applies a minoritizing discourse to his discussion of Whitman's political, social, and literary value, authorizing the homosexual to make evaluative claims—to stake out some kind of canon, one here that is both aesthetic and clearly political—as to what that minoritized category of value will be. Symonds demonstrates this link as he focuses his discussion of Whitman around the poet's notion of comradeship, seeking this "meaning" in identitarian language very similar to the "sense" and "secret" frequently mentioned by Pater and Wilde:

> It therefore becomes of much importance to discover the poet-prophet's *Stimmung*—his radical instinct with regard to the moral quality of the feeling he encourages. Studying his works by their own light, and by the light of their author's character, interpreting each part by reference to the whole and in the spirit of the whole, an impartial critic will, I think, be drawn to the conclusion that what he calls the "adhesiveness" of comradeship is meant to have no interblending with the "amativeness" of sexual love. (118)

Symonds further reports that he wrote Whitman about the intentions behind the "Calamus" poems and that Whitman denied intending any reference to sexual inversion in his poetry, with Whitman responding with evasive formalism in a letter dated 19 August 1890 that his poetry "is only to be rightly construed by and within its own atmosphere and essential character" (quoted in *Modern Ethics*, 119).[14]

We see that the *Stimmung*, that entity that, like Pater's "sense" and Wilde's "secret," best represents the text as a whole, is mediated through the queer critic's "sensitive," anal ability to interpret. In Symonds' essay in particular, there exists an insistence on reading the author's text for that grain of the voice, to invoke Barthes' idea, that carries the imprint of the male author's—here the queer author's—identity. It seems that Whitman's *Stimmung*, that element that bears the imprint of his voice, reflects not just a formalist and queer biographical search but also a search based on sexological essentialism, a pathological and clinical kind of reading that can discover the poet's "radical instinct"— a coupling of words quite ambiguous, implying political radicalism or the text's minoritizing difference—and one which, at the very least, minoritizes and pathologizes the author's literary value, which inheres precisely in the "instinct." The word instinct to describe homosexual inclinations abounds in sexological discourse, and the use of the identitarian and sexological word here to determine literary value suggests that it is a minoritizing and culturally privileged idea of the homosexual as a superior human—a more refined being that we have already noticed in Symonds and in Carpenter—that allows Symonds to make a canonizing judgment of Whitman's character and writing and that places the homosexual at the center of culture and canon. This judgment suggests that literary "excellence," as it has been defined in the traditional canons of this century, relies on a certain "queer" notion of pathological (or, in literary critical pathology, defamiliarized) deviations from normalizing definitions of common discourse. A queer critic is able to understand the queer *Stimmung* of the author. This understanding is crucial to Symonds' construction of a queer canon in which the queer critic's perception of the *Stimmung* creates a queer understanding of the canon. In this sense does the queerness of the critic (his homosexuality) dovetail with the queerness of the work (its exceptionality), coupling queer and canon.

I am extending here Eve Sedgwick's notion of a "minoritizing" discourse of the homosexual—of a historically fairly stable minority or "ten percent"—to categories of literary value.[15] I would therefore submit that this sexological and pathological construction ironically authorizes the homosexual critic, himself the "pathological" deviation from the "majority" (or again, in Nordau's words, "*a morbid deviation from an original type*"), to exercise literary judgment, to determine a canonical "ten percent." As the closet is that queer product of the nineteenth-century binary, public/private, as well as that place that marginalizes and culturally legitimates the aesthete/homosexual invested with academic and cultural capital, it is a particularly appropriate rubric for historicizing patterns of canon formation. As Sedgwick says in an evocative recollection of Allan Bloom's teaching, "Bloom is unapologetically protective of the sanctity of the closet, that curious space that is both internal and marginal to the culture: centrally representative of its motivating passions and contradictions, even while marginalized by its orthodoxies" (56). This minoritizing language, used here to describe a distant and elite culture and, consequently, the minoritizing and canonizing language such a profession will develop, situates precisely the reconciler/interpreter Carpenter delineates as the very figure of high culture—interpreting it because proscribed by it. Thus the privatizing notion of the closet parallels the growth of professionalization in the nineteenth century, as the move toward close analysis, one requiring a professional's gaze, itself involves an elite minority, rather than a lay citizen. The homosexual's minoritized status in sexological discourse, then, along with his experience of the closet and the private, authorizes him to uncover equally closeted textual secrets; his queer "specialness" to determine the "specialness" of texts. Such a figure therefore underwrites nearly every formalist critical paradigm of text- and reader-centered criticism within this century.

But though the queer critic here clearly glorifies the homosexual and fairly blankly identifies himself with the very subject position he praises, he does so through an equally clinical, self-authorizing reserve, for only by practicing the queer reading practice he outlines can the "impartial critic" access impartiality and the "meaning" of the work. Thus there exists in the *Stimmung* passage an organic coupling of putatively "objective" and "subjective" methods of evaluation, both organically linked to one another. The impartial critic, nevertheless employing the very partial method of queer formalism, excavates the text's secrets and reconstructs its larger textual contexts—not just the reading of the lines but the larger textual and political patterns they reveal.

Accessing this tone, however, relies not only on textual analysis but also on a truly structural analytic practice: "interpreting each part by reference to the whole" as well as "by their own light." So there is a New Critical disdain for biography here ("By their own light"), but also, in that same sentence, a bio-graphical and queer historical need to find the author in the work, a resistant queer formalism. For however important it is to study "works by their own light," Symonds highlights a contrast with "And by the light of their author's character" (118). In this sense gay formalism is not just formalism; it is the "spirit of the whole," the *Stimmung,* the sense and the secret deeply interwoven with the queer and desired male authors who produce them. However imag-ined, however bound to the text, there exists here a trace of a living, breathing queer, of that "language lined with flesh," Barthes called it,[16] barely audible except to the initiated, increasingly becoming, in such an economy, the male homosexual critic. Though this reading practice is no less formalistic in that it still focuses on the text, it focuses on a textual body, moves out of and destabi-lizes the text. Such a formalism, therefore, is not anti-contextual. The impar-tial queer critic makes his confident and sexologically "objective" argument through the text, for in an increasingly identitarian view of homosexuality, the evidence of homosexual identity is not sexual, is not evidence of genital acts, but, with Foucault in tow, textual, the trace of the homosexual's identity, whether he ever had or knew he wanted to have homosexual sex. In the same way that many gay and lesbian people can answer their parents' question, "But how do you know if you've never slept with a member of the same sex?" Sy-monds here invokes the distant method of textualism to assert the queer iden-tity of people he's never known, knows nothing about, and/or has never slept with. In this sense the move toward homosexual identity is necessarily cotermi-nous with the increasing textualism of the nineteenth century.

"(You) goe, little book!"

If modern gay identity is partly, as John D'Emilio claims, the product of urban capitalism—the anonymity attending the growth of an urban and mobile middle class[17]—and if, as we have noticed, the most common and visible nar-rative of queer identity in this century has been middle-class, effete, ironic, and urbane, then it should not surprise us that the growth at the fin de siècle of the homosexual as an identity category emerges with textualism. As Linda Dow-ling suggests, the nineteenth century witnesses a battle over whether English is primarily a spoken or a written language, one tipping toward the side of the

text by the end of the century, especially with continental comparative philology and the need of figures like Carlyle textually to preserve a rapidly changing
culture.[18] This conflict between oral and written cultures, already fraught with
the distinction between public citizen and private invert, public and private
man of letters, constructs—as does Wilde's strategic privileging of art over
life—the text, that world of the possible and the mediated, as the discourse
which the emergent, identity-based homosexual improvises. Thus textualism
grows in symbiotic relation to homo(text)ualism, and if Symonds affects an
argument at once minoritizing (we're a fixed ten percent) and universalizing
(we are everywhere in every time)—that is, we are small but everywhere—this
relay between the two discourses must owe much to the "texting" of homosexuals at this crucial historical juncture, confined to literature and print at exactly
the same time as their numbers are confined and reduced from anyone (under
a discourse of acts) to a fairly visible, literate, and literary minority (under a
discourse of identity). As gays and lesbians are not born into their culture but
must access it later, often through alien texts, this universal but literate minority, as Symonds has constructed it through the medium of the text, nevertheless
reaches to all four corners of the globe (with Symonds' anthropological universalism), where it globe-trots textually: "(You) Goe, little book!"

In tandem with psychoanalytic theories like Lacan's of the text and language
as loss, of an imperfect and mediated form of communication, queer "texts"
here become any displacement and sublimation. As Thomas E. Yingling evoc-
atively recalls, the narrative of queer identity is therefore "always already post-
structural, a personal narrative experienced as absence and denial."[19] In a word,
such an identity is textual. Recalling that the second kind of sodomite Mantegazza describes is essentially emotional and psychic and sensitive rather than
bodily ("psychical . . . 'not a vice, but a passion'"), we see that the rarefied quality of this anal identity, its tendency toward the subtle and the complex, renders
it not only private but also textual. As Guy Hocquenghem, a pioneer in gay
and lesbian studies and one who feels psychoanalytic queer appropriations can
liberate the homosexual, opines, "anality is the very movement of sublimation
itself" and is, because excremental, "chiefly private."[20] These descriptions also
recall the increasingly textual orientation of the nineteenth century. To have an
identity is to read for the subversive traces of it, and to read is to search for the
identity of the author, as we do in biographical and much contextual and even
textual analysis. Reading mediates identity in ways quite different from its
function—and oral discourse's function—in a pre-identitarian world. The homosexual or homosexually sympathetic critic is "impartial" precisely because
the homosexual "threat" is at a distance of a few textual removes. Through the
text, the homosexual becomes mediated over time and space, and, in Whitman's case, the ocean. As a textual and problematically contained trace and

figure of resistance, his presence here, like the decrease in numbers of subjects of male–male desire with the Foucauldian shift from acts to a circumscribed identity, is minoritized by the text. As a textual rather than a sexual trace, and as a trace of identity rather than, as Symonds later says, "the 'amativeness' of sexual love," the homosexual can be the impartial critic because he has an identity rather than being a subject of a specific sexual act.

In the shift from acts to identity, however liberating the move from body to head and culture may seem, the homosexual becomes a subject of rather fixed demographic tyranny: ten percent, Greenwich Village, the academy. The consequences of a minority identity within Western, democratic notions of citizenship are enormous and herald one primary minority political strategy: assimilation. That is, Symonds allows, through his "legitimation" of the homosexual by placing him at the center of reading and culture, the participation of the new queer in culture, but along the lines of inclusion: majority rule with minority rights. With this move to identity, fixed numbers, and assimilation, the possibility of shifting numbers of subjects of same-sex acts is drastically limited. Thus however much I should like this essay to be a revisionist and utopian history of queer close reading, we must attend to the double bind by which the homosexual both disciplines a homo(text)uality and is *disciplined* by the very structures of power inherent in the close reading he both dispenses and is circumscribed by.

The homosexual is codified and disciplined even as he begins to underwrite a discipline. When Edward Carpenter claims that "much teaching and instruction on the subject [of homosexuality] is needed" and that "it needs a strict self-control" (*Intermediate Sex*, 220), he demonstrates that the very lack of disciplining the homosexual, of his inability to be codified and "read," highlights precisely the necessity for a discipline about him, a sexological discipline of reserve that resembles the disciplining of the homosexual that takes place in close reading. The late-Victorian and modern, identity-based homosexual, always already "texted," is interpellated within the discourse of close reading, both "empowered to speak, but unable to say,"[21] both resistant to and implicated in the very discourse that calls him into being.

Notes

1. I wish to deploy this and other words in the vocabulary of sexual subjectivity with some precision. I will frequently use the term "homosexual" to describe a particular kind of male sexual subject who understands his identity as an innate part of himself, a homosexual who, as Foucault notes in *The History of Sexuality, volume 1* (Trans. Robert Hurley. New York: Vintage, 1990), emerges in the nineteenth century as "a personage, a past, a case history, and a childhood, in addition to being a type of life, a life form,

and a morphology, with an indiscreet anatomy and possibly a mysterious physiology"
(43). Despite its origins in oppressive sexological discourse aimed at codifying and con-
trolling sexually marginal subjects, I nevertheless use the term precisely because many
late-nineteenth-century sexual subjects applied the term to themselves and found explanatory power within it. "Sexual subject" also defines a certain kind of person who
sees him/herself as an agent of some kind of sexuality, though the term's historical specificity is less distinct than "homosexual." I often use "sexual subject" with figures who
predate the end of the nineteenth century and its paradigm shift (noted by Foucault
above) from agents of sexual acts, such as sodomites, to subjects possessing essential
sexual identities, such as "homosexuals." I will often also assign to the milieu that pre-
identity sexual subjects inhabit the more diffuse label "homoerotic," and I preface the
actions and texts of such figures as "male–male" or "same-sex." Because the primary
figure of this paper dabbled in the emergent discourse of sexology, I occasionally delve
into the rhetoric of sexology and self-consciously refer to sexual subjects within that
pathologizing vocabulary, with words like "invert" to describe the reversal of heterosexual instinct, a reversal sexologists deemed to be the basis of homosexual identity. Finally,
the academic vogue of the last several years has privileged the term "queer" as a way to
appropriate a despised label, celebrating our unapologetic difference, and to build larger
coalitions beyond the limiting minority logic behind the "one in ten" concept of "homosexual." There are times when, out of a need to express one or more of these motives, I
shall deploy this term, but I want to stress that my usage of "queer" nearly always refers
to the strangeness and instability of personal, political, and textual features. I mean to
foreground the "queer" critic as the one best able to identify the text's "queerness"—its
making strange or exceptional. Finally, because the figures I consider had considerable
access, through their closets, to racial, gender, class, and institutional power, "homosexual" and other terms for sexual subjects in this chapter almost always mean men; in
rare exceptions, such as Edward Carpenter's feminist and labor activism, the term also
includes women. In cases where the writer intends "homosexual" or another term to
include women, I use explicit pronouns. It should be the subject of ongoing inquiry and
critique, however, that lesbians, then as now, do not possess the cultural power, wield
the visibility, or invoke the surveillance that these sexually dissident male subjects do.

2. Symonds' pseudo-scientific terminology, borrowed largely from Ulrichs and other
sexologists, is complex and occasionally comical. He uses the term "invert" to describe all
his sexual subjects, among whom there are "acquired" and "congenital" types. The former
he subdivides, borrowing from a chart of Richard Krafft-Ebing's, into "persistent" and
"episodical." The latter category includes the "Urnings," who represent an inversion of
male and female qualities. Of these, "Mannlinges" are male sexual subjects who resemble
women only in their sexual appetite for men, while their more Wagnerian-sounding cousins, the "Weiblinges," are effeminate as well.

3. John Addington Symonds, *A Problem in Modern Ethics* (1891; n.p., London:
1896), 102. Subsequent references to this work are in parentheses in the text.

4. Max Nordau, *Degeneration* (1892; reprint, Lincoln: University of Nebraska Press, 1993), 16.

5. Pathology is, in the history of medicine, generally described as just such an inversive state. Foucault defines pathology as the opposite of an organic, normal state, arguing that "[a]t the heart of all" biological concerns "is error," "anomaly," "mutations"— in a word, queerness (introduction to Georges Canguilhem, *The Normal and the Pathological*, trans. Carolyn R. Fawcett [New York: Zone Books, 1991], 22). In *The Birth of the Clinic*, Foucault also addresses how, in eighteenth-century medicine, bodily functions like coughs formed an "'essential symptom,' since they made it possible to designate a pathological state (in contradistinction to health), a morbid essence" (trans. A. M. Sheridan Smith [New York: Vintage, 1975], 90). Thus the language of pathology is precisely that of homosexual inversion.

6. Edward Carpenter, "Homogenic Love," in *Sexual Heretics: Male Homosexuality in English Literature from 1850–1900*, ed. Brian Reade (New York: Coward-McCann, 1970), 343. Further reference to this work in parentheses in the text.

7. *The Intermediate Sex*, in *Edward Carpenter: Selected Writings*, ed. Noël Greig (London: GMP, 1984), 194. Further references to this work are in parentheses in the text.

8. The tension between the critic as representative of or ruler for a culture has a long history in the nineteenth century. Wordsworth says in his 1802 Preface to the *Lyrical Ballads* that he endeavored to describe situations "in a selection of language really used by men; and, at the same time, to throw over them a certain colouring of the imagination, whereby ordinary things should be presented to the mind in an unusual way," an intention revealing the elitist role of the poet in handling the crude emotions of those he represents (*The Norton Anthology of English Literature*, 5th ed., The Major Authors, ed. M. H. Abrams et al. [New York: Norton, 1987], 1383). Whitman reveals similar motives when he says in the 1855 Preface to *Leaves of Grass* that "The sailor and traveler . . . the anatomist chemist astronomer geologist phrenologist spiritualist mathematician historian and lexicographer are not poets, but they are the lawgivers of poets and their construction underlies the construction of every perfect poem" (*The Harper American Literature*, ed. Donald McQuade et al. [New York: Harper and Row, 1987], 1007).

9. John Churton Collins, *The Study of English Literature: A Plea for Its Recognition and Organization at the Universities* (London: Macmillan, 1891), 33.

10. Franklin E. Court, *Institutionalizing English Literature* (Stanford: Stanford University Press, 1992), 123–31. Court is the most recent authority on this matter. In another racial and ethnic context, though, Gauri Viswanathan argues in *Masks of Conquest* (New York: Columbia University Press, 1989) that the institutional teaching of English literature developed quite early in the century in India, in order to displace the situation of colonial struggle and impose English rule.

11. David T. Evans, *Sexual Citizenship: The Material Construction of Sexualities* (London: Routledge, 1993), 64.

12. Ed Cohen, *Talk on the Wilde Side: Toward a Genealogy of a Discourse on Male Sexualities* (New York: Routledge, 1993), 106.

13. However homoerotic, Whitman's elegy for President Lincoln, "When Lilacs Last in the Dooryard Bloom'd," represents a public act of national mourning. Similarly, in "Scented Herbage of My Breast," from the homoerotic "Calamus" poems, the speaker cries, "I will sound myself and comrades only, I will never again utter a call only their call, / I will raise with it immortal reverberations through the States," raising the private homoerotic gaze to the very type of the national (*Harper American Literature*, 1068–69).

14. The association between "aestheticism" and homosexuality at the end of the nineteenth century is pervasive. This need to separate a vague "comradeship" in art from the "amativeness" of sexual love protests too much that the artistic product must bear only aesthetic, not sexual, traces. In a dramatic example of such strategic formalism, Wilde in his trials insisted against his interrogators that his and other homosexual authors' works could be understood solely on literary terms, even as the cross-examiner attempted to fix his identity and crime through literary texts. Confronted with his decadent statements in the Preface to *The Picture of Dorian Gray*, such as "There is no such thing as a moral or an immoral book," Wilde consistently evacuates the text, in proto-New Critical fashion, of political significance, responding that "No work ever puts forth views of any kind. Views belong to people who are not artists" (Cohen, *Talk*, 161–62). Critiquing his cross-examiner's naïve biographical reading practice that fixes text to authorial identity, Wilde's formalism resembles Symonds' evasive retreat into the text's rarefied atmosphere or *Stimmung*, an especially strategic move, in Wilde's case, for a man who stands in the dock, his life on the line.

15. Eve Kosofsky Sedgwick, *Epistemology of the Closet* (Berkeley and Los Angeles: University of California Press, 1990), 1.

16. Roland Barthes, *The Pleasure of the Text*, trans. Richard Miller (New York: Noonday, 1990), 66.

17. John D'Emilio, "Capitalism and Gay Identity," in *Powers of Desire: The Politics of Sexuality*, ed. Ann Snitow et al. (New York: Monthly Review Press, 1983), 100–13 passim.

18. Linda Dowling, *Language and Decadence in the Victorian Fin de Siècle* (Princeton: Princeton University Press, 1986), xi, 34.

19. Thomas E. Yingling, *Hart Crane and the Homosexual Text: New Thresholds, New Anatomies* (Chicago: University of Chicago Press, 1990), 36.

20. Guy Hocquenghem, *Homosexual Desire*, trans. Daniella Dangoor (London: Allison and Busby, 1978), 82.

21. Yingling, *Hart Crane*, 26.

ELEVEN

The Romance of Boys Bathing: Poetic Precedents and Respondents to the Paintings of Henry Scott Tuke

JULIA F. SAVILLE

The motif of boys bathing *en plein air* as it occurs in Victorian poetry, painting and photography is not merely a popular theme.[1] A particular concatenation of cultural circumstances converges to make this motif a matrix of political, aesthetic, and psychosexual tensions among which a key issue at stake is the potential for displaying and admiring the male body as in itself an object of beauty and eros. In its full scope this project traces the development of the bathing motif over roughly seventy years, from the 1840s until the first decade of the twentieth century. This essay will focus on a crucial aesthetic moment at the turn of the century, when the overdetermination of the bathing motif allows it to become a site at which a particular group of male poets and painters are able to convene and experiment with a new, volatile aesthetics of male beauty. In other words, in the climate of fin-de-siècle Britain, where new discursive spaces are opening for the articulation of an increasing multiplicity of sexual difference, the motif of bathing *en plein air* makes publicly possible a specifically male erotic pleasure in the nude male form.

In studying this aesthetic moment, I consider two particular issues: first, on a formal level, I am interested in the re-emergence in the 1890s of a dialogue between the sister arts that had been particularly lively among the Pre-Raphaelites earlier in the century. The painter who seems to initiate this dialogue, Henry Scott Tuke, is not quite a household name today, although several of his paintings hang in the Tate and other leading British galleries. Tuke was the younger son of the physician Daniel Hack Tuke and descendant of a long line of eminently respectable Quaker philanthropists. His mother, Esther Maria Tuke, born Stickney, was the niece of Sarah Stickney Ellis, renowned for her conduct manuals for middle-class women. From the 1880s through the early 1900s, Tuke produced a substantial series of paintings repeatedly exploring the motif of adolescent boys bathing in the sea. These paintings, several of which drew on literary antecedents, provoked a responding cluster of poems by the "Uranians"—an appellation chosen by critic Timothy d'Arch Smith to name a group of poets who celebrated an idealized love for young boys.[2] Charles Kains-Jackson, John Gambril Nicholson, Alan Stanley, Frederick Rolfe (alias Baron Corvo), and several others took up and elaborated the bathing boys motif. While these poets were clearly a marginal group of writers, publishing in fringe journals, Tuke was well known and highly acclaimed in mainstream art circles, which brings me to my second, more political focus of interest. What is it about Tuke's aesthetic that enables him to paint the male nude repeatedly *en plein air*, at a time when even in studio painting, male nudity had been almost completely displaced by the female nude? More than this, how was he able to achieve broad public acclaim while at the same time contributing to the climate of dissidence that produced new liminal spaces for the performance of sexual difference? For it seems remarkable that Tuke's paintings should not have been treated with more suspicion in the decades when the Labouchère Amendment (1885) and its spectacular implementation during the three trials of Oscar Wilde (1895) had heightened the British public's perception of male same-sex passion as criminal.[3] I propose that the popular success of Tuke's work lies in his singular ability to manipulate in painting a dialectics of romance that in poetry and prose was far more threatening to a middle-class sense of sexual propriety. Let me outline briefly what I mean by this "dialectics of romance."

The Dialectics of Romance in Victorian Poetry and Painting

My conception of the romance mode is taken from Patricia Parker's study of it as an organizing principle—a form "which simultaneously quests for and postpones a particular end, objective, or object."[4] In poetic texts, romance occurs in moments of dilation or delay that postpone the forward movement of the narrative quest for truth or closure. Associated with the figurative, picture-making power of lyric poetry (7), romance is moralized as complicit with the enervating effects of idleness; it takes the form of dalliance, a pandering to the senses or straying from the point that intrudes into, and suspends, the rational striving typical of epic narrative (38). More than this, the moral overtones of romance are complicated with gender coding: its deferring, postponing strategies are associated with feminized powers of seduction, for instance with Scheherazade's postponement of death by storytelling (37). They may also be opposed to the putatively male urge toward active completion of the quest, as in the ability of Acrasia—Spenser's harlot of romance—to hold knights in thrall (59).

For the purposes of this project, Parker's theory of romance has two particular advantages: First, it offers the hypothesis that romance provides an emblem for the preapocalyptic or threshold nature of language itself.[5] In other words, there is a dual impulse inherent in language: a linear impulse associated with narrative unfolding that hastens toward revelation is offset by detours, postponements, and suspensions in embowered spaces associated with lyric con-

templation. Applied to a morally charged problem such as the erotic representation of the male nude in late-Victorian England, Parker's hypothesis might
be extended further. One could surmise that a eulogy to the male nude expressed in words bears with it the threat that, regardless of the postponements
it performs, its linearity proceeds toward an inevitable revelation of some truth
concealed because morally questionable: for instance, the possibility that the
body eulogized is an object of sexual desire. In contrast, painting or the plastic
arts have the power to engage romance strategies more exhaustively, stalling
narrative progress indefinitely. In painting, revelation of truth can be perpetu-
ally suspended as implication. This theory, as we shall see, helps to explain the
dual success of Tuke's bathing studies both as popular and as dissident art.

A second advantage of Parker's version of romance lies in its capacity to
comprehend historical difference even as it reveals certain structural affinities
in the poetic texts studied. Whether, for instance, emphasis will fall on arrival
or on delay, and whether such dynamics will be interpreted as morally laudable
or threatening will be determined by the context in which the romance principle operates, so that it should not be considered either as a fixed generic pre-
scription, nor a trans-historical category, but rather as a recurrent dialectic with
shifting, tractable terms. This dialectic is observable in Victorian culture in
both general and highly specific forms.

Generally speaking, the dominant middle-class ideology of utilitarianism
and industrialism in Victorian Britain forced the arts, and in particular poetry,
to stand as an alternative to the acquisitive preoccupations of the market economy and expansion of empire.[6] Following the separate gendering of public and
private spheres—the public being allied with the putatively male involvement
in market activity and the private coded as feminine and domestic—art, literature, and in particular poetry assumed a feminized romance function. This was
often in protest against the activities of manufacturing and industry—the
fields where manliness could be most readily played out. Aesthetic culture thus
came to involve an ambivalence toward the category of the feminine on which
it depended but which, to defend its worth, it simultaneously felt obliged to
disavow.[7]

On a more local level, such ambivalence is apparent in the poetry and painting of the Pre-Raphaelites, where poets such as Dante Gabriel Rossetti
and Algernon Charles Swinburne, following John Keats and Alfred, Lord
Tennyson, repeatedly use the figure of woman to develop a new dimension
to Romanticism's fascination with the motif of sublime revelation. The Pre-
Raphaelites create feminized spaces that operate to suspend the potentially
ominous closure toward which manly action leads. The dreamlike suspension
of their verse creates a pictorial effect that translates very successfully into visual images. Thus lyrics like Keats's "La Belle Dame Sans Merci" and "The

Eve of St Agnes" or Tennyson's "The Lady of Shalott" and "Mariana" provoke innumerable representations by William Holman Hunt, D. G. Rossetti, John Everett Millais, and others. Alternatively, romance appears as a poised suggestiveness in painting and sculpture, which poets seem provoked to counter with language's linear, syntactic movement toward revelation. In this Pre-Raphaelite dialogue between poetry and painting, the alliance of romance suspension with the ambiguous femininity that Parker theorizes is perpetuated to shrewd political ends. The female figure is constructed with the dual potential to be both morally elevated (the angel or madonna) or morally corruptive (the prostitute or seductive "Magdalen"). Thus, as Kathy Alexis Psomiades has shown, the figure of woman can be used to finesse a basic contradiction underlying the Victorian artwork: it is supposedly priceless and yet it is a marketable commodity bearing a price tag.[8]

Toward the end of the century, the morally ambiguous female figure is displaced from the embowered space of romance by the volatile figure of the effeminate young man,[9] a striking illustration being Dorian Gray as he dallies with Lord Henry Wotton in Basil Hallward's *hortus conclusus* in the opening chapters of *The Picture of Dorian Gray*. Like femininity earlier in the century, effeminacy becomes a remarkably unstable category by the turn of the century, as both Sinfield and Joseph Bristow have recently demonstrated.[10] It can, for instance, be used to invoke the foppish effeteness of the nonetheless securely heterosexual gentleman of leisure (the dandy) but is as easily appropriated as characteristic of the aesthete whose delight in sensual pleasures is increasingly associated with male same-sex passion.

The motif of boys bathing *en plein air* flirts with effeminacy with peculiar suggestiveness, for while its secluded spaces can evoke the tradition of romance, they simultaneously eschew both dandyism and brooding or languid sensuality. It is Henry Scott Tuke's ability to combine the principles of romance feminization with a Victorian aesthetic of athletic manliness that assures his simultaneous status as acclaimed Academician and contributor to the unsettlement of stable and conventional sexual categories. Let us turn now to a close scrutiny of his techniques.

Tuke and His Lyric Precedents: Swinburne against Symonds

An unusually versatile painter, Tuke was a member of both the Royal Academy and the Royal Water Colour Society, a renowned portraitist, and painter of nautical subjects such as tall ships. In spite of this, his public reputation was chiefly founded on his paintings of boys bathing in the sea. In her biography of her brother Harry, Maria Tuke Sainsbury remarks that "there was nearly always a bathing picture or a nude in some form on the way each summer" and

Figure 1 *August Blue,* by H. S. Tuke (1893–94). Oil on Canvas. Reproduced
with the kind permission of the Tate Gallery, London.

that, at his memorial exhibition after his death in 1929, many people "expressed surprise at the range of his work, having always regarded him merely
as the painter of bathers."[11] The array of paintings on which I might draw to
illustrate this argument is therefore vast. In fact I have chosen to focus on two
of the earlier studies, *August Blue* (fig. 1) and *Ruby, Gold, and Malachite* (fig. 2)
for the following reasons: First, these were exhibited at the Royal Academy
and achieved public acclaim when Tuke was not yet an Academician and was
still establishing his reputation as an artist. Second, the two paintings mark an
expansion of his repertoire from pictorial narrative toward color compositions.
While the narrative paintings dwelt on manly activity—exemplified for instance in *All Hands to the Pumps!* of 1889 (fig. 3) and *The Run Home* of 1902
(fig. 4)—the color compositions suggested the contemplative suspension of activity in a moment of romance deferral.

To the eye of the art historian, the obvious precedent for preoccupation with
color might be James Whistler's "symphonies" and "harmonies,"[12] and this
connection is certainly endorsed by Tuke's early diary entries. In 1877, for instance, after a visit to the first show at the new Grosvenor Gallery, he writes,

Figure 2 *Ruby, Gold, and Malachite,* by H. S. Tuke (1901). Oil on canvas. Reproduced with the kind permission of the Guildhall Art Gallery, Corporation of London.

"Whistler has some very singular 'arrangements' and 'harmonies'"; and in March 1884, "called on Whistler at Tite Street and saw some lovely things, especially a blue girl, full length."[13] However, elaborating on a fleeting suggestion made by Emmanuel Cooper,[14] I want to argue that Tuke's color compositions—*August Blue* (1894), *Ruby, Gold, and Malachite* (1902), and the later *Blue and Gold* (1912), *Green and Gold* (1922), and *Aquamarine* (1929)—are also echoes of and responses to another, later, and less obvious precedent: John Addington Symonds's contemplation of color as a medium for exploring male eros in his discourse "In the Key of Blue." Building on this hypothesis, I will then argue that, in the press reviews of the two paintings, a debate over what on the surface might appear to be purely formal issues reveals some of the moral stakes involved in these images of the youthful male nude bathing *en plein air.* Indeed, these moral stakes are more directly spelled out when the Uranian poets respond to Tuke in verse form.

I begin my reading of *August Blue* and *Ruby, Gold, and Malachite* by considering their relations to the verbal precedents alluded to in their titles. Following

Figure 3 *All Hands to the Pumps!*, by H. S. Tuke (1888–89). Oil on canvas.
Reproduced with the kind permission of the Tate Gallery, London.

Figure 4 *The Run Home,* by H. S. Tuke (1901–2). Oil on canvas. Reproduced with the kind permission of the Royal Institution of Cornwall, The Royal Cornwall Museum, Truro. The painting was a gift to the museum by Alfred de Pass in 1930.

the pattern of romance principles already outlined, I suggest that these pictorial images suspend the linear, forward movement implicit in their verbal prece- dents to fine political effect. The title *August Blue* is generally recognized as a quotation from Algernon Charles Swinburne's lyric "The Sundew," published in *Poems and Ballads* in 1866.[15] The opening lines of the poem describing "A little marsh-plant, yellow green, / And pricked at lip with tender red" have also been suggested as the textual source of *Ruby, Gold, and Malachite.*[16] This would situate both paintings in the context of youthful, heterosexual love, for the small marsh-plant is named as sole witness to the lyric speaker's passionate spring courtship. The sundew is privy to the identity of the speaker's lady-love, and yet as the heat of the summer and by extension the lovers' passion intensi- fies, the moss-water in which the flower grows becomes stagnant. The spoiled flower, apparently too fragile to honor the memory of the speaker's beloved, is therefore impatiently dismissed as unworthy of experiencing the full sensual richness of midsummer:

> The hard sun, as thy petals knew,
> Coloured the heavy moss-water:
> Thou wert not worth green midsummer
> Nor fit to live to August blue,
> O sundew, not remembering her.[17]

In this context, the titles *August Blue* and, more obliquely, *Ruby, Gold, and Malachite* would seem to evoke the peak of summer beauty—the period in which the turn and decline of the season into fall and decadence is just immanent—while the sundew suggests the fragility and transience of spring and young love.

Certainly Tuke's painting evokes a moment of summer perfection exploiting painting's capacity to suggest time suspended, or the "moment's monument." *August Blue* in particular suggests the very minimum of movement; none of the four boys is doing anything concerted. The dominant figure, standing, seems poised in contemplation, his vertical stance repeated by the distant masts of the tall ships, sails furled, at anchor in the background. One boy reclines in the stern of the boat, one leans forward on his oars, and a fourth, in the water, rests his arms on the side of the boat. The striking feature of the painting is its impressionistic suggestion of light through color: blue is dominant, its varying shades in the sky, water, boat and rower's shirt broken only by the complementary gold of the boys' bodies and hair. Yet even after one has paid close attention to both Swinburne's poetic text and Tuke's painting, the connection between the two seems unsatisfactorily tenuous, prompting one to ask why Tuke would have alighted on this poem or selected this particular phrase for his title. If, however, one pauses to consider how Tuke might have felt about Swinburne at the time he was painting *August Blue,* if one takes into account the convoluted personal interactions between Swinburne and Symonds, and Symonds and Tuke, one might suspect that Tuke's title is more than an innocuous, chance citation of verse.

Swinburne and Symonds shared a brief literary friendship that on Symonds's part progressed from prudish disapproval of Swinburne's poetic subjects, to passionate admiration of his moral daring, and finally to disillusionment particularly with Swinburne's denunciation of Walt Whitman.[18] Both Symonds and Swinburne had studied under Benjamin Jowett at Oxford, and when Symonds died in April 1893, Jowett wrote his epitaph, concluding it with the words "Farewell, my dearest friend. No one in his heart sustained his friends more than you did, nor was more benevolent to the simple and unlearned."[19] When Jowett himself died a few months later (October 1, 1893), Swinburne wrote a memorial essay, "Recollections of Professor Jowett," which was published in *The Nineteenth Century* in December 1893. In that essay, he took the opportunity to lash out at Symonds, perhaps avenging himself for the latter's unenthusiastic reviews of his work, and possibly also expressing jealousy of the intellectual respect that Jowett had always shown toward Symonds. In a strangely charged defense of his mentor's judgment, Swinburne observes that even if Jowett's sharp intelligence was occasionally affected by the "foggy damp of Oxonian atmosphere," he would certainly never have succumbed to the views of "such renascent blossoms of the Italian renascence as the Platonic amorist of blue-breeched gondoliers who is now in Aretino's bosom." Then, with a cutting allusion to Symonds's admiration of the comradeship advocated by Whitman in the "Calamus" section of *Leaves of Grass,* he adds, "The cult of calamus, as expounded by Mr. Addington Symonds to his fellow-calamites, would have found no acceptance or tolerance with the translator of Plato."[20]

Symonds, for all his unorthodox views on male sexuality, was such a paragon of personal discretion and tact that to portray him as an acolyte of Pietro Aretino, "that notorious ribald of Arezzo" (to use Milton's phrase), seems an unwarranted cruelty. And as Grosskurth, citing Faber, remarks, the neologism "calamites" with its evocation of "catamites" is in equally poor taste,[21] but Swinburne was given to vicious humor, even referring on one occasion to "the late Mr. Soddington Symonds."[22] Given the strained relations between Symonds and Swinburne and the launching of this caustic attack so soon after Symonds's death, one is provoked to wonder whether Tuke did not deliberately appropriate the poetic phrase from Swinburne's poem to nettle the poet, while celebrating precisely a form of manly beauty that the "Platonic amorist of blue-breeched gondoliers" would have appreciated. The fact that in Swinburne's opinion "The Sundew" was "the most juvenile of all my effusions of past years" adds piquancy to the jest.[23]

For the friendship between Tuke and Symonds, if shortlived, was apparently very tender and mutually appreciative. Their fathers, both medical men, had been friends, as Symonds explains in his first letter to Tuke written in the fall of 1890 from Switzerland. There he had been visited by Horatio Forbes Brown, the historian of Venice and later Symonds's literary executor and biographer, who had described the young Falmouth painter and his work with great enthusiasm. Symonds, impressed by a photograph of Tuke's painting "Perseus and Andromeda," exhibited at the Royal Academy in February 1890, felt compelled to write to the young artist using their paternal connection and their mutual friendship with Brown as an introduction. Subsequently, in various letters, he refers with admiration to Tuke, and in August 1892 visited Falmouth for several days, bringing with him his close companion of some eleven years, the Venetian gondolier Angelo Fusato.[24] Symonds and Fusato stayed at the local hotel, where Tuke met them, enjoying a moonlight stroll one night and then entertaining them at his Swanpool cottage for the following two days.[25]

Earlier, in the spring of that year, Symonds had been composing "In the Key of Blue," which in June 1892 he describes to the young poet Arthur Symons like this:

> At Venice last month I tried my hand at nine studies (Verse) "In the Key of Blue," with a prose setting. Something in the line of impressionism. I have a friend there, who is a facchino [porter] of 20, and dresses in a costume of three modulated blues. He poses in my studies, in combination with other colours. Of things like this, I have always been doing plenty, and then putting them away in a box. The public thinks them immoral. You ought not to be attached to a young man in a blouse, and see how beautiful he is combined with blacks and reds and golds, etc.[26]

From our perspective, it is particularly worth noting first that the color blue is the focus of Symonds's study, and second that his model should coincidentally be named *Augusto* Zanon.

In January 1893, Symonds published the essay in a collection entitled *In the Key of Blue and Other Prose Essays;* in April that year he died; and in the summer Tuke began work on what was to become *August Blue.* It appeared with that title when exhibited at the Academy the following spring (May 1894) after Jowett had died and Swinburne's vindictive remarks about Symonds had appeared in *The Nineteenth Century.* Aside from these historical coincidences, compelling material appears in Symonds's text itself to endorse the hypothesis that "In the Key of Blue" is the verbal antecedent of *August Blue,* of *Ruby, Gold, and Malachite,* and perhaps of Tuke's later color compositions.

The essay opens by protesting the inadequacy of language to represent the fine gradations of the color spectrum. For Symonds, green is the color most poorly served by distinguishing terms, while "blue fares better . . . yellow is still more fortunate," and "red stands at the head of the list." Then, in the time-honored strategem of translating disadvantage to empowerment, he argues that the very poverty of language provokes the stylist to greater exercise of both fancy and imagination. Alighting on the color blue, the color apparently favored in the nineteenth century by the watermen of Venice—the fishermen, stevedores, porters, and boatmen who wear "blouses, sashes and trousers of this colour"—he undertakes "a series of studies of what might be termed 'blues and blouses'."[27]

What we read are supposedly the "notes taken for these studies . . . caught by accident, not sought deliberately," in which language is the medium of representation, while color and clothing—"blues and blouses"—are the matter under discussion. However, as the essay progresses, it takes on more and more clearly the structure of a romance quest in which the power of prose to hasten toward apocalyptic revelation or unveiling of the truth is set in tension with the picture-making power of verse to stall that forward movement. On the one hand, the prose passages provide a simple narrative in which the two men— the nineteen-year-old Augusto and the much older speaker—meet on a hot summer night in Venice and then undertake a journey into the country so that the young *facchino* can have a glimpse of rural life he has never before had the opportunity to experience. On the other hand, the verse passages suspend narrative progress to record Augusto in blue at various moments and in various settings.

What is striking about each poetic description is the contemplative indifference of the belovèd to the poet's admiring eye. Sometimes he is self-absorbed, sometimes he dances with another, once he dandles a little girl on his knee, so that an aura of inaccessibility constantly surrounds him. At length, Symonds articulates his covert desire to treat Augusto as more than a mere clotheshorse and vehicle for specular pleasure, so that the final "symphony" represents a coming to the point after repeated deferral and postponement. In this verse, a walk through the old town of Castelfranco and a sudden thunderstorm that gives way to a moonlit night in which the comrades walk and talk closes climactically in the seclusion of the bedchamber:

> Hushed was the night for friendly talk;
> Under the dark arcades we walk,
> Pace the wet pavement, where light steals
> And swoons amid the huge abeles:
> Then seek our chamber. All the blues
> Dissolve, the symphony of hues
> Fades out of sight, and leaves at length
> A flawless form of simple strength,
> Sleep-seeking, breathing, ivory-white,
> Upon the couch in candle-light.[28]

In this closing scene, the literal act of undressing for bed becomes the moment at which the veil of blue dissolves, revealing the nude male body as the climactic image or endpoint of the study. In its inaccessibility, its perfection is sustained—"A flawless form of simple strength"—and it continues to be an image of resolute, distant indifference: "Sleep-seeking, breathing, ivory-white, / Upon the couch in candle-light."

Only in the envoy to this fantasia does Symonds relinquish his distance from the desired object. Reversing the priority of the color and the image which it veiled, he confesses openly that he has been absorbed less in the aesthetic problem of representing color through words, than in representing the physical beauty of the *facchino* whom he admires:

Come back, my Muse, come back to him
Who warmed the cold hue, bright or dim.
Those ivory brows, those lustrous eyes,
Those grape-like curls, those brief replies;
These are thy themes—the man, the life—
Not tints in symphony at strife.[29]

In this moment of revelation, aesthetic equilibrium gives way to political urgency. As if no longer able to resist the impulse of language to hasten toward apocalypse, Symonds admits the transgressive nature of his passion which up to this point he veils behind implicitly heterosexual aesthetic conventions. His initial thesis—that language is inadequate to the subtle representation of color—has obliquely addressed another, more fraught aesthetic problem: the difficulty in 1890s England of composing a verbal eulogy on the allure of the nude male body without thereby compromising its moral integrity. It is this aesthetic problem that Henry Scott Tuke addresses more successfully through the medium of painting. Eluding the compulsion toward revelation evident in the verbal art of Symonds, Tuke takes advantage of the visual image's capacity to stall linear progression. Using color to produce unusual lighting effects that stall the viewer's eye on the nude male body, his compositions provoke uneasy responses in his viewers. While they praise his use of color, they disapprove of his rendering of the nude form. This ambivalence is particularly apparent in the critical evaluations that followed *August Blue*'s exhibition at the Royal Academy in the spring of 1894.

Some Implications of Critical Ambivalence

August Blue received mention in most of the leading London art journals: *The Academy, The Athenaeum, The Magazine of Art, The Spectator, The Fortnightly Review, The Times Weekly Edition,* to name only a few; and from these it earned a fair share of praise. To Claude Phillips of *The Academy,* it was "[o]ne of the most brilliant *plein air* pieces at Burlington House"; to D. S. MacColl of *The Spectator,* "The illumination is high pitched in a golden key, and the merit of the picture is the way in which this orange light is carried through every part."[30] Two others refer to the painting as "brilliant." Yet while the sensual appeal of Tuke's work as a color composition is acknowledged, his treatment of the nude is relentlessly criticized. Each critique points to a formal negligence in his execution, implicitly reading it as a signal of moral laxity. To the anonymous reviewer from *The Athenaeum,* whose general assessment of the Exhibition is peppered with complaints about poor composition, crude draftsmanship, and dirty coloring, Tuke's nudes are executed "with a light hand, but thinly"; they are "drawn with tolerable correctness, but no unusual spirit."[31]

The same reviewer trivializes the painting as "a large *ad captandum* sketch"—by implication, work hastily and roughly executed for the purpose of pleasing the crowd. MacColl complains that Tuke "has not yet gained enough command over his material to give his group a look of being caught in natural action." He continues, "The defect may be partly due to the study of figures posed to imitate a somewhat momentary action, but it depends still more on slackness in the composing faculty."[32]

One might assume that the point at issue here is the British critics' defense of painstaking composition and draftsmanship—associated with academic and studio technique—against the unpolished but suggestive sketchiness of open-air painting assimilated by a new generation of English artists from the French *plein air* painters and Impressionists. But what is interesting about this particular debate is that it should circulate around a painter who had received such a solidly academic studio training. For Tuke had started his education at the Slade School of Art in London under E. J. Poynter, later Sir Edward Poynter, Director of the National Gallery and President of the Royal Academy. This was followed by study in Paris at the studio of Jean Paul Laurens, a master renowned for careful painterly modeling in the neo-classical, tragic tradition of Jacques Louis David. Only later, under the influence of the English artist Arthur Lemon, did Tuke become absorbed in *plein air* painting, following Jules Bastien-Lepage, an artist sometimes loosely associated with Manet and Millet as a leader of the movement to take art out of the studio and the academies and expand its possibilities in the open air.[33]

Tuke's foregrounding of the nude male form could be read as a reflection of his neo-classical training, but his use of complementary colors to achieve the light and shadow effects that create such foregrounding is impressionistic. Unlike W. A. Bouguereau, celebrated for his rendering of the female nude, Tuke does not produce "the exquisitely modelled and perfectly drawn" flesh so admired by the *Athenaeum*'s reviewer in *Amour Piqué,* the French artist's contribution to the 1894 Exhibition. Instead the very corporeality of Tuke's boys seems an ephemeral effect of light and shade caught in color that deliberately resists appropriation by a fin-de-siècle discourse of high aestheticism. Tuke avoids a preoccupation with classical form of the kind invoked and critiqued by Oscar Wilde in the figure of Basil Hallward;[34] for where Hallward's admiration of Dorian Gray risks effacing eroticism by a protomodernist attention to aesthetic form, Tuke blends impressionistic innovations in the representation of light through color with a neo-classical focus on figure painting, producing a new, sensualized rendition of the male body that cannot be unequivocally appropriated to mainstream political purposes. In so doing, he could be said to pursue "the claims of bodies, pleasures, and knowledges" that Michel Foucault was to advocate some seventy-four years later as a means of rallying against the hegemonic deployment of sexuality.[35]

Little wonder that the responses of Tuke's critics reflect anxiety about the formal implications of *August Blue*. The choice of terms such as "slackness" and "defect," and phrases such as "not . . . enough command" and "no unusual spirit" suggest that the reviewers' discomfort lies more with the moral implications of the subject matter than with the painting's formal execution. Just as the liberties which Walt Whitman took with the rules of meter and scansion in *Leaves of Grass* could be readily translated into "bad morals";[36] just as Swinburne's "unpruned exuberance of language and imagery" could be used to infer "perverted moral perceptions";[37] so in Tuke's painting, innovative emphasis on light effects through color when portraying the male nude could be moralized as a tendency toward effeteness or a lack of manly control. Yet even as it seems on the verge of critical disparagement, *August Blue* ironically receives ratification from a most respectable quarter: the trustees of the prestigious Chantrey Fund chose to buy it for the nation.

The Chantrey Fund had been established by the successful sculptor Sir Francis Chantrey (1781–1841) and had come into effect in 1877 on the death of his widow. According to his will, income from Chantrey's estate was to be used for the "encouragement of British Fine Art" through the purchase of works "of the highest merit in painting and sculpture that can be obtained either already executed or which may hereafter be executed by Artists of any nation provided . . . the same shall have been entirely executed within the shores of Great Britain."[38] In 1889, Tuke's dramatic narrative painting *All Hands to the Pumps!* (fig. 3) had been bought by the Chantrey bequest, and its representation of manly resilience in the face of nautical disaster seems in keeping with the nationalistic sentiments expressed in the will.[39] *August Blue* could well have been viewed as another perspective on British nautical life, for it combines a cluster of features that would have conformed perfectly to the nationalistic spirit of Chantrey's endowment. Not only is the painting cast as a seascape, "the department in which an English exhibition is always richer than in any other,"[40] but it is a twofold celebration of that rare perfection, the clear English summer day and the capacity of healthy youth to enjoy it. This discrepancy of opinion between the skepticism of the critics and the enthusiasm of the Chantrey trustees is an indication of the fine line Tuke walks between conforming to a mainstream paradigm of athletic masculinity, while opening up the possibilities for the recognition of homoeroticism in the admiration of manliness.

Tuke's next color composition of nude bathers, *Ruby, Gold, and Malachite*, exhibited at the Royal Academy in the spring of 1902, harks back to the lists of color terms in the opening paragraph of Symonds's essay: the "*emerald-green*, sage-green, *jade*-green" or the "topaz, *gold*, orange, citron . . . rose and cherry, *ruby* and almandine, blood and flame" (emphasis added) even as it might also ironically echo Swinburne's "little marsh-plant, *yellow green*, / And pricked at lip with tender *red*" (emphasis added). The unusual "malachite" in particular seems to answer to Symonds's complaint that "green is the color most poorly served by distinguishing terms." But besides echoing a literary precedent, *Ruby, Gold, and Malachite* also explores a slightly different version of adolescent male beauty than that exemplified in *August Blue*. The boys of the latter are young, combining a fragile ethereal innocence with the potential for dangerous transgression that Martha Vicinus has identified in her study of the adolescent boy as *fin-de-siècle femme fatale*.[41] *Ruby, Gold, and Malachite*, however, focuses on slightly older boys, the "rough lads" idealized by Oxbridge social reformers in the 1880s and 1890s.[42] It is perhaps because his figures invoke the latter mainstream paradigm that Tuke received more assured praise from his reviewers for this painting, although several other factors might have contributed to making him a far safer bet for critical acclaim than he had been in 1894.

First, he had been elected an Associate of the Royal Academy in 1900; second, along with his color composition, he exhibited a yachting study, *The Run Home*, and a formal portrait, *Portrait of Alfred de Pass*, a wealthy South African who had built a holiday home in Falmouth in 1895 and was to become a close friend of Tuke. While *Ruby, Gold, and Malachite* is daring in its presentation of the male nude in an embowered space the intimacy of which is increased by the absence of horizon, the other two works stand as alibis for the painter's respectability, both as the athletic participant and promoter of British manliness exemplified in seamanship, and as an acclaimed portraitist much in demand by wealthy patrons of the arts. The reassurance to be derived from these alibis is evident in the following comment by an anonymous reviewer in *The Illustrated London News:*

> Mr. Henry Tuke is a yachtsman as well as a painter of the sea, and he may be said to show his strength in both capacities in "The Run for [*sic*] Home." What is unusual in a sea-painter is his delightful feeling for decorative beauty, showing itself here in the scheme of colour, in the almost idyllic figures of his sailors and boys, and again expressed in the title of a second delightful picture, "Ruby, Gold, and Malachite."[43]

The potential danger of effeteness or effeminacy implicit in the phrase "the delightful feeling for decorative beauty" is negated in Tuke's case by his credentials as a sea painter. With such overt guarantees of his manliness, the painter's reviewers can even go so far as to study the beauty of specific parts of the nudes, as does "H. S." of *The Spectator,* who observes,

> A specially beautiful piece of painting is the colour and tone of the thigh of the nearest figure; it is as subtle and delicate as the red shirt of the figure in the boat is gay and brilliant.[44]

Just as the reviewer for *The Illustrated London News* can accept the "decorative beauty" of *Ruby, Gold, and Malachite* in the context of the manly vigor of *The Run Home,* so "H. S." can extol the beauty of a nude's thigh as especially "subtle and delicate" by contrasting it to the gaiety and brilliance of the red shirt. Color is once again the medium whereby Tuke can arrest the viewer's eye, focusing on the active male body suspended in time. This intense focus could be construed as a form of romance dalliance complicit with the trend toward idolizing working-class boys that middle-class men indulged at the turn of the century. For Tuke captures a peculiarly rare and forbidden form of beauty: the ephemeral, supposedly aboriginal, boyish grace that has heightened allure when embodied in the working-class lad. Eluding accusations of immorality that Symonds incurs for his "blues and blouses," Tuke is simultaneously able to resist assimilation into the pathologizing sexological discourses proliferating at the turn of the century to which Symonds made himself vulnerable.

For one thing, Tuke shrewdly shifts focus from the single, adult male nude to the group of adolescents—a shift from the overtly homoerotic to the less threateningly homosocial. He sets his scenes not in the candlelight of an Italian bedchamber, but in the brightest light of an English summer's day. In this treatment, his bathing boys are legible as healthy, working-class "rough lads" from Cornish villages participating in the invigorating activity of open-air swimming so staunchly promoted by the eminently respectable, public-school tradition of Dr. Thomas Arnold. Thus, in post–Boer War Britain, when public opinion linked failing imperial strength to a perception of working-class urban youths as degenerate hooligans,[45] Tuke's boys present a fantasy of possible heirs to the empire who, even at play, are apprentices in seamanship, qualifying to man the vessels of the British Navy and fishing industry. Through this very ambiguity in his paintings—the suspension of manly activity in a moment of romance dalliance—Tuke is able to articulate a mainstream paradigm of athletic masculinity that conforms to the Victorian heterosexual ideal of imperial manliness, while simultaneously opening the possibility of same-sex eros in such manly beauty. It is, I would argue, this quality of suspended ambiguity in his work that prompts the Uranian poets to translate the pictorial back into the verbal, spelling out in the linearity of verse the covert significance of Tuke's color compositions for their particular fin-de-siècle subculture.

Tuke's "Uranian" Respondents

One of the first of the responses to Tuke's bathers is a sonnet by Charles Kains-Jackson, a London lawyer and editor of *The Artist and Journal of Home Culture*, an apparently mainstream journal which nevertheless managed to publish a large body of Uranian material.[46] Appearing in this journal in May 1889, the sonnet bore the heading "On a picture by H. S. Tuke in the present exhibition of the New English Art Club."[47] It runs as follows:

> Within this little space of canvas shut
>   Are summer sunshine, and the exuberant glee
>   Of living light that laughs along the sea,
> And freshness of kind winds; yet these are but
> As the rich gem whereon the cameo's cut;
>   The cameo's self, the boyish faces free
>   From care, the beauty and the delicacy
> Of young slim frames not yet to labour put.
> The kisses that make red each honest face
>   Are of the breeze and salt and tingling spray.
> So, may these boys know never of a place
>   Wherein, to desk or factory a prey,
> That colour blanches slowly, nature's grace
>   Made pale with life's incipient decay.[48]

Kains-Jackson dwells on an issue that Tuke, working within the "little space of canvas," can defer addressing: the fact that the progression of time will transform the sensual freshness that the boys now embody. The images of gem and cameo, and terms such as "beauty" and "delicacy" used in the octave, convey a sense of the boys' value to the lyric speaker. In the first two lines of the sestet ("The kisses that make red each honest face / Are of the breeze and salt and tingling spray"), there is a hint that change might take the form of sexual corruption—that the future might hold caresses less innocent than the kisses of breeze and salt spray—but more strongly emphasized is the threat of clerical or factory drudgery that will be detrimental to the boys' health and therefore to their physical beauty. Resonant with Edward Carpenter's democratic comradeship, the sonnet uses an issue of class to negotiate the subversiveness of its aesthetics: it uses an attack on the capitalist work ethic, venerated by middle-class respectability, as an alibi for eulogizing working-class male adolescent beauty; for it represents that beauty as threatened by the adverse effects of excessive labor. At no point, however, are the boys cast as objects of the speaker's lust; rather, reminiscent of Symonds's Augusto, they are inaccessible and therefore sublime embodiments of a rare form of beauty. Even as it distributes attention over a group rather than focusing on a single object of admiration, the sonnet thus appropriates and refashions the dynamics of the courtly, Petrarchan tradition to homoerotic ends.

The second poem, "August Blue," was published the year Tuke's painting was exhibited. It was included in a collection entitled *Love Lyrics* by an enigmatic figure, Alan Stanley, about whom we know very little.[49] Unlike Tuke and Kains-Jackson, Stanley heightens the homoerotic implications of his lyric by singling out one boy—the standing boy of Tuke's study—instead of representing a group in more homosocial terms.

Silver mists on a silver sea,
And white clouds overhead
Sailing the grey sky speedily
To where the east turns red.
And one lone boat her sails has spread,
Sails of the whitest lawn,
That seem to listen for the tread
Of the tender feet of dawn.

The risen sun now makes the sky
An arching roof of gold,
Amber the clouds turn as they fly
Uncurling fold on fold;
The sun a goblet seems to hold
A draught of fervid wine,
And the young day no longer cold
Glows with a fire divine.

Stripped for the sea your tender form
Seems all of ivory white,
Through which the blue veins wander warm
O'er throat and bosom slight,
And as you stand, so slim, upright
The glad waves grow and yearn
To clasp you circling in their might,
To kiss with lips that burn.

Flashing limbs in the waters blue
And gold curls floating free;
Say, does it thrill you through and through
With ardent love, the sea?
A very nymph you seem to be
As you glide and dive and swim,
While the mad waves clasp you fervently
Possessing every limb.

King of the Sea, triumphant boy,
Nature itself made thrall
To God's white work without alloy

On whom no stain doth fall.
Gaze on him, slender, fair, and tall,
And on the yearning sea
Who deigns to creep and cling, and crawl,
His worshipper to be.[50]

Of these five stanzas, the central or third seems a verbal interpretation of Tuke's painting, while on either side, the first and second stanzas and the fourth and fifth act as the preceding and succeeding frames in a narrative progression.

The first two stanzas set the scene, suggesting the growing warmth of the day (and by implication, the growing passion of the speaker/observer) through the spectrum of color. Emphasized by the predominantly iambic rhythm, silver, white, and grey are transformed to gold and amber by the red of the rising sun. The third stanza rests on the image of the standing boy in Tuke's painting. Many of the terms used to describe him ("tender form," "throat and bosom slight," "slim"), combined with the colors of the Holy Virgin (blue, white, and gold), suggest a moral purity, fragility, and femininity that are besieged by the "glad waves," personifications of lovers impassioned by the indifference of the boyish *femme fatale*. In the fourth stanza we witness what might be the next frame to Tuke's painting as the boy plunges into the sea. The eroticism that is latent in both Tuke's and Kains-Jackson's work, and the violence inherent in same-sex relations at this time,[51] are more clearly articulated in the fantasy of the feminized boy engulfed in the power of the "mad waves." However, in a sudden shift of gender, the boy is transformed in the fifth stanza from fragile maiden to triumphant monarch. As if resuming the position in which Tuke painted him, he becomes once again an embodiment of virginal purity and therefore moral conquest while his admirers, no longer besieging him, are subservient and powerless. On the verge of a fantasy of passionate coercion, Stanley retracts, returning to the idyllic quality that Tuke consistently preserves.

It is as if Stanley, and to a lesser extent Kains-Jackson, feels compelled to disrupt romance deferral and accentuate the erotic suggestiveness in Tuke's visual images. Combining the linearity of language with the pictoriality of lyric verse, each poet then creates fantasies that approach more closely the overt articulation of forbidden desire. Whether we, as readers, are comfortable with the particular form of eros proposed by the Uranians is perhaps less to the point than how the dialogue between poetry and painting circulating around the image of the adolescent boy gradually opens up a space in Victorian aesthetic culture in which the nude male figure can become the subject of a homoerotic discourse. This development, I would argue, is in large part attributable to Henry Scott Tuke's ingenuity in manipulating the aesthetics of romance.

Notes

A condensed version of this paper was given at the 1996 MLA Convention in Washington, D.C., for one of three panels under the rubric *Victorian Sexual Dissidence*. I wish to thank participants at the session, especially Richard Dellamora and Martha Vicinus, for their comments; I also thank Richard Howard, David Alexander, Elizabeth Heckendorn Cook, and Deidre Lynch for their contributions to this work.

1. Although a number of critics have recently drawn attention to the bathing motif and the dialogue between poetry and painting that it generates, nobody to date has studied the possible ideological implications of this formal interaction. See Timothy d'Arch Smith, *Love in Earnest: Some Notes on the Lives and Writings of English 'Uranian' Poets from 1889 to 1930* (London: Routledge and Kegan Paul, 1970), 169–72; Joseph Kestner, *Masculinities in Victorian Painting* (Aldershot: Scolar Press, 1995), 255–67; and Robert Bernard Martin, *Gerard Manley Hopkins: A Very Private Life* (New York: Putnam's, 1991), 390–92.

2. The adjective "Uranian" is drawn from Plato's *Symposium*, where Pausanius argues that there are two Aphrodites: the "heavenly" and the "common" Aphrodite. The heavenly Aphrodite is the older, motherless daughter of Uranus, and the love that accompanies her "does not share in the female, but only in the male—this is love for young boys." Pausanius then goes on to describe in some detail the superior nature of this love. See Plato, *The Symposium*, in *The Symposium and the Phaedrus: Plato's Erotic Dialogues*, trans. William S. Cobb (Albany: SUNY Press, 1993), 180c–181e.

In Europe at the turn of the century, "Uranian" was a fairly commonly used term. It was supposedly first used by Karl Heinrich Ulrichs, the German lawyer and author of pioneering theories about homosexuality. In a more literary context, it was used, for instance, by John Addington Symonds in a poem, "To Leander," published in the Oxford undergraduate journal of which Lord Alfred Douglas was the sometime editor: "Thou standest on this craggy cove / Live image of Uranian love" (*The Spirit Lamp* 3, no. 2 [1893]: 29). It appears in the title of André Raffalovich's book *Uranisme et unisexualité* (1896); and in a letter dated 18 February 1898, Oscar Wilde writes: "To have altered my life would have been to have admitted that Uranian love is ignoble" (see *The Selected Letters of Oscar Wilde*, ed. Rupert Hart-Davis [Oxford: Oxford University Press, 1979], 327). D'Arch Smith chooses this term because it is free from the derogatory associations of alternatives such as "homosexual," "paederast," and "catamite" (*Love in Earnest*, xx).

3. "The Labouchère Amendment" was the name given to the eleventh clause to the Criminal Law Amendment Act, a rash piece of legislation which ruled that those committing "acts of gross indecency" in public *or in private* would be liable for prosecution and a sentence of two years' imprisonment with or without hard labor. For details on the passage and effects of this law, see F. B. Smith, "Labouchère's Amendment to the Criminal Law Amendment Bill," *Historical Studies* 17 (1976): 165–75.

4. Patricia A. Parker, *Inescapable Romance: Studies in the Poetics of a Mode* (Princeton: Princeton University Press, 1979), 4.

5. Parker points to the "echoes of romance *données* in modern theories of linguistic errancy and narrative structure" (219). She illustrates this observation by citing Saussure's "diacritics," Jakobson's "binary opposition," and Derrida's *"différance."* Elsewhere, I have argued that Lacan's dialectic of desire can be read in terms of the romance mode as Parker describes it (Saville, "'The Lady of Shalott': a Lacanian Romance," *Word and Image* 8, no. 1 [1992]: 73–76).

6. See Alan Sinfield, *The Wilde Century: Effeminacy, Oscar Wilde and the Queer Moment* (New York: Columbia University Press, 1994), 85.

7. Ibid., 87.

8. Kathy Alexis Psomiades, "Beauty's Body: Gender Ideology and British Aestheticism," *Victorian Studies* 36, no. 1 (1992): 31–52.

9. Very suggestive in this context is Martha Vicinus's essay "The Adolescent Boy: Fin de Siècle Femme Fatale," *Journal of the History of Sexuality* 5, no. 1 (1994): 90–114.

10. See Sinfield, *Wilde Century,* and Joseph Bristow, *Effeminate England: Homoerotic Writing after 1885* (New York: Columbia University Press, 1995).

11. Sainsbury, *Henry Scott Tuke R.A., R.W.S.: A Memoir* (London: Secker, 1933), 90, 100.

12. See, for instance, David Wainwright and Catherine Dinn, *Henry Scott Tuke: Under Canvas* (London: Sarema Press, 1989), 56.

13. Sainsbury, *Memoir,* 28, 71.

14. See Cooper, *The Life and Work of Henry Scott Tuke* (London: Gay Men's Press, 1987), 29.

15. See Sainsbury, *Memoir,* 111; Cooper, *Life and Work,* 29; Wainwright and Dinn, *Under Canvas,* 56; and Kestner, *Masculinities,* 262.

16. Wainwright and Dinn, *Under Canvas,* 56.

17. Swinburne, *Poems and Ballads* (1866; reprint, London: Chatto and Windus, 1906), 213.

18. See Phyllis M. Grosskurth's account of this progress in "Swinburne and Symonds: An Uneasy Literary Relationship," *Review of English Studies,* n.s., 15, no. 55 (1963): 257–68.

19. Jowett in Symonds, *The Letters of John Addington Symonds,* ed. Herbert M. Schueller and Robert L. Peters, 6 vols. (Detroit: Wayne State University Press, 1969), 3:841.

20. Swinburne, "Recollections of Professor Jowett," in *Studies in Prose and Poetry* (1894; reprint, London: Chatto and Windus, 1915), 34.

21. Grosskurth, "Swinburne and Symonds," 268.

22. Swinburne, *The Swinburne Letters,* ed. Cecil Y. Lang, 6 vols. (New Haven: Yale University Press, 1982), 6:74. Richard Dellamora has similarly documented a pattern of abusive wit in Swinburne's letters whereby the Cretan term for the male lover in

pederasty [φιλήτωρ] is transliterated through the term "fellator," whose root is Latin rather than Greek—from the verb "fellare," to suck. Swinburne thus makes crudely explicit a physical dimension in male intimacy that C. O. Müller and J. A. Symonds treat with allusive discretion. See Dellamora, *Apocalyptic Overtures: Sexual Politics and the Sense of an Ending* (New Brunswick, N.J.: Rutgers University Press, 1994), 51–52.

23. Swinburne's opinion of "The Sundew" is cited by Philip Henderson, *Swinburne: Portrait of a Poet* (New York: Macmillan, 1974), 263.

24. A detailed account of the relationship between Symonds and Fusato is given in Symonds's final chapter of *The Memoirs of John Addington Symonds*, ed. Phyllis M. Grosskurth (New York: Random House, 1984).

25. Sainsbury, *Memoir*, 107.

26. Symonds, *Letters*, 3:691.

27. Symonds, *In the Key of Blue and Other Essays* (1893; reprint, London: Elkin Matthews, 1918), 4.

28. Ibid., 15.

29. Ibid., 16.

30. Claude Phillips, "The Royal Academy II," *The Academy* 45, no. 1151 (May 26, 1894): 441; and D. S. M. [D. S. MacColl], "The Academy," *The Spectator* 88 (May 12, 1894): 652.

31. "The Royal Academy: Second Notice.—Figure Pictures and Portraits," *The Athenaeum*, 3473 (May 19, 1894): 652.

32. MacColl, "The Academy," 652.

33. Wainwright and Dinn, *Under Canvas*, 24.

34. Dellamora points out that Wilde, along with writers such as Walter Pater and Edward Carpenter, was concerned to distinguish between an emergent male homosexual culture and the male homosocial culture in which homosexual desire was regularly introduced, only then to be directed to hegemonic purposes. Basil Hallward is an illustration of the latter impulse when he attempts to validate his attraction to the handsome young Dorian by placing it in the service of high art (see Dellamora, *Apocalyptic Overtures*, 43).

35. Foucault, *The History of Sexuality*, Vol. 1, *an Introduction*, trans. Robert Hurley (1978; reprint, New York: Vintage, 1990), 157.

36. See Gerard Manley Hopkins's paraphrase of the editor of the Jesuit journal *The Month* who agrees to publish Hopkins's ode "The Wreck of the *Deutschland*" on condition that it "rhymes, scans and construes" and does not—like the "new sort of poetry" in America—"make nonsense or bad morality" (*Further Letters of Gerard Manley Hopkins*, ed. Claude Colleer Abbott [London: Oxford University Press, 1956], 138).

37. Thomas Spencer Baynes in "Swinburne's Poems," quoted by Thaïs E. Morgan, "Mixed Metaphor, Mixed Gender: Swinburne and the Victorian Critics," *The Victorian Newsletter* 73 (spring 1988): 17.

38. See "Foreword," in *Within These Shores: A Selection of Works from the Chantrey*

Bequest, 1883–1985 (London: Tate Gallery in Association with Sheffield City Art Galleries, 1989), 24.

39. Joseph Kestner hypothesizes a classical Greek significance to this and several of Tuke's other marine paintings, identifying a Spartan pedagogic element in the relation between the older sailors and the ephebiate youths (*Masculinities*, 261). While Kestner's point is well taken, it should be noted that the discrepancy in ages on which this Greek allusion depends is precisely a characteristic missing from the bathing pictures where an adult male presence never intrudes on the adolescent group, except insofar as it might be inferred in the position of the artist or viewer.

40. "The Royal Academy: 126th Annual Exhibition," *The Times Weekly Edition* (May 11, 1894): 369.

41. The bathing boys photographed by Frank Meadow Sutcliffe in, for instance, his medal-winning composition "Water Rats" at Whitby (1886) or "Sea Urchins" at Saltash are pre-adolescent and therefore present a less ambiguous aesthetic, quite different from that developed by Tuke. As the titles of Sutcliffe's compositions imply, his images portray boys as rascally little animals rather than as sensual nude forms.

42. See Seth Koven's study of the sexual and class dynamics whereby working-class boys were idealized as "rough lads" in the 1880s and 1890s only to be recast as "hooligans" in the first decade of the twentieth century ("From Rough Lads to Hooligans: Boy Life, National Culture and Social Reform," in *Nationalisms and Sexualities*, ed. Andrew Miller, Mary Russo, Doris Sommer, and Patricia Yaeger [New York: Routledge, 1992], 365–91).

43. "The Royal Academy: First Notice," *Illustrated London News* (May 10, 1902): 688. In the pictorial supplement to this issue, *The Run Home* and *Ruby, Gold, and Malachite* are printed side by side at the bottom of page III, as if to insist on their status as a nautical pair.

44. H. S., "The Academy—I," *The Spectator* 72 (May 3, 1902): 687.

45. Koven, "Rough Lads," 376.

46. D'Arch Smith, *Love in Earnest*, 17.

47. It is difficult to determine precisely which of Tuke's paintings this sonnet responds to. In her chronological list of Tuke's work (*Memoir*, Appendix II, 190–94), Sainsbury lists *Bathers* as the painting exhibited at the New English Art Club (NEAC) in 1889 and locates it at Leeds. However, Wainwright and Dinn argue that *The Bathers* was the painting to which Martin Colnaghi (owner of the Marlborough Gallery in Pall Mall) objected when he withdrew his support from the NEAC just before its opening exhibition in April 1886. They describe *The Bathers* as "depicting nude boys on the rocks at Newporth Beach" (*Under Canvas*, 34) and in a footnote (68 n. 12) they argue that Sainsbury confuses *The Bathers* with *Two Falmouth Fishing Boys*. This does not clarify matters, for two other critics offer different information. Emmanuel Cooper provides an illustration of *The Bathers*, which he dates 1885 and records as exhibited at the NEAC in 1886 (not 1889), and now in the City Art Gallery at Leeds. Cooper's illustra-

tion differs from the description of *The Bathers* given by Wainwright and Dinn but corresponds to Joseph Kestner's description: "Three naked boys are on deck one of whom points to a figure emerging on the left (*Masculinities*, 261). Like Cooper, and Wainwright and Dinn, Kestner dates this painting at 1885, and while he mentions Kains-Jackson's sonnet, he shrewdly does not attempt to link the poem with any particular painting.

48. The sonnet is reprinted in Brian Reade, *Sexual Heretics: Male Homosexuality in English Literature from 1850–1900* (London: Routledge and Kegan Paul, 1970), 225–26.

49. Timothy d'Arch Smith offers a brief account of Stanley in *Love in Earnest*, 92–93, 172.

50. This lyric is also reprinted in Reade, *Sexual Heretics*, 347–48.

51. See Vicinus, "Adolescent Boy," 107.

TWELVE

The Dance of Life: Choreographing Sexual Dissidence in the Early Twentieth Century

ANDREW HEWITT

In *Culture and Anarchy*, Matthew Arnold excoriates the dissident journal *The Nonconformist* for espousing what it vaunts as a "dissidence of dissent and the Protestantism of the Protestant religion."[1] Arnold's polemic serves as proof that in the cultural debates of Victorian England, the very concept of dissidence is itself contested. Whereas dissidence might normally be understood as an opposition to hegemonic social and sexual structures, at least one cultural critic saw dissidence itself as the prevailing ideological fact of British intellectual life.[2] At the point where it becomes a purely negative principle, Arnold is suggesting, dissent in fact effects a dialectical *Umschlag*, ontologizing critique as a positive principle. Politically, this reversal opens dissidence up to a variety of troubling possibilities: by way of example Arnold points out *The Nonconformist*'s collaboration with capitalist exploitation in opposing the liberal labor reforms of the Factory Act of 1843. I cite Arnold, however, not to follow through his ultimately statist arguments, but merely to demonstrate what we might call "the dialectic of dissent"—a structure permitting dissent to join forces with the status quo. Arnold is further useful in reminding us of the intimate connections between a culture of dissent and Puritanism.

In similar vein, Jonathan Dollimore has demonstrated the operation of Puritan dissent with respect to sexual politics, arguing for the operation of two modes of sexual dissidence—identified with Gide and Wilde respectively.[3] The Gidean "Protestantism of the Protestant religion"—if we may so annex his position—takes issue not with the valorizing binaries of the hegemonic order, but with their application: it seeks to install the putatively unnatural at the very heart of the natural order itself. In this model, "nature" retains its legitimizing force. Wildean play, meanwhile, is deconstructive in arguing for culture and artifice over and against nature. In this chapter I seek to demonstrate how, in at least one tradition of dissent, some of Dollimore's binaries are overcome. Examining the trope of dance in the later writings of Havelock Ellis, I will argue that an implicit "Protestant work ethic" is displaced by the ontological category of play. In Ellis's writing, Wildean tropes of play acquire a high seriousness when bodied forth as dance; in the work I shall focus on, *The Dance of Life*, dance is celebrated as "the art that is most clearly made of the stuff of life and so able to translate most truly and clearly into beautiful form the various modalities of life."[4]

Bearing in mind the ways in which "the dissidence of dissent" became conservative for Arnold, we might note that in Ellis's writings on dance, "the stuff of life" occupies the position that market forces occupied in the implicit social agenda of the nonconformists: it is lawlessness become law. I seek to show how "the stuff of life"—as an irreducibly material residue and origin of history—is traduced precisely as it is ontologized in an early twentieth-century vitalism. I will demonstrate how an emergent philosophical strain of vitalism in the early part of this century marked the disappearance of sexuation from biologizing accounts of sexual life. The trope of dance figures as a pre-social impulse that itself grounds the possibility of social order. At the same time, dance as a medium for reflection on sexuality removes the sexual from the social and political realm. When sexuality is understood as but part of an over-arching life force, I will argue, the biological ceases to resist metaphysics and becomes instead its grounding principle.[5] Looking forward into the twentieth century, in this essay I aim to show how a socially oriented dissident tradition generated from within itself a vitalistic discourse that made the body—as a biological principle—the grounding vital force of history rather than an object of contestation. More specifically, in examining *The Dance of Life*, I will argue that reflections on dance both as an anthropological datum and as a reemergent cultural form provided a medium for ontologizing life, motion, rhythm, and change as principles that undercut all political positionality.

In this essay, then, I examine ways in which a tradition of Victorian sexual dissidence was recuperated and revamped for a twentieth-century modernism. The strategies of recuperation were by no means uniform: it was not simply a question of restoring a normative, heterosexual, procreative sexuality, for example. Indeed, as I will show, the very fecundity and materiality of the sexual as a material and specifically historical productive force posed a threat to what constituted, in the early years of the century, a veritable metaphysics of sex.[6] Nevertheless, it will be a central element of my argument that the recuperation of sexual dissidence certainly also resulted in the de-queering of a late nineteenth-century decadent proto-modernism that had found expression through a curious linkage of Decadence and Neo-Classicism. Furthermore, I will argue that the process of recuperation—which I identify with philosophical vitalism—was already under way from within the ranks of the dissidents. To this end, I focus on *The Dance of Life* not only in order to show how metaphysical metaphors of dance served to de-sex the sexual, but also to show how sexual dissidents—who were, as has been argued in this volume, forerunners of modernism both ideologically and aesthetically—failed to respond to the challenges of a new century and new aesthetic forms.

I should first outline what I take to be the stakes of approaching questions of sexuality through the prism of dance. Both are, of course, specifically physical experiences that have nevertheless been co-opted to address metaphysical concerns. If the move from Ellis the sexologist to Ellis the theorist of dance seems abrupt, however, we would do well to remember the humble origins of Ellis's work *Sexual Inversion*. The impetus for the work came from Ellis's collaborator J. A. Symonds (whose name—subsequent to his death and prior to the volume's publication—would be removed from the work). Shy of approaching Ellis himself with the proposal, Symonds invoked the help of his friend Arthur Symons, who suggested the project to Ellis one night in 1892, at the music hall.[7] Symons, we know, was the leading cultural supporter of theatrical dance, albeit of the music-hall variety, in Britain in the 1890s. His *Studies in Seven Arts* would privilege dance above all other arts. The idea for *Sexual Inversion*, we may surmise, was hatched during an evening of dance, and for Ellis dance would consistently figure as the form that most directly translated the bio-sexual nature of man into aesthetic form.

It will not be my aim in this essay to recontextualize Ellis's work within a tradition of Victorian writing about dance and the body. My trajectory is toward the future: to ask what became of the sexual dissidence of thinkers such as Ellis in the twentieth century. Toward the end of the essay, I will read Ellis's reformulations of "classical" and "romantic" with regard to dance alongside the more polemical and bellicose formulations of T. E. Hulme. My aim in so doing is to read the proto-modernism of a Victorian dissident—a modernism, I would argue, both enabled and limited by its exploration of neo-Classical notions of homosocial order—alongside a seminal twentieth-century modernist. At the same time, however, it should be acknowledged that we are dealing here with two different senses of "the modern": clearly, Ellis's commitment to social and sexual "progress" cannot simply be equated with Hulme's aesthetic modernism, which was linked to ostensibly "reactionary" political positions. This movement between discourses, however, is crucial for two reasons: first, it demonstrates how the logic of aesthetic modernism was radical in a way that the political and social work of reformists such as Ellis ceased to be; second, it allows us to see how works such as *The Dance of Life*—essentially anthropological, or even ethnological, in its treatment of world dance forms; and clearly susceptible to a reading informed by the concerns of post-colonial theory—nevertheless responded and contributed to aesthetic debates central to the shift from symbolism and aestheticism to a modernism more strictly defined.

By placing Ellis alongside Hulme, I wish to show how even such a misogynistic and patently "un-queer" avatar of the modern as Hulme necessarily poses questions of sexual identity that have fallen away in the work of the erstwhile pioneer, Ellis. This falling away from the more radical project of sexual dissidence in Ellis's work I trace to an evisceration of the concept of the classical. It is the classical as a "life-alien" form that paradoxically rescues "the stuff of life" by fixing and isolating it outside the flow of a vitalism that merely makes the contingence of life itself a fundamental principle.[8] It is not, I will argue, because Hulme privileges—or would even be interested in privileging—the sexual as a vehicle for subverting social structures that his work takes up where the project of radical Victorian sexual dissidence leaves off. Instead, it is a working through of the problem of the classical as an aesthetic possibility as well as a model of homosocial order that makes his work so challenging. This comparison of Hulme and Ellis will engage me in a reevaluation of the three categories "classical," "romantic," and "decadent" as I argue that Hulme's polemical binary of classical and romantic needs to be triangulated through the category of the decadent. This category itself, however, needs to be reconfigured in the light of the classical–romantic debate and is far from unproblematic. Showing how Ellis's understanding of "the decadent" shifts from work to work, I trace these shifts to specifically sexual anxieties concerning the construction of gender identities.

Returning to Dollimore's distinction of Gidean Protestantism and Wildean playfulness, it is clear that figures such as Ellis were always ambiguous. Certainly, his liberal project was reformist and "protestant" in its sexual dissent, but certainly in his later writings Ellis would consistently stress what he calls, in one essay, "the play function of sex."[9] This play function, "while it extends beyond the sexual sphere, . . . yet definitely includes that sphere" (*LE*, 119). Ellis's linkage of sex to play certainly opens up what we might call a "Wildean" space of sexual experimentation by opening up the sexual to the aesthetic. Quite what form of aesthetic is implied, however, needs to be clarified. Play, Ellis argues, "is not concerned with the construction of objective works of art, although—by means of contact in human relationship—it attains the wholesome organic effects which may be indirectly achieved by artistic activities" (*LE*, 120). His "aestheticization of sex" is specifically non-artifactual: it is an "organic" aesthetic of the creative subject rather than an aesthetic of the work or object. Reapplied to the sexual realm, I will argue, Ellis's "playful" understanding of sex clearly does not foreground the act of (re)production as an act that will create an object—or child—as its completed work. Moreover, I would argue, dance becomes important to Ellis as the aesthetic form that best approximates this condition of organic—and biological—play divorced from any object that would result from it. Completing the circle, we might say that dance figures as a form of non-reproductive sexuality, or rather, it tropes the passage of the sexual into the aesthetic. It is not disembodied like music—but nor is it oriented toward the (re)production of bodies: it is the "activity" of "human relationship." In what follows I wish to suggest parallels between dance as a non-mimetic aesthetic form and non-reproductive sexuality in Ellis's thought. Rather than suggesting some "queering" of the already rather queer Mr. Ellis, however, I will in fact suggest that his antipathy toward aesthetic artifact extends, finally, to the body of the dancer him or herself as sexed entity. In other words, the ontologizing of play does the work of de-sexing.

Published in 1923, *The Dance of Life* is the result of interests stretching back fifteen years and at times returns to interests harbored by the author from the earliest period of his studies. That the work should have been conceived and published over this particular span of time interests us primarily because it means that the work matured throughout the heroic period of the Ballets Russes. It seems to partake of two distinct discourses; on the one hand, the ethnographic and anthropological (in which respect the work fits quite clearly into Ellis's anthropologically oriented sexological writings); and on the other, a critical discourse facilitated by the reemergence of theatrical dance as a viable aesthetic form. Ellis himself quotes an unnamed critical source from 1906 to demonstrate the parlous state of dance at the turn of the century; "The ballet is now a thing of the past," the critic writes, "and, with the modern change of ideas, a thing that is never likely to be resuscitated." (quoted 53–54). What effect did the resuscitation of theatrical dancing under the Ballets Russes have on theories of dance; and how, given the role that such theories had acquired within an ethnological and anthropological discourse, did theatrical dance begin to reshape the world view of thinkers of the time?[10]

The importance of the dancer as a romantic image of aesthetic sublation— the taking up of inert bodily matter into the movement of the spirit—has been most notably elaborated by Frank Kermode in his 1957 study, *Romantic Image*.[11] Masterfully establishing a tradition of writing about dance that passes through the Symbolists to the romantics, harking back also to Blake, he demonstrates how in a very real sense dance—and here he quotes R. G. Collingwood's *Principles of Art*—"is the mother of all languages" (62). After the chapters devoted to "The Image" and "The Dancer," however, Kermode's study falters quite noticeably as it enters the twentieth century, when Symons—author of the influential *The Symbolist Movement in Literature* and friend of Ellis—is accorded a disproportionate significance. Meanwhile, the writings of T. E. Hulme are shuttled off rather hurriedly before Eliot takes center stage. I wish to argue that Kermode's analysis, though brilliant, is too assimilative, stretching the terms of Romanticism to cover developments that really do not quite fit his scenario. We might begin our disruption of Kermode's eviscerating genealogy by returning to his epigraphic quotation from Collingwood: "Dance is the mother of all languages." What Kermode seeks to demonstrate in the chapter that takes this statement as its motto is the validity of the claim with which he has just closed the preceding chapter; namely that in the image, "as in the dance, there is no disunity of being; 'the body is the soul'" (61). Investigating the context of Collingwood's statement, however, we are obliged to understand it in a way that turns Kermode on his head. Collingwood introduces into his aesthetics an anthropological and ethnological (not to say eugenic) interest in dance as "essentially a courtship-ritual."[12] Kermode's "image," let us recall, permitted of no "disunity of being" (61), nothing, that is, that exceeds the immanence of its own performance. Collingwood's instrumentalization of dance as a courtship ritual obliges us to question this assumption, however, since for him dance works "to arouse in the young of each sex an interest in some member of the other sex. . . . This interest, so far from being satisfied and therefore exhausted in the dance itself, is intended to fructify in a future partnership" (75–76). What Collingwood attunes us to, then, is a concept of dance that produces a residue (a progeny) beyond itself: an aesthetic experience that is not self-consuming and self-producing in the manner suggested by Kermode.

I am not invoking dance's status as courtship ritual in order to reinstate an anthropology, but rather to question the economy of Kermode's "image." Whereas for Kermode the image is self-sufficient, it is clear that for the authorities he cites it is not; rather, it is "far from being satisfied and therefore exhausted in the dance." It is the re-sexualization of dance, I would argue, that reintroduces a dissident voice: the trace left by the dance is figured as progeny. The task of procreation—as a context for dance—demonstrates how this grounding aesthetic form is "interested" in the radical sense. That is to say, while dance might seem to offer itself as an image of a radically disinterested performance in which the performer ceases to exist in embodied form—and its status, indeed, as performative rather than denotative guarantees its centrality to the abstract impulses of Romanticism—it can nevertheless be re-subsumed under a discourse of production when framed anthropologically. If a disinterested aesthetic is one that takes no interest in the actual physical existence of its object, completing itself spiritually through reflection, surely this dance that is oriented—in Collingwood—toward the production and reproduction of the species cannot be taken as "disinterested." Dance—at least in Collingwood—is an "interested" aesthetic form insofar as it produces a result, and this interest is figured as a heterosexual coupling. In the passage from Collingwood to Kermode, it is the dissident voice of the sexual that has been silenced.

This excess produced in and through the dance as image—embodied, so to speak, in the child—puts at risk precisely the transcendentalism of Kermode's romantic aesthetic. Indeed, Kermode's own presentation of dance as the "mother" of all languages already suggests a procreative scenario in which language itself is a product of excess, the non-closure of the dance. Dance, it would seem, might also be invoked to ground a counter-aesthetic of worldliness. To put in a nutshell the distinction I am making with reference to Collingwood and the reproductive functions of dance, we might quote Kermode on Yeats: "The Dancer, in fact is, in Yeats's favourite expression, 'self-begotten,' independent of labour" (99). Anthropology reinserts, I would argue, the concept of labor (or what I would term, more precisely, "work") in the guise of biological reproduction; and this link is already implicit in Yeats, for whom independence from labor was marked by the act of self-begetting.

Dance as a ritual oriented toward begetting introduces alterity at the origin. We need to stress the anti-metaphysical, anti-ontological perspective introduced into theories of dance by the emerging discourses of anthropology and sexology. The Dancer is not self-begotten, but the product of a worldly, social ritual. Moreover, his or her dance is itself oriented toward the act of begetting. It is important to think dance through the prism of anthropology not in order to establish a discourse that might ground theatrical dance in some more fundamental, trans-historical human impulse and establish a new metaphysics of "human nature" behind social practice, but for entirely opposite reasons. Such a reframing undoes the romantic transcendentalism of The Dancer as subject and "image": time and history re-enter. Even though anthropological discourse dominated much thinking about dance in the latter period of which he writes, Kermode does not engage it.

Reframing these questions in terms of a literary historical narrative or genealogy, we can see how the very history of Ellis's *The Dance of Life* dramatizes its own emergence from and out of a twin set of anxieties: a primary concern with the feasibility in the twentieth century of late nineteenth-century symbolist and aestheticist cultural ideals and, linked to this, secondary anxieties about a writerly ethic that Ellis implicitly will trope in terms of a heterosexual coupling. Of particular importance for my claim that *The Dance of Life* was a transitional text—a failed translation of Victorian sexual dissidence into twentieth-century cultural modernism—is a consideration of its history. The history of the book's own publication might be read as a metaphor for the fate of Victorian sexual dissidence in the first two decades of this century. In the preface to the work, Ellis tells us that it was first conceived—and elements of it first began to appear—in 1908, and that its subsequent form was dictated by its slow emergence over a period of fifteen years. These fifteen years are, essentially, the high point of the Ballets Russes of Diaghilev and the emergence of dance as a privileged modernist form. Ellis's own interest in dance is, in essence, "pre-modernist" (and popular/low-cultural) and yet formulates itself during a time when an erstwhile low cultural form (first considered by serious cultural thinkers during the 1890s in both France and Britain) was assimilated to the cultural pantheon of modernism.

In his preface to the work, Ellis will argue that "slowness is beauty, and certainly it is the slowest dances that have been to me the most beautiful to see, while, in the dance of life, the achievement of a civilisation in beauty seems to be inversely to the rapidity of its pace" (v). The slow emergence of the work itself, then, is to be thought of as a dance, as a slow emergence from the cultural milieu that produced *Sexual Inversion* into a new aesthetic. To comprehend the broader implications of this rupture—and likewise this limitation—in Ellis's reconceptualization of dance, we might begin by examining the status of dance as a rhetorical organizing principle in his work. Stability is most important to Ellis; what he seems most to value in dance is not movement but stasis. This privileging of stasis within dance even leads him to quote the sculptor Rodin for his aesthetic credo: "Slowness is Beauty" (v).[13] This could hardly be further from the symbolist-romantic aesthetic extrapolated by Kermode from Symons's essay on "Ballet, Pantomime and Poetic Drama," where according to Kermode "It is the dancer's movement (contrasted with the immobility of sculpture) and the fact that this movement is passionate, controlled not by intellect but by rhythm and the demands of plastic form, that make her an emblem of joy" (87). Kermode's opposition of dance and sculpture, however, is already overstated, even in the context of Symons. In his appreciation of Rodin, for example, Symons quotes Baudelaire's dictum, "L'énergie, c'est la grâce suprême" (11), privileging the quality of *energeia* over any actual kinetic movement. It is the potential for movement rather than movement itself that is valued: power rather than motion. Stasis, indeed—that is, as energy, or the possibility for motion—becomes the privileged modality of vitalism as it passes from late Romanticism into the classical modernist tradition. Precisely the transcendentalism of the romantic image of dance necessarily returns it to a celebration of energy over actual movement. Movement implies a rootedness in time and space that constantly undermines what the movement was meant to trope: the *idea* of movement replaces movement itself. This logical move is at the very heart of vitalism.

It is impossible to ignore how Ellis's conception of his project moves him—slowly, perhaps—away from what we might call a symbolist aesthetic embodied in the idea of the book itself as an ideal form. He begins his preface to *The Dance of Life* by arguing that it is not "complete," that it is somehow fragmentary. This avowal, however, should not immediately be read as Ellis's passage into an aesthetic of modernist fragmentation; for this incompletion is mapped not synchronically or spatially—figuring the work as a form of collage, that is—but diachronically and historically. Incompletion, for Ellis, is the aesthetic outcome of the passage of history into the very composition of the work itself. Implicitly, he sees history entering the project of writing through the medium of dance, breaking down both the Aestheticists' ideals of finished form and the resistance of their works to history. His essays, Ellis argues, are not a "Book." He elucidates his meaning by saying that *The Dance of Life* is not a book "in the sense that a Bible means a book" (xiii), but the reference to Mallarmé's avowed and impossible aesthetic goals is unmistakable: "a book," Ellis writes, "must be completed as it had originally been planned, finished, rounded, polished" (v). For all the privileging of stasis in dance, Ellis implicitly distinguishes his work from the sculptural unity of the aestheticist "Book." Taking as countermodels to his own work both the aestheticist notion of a "finished, rounded, polished" work and the Bible (a work, if ever there was one, that was also written over a great period of time and by many authors) Ellis effects one of those curious inversions that I see as typical of his work: the alignment of Aestheticism and Christianity.

What begins as a conventional rhetorical apologia for the inconsistencies of *The Dance of Life*, however, soon becomes a compositional statement of the aesthetic the book seeks to espouse: "A part of the method of such a book as this, written over a long period of years, is to reveal a continual slight inconsistency" (vi). The "slow movement" of the dance is a movement that produces inconsistency by admitting history—and difference—into the compositional method. More than a fleeting acquaintance with new Bergsonian trends in philosophy is suggested by Ellis's embracing of dance as flux, but inconsistency further suggests more troubling uncertainties, as Ellis almost inadvertently notes by comparing his own method to that of the logically consistent Book:

> The man who consistently—as he fondly supposes, "logically"—clings to an unchanging opinion is suspended from a hook which has ceased to exist. "I thought it was she, and she thought it was me, and when we come near it weren't neither one of us"—that metaphysical statement holds, with a touch of exaggeration, a truth we must always bear in mind concerning the relation of subject and object. They can neither of them possess consistency; they have both changed before they come up with one another. (vi)

I take this down-home "metaphysical statement" as an important indicator of a shift that Ellis's later work necessarily faces but fears to articulate: the collapse of a philosophical construct of subject-object thinking predicated on the certainty of a heterosexual compact. *The Dance of Life* inhabits the fear that the embrace of the heterosexual couple—"I" and "She"—will prove impossible, for neither one of us is what we seemed. In what follows, I wish to show that Ellis does, indeed, "dance around" this problem and to suggest that his maneuvers are typical of the ways in which Victorian sexual dissidence would be recuperated and revised for various modernist projects. At the same time, I wish to bear in mind the coterminous failure of the "heterosexual metaphysic"—as it is presented here—and the aestheticist fantasy of the Book, to suggest that sexual and aesthetic crises are intimately linked. The book can be no more complete and self-enclosing than "she" and "I" in our failed embrace. What I mean to suggest by this is a compositional recognition in Ellis's late work of a "queering" (but one, as we have noted, that can find form just as easily in reproductive sexuality—as excess—as it can in any homosexual positionality per se) that is consistently foreclosed at the level of content. By contrast, Ellis's linkage of two failures—the failure of the biblical/aestheticist project and the heterosexual encounter—obliges us to rethink aestheticism as an aesthetic that foregrounds the queer at the level of substance while foreclosing it at the level of composition.

I have traced this development in Ellis's work to a confrontation with aestheticist notions of "the Book," but we need to go further back fully to contextualize Ellis's polemic in this work. "If we survey the development of dancing as an art in Europe," he observes, "it seems to me that we have to recognise two streams of tradition which have sometimes merged but yet remain in their ideals and their tendencies essentially distinct" (48). These, of course, are the classical and the romantic, and it is instructive to note the implications of what I take to be an insistent but subtle privileging of the classical in Ellis's work. The classical, we read, is "the more ancient and fundamental" (48), originating in Egypt, "the most influential dancing-school the world has ever seen" (49). The linkage of the classical tradition to Egypt is itself somewhat startling, especially as Ellis will go on to argue that "Greek dancing had a development so refined and so special . . . that it exercised no influence outside Greece" (51). We will encounter this filtering of the classical through Egypt once again in Hulme, most clearly in the 1914 essay on "Modern Art and its Philosophy," where he argues that

> you have first the art which is natural to you, Greek art and modern art since the Renaissance. In these arts the lines are soft and vital. You have the other arts like Egyptian, Indian and Byzantine, where everything tends to be angular, where curves tend to be hard and geometrical, where the representation of the human body, for example, is entirely non-vital.[14]

Ellis's reconfiguration of terminologies mirrors very closely Hulme's own taxonomic difficulties. As Michael Roberts has noted, "Hulme is compelled to take Egyptian, Indian, and Byzantine art to illustrate his conception of Classicism; he regards Greek architecture as humanist, not classical; and his description of the humanist is exactly parallel to Worringer's account of classical man."[15] Furthermore, the linkage of curves to vitality and angularity to the life-alien principles of Egyptian art in Hulme's formulation perhaps allows us to speculate on Ellis's usage of the same binarism in 1923. The privileging of a (mortified) male angularity over female curves is the only indication of a foregrounding of the male body or the life-alien in Ellis's work: elsewhere all is curves, all is a more traditionally romanticized "classical" affirmation of life. The male body will only be displayed as a corpse. Likewise, Ellis exhibits no love of the new angular modernist forms introduced into dance by Nijinsky and the Ballets Russes. It is as if Ellis contemplates the possibility of an aesthetic grounded in the male body only to retract, realizing that that way death lies.

When we turn to consider the reconfiguration of the terms "classical" and "romantic" in Ellis's writings on dance, it will become clear that his taxonomies reflect a shift in sensibility most often associated with the writings of Hulme. A major difference, however, is Ellis's investment in life, in an embodied vitalism. Hulme, for his part, is more profoundly influenced by Worringer's notion of "life-alien" function of art in certain societies, and this notion of alienation informs even his thinking about the body. If Ellis seeks in dance an embodied aesthetic—albeit, as we shall see, an aesthetic embodied only in certain types of body—Hulme is more fundamentally distanced from the body. His work is full of images of gender-transgression attesting to that. Nevertheless we need to acknowledge what links and divides Hulme and Ellis as antipathetic prophets of a new modernist Classicism. This con- and divergence is crucial, I believe, because it allows us to see how classicizing tendencies in late Victorian sexual dissidence prefigure, but do not exhaust the possibilities of, a modernist Classicism. In the terms Kermode uses to gloss Hulme on Worringer, "If you compare Egyptian art with Greek you find the first life-alien and the second life-worshipping, the first abstract and the other dependent on empathy" (137). Though Ellis shares Hulme's formulations of romantic and classical and frees the classical, in similar fashion, from its reliance on Greek humanism, he does not take on board the distinction of life-worshipping and life-alien art derived from Worringer. No one could be more life-affirming than Ellis, who lacks the hard, formal, structuring edge of Hulme and seems much more closely linked to romantic organicism in his presentation and privileging of the classical.

A history of the dance, it would seem, is Ellis's medium for rewriting historical aesthetic taxonomies: a Classicism without Greece. Later in *The Dance of Life*, Ellis quotes a Nietzschean scholar of classics to argue that there was "much in the religious life of Greece which seems not to harmonise with what we conventionally call 'classic'" (190–91). "In its pure form," we read, the classical is "solo dancing" that is "based on the rhythmic beauty and expressiveness of the simple human personality" in order to produce "measured yet passionate movement" (48). The romantic, meanwhile, is "of Italian origin, chiefly known to us as the ballet" (48) and consists of "concerted dancing, mimetic and picturesque, wherein the individual is subordinated to the wider and variegated rhythm of the group" (48–49). One suspects that Ellis objects to the collective nature of such dance and its flirtation with what will elsewhere be character-ized as "the supremely false dictum: 'Art is, above everything, a phenomenon of sociability,'" and the related heretical view "that art is 'expression,' for 'ex-pression' may too easily be confused with 'communication'" (302). Particularly startling, however, is Ellis's genealogy of the romantic, for "the germ of the ballet," he asserts, "is to be found in Rome where the pantomime with its con-certed and picturesque method of expressive action was developed" (52). In other words, not only are those cultures generally considered "classical" ex-empted from Ellis's definition, but one of them, the Roman, is made the fun-dament of Romanticism. Romanticism, moreover, is being identified with the "picturesque" (i.e. figurative) and (panto-)mimetic elements in dance. As he develops a modern theory of the dance, Ellis seems engaged in nothing less than a reformulation of what have since become commonplaces in our own genealogies of the modern. His own romantic terminology notwithstanding, Ellis rejects the necessary link to the romantic project by harnessing Romanti-cism to mimesis.

Perhaps our trope of genealogy is particularly appropriate here, for one of Ellis's major concerns throughout *The Dance of Life* is a form of negative eu-genics, which consists less in propagating what is best than in weeding out what is feeble. Viewed in these terms, romantic dance (the ballet) is miscege-nated and encourages miscegenation: "Romantic dancing, to a much greater extent than what I have called Classic dancing, which depends so largely on simple personal qualities, tends to be vitalized by transplantation and the ab-sorption of new influences" (52). The collectivity of romantic dance, therefore, should not be thought of in terms of a national collective or the self-creation of the collective through ritual and festival.[16] It is not a ritual producing a ho-mogeneous national collective.

If Ellis's reconfiguration of romantic and classical is remarkable for its eccen-tricity (Greece's disappearance from Classicism being the most notable point, along with the etymological linking of Romanticism to Rome) it is no less remarkable for the rigidity of its binarisms—this in a book that stresses fluidity and inconsistency. It is as if the very rigor of the opposition is serving to mark a tension in the book, inviting further scrutiny. Even the terms classical and romantic have shifted from Ellis's other writing. We might surmise that these terms feed off new debates within modernism, debates we here identify with the figure of Hulme. Elsewhere in Ellis's writings, however, he opposes Classi-cism to Decadence rather than to Romanticism (or rather, he sees Decadence as an elaboration of Classicism, a sort of delirious rigor). Whereas *The Dance of Life* implicitly privileges the classical over the romantic, Ellis elsewhere priv-ileges the decadent over the classical. For example, in his preface to Huysmans's *A Rebours*—a classical statement of nineteenth-century sexual dissidence if ever there was one—Ellis in fact suggests a Romanic or romantic derivation for the decadent. Reading Huysmans, he writes,

> I find myself carried back to the decline of the Latin world. I recall those restless Africans who were drawn into the vortex of decadent Rome, who absorbed its corruptions with all the barbaric fervor of their race, and then with a more natural impetus of that youthful fervor threw themselves into the young current of Christianity, yet retaining in their flesh the brand of an exotic culture, . . . a fantastic mingling of youth and age, of decayed Latinity, of tumultuously youthful Christianity.[17]

In effect, Ellis synthesizes two models of decadence here: one seeing the decadent as an atavism ("Africans . . . barbaric fervor") and the other seeing it as the result of over-refinement (Rome's "corruptions"). With regard to the British scene, however, we can only speculate as to why Ellis would be interested in "the fervent seeker of those early days, indeed, but *à rebours!*" (v). What are we to make of this figure of the inverted seeker—of the invert, indeed, as a seeker? As Ellis presents it, the salient inversion is a historical one: youthful Christianity now takes the role of the older partner that the decadent will overthrow and embrace (the potentially paederastic language is of interest here also) as the British aesthetes of the late nineteenth century did, indeed.[18]

"Technically," Ellis argues in the preface to *Against the Grain,*

> a decadent style is only such in relation to a classic style. It is simply a further development of a classic style, a further specialization, the homogeneous, in Spencerian phraseology, having become heterogeneous. The first is beautiful because the parts are subordinated to the whole; the second is beautiful because the whole is subordinated to the parts. (xiv)

Defining Decadence as the inversion of a classical relation of part to whole became a critical commonplace in writings influenced by Bourget (whom Ellis quotes at some length). Ellis, however, sees the relation not as an inversion, but as a "development." In other words, classical and decadent are more intimately related than we thought. In general, indeed, "all art is the rising and falling of the slopes of a rhythmic curve between these two classic and decadent extremes": the figure of a dance, a rising and falling, blurs the binarisms of *The Dance of Life*.

If we attempt to overlay the binarisms romantic–classical and decadent–classical, however, we arrive at some interesting incongruities. For example, whereas the classical privileges the whole and Romanticism the part (in the preface to *À Rebours*), in *The Dance of Life* it is not the classical but rather the romantic that produces "concerted dancing, mimetic and picturesque, wherein the individual is subordinated to the wider and variegated rhythm of the group"

(48–49). Here, the classical is identified with "in its pure form, solo dancing" (48). Ellis's concept of totality is clearly individual rather than social: the totality of romantic dancing is, after all, "picturesque" and "mimetic"—a merely collective or social *representation* of true totality. We need, somehow, to triangulate—or dialecticize?—classical, romantic, and decadent. In such a reading, the classical—which here champions the individual, the part, over the social or concerted whole—would stand in for the decadent. Classicism, as reconstructed through an overlaying of these texts, has always been predicated upon decadence: it is as if the classical camouflage so popular with the Victorian sexual dissidents has come into its own as an aesthetic project—a project by now necessarily over-determined, as we shall see, by modernist polemics around the binarism classical–romantic. By recurring to an opposition of classical and *romantic* (rather than decadent) and rooting the romantic in Rome, Ellis creates a Classicism from which any hint of sexual dissidence has been erased through the excising of both Greece and Rome. What is it that is occluded in this reconfiguration?

As Kermode has pointed out, Symbolism effectively worked through certain dialectical tensions in the tradition of the romantic image. Most notably, the moment of transsubstantiation and spirituality central to Romanticism is reassessed in the light of the trace of sensuality—the female body—that necessarily embodied it. By the late nineteenth century—at least in Kermode's reading, which I contest—the sensual becomes the mode of embodiment of the spiritual rather than that which must simply be negated. The earliest example cited by Kermode for the identification of the romantic image with the persona and activity of The Dancer is the work of Heine—more specifically, *Die Bäder von Lucca* and *Florentinische Nächte*. In the latter work Heine describes the performance of a London street dancer, who acquires a privileged position in his own and subsequent romantic aesthetics; "Madame Laurence was not a great dancer, but she was a natural one" (quoted by Kermode, 81). The image of The Dancer in Kermode's presentation is clearly linked to a fantasy of natural language, figured here as the immanent language of the body; Mme Laurence's gestures "seemed to be trying to say something, like words in a special language" (81). On the surface at least, Heine's dancer seems to bring the body to speech, but this association of bodily and linguistic articulation is clearly strained; the gestures only "seemed to be trying" to articulate. This immanent bodily language remains below the threshold of language, even as it claims to speak for the spirit through the body.

This failure is explicitly linked to questions of gender, I would contend. The reemergence of the body in literary reflections on dance figures a return to questions of materiality, the materiality of the bodily or linguistic signifier. Ignoring this complication, Kermode's privileging of the dancer as "self-begotten" elides the labor of procreation that is the specific work of the female body. For example, he confronts Yeats's notorious social conservatism with regard to gender by insisting that "the lighthearted talk about the education of women"—Yeats, we should remark, was against subjecting women to the alienating regimen of mechanical "scholarly" learning—"is no mere *jeu d'esprit.* . . . In women, as in poems, the body as a whole must be expressive; there should be no question of the mind operating independently of the whole body" (66–67). If, in Kermode's reading of Yeats, men stand for the alienation of body and soul through commemorative rather than creative learning, women stand for the possibility of natural grace, embodying "an organic, irreducible beauty, of which female beauty, the beauty of a perfectly proportioned human body, is the type" (63). The Dancer—that quasi-Platonic form—is necessarily sexed: she is necessarily a woman. Of course, the importance of sexing foregrounds the importance of the body, bringing into the dance sensual elements that will eventually undermine its transcendental pretensions.

The issue of play and labor, then, is intrinsically linked to questions of sexuality for Ellis. I suggest that the most important historical shift occurring in dance at the time of Ellis's preparation of *The Dance of Life* was the emergence of the male dancer under the Ballets Russes. Recontextualizing Ellis's study from its ostensible ethnographic concerns and addressing instead precisely the European cultural developments he studiedly ignores, I will argue that a horror of contemplating the male body as a sensuous embodiment—rather than as rational cognition of truth—is responsible for many of the distortions to be encountered in Ellis's work. This is something more than a simple homosexual panic. In making this suggestion, I posit not a simple homophobia unable to countenance the erotic display of male bodies, but rather a more radical epistemological shift that disrupts Yeats's parsing of knowing and being in terms of masculine and feminine. Provisionally, we might venture the hypothesis (in support of our observations on Nijinsky) that the birth of a new—"modernist"—Classicism at the beginning of the century was directly related to the resurgence of the balletic tradition, and to the new role conceived within that ballet for male dancers.[19] To this extent, we need to look beyond the decadent—"symbolist"—trappings of the Ballets Russes in order to appreciate the radical, classical shift that their productions reflect or indeed help bring about. Aesthetically and historically, the Ballets Russes were important for the transition they effected from a late-nineteenth century "decadent" or symbolist aesthetic to a stripped-down twentieth-century modernism. It is as if, in the Ballets Russes, the implicit strategy of the Victorian dissidents—the linkage of Decadence and Classicism as a mode of modernism—became an explicit aesthetic project.

It might seem odd, given that the classical ballet was revived by the Russians, that Ellis identifies the classical with Isadora Duncan, Ruth St. Denis, and the U.S.A., and the romantic with Russia. Clearly, though he is elaborating his aesthetic with regard to dance, Ellis is not deriving his terms from the vocabulary of dance. His "classical" dance, in the guise of Isadora, seems uncannily close to the "free dance" of Mme Laurence and the women who stood in for her in the Kermodian romantic tradition. Given my thesis that the new Classicism and the reemergence of classical ballet (in the more limited sense) encouraged and facilitated each other, Ellis's binary oppositions clearly pose problems. For here the Russian Ballet tradition is identified with the romantic, and Duncan's dance with the classical.[20] The confusion, I would argue, results from Ellis's embarrassment at the historical necessity of contemplating the male body offered up to critical gaze by the Russians. Still tied, for all his incipient modernism, to the romantic trope of an embodied aesthetic, he is unable or unwilling to cast his critical gaze on the male body. Consequently, the "romantic" tradition of the Russians remains strangely disembodied. It finds no concrete synecdochic form within the text: Nijinsky dances unnoticed and without a footnote. When a figure is, finally, invoked as bearer of the romantic tradition, it is a woman, Taglioni. Even then she figures as "the most ethereal embodiment of the spirit of the romantic movement *in a form that was genuinely classic*" (53; emphasis added). The male body—Nijinsky's body—is doubly distanced: first, it will not be identified with the classical renaissance at all; and second, the romantic will be granted only a grudging embodied form in the figure of a woman, Taglioni. The American "classical" tradition is embodied in Ellis's writing in a way that the Russian romantic tradition can never be. It is the dance of Isadora Duncan and Ruth St. Denis. Ellis's reluctance to contemplate the male body of the Russian Ballet obliges him to scramble his terms—to see in Isadora the possibility of talking without compromise about bodies and, therefore, of embodying his own aesthetic in a classical and sexually uncompromised form. His reconfiguration of romantic and classical is entirely subservient to a romantic tradition of thinking and visualizing the female body.[21]

If, as I am suggesting, twentieth-century classicist modernism is invested in male bodies to the same extent that Romanticism is in the female body, an array of cultural assumptions need to be questioned. Yeats's recognition, quoted by Kermode, that "Man can embody truth but he cannot know it" (62) suddenly acquires gender specificity. Woman can embody truth but cannot know it—Man can know it but cannot embody it.[22] The body of the male dancer becomes scandalous in a radical sense, for what absence of knowledge does his body suggest, what break with a rationalism that confines the irrational to the female body? Can a man who dances be the subject of a knowledge? In the radical sense, can Nijinsky legitimately claim to be a philosopher who dances?[23]

Furthermore, can this seepage of the irrational into the cognitive function of masculinity—through the body of the male dancer—be figured as homosexual? Does the dancing male body—the homosexual body—challenge Enlightenment? Would this be the lurking fear that limits and impels classical modernism, the sensual reemergence of masculinity?

Of course, to hypothesize a historically specific break—I have been suggesting the Ballets Russes here, and the fetishizing of Nijinsky's body—does not mean that elements of this new "masculine" Classicism had not already begun to make themselves felt within the romantic tradition of which Kermode writes. But again, I think we need to be aware, in a way Kermode is not, of the gendering of the Image-Dancer and the sexual economies put in play. Kermode's Romanticism, I would argue, is riven with such issues of sexuality. For example, is Pater really the most obvious place to look for a romantic privileging of "feminine," "organic" beauty? And is there no irony in the fact that "Yeats thanks Verlaine for awakening him" (63) to an appreciation of organic femininity and a condemnation of the alienation of feminine beauty through over-education? Let us make no mistake: writing about male bodies—the task imposed on the modernist conversant with balletic as opposed to "free" dance—brings with it a whole series of anxieties that finally explode the symbolist aesthetic. If what I am calling the "classical" ballet (by which I mean "classical" in a broader cultural sense than the term usually implies in dance history) opens up the male body to the gaze and to the pen, the inverse is also true. The emergence of this body in dance positively obliges the cultural critic to consider what had been unspeakable heretofore. In other words, the homosexual camouflage of ballet was something more than a sub-code for a small group: it was a cultural obligation to *all* critics. (One does not imagine Hulme lingering with any particular relish over the male dancer's torso, and the avoidance of such attentions seems to have perverted Havelock Ellis's perceptions of the new Classicism.)

I am suggesting, then, that that which must remain unarticulated in the new dance-aesthetic of the classical modernists is the male body as an object of desire, as a sexuated "embodiment." The implications of any such gazing at the male body go beyond homosexual panic, however, suggesting a broader epistemological concern with the parsing out of cognition and embodiment. Thus, for example, it is in the work of the otherwise liberal sexologist—Havelock Ellis—that this fear of male embodiment leads to the most notable distortions, suggesting that the fear cannot be reduced to purely sexual motives. By contrast, T. E. Hulme's fragmentary writings seem more willing to reconsider the tropological function of the male body, even though his sexual politics are by no means ostensibly sympathetic to encroachments from "the queer." In what follows I offer an unorthodox reading of Hulme in order to show how in his work an explicit and binary polemical opposition of romantic and classical necessarily, or even inadvertently, leads to a radical gender realignment that the otherwise much more liberal Ellis cannot articulate. This is not, I should add, to downplay Hulme's misogyny: indeed, we might ask whether the often asserted alliance of misogyny and homosexuality needs to be rethought. Whether, in other words, it is not a question of "the homosexual" necessarily flirting with misogyny, but rather of misogyny—in a social order predicated on however momentary an overcoming of misogyny in heterosexual reproduction—always necessarily confronting the possibilities of a queer sympathy with the feminine.

In turning to Hulme, we must be careful not to conflate his observations on dance and his poetics. For while I contend that the emergence of dance as a theatrical form necessarily mediates his reception—and rejection—of romantic and Symbolist predecessors, the role played by dance in his poetic reflections is by no means straightforward. Within his general theory of artistic innovation, Hulme draws important distinctions between the various arts. These distinctions follow in a tradition of aesthetic theory concerned with the nature of temporality and performance in the various art forms. "It would be different," Hulme writes in the early piece "A Lecture on Modern Poetry," "if poetry, like acting and dancing, were one of the arts of which no record can be kept and which must be repeated for each generation" (FS, 69). No clearer statement could be possible of dance's problematic relation to writing and poetics. Dance is invoked as a counterexample of his historical dialectic of poetic forms: "as poetry is immortal, it is differentiated from those arts which must be repeated" (FS, 69). Poetry is "immortal" and therefore constantly new. Dance, meanwhile—and the arts of performance—are strictly temporal and can therefore be preserved only in memory through a *repetition* of inherited forms. This is a complex relation indeed. Poetry is "immortal" and therefore must rejuvenate itself with each generation; dance is not, and so can continue forever in the same form. There is, of course, an odd reversal in all of this: that which is immortal is subject to the laws of novelty, whereas that which is not can continue eternally in unchanged form. "Those arts like poetry, whose matter is immortal, must find a new technique each generation" (FS, 69). The immortality of Hulme's Classicism derives not from its duration across time and the negation of its own historical situation, but from its absolute origination. Here, perhaps, we see an example of Hulme seeking not, as Kermode argues, new polemical terms to express essentially the same old romantic ideas, but rather the clumsy use of essentially romantic terms ("immortality") to express fundamentally new ideas.

In terms of the distinction Hannah Arendt draws, in *The Human Condition*, between immortality and eternity, the "immortality" of poetry is a form of worldliness. "Immortality," she argues, drawing on the distinction operative in Greek thought, "means endurance in time, deathless life on this earth and in this world as it was given, according to Greek understanding, to nature and the Olympian Gods."[24] The eternal, meanwhile—which Arendt identifies with either Socrates or Plato, and which is, ultimately, responsible for the denigration of human activity—is "the true center of strictly metaphysical thought" (20). "It must be admitted," Hulme writes, that verse forms, like manners, and like individuals, develop and die" (68). They are essentially mortal, and yet "it is necessary to realize that . . . poetry is immortal" (69). Verse forms are mortal, whereas poetry is immortal. Rather than stressing the distinction between the mortal and the immortal, however—and thereby reinscribing Hulme into a romantic tradition he claims to be rejecting—we should stress instead the operation of his poetics within the problematic of mortality as opposed to *eternity*. The "immortality" of Hulme's poetics is distinctly worldly and antimetaphysical. What might at first appear as an invocation of romantic terminology functions, instead, as a rejection of metaphysical and ahistorical notions of history. This indeed is the very domain of writing as opposed to any dance that might exhaust itself in the performance. To cite Arendt, "No matter how concerned a thinker may be with eternity, the moment he sits down to write his thoughts he ceases to be concerned primarily with eternity and shifts his attention to leaving some trace of them" (20). For Hulme, the poetic act is both that which records and that which is recorded; "even the Greek name *poeima*," Hulme writes, "seems to indicate the thing created once and for all" (*FS*, 71).

Dance, meanwhile, figures as an aesthetic of the eternal, a set of techniques that do not record and must, therefore, repeat. Precisely because it leaves no trace, it cannot be "immortal." Whereas for the Symbolists and romantics, dance tropes the immanence of origin and performance, the absolute uniqueness of the poetic moment, for Hulme it means quite the opposite. Dance is eternity thought only from the perspective of a necessary iterability, a metaphysics paradoxically tied to historical instantiation and repetition. It is the historical repetition of the same, whereas poetry is intrinsically originary precisely because it exists through historical time. In other words, the possibility of *recording* history—of writing as the recording of its own history—necessitates the ahistorical poetic moment of absolute origin. Dance, precisely because it can record no narrative, must constantly retell that narrative; it exists, so to speak, at the same level as oral culture, which tells its own history repeatedly because it does not, in effect, have one.

Several points need to be made here. Dance no longer tropes the inspired moment of literary creation; quite the reverse. Dance, refigured as a condition of poetry, would be a stale repetition: it is impervious to history because it can *write* no history. Poetry, on the other hand, is historical because its writing and recording frees it from the weight of historical reiteration and impels it, instead, toward the *generation* of history. Every performance of a dance is the writing of a history that is immediately erased, to be reestablished only through iteration. Certainly, Hulme's insistence on the necessity of poetic originality, in the radical sense, is entirely commensurate with romantic notions of the "self-begotten" image, but the location of the originality has shifted. The poem will no longer be likened to dance, because dance itself, in fact, is no longer seen as the trope for a natural (embodied) language, but as a form whose historicity must be repeatedly reiterated. To reframe these questions of eternity and immortality in terms of Yeats's elision of labor in dance, I would argue that the leaving of a trace—the aesthetic artifact, or the child—is what makes of an art form a writing. Rather than demonstrating how writing can become dance, Hulme, we might say, shows how dance will seek—and fail—to become a writing.[25]

Clearly, if Hulme's refiguring of dance as a trope cannot itself be linked to the explosion of ballet at the beginning of this century, it is nevertheless balletic dance—dance, that is, as a technical and grammatical system, rather than as a mode of immanent self-expression—that he has in mind. This anti-metaphysical reading of Hulme through "classical" distinctions derived from Arendt obliges us, I think, to acknowledge, as the Greeks did, that "the mortality of men lies in the fact that individual life . . . arises out of biological life" (Arendt, 19). In other words, the anti-metaphysical aspect of Hulme's thought leads to an embodiment and sexuation—to biology as a reproductive system. In what follows I wish to foreground necessary shifts in the conceptualization of *physical*—not just *metaphysical*—existence and to suggest points of biological distinction separating Hulme and Ellis. The return to biology should not automatically be taken as a return to procreative sexuality: "Men," Arendt will claim, "are 'the mortals,' the only mortal things in existence, because unlike animals they do not exist only as members of a species whose immortal life is guaranteed through procreation" (18–19). If the question of immortality—unlike the question of eternity, which would necessarily ignore such issues—"cuts through the circular movement of biological life" (19), it also seems to cut across the distinctions of gender upon which such biological life depends. Hulme's writings reject not only the Yeatsian ideology of the "self-begotten" but the very technology of begetting; and it is precisely in his reflections on the historical generation of forms, furthermore, that Hulme throws his wrench into the machinery of procreation and scrambles gender.

"To the artist," Hulme points out, "the introduction of a new form is, as Moore says, like a new dress to a girl; he wants to see himself in it" (68): neatly parceled out by simile, the modernist's desire nevertheless suggests a transvestite impulse, trying on new forms like new dresses.[26] Clearly, if the male is not to be countenanced as an object of desire—leaving the balletic tradition "disembodied," as in Ellis—Hulme at least seems ready to try out the subject-position of the woman.[27] The "Notes on Language and Style" are also riddled with images of cross-dressing, and in "Cinders" Hulme implicitly acknowledges the tropological importance of dress in his "general theory" when he observes how "most of our life is spent in buttoning and unbuttoning" (S, 224). It might seem perverse indeed to read Hulme as a "queer" writer in any sense of the word, and yet there are moments in his writing where he contemplates the male in a way Ellis, the sexologist, cannot. Take, for example, the apparently arbitrary citation of a line from Shakespeare as typical of the "dynamic classical" and Hulme's comment on the line. Seeking to establish rhetorical distinctions between the romantic and the classical, Hulme glosses Shakespeare as follows:

> "Golden lads and girls all must
> Like chimney sweepers come to dust"

> Now, no romantic would have ever written that. . . . I think quite classical is the word lad. Your modern romantic could never write that. He would have to write golden youth, and take up the thing at least a couple of notes in pitch. (S, 121)

While the homosexual cult of the "lad" only reached its apogee in the trench poetry of World War I, it had already acquired distinctly homoerotic overtones before that.[28] The suggestion of a link between the classical impulse and the homo-social/homo-sexual is startling and revealing, a covert acknowledgment of modernism's implication in a fin-de-siècle homosexual decadence. Hulme does not know how right he is—no romantic *would* have written this. My argument, then, is not that Hulme engages in any wholesale queering of modernist Classicism, but that his disinterested rigor in presenting terms inherited from the nineteenth century allows him to lay bare a hidden sexual agenda. It is precisely because he *does not* use classical rhetoric to justify a sexual agenda that he can bring that agenda to the fore.

It is particularly notable that in Hulme dance has been taken off the street and framed theatrically. This is not the unrestrained free dance of Heine, with its fantasy of a natural language of the body. This dancer is entirely artificial and regulated, dependent on the capacities of poetry to recapture, through artifice, the shock of the new that can rejuvenate language. Contrasting Hulme with Symons—who represents, for Kermode, the symbolist tradition in its decadent mode, and who passes that tradition on into twentieth-century modernism—we are struck all the more by the importance of "staging" in Hulme's conceptualization of dance. In his *Studies in Seven Arts*, Symons states in his introduction an intention to focus on "painting, sculpture, architecture, music, handicraft, the stage (in which I include drama, acting, pantomime, scenery, costume, and lighting) and, separate from these, dancing." Dancing is quite clearly privileged and set apart from the other arts, most specifically from the stage. Dance in this symbolist tradition is the passage of art into life and the revivification of art itself. The problem for Hulme, on the other hand, is going to be how to take the dance of philosophy out of the theatrical frame and into the world. Though he asserts that "the effort of the literary man to find subtle analogies for the ordinary street feelings he experiences leads to the differentiation and importance of those feelings" (FS, 93–94), in fact the problem he faces is the reverse—how to take ideas from their stage and place them on the street without their prostituting themselves as street-walkers.

If he were not a philosopher, would Hulme be a dancer? Like Nijinsky, perhaps, the philosopher who dances? Probably not; as Michael Roberts notes, Hulme was fond of remarking, "I am a heavy philosopher." If dance allows for modifications in Hulme's poetics, it is not the condition toward which that poetics aspires. No—Hulme's philosophy is sedentary, finally, an aesthetic and philosophy of "dwelling" and prolongation. But dance will serve to trope this mode of thinking:

> Perhaps the difficulty that is found in expressing an idea, in making it long, in dwelling on it, by means of all kinds of analogy, has its root in the nature of ideas and thought itself.
> Dancing as the art of prolonging an idea, lingering on a point. (FS, 91)

Dancing is the analogy Hulme uses to express the analogical function of philosophy: it is, after all, the modus operandi of the philosopher. Clearly, the "dwelling on a point" as a philosophical mode of dance suggests the feminine dance on *pointe*, and it is important to note the maintenance of a traditional feminine coding of dance in Hulme. I would like now, however, to trace this notion of dance as it moves across genders and levels of aesthetic performance.[29] Returning to Hulme's notion of "trying on" new poetic forms like so many girls' dresses, it is clear that tropes of clothing and footwear are, for Hulme, "symbolic of the world organized (in counters) from the mud" (S, 227); symbolic, that is, of the precarious aesthetic endeavor that creates meaning from chaos. The tropes undertake this work only through the organization of "counters," however—that is, through precisely those linguistically reifying practices Hulme abhors. Dance, then—as a dwelling—tropes the possibility of a creation of meaning that would not be merely formulaic and that would reconstruct gender beyond the formalities of transvestism.

Thus, Hulme will reject "W. B. Yeats' attempts to ennoble his craft by strenuously believing in supernatural world, race-memory, magic, and saying that symbols can recall these where prose couldn't" (*FS*, 98). The break with Symbolism is effected in the name of analogy. Thus, Hulme suggests in place of Yeats's symbols that "the analogies a man uses to represent a state of soul, though personal, can be replaced to produce almost the same effect. *No one* mistakes the analogies for the real thing they stand for" (*S*, 235). Though he despises language thought as "counter-pushing," Hulme can at least cling to the negative presence of the thing signified by insisting that no conflation of signifier and signified (typical of the symbol) be allowed to take place. Analogy does not allow for embodiment, for "all these sudden insights (*e.g.* the great analogy of a woman compared to the world in Brussels)—all of these start a line, which seems about to unite the whole world logically. But the line stops. There is no unity" (*S*, 235). The rejection of symbol—of analogy, that is, pushed to the point of identity—is figured as a rejection of the female body as a moment of representational closure. The body—the *female* body—suggests the closure of a system of analogies—and it is this that Hulme resists. Could it be that the male body would resist such closure in its presentation of analogy as a non-identical structure of logic opposed to the (female) symbol?

If Hulme is a heavy philosopher, and if to philosophize is, after all, to dance, he will need to find some other mode of dancing—one that stresses stasis and the energy contained within it. Dwelling on a point, refusing the transcendent moment of movement, this is Hulme's dance. As he notes in the epigraph to the poem "Mana Aboda," "beauty is the marking-time, the stationary vibration, the feigned ecstasy of an arrested impulse unable to reach its natural end" (*S*, 266). We encounter a similar notion of "vibration" in Nijinsky's writings: a "marking-time" that asserts its own temporality and worldliness even as it seems to hover above it. Time is, as it were, transcended yet marked. The dance, rather than transcending the temporality and historicity of the dancer in "symbolist" fashion, inserts the passive temporality of a dwelling into the dwelling—the room—of philosophy. Finally, the two senses of dwelling rejoin each other; "gradually one learns the art of dwelling on a point, of decorating it" (*FS*, 92). Through tropes of decoration and vestment, then, we return to the centrality of dance.

Hulme is constantly torn between wonder at man's ability to create himself out of mud and chaos, and disgust at the pretensions involved in that self-creation. Notably, the disgust is generally bodied forth in female figures. Thus, for example, his philosophical "dwelling on a point"—the aesthetic dance on *pointe*—is parodied by "two tarts walking along Piccadilly on tiptoe," who cause him to "worry until [I] could find the exact model analogy that will reproduce the extraordinary effect they produce" (*FS*, 82). He finally identifies the aesthetic effect as "disinterestedness, as though saying: We may have evolved painfully from the clay, and be the last leaf on a tree. But now we have cut ourselves away from that. We are things-in-themselves. We exist out of time" (*FS,* 82). Taken out of the theatrical framework of balletic dance, the "dwelling on a point"—walking on tiptoe—reveals itself as the pretension of a tart. "In a sense all ideals must be divorced, torn away from the reality where we found them and put on a stage" (*FS,* 90), Hulme writes, but the problem ultimately will be, precisely, one of staging. What becomes of philosophy once abstracted from the stage? Then, the ideals "must wear high-heeled shoes" (*FS,* 90) like the tarts: "The separation of the high heel and the powdered face is essential to all emotions, in order to make a work of art" (*FS,* 90). The prostitute becomes the figure for worldly philosophy. The coquettish symbolist dancer now reveals herself for what she always was; and what makes her base and prostituted is precisely her *separation* from the earth, the "high-heeled shoes that make them appear free movers" (*FS,* 90). We are a long way—or are we?—from the free movements of Mme Laurence.

What is left, if philosophy is to operate in the world without prostituting itself? In the end, it seems, the transference of the "image" from ballet stage and music hall to life is the work of men. If it is the women who continue to dance, it is the men who carry the affect of dance out of the theater:

> Each dancer on the stage with her effects and her suggestions of intensity of meaning which are not possible, is not herself (that is a very cindery thing) but a synthesized state of mind in me. The red moving figure is a way of grouping some ideas together, just as powerful a means as the one called logic which is only an analogy to *counter-pushing.* (*FS,* 89)

Hulme rejects any notion of the dancer's self-sublation in the dance—it is the synthesizing effect in the mind of the male spectator that is important. Moreover, the dance itself is likened to the dreaded counter-pushing of logic: it is only the ana-logic synthesis that counts. In a counter-piece, almost, to the two tarts in Piccadilly, Hulme observes another scene:

> Complete theory, what was thought, in the old book, of relation between the poet and the reader seen suddenly at a glance in listening to boys going home from music-hall whistling a song. Chelsea Palace. Here a new way (a mental dance) found for them of synthesizing certain of their emotions. (*FS,* 93)

The boys have moved from being spectators at a theatrical performance to being themselves the objects of the philosopher's observations. In this instance, though, the dance—the "mental dance" of their whistling—*is* synthetic. Hulme can philosophize not by *looking* at the dance of the boys, but by *listening* to it: the anxiety of embodiment is overcome. Whistling achieves what the female theatrical dancer cannot. The passage from logical counter-pushing to the work of analogy is the passage from dance—through analogy—to music.

One might say that any necessary relation of dissidence to dissonance has been broken by the lads' synthetic whistling. This passage frees the boys up for Hulme's analysis; the furtive "glance" he casts on the boys is merely a glance at a "relation." As we find ourselves back where we started, in the vibrant, vital, London Music Hall, the philosopher's gaze is muted to the modality of listening. Gazing at—or, rather, listening to—the boys leaving the Chelsea Palace, Hulme suggests that this modernist philosophical method will be—in a sense quite different from Ellis's pathologies of sexual inversion—"musical."

Notes

1. Matthew Arnold, *Culture and Anarchy: An Essay in Political and Social Criticism*, in *Culture and Anarchy and Other Writings*, ed. Stefan Collini (Cambridge: Cambridge University Press, 1993): 68.

2. Since we are concerned here with tracing the tradition of dissidence into the modernist project, we would do well to note also the persistence of a countertradition. Arnold's critique of the hegemony of dissidence is taken up by Wyndham Lewis in *The Art of Being Ruled* (New York: Harper and Bros., 1926).

3. Jonathan Dollimore, *Sexual Dissidence* (Oxford: Oxford University Press, 1991).

4. Havelock Ellis, *The Dance of Life* (London: Constable, 1923): 32. Subsequent references noted in the text.

5. This linkage of dance and vitalistic impulses in early twentieth-century aesthetics can be remarked elsewhere. In the essay "The World as Ballet," for example, Arthur Symons writes that "the abstract thinker, to whom the question of practical morality is indifferent, has always loved dancing, as naturally as the moralist has hated it. . . . The dance is life, animal life, having its own way passionately" (*Studies in Seven Arts* [New York: Dutton, 1907], 387). If, for the romantic tradition, the dance marked the taking up of flesh into the spirituality of movement, clearly for the Symbolists—the dancers post-Salomé, let us say—dance will feature as the *revenge* of the body. It is as the expression of life that dance will be celebrated—dance's worldly passion is now what distinguishes, rather than denigrates, it. "The dance, then, is art," Symons will proclaim, "because it is doubly nature" (388). Its very excess negates its own negation of nature: it is doubly nature, but nature, of course, would be that which has no double. Symons's decadence stems, in fact, from an excess of nineteenth-century naturalism, a privileging of nature to the point where nature can no longer bear the burden imposed on it and must be remade as an artificial construct.

6. The figures I have in mind are people like Otto Weininger, *Sex and Character* (London: Heinemann, 1906); Georg Simmel, *Georg Simmel on Women, Sexuality and Love*, trans. Guy Oakes (New Haven: Yale University Press, 1984); Hans Blüher, *Die Rolle der Erotik in der männlichen Gesellschaft*, 2 vols. (Jena: Eugen Diederichs Verlag, 1917); Paul Charles Bourget, *Physiologie de l'amour moderne* (Paris: Plon, 1902); Rémy

de Gourmont, *The Natural Philosophy of Love* (New York: Liveright, 1932). For a consideration of elements of this strain of thought see my *Political Inversions: Homosexuality, Fascism and the Modernist Imaginary* (Stanford: Stanford University Press, 1996).

7. Details of Symonds's mediated connection with Havelock Ellis can be found in Phyllis Grosskurth, *Havelock Ellis: A Biography* (New York: New York University Press, 1985).

8. The concept of the "life alien" is derived by Hulme from Wilhelm Worringer, *Abstraction and Empathy: A Contribution to the Psychology of Style* (Cleveland: World Publishing, 1967). On the question of vitalism in early twentieth-century cultural life see Siegfried Kracauer, "Those Who Wait," in *The Mass Ornament: Weimar Essays,* trans. and ed. Thomas Y. Levin (Cambridge: Harvard University Press, 1995). Here Kracauer argues that "this doctrine recognized life-transcending norms and values only for the time being, so to speak, and destroyed the absolute in the very act of making the ebb and flow that is indifferent to value—in other words, the process of life—into an absolute. It was an act of desperation on the part of relativism" (131).

9. Havelock Ellis, *Little Essays of Love and Virtue* (New York: George H. Doran, 1921): 116–33. Further references noted in text as *LE.*

10. Of course, we can observe the interplay of aesthetic production and anthropological interests throughout the oeuvre of the Ballets Russes; from Nijinsky's interest in Greek sculpture in *L'après-midi d'un faune* and the interest in dance as ritual in *Le Sacre du printemps,* through to the predominance of mythological libretti—both Russo-Slavic and Orientalizing—in the repertoire of the ballet as a whole. That a certain anthropology of dance influenced those producing dance at the turn of the century—and since— can hardly be doubted. I would like to examine here the possibility of a retroaction and to ask, as well, what work dance was doing in the writings of such as Havelock Ellis.

11. Frank Kermode, *Romantic Image* (London: Fontana, 1971).

12. R. G. Collingwood, *The Principles of Art* (Oxford: Clarendon, 1938), 75. Subsequent references in the text.

13. In terms of dance's position within the *ut pictura poeisis* debate—as a form divided between the plastic and the temporal-musical—it is significant to note that the most influential cultural supporter of Nijinsky's *L'Après-midi d'un faune*—which had been attacked in *Le Figaro*—was the sculptor Rodin. See "La Rénovation de la Danse," reprinted as "The Rebirth of Dance" in *Afternoon of a Faun: Mallarmé, Debussy, Nijinsky,* ed. Jean-Michel Nectoux (New York: Vendome Press, 1989), 51.

14. T. E. Hulme, *Speculations: Essays on Humanism and the Philosophy of Art,* 2d ed., ed. Herbert Read (1924; reprint, London: Routledge and Kegan Paul, 1987), 82. Subsequent references to this text are noted in the text as *S.* References to T. E. Hulme, *Further Speculations,* ed. Sam Hynes (Lincoln: University of Nebraska Press, 1962) are noted in the text as *FS.*

15. Michael Roberts, *T. E. Hulme* (1938; reprint, New York: Haskell, 1971), 59.

16. Ellis writes of the Chinese that "the sphere in which ceremonies act is Man's

external life; his internal life is the sphere of music. It is music that moulds the manners and customs that are composed under ceremony" (23).

17. Ellis's Introduction to J.-K. Huysmans, *Against the Grain* (New York: Dover, 1969): v.

18. We find similar gestures in Pater's *The Renaissance,* specifically, in the Winckelmann chapter, where Greece is represented as an age of immaturity to be cherished by the later world. In other words, the writing of history itself is implicitly couched in terms of a paederastic wooing: "Let us not regret that this unperplexed youth of humanity, satisfied with the vision of itself, passed, at the due moment, into a mournful maturity" (167).

19. However, we need to acknowledge from the outset an alternative reading of this phenomenon: one that allows for the emergence of the male dancer—the male body—from *within* the epistemological structure I claim he supplants. As we have seen, all the anthropological and philosophical discourses brought to bear on dance at the time led back to the act of procreation: for Yeats's "self-begotten" dancer, the ball was already over. It might be argued—in a way that runs counter to my primary argument but allows perhaps for some of the blurring of the lines, some retention of romantic pathos in the Classicism of even so polemical a figure as Hulme—that only the homosexual male serves now to embody the possibility of self-begetting: a dance that produces the dancer but no excess, no progeny. We might bear in mind Cyril Beaumont's observation that in such roles as that of the *Spectre de la rose* Nijinsky "did not so much dance to the music, he appeared to issue from it. His dancing was music made visible" (Cyril W. Beaumont, *Bookseller at the Ballet: Memoirs 1891–1929* [London, 1975], 100). Thus, if the male dancer in one way troubled a tradition of thinking about dance as the physical transcendence of the physical, in other ways he served to perpetuate it.

20. We should note that Ellis is not merely naive in this respect. He ridicules attempts to reconstruct ancient Greek dances and music. Isadora is not celebrated because she is mimetically close to Greece. Quite the contrary, it would, of course, be impossible to approach the Greeks through mimesis since they represent the possibility of a nonmimetic being.

21. Ellis's observations in this regard are displaced into the realm of primitive anthropology. He acknowledges that dance is primarily a male function in primitive societies "for man is naturally the ornamental sex and woman the useful sex" (13).

22. In such diverse thinkers of the early part of this century as Weininger and Simmel, the romantic tradition lives on only through the desired (Simmel), or despised (Weininger), female body. See note 6.

23. In Vaslav Nijinsky, *The Diary of Vaslav Nijinsky,* ed. Romola Nijinsky (London: Quartet, 1991), Nijinsky often refers to himself as a philosopher. "I am a philosopher who does not reason—a philosopher who feels" (148).

24. Hannah Arendt, *The Human Condition* (Chicago: University of Chicago Press, 1958), 18. Subsequent citations in the text.

25. The locus classicus for this debate in terms of contemporary theory is, of course, Jacques Derrida's conversation with Christie V. McDonald, "Choreographies," trans. Christie V. Macdonald, *Diacritics* 12, no. 2 (summer 1982): 66–76.

26. Perhaps the most startling example of this tendency is revealed by what we might call an "editorial parapraxis" in Herbert Read's edition of the "Notes on Language and Style." In the version published in *Further Speculations*, Hulme notes, in keeping with the notion of the life-alien function of art, "the beauty of London only seen in detached and careful moments, never continuously, always a conscious effort. On top of a bus, or the sweep of the avenue in Hyde Park. But to appreciate this must be in some manner detached, e.g. wearing workmen's clothes" (99). In Read's version this is transcribed as "wearing women's clothes." Strangely, Read's version might be said to tie in more closely with the tropology of the notes as examined in the body of this chapter. In either case, it is clear that cross-dressing of some sort—across gender or class lines—is crucial to Hulme's aesthetic, which is life-alien not only in its potentially reifying relation to the aesthetic object, but in its assault on the integrity of the poet as a gendered or class-specific aesthetic subject.

27. Though he differed but little from Yeats in his attitude to women otherwise.

28. On the cult of the "lad" in pre–World War I and wartime writings, see Paul Fussell, *The Great War and Modern Memory* (New York: Oxford University Press, 1975), and Richard Dellamora, *Apocalyptic Overtures: Sexual Politics and the Sense of an Ending* (New Brunswick, N.J.: Rutgers University Press, 1994).

29. It is perhaps interesting to note that this gender play was clearly intended in some of Nijinsky's works. *Jeux*, for example, was originally conceived as a ballet on pointe for men. This was in keeping with the subject matter as elucidated in Nijinsky's *Diaries:* "*Jeux* is the life of which Diaghilev dreamed. He wanted to have two boys as lovers. . . . In the ballet the two girls represent the two boys and the young man is Diaghilev. I changed the characters because love between three men could not be represented on stage" (123).

CONTRIBUTORS

Oliver Buckton was born in London, England, and educated at Cambridge University and Cornell, where he received his Ph.D. in 1992. He is an assistant professor of English at Florida Atlantic University, where he teaches Victorian literature, film, and critical theory. He is the author of *Secret Selves: Confession and Same-Sex Desire in Victorian Autobiography* (University of North Carolina Press, 1998).

Richard Dellamora is currently affiliated with the Department of English at New York University as a Guggenheim Fellow. He is the former acting director of the Graduate Program in Methodologies at Trent University in Peterborough, Ontario. Dellamora is the co-editor of *The Work of Opera: Genre, Nationhood, and Sexual Difference* (Columbia University Press, 1997) and editor of *Postmodern Apocalypse: Theory and Cultural Practice at the End* (New Cultural Studies series, University of Pennsylvania Press, 1995). He is the author of *Apocalyptic Overtures: Sexual Politics and the Sense of an Ending* (Rutgers University Press, 1994) and *Masculine Desire: The Sexual Politics of Victorian Aestheticism* (University of North Carolina Press, 1990). He is currently writing a book on desire, citizenship, and the novel in Victorian England.

Dennis Denisoff is assistant professor of English at the University of Waterloo. He recently held a Social Sciences and Humanities Research Council of Canada post-doctoral fellowship in the Department of English at Princeton University. He has edited *Queeries: An Anthology of Gay Male Prose* (Arsenal Pulp, 1993) and co-edited *Perennial Decay: On the Politics and Poetics of Decadence* (University of Pennsylvania Press, 1998).

Regenia Gagnier is Professor of English at the University of Exeter, where she teaches Victorian Studies, especially the fin de siècle; social theory; feminist theory; and interdisciplinary studies. Her books include *Idylls of the Marketplace: Oscar Wilde and the Victorian Public* (Stanford University Press, 1986), *Subjectivities: A History of Self-Representation in Britain, 1832–1920* (Oxford University Press, 1991), and an edited collection, *Critical Essays on Oscar Wilde*

(Macmillan, 1992). Most recently she has published essays on the comparative histories of economics and aesthetics in market society in *Feminist Economics, Journal of Economic Issues, Journal of Victorian Culture, Victorian Studies, Victorian Literature and Culture,* and *Political Theory.*

Eric Haralson is assistant professor in the Department of English at the State University of New York at Stony Brook. He has published essays on Victorian and modern masculinity in *American Literature, Nineteenth-Century Literature,* the *Arizona Quarterly,* and the *Henry James Review,* as well as in the collections *Queer Forster* (University of Chicago Press, 1997), *The Cambridge Companion to Henry James* (1998), and the *Historical Guide to Henry James* (forthcoming from Oxford University Press). His book-in-progress is entitled "Henry James and the Making of Modern Masculinities."

Andrew Hewitt, associate professor of comparative literature at SUNY Buffalo, is the author of *Fascist Modernism: Aesthetics, Politics, and the Avant-Garde* (Stanford University Press, 1993) and *Political Inversions: Homosexuality, Fascism, and the Modernist Imaginary* (Stanford, 1996). He is currently writing a book on dance in Modernism.

Christopher Lane is associate professor of English at Emory University. He is the author of *The Ruling Passion: British Colonial Allegory and The Paradox of Homosexual Desire* (Duke University Press, 1995) and *The Burdens of Intimacy: Psychoanalysis and Victorian Masculinity* (University of Chicago Press, 1999), and editor of *The Psychoanalysis of Race* (Columbia University Press, 1998).

Thaïs E. Morgan, associate professor of English at Arizona State University, writes in the fields of Victorian poetry and nonfiction prose, Aestheticism, the history of criticism, and contemporary critical theory. Her books include *Victorian Sages and Cultural Discourse: Renegotiating Power and Gender* (Rutgers University Press, 1990); *Men Writing the Feminine: Literature, Theory, and the Question of Gender* (SUNY Press, 1994); and an analytic translation of Gérard Genette's *Mimologiques* (as *Mimologics,* University of Nebraska Press, 1995).

Yopie Prins is associate professor of English and comparative literature at the University of Michigan and specializes in relations between Victorian poetry and Classical Greek. She is the author of *Victorian Sappho* (Princeton University Press, 1999) and co-editor of *Dwelling in Possibility: Women Poets and Critics on Poetry* (Cornell University Press, 1997).

Kathy Alexis Psomiades, associate professor of English at the University of Notre Dame, is currently writing about femininity, knowledge, and the late Victorian novel. She is the author of *Beauty's Body: Femininity and Representation in British Aestheticism* (Stanford University Press, 1997) and coeditor with Talia Schaffer of *Women and British Aestheticism* (forthcoming, University Press of Virginia).

Julia Saville, assistant professor of English at the University of Illinois at Urbana-Champaign, was educated at the University of Cape Town and at Stanford University. She has published in journals such as *Word and Image* and *American Imago* and is currently working on a book entitled *A Queer Chivalry: The Homoerotic Ascesis of Gerard Manley Hopkins.*

Robert Sulcer, Jr. received his Ph.D. in English from the University of Texas at Austin in 1997. He is currently writing a book that links the dual emergence at the fin de siècle of male homosexuality as an identity category and literary study as an institution.

Martha Vicinus is the Eliza M. Mosher Distinguished University Professor at the University of Michigan at Ann Arbor. Vicinus is the author and editor of numerous books on Victorian women, the history of sexuality and popular culture, including *Independent Women: Work and Community for Single Women, 1850–1920* (1985), *Hidden from History: Reclaiming the Gay and Lesbian Past* (co-edited, 1989), and *Lesbian Subjects: A Feminist Studies Reader.* (1996).

INDEX

Abbot, Henry Ward, 222
Ackerman, Robert, 76n.40
Adams, James Eli, 112–13, 151, 201
adventure stories: homoerotic violence in, 88; and male homosocial, 86
Aeschylus, 74n.14
aesthete, 235–36, 256. *See also* Aestheticism; dandy; decadence
aesthetic: term, reification of, 131, 141, 143n.14
Aestheticism: and anti-Semitism, 154; and art for art's sake, 156; and chinamania, 151, 158, 166n.18; and Christianity, 287; and family, 152; feminist critique of, 8, 21, 23; gendering of, 255; and heterosexuality, 9, 22, 152, 196; and history, 286; as homoapologetic, 21; and male homosexuality, 253n.14; and homosocial, 197; in *Jude the Obscure,* 133; and male-male desire, 157, 197; and modernism, 11, 281; Oxford, 2; as queer, 288; refusal of natural body in, 24; and sexual dissidence, 153, 155, 157; sexual politics of, 21, 197; spoofed in *Punch,* 166n.18; and Symbolism, 285; in works of James, 197. *See also* dandy; decadence
aesthetics: applied, 135–36; and body, 135, 156, 289; of consumption, 130, 136–41; and creativity, 211; and daily life, 136; defined, 130; and economics, 140–41; embodied, 289, 294; and empiricism, 137; and eroticism, 156; ethical, 130–34; of evaluation, 130; and

female body, 30–37; and female narcissism, 36; formal, 8; Foucault on, 6, 133; gendered, 131, 221, 255; and individual, 131; laissez-faire, 140; Marxist, 134; medicalization of, 32; missionary, 139; and nationalism, 130; and natural selection, 137; opposed to social institutions, 140; Paterian, 138; perverse, 138; phenomenological, 219; physiological, 30–37, 40n.26, 136–38; and pleasure, 136–38; of production, 130, 134–36; psychological, 33–37, 130, 139, 211, 219; and ritual, 284; and sexuality, 211, 220; and sublimation, 36, 211; symbolist, 286; and sympathy, 161, 168n.48; and taste, 129–30, 136; as waste, 220; Wilde's transgressive, 10
Allen, Grant: "The New Hedonism" (1894), 138; *Physiological Aesthetics* (1877), 40n.26, 136–38
Alma-Tadema, Sir Lawrence, 49–51, 65, 74n.15
androgyny: and adolescent boy, 86, 90; as hermaphrodism of the soul, 2; in *Miss Brown,* 28; in *Trilby,* 161–62; and virginity, 90; in *A Woman Appeared to Me,* 94
Anglo-Saxon: and nationalism, 240
animalism, 120n.27
anonymity: and capitalism, 247
Anstruther-Thomson, Clementina (pseud. Kit), 22, 30–37; aesthetic experiments of, 139; collaboration with Vernon Lee, 30–37, 39n.23, 99–100;

Chantrey, Sir Francis, 267
Chantrey Fund, 267
chinamania: and Aestheticism, 151, 158,
　166n.18
Christianity: and Aestheticism, 287; and
　decadence, 291; and Hellenism,
　223–24; and sexual dissidence, 2, 87;
　in works of Santayana, 223–24
cigarette: as perfect commodity, 129
citizenship: and assimilation, 249; and
　male homosexuality, 242
civic masculinity: classical sources for,
　110–12, 116; and gender deviance,
　117–18; heterosexism of, 113
class: of adolescent boy, 87, 270; and
　aesthetics, 137–38
Classicism: in dance, 288–92; and deca-
　dence, 290–93; and Egypt, 288; and
　homosocial, 282; as life-alien, 282,
　288–89; as modernist, 289, 293, 299;
　privileges whole, 291; and Romanti-
　cism, 288–89, 291–92; and sexual dissi-
　dence, 289, 292; in works of Ellis,
　288–92. See also Hellenism; Neo-
　Classicism
Clemens, Cyril, 216
close reading: as queer, 237–38, 246–49
closet: and culture, 242; epistemology of,
　4; and Foucault on silence, 4; and pro-
　fessionalization, 246; and public/
　private dichotomy, 246
Clough, Anne Jemima, 73n.4
Cobbe, Francis Power, 47
Cohen, Ed, 118n.4, 156
Cohen, William, 1, 117, 122n.63
Coke, Edward, 243
Colby, Vineta, 105n.44
Colette, Sidonie Gabrielle, 98, 101
Collingwood, R. G., 283–84
Collini, Stefan, 119n.17
Collins, John Churton, 240
Colnaghi, Martin, 276n.47
color: and male eros, 258
Colvin, Sidney, 117
comfort: and consumption, 129–30
coming-out narratives, 11

commodification: focus on, in scholar-
　ship, 127
commodity: and labor theory of value,
　135
Conner, Frederick W., 230n.14
Connor, Steven, 143n.14
Conrad, Joseph, 203
consumption: aesthetics of, 127; and
　dandy, 158; and economic liberalism,
　140–41; and gender, 128; as liberating,
　128; middle-class, 2; and modernity,
　130; moral, 135; shift from production
　to, 128, 130; in works of Wilde,
　175–76
Contagious Diseases Acts (1860s),
　66
contralto: as homoerotic icon, 160
Cooper, Edith (pseud. Michael Field), 9,
　44, 54–61, 86, 91; conversion to Ca-
　tholicism, 60; male friends of, 92–93;
　meeting with Pater, 59; relationship
　with Bradley, 46, 54–55, 93; as spin-
　ster, 93. See also Bradley, Katherine;
　Field, Michael
Cooper, Emmanuel, 258, 276n.47
Cornford, Frances, 70
Cornford, Francis, 70
Cory, Daniel, 216
Court, Franklin E., 252n.10
Crackenthorpe, B. A., 102n.3
Craft, Christopher, 4
Cram, Ralph Adams, 11
Crawford, Robert, 75n.20, 76n.44
creativity: and aesthetics, 130; Marxist
　critiques of, 128
Creech, James, 208n.22
Criminal Law Amendment Act (1885),
　191, 194, 254, 273n.3
Crisp, Quentin, 235
critic: cultural role of, 252n.8
cross-dressing, 2; and effeminacy,
　116–17; as life-alien, 306n.26; in op-
　era, 160; in Trilby, 160; in works
　of Hulme, 298
Curzon, George, 194
Custance, Olive, 94

Dowgun, Richard, 74n.14
Dowling, Linda, 12n.6, 43, 76n.44, 110, 119n.5, 247
dromenon, 67
DuBois, Page, 120n.24
Du Maurier, George, 2, 147–64; as bohemian, 148; cartoons for *Punch*, 148–53; conservatism of, 148; men in works of, 155, 158; studies in Paris, 148; women in works of, 155
Works:
—*The Martian* (1897), 2, 147–48, 162–64; sexual ambiguity in, 162
—"Nincompoopania" (1879), *152,* 153, 164
—"A Rising Genius" (1878), *150,* 151–52
—*Trilby* (1894), 2, 83, 147, 153–62, 164; anti-Semitism in, 153–54, 163; cross-dressing in, 160; dramatic versions of, 163; effeminacy in, 155; gender ambiguity in, 160–62; genius in, 153–62; homosocial in, 156; male body in, 156; mesmerism in, 153, 158; misogyny in, 158; music in, 158, 160–62; popularity of, 163; spoofs of, 160, 163; Svengali in, 153–54, 157–58, *159,* 163
Duncan, Isadora, 294

Eagleton, Terry, 10, 143n.14
economics: and aesthetics, 134–36, 140–41; and consumer culture, 140–41; Victorian, 127–31, 141
Edelman, Lee, 200
education, 72n.3
effeminacy, 2, 90, 109–18; as aesthetic minoritizing discourse, 118; of bathing boy, 256; and cross-dressing, 116–17; of dandy, 200; and femininity, 113; and flamboyance, 200; as gender deviance, 120n.25; opposed to civic masculinity, 110–12; and self-control, 112; shifting definitions of, 116–18, 121n.32, 123n.71, 149, 165n.13, 256;

as sign of sexual dissidence, 109, 118, 118n.4
effeminatus, 111–12
Egerton, George, 9
Eliot, George, 235–36, 243
Eliot, T. S., 9
Ellis, Havelock, 84, 279–303; collaboration with Symonds, 281; on decadence, 290–91; as queer, 283
Works:
—*The Dance of Life* (1923), 279–80, 286–94; as anthropological, 281, 283, 305n.21; as book, 286–87; Classicism in, 288–90; eugenics in, 290; male body in, 293–95; post-colonial perspective in, 281; queering of, 288; Romanticism in, 291–92; as transitional text, 285; vitalism in, 286, 289
—Introduction to *A Rebours,* 290–91
—*Sexual Inversion* (1897), 281, 286
Ellis, Sarah Stickney, 253
Ellmann, Richard, 11, 171, 191
embodiment: and cognition, 295; in dance, 298; and language, 292–93; of male body, 295
Engelbrecht, Penelope J., 105n.39
Epstein, Joseph, 221–22
ethics: and aesthetics, 130–34
Euripides: Victorian reception of, 67, 74n.14; *Bacchae,* 49, 51, 62–63, 65–66
Evans, David, 242
evolution, 3, 32; and aesthetics, 137–38

Factory Act (1843), 279
Faderman, Lillian, 102n.7
family: and Aestheticism, 152; redefinitions of, 72
fantasy: and meaning, 219–20
Fawcett, Millicent Garrett, 73n.4
Felski, Rita, 9, 21, 142n.2
female body: and closure, 301; in dance, 292–93, 301; and hypersensation, 8; in Lee's aesthetic theory, 22, 30–37; as metonym for society, 121n.40; in Modernism, 9; in painting, 254; in Romanticism, 292, 294; in Rossetti's work,

prosopopoeia, 178–79, 181
prostitute: as figure for philosophy, 302
pseudonyms: of fin-de-siècle lesbian writers, 91
Psomiades, Kathy Alexis, 142n.2, 166n.17, 256
psychology: and aesthetics, 130, 135–38, 211; associationist, 137
public/private dichotomy: and closet, 246; gendering of, 255
Puerner, Charles, 163
Punch, 2, 8; Aestheticism spoofed in, 166n.18; body represented in, 165n.13; cartoons from, 44, *45*, 149, *150, 152,* 158, *159;* dandy represented in, 149–51, 163, 200–201; elitism of staff, 149; as masculine community, 148–49; women represented in, 165n.9
Puritanism: and dissent, 279
purity: and adolescent boy, 90; as polemic, 29–30; and sexual dissidence, 25, 27, 29, 36; and social body, 38n.15

Queensberry, marquess of, 180, 194
queer: and Aestheticism, 288; body, 237–38; canon, 246; close reading as, 238, 246–47; criticism, 237, 245–47; dandy as, 200; and femininity, 296; formalism, 246–47; geneaology, 47; term, privileging of, 250n.1; term, in Victorian usage, 192

race: and aesthetics, 130–31
Raffalovich, André, 273n.2
Read, Herbert, 307n.26
Reade, Brian, 155
Reform Bill (1832), 132
reproduction: and beauty, 220; and biology, 298; and labor theory of value, 134–36; and pleasure, 138; and production, 134–35; and work, 285
Reynolds, Margaret, 160
Richards, I. A., 9, 11, 33
Richards, Jeffrey, 87
Ricketts, Charles, 92
Roberts, Michael, 288, 300

Robinson, A. Mary F., 59
Rodin, Auguste, 286, 304n.13
Rohde, Erwin, 62
Rolfe, Frederick (pseud. Baron Corvo), 87, 253
romance mode: as deferral, 254; as dialectic, 255; as emblem for language, 254–55; gendered, 254–55; in painting, 255–56, 269, 272; in poetry, 254–56
Romanticism: of ballet, 289–90; and Classicism, binary of, 282, 288–89; in dance, 288–92, 297; and decadence, 282, 291–92; female body in, 292, 294, 305n.22; and mimesis, 290; organicism of, 289; privileges part, 291; and Symbolism, 292
Rosebery, Lord, 194, 201
Ross, Robert, 172, 194
Rossetti, Christina, "In an Artist's Studio," 23
Rossetti, Dante Gabriel, 1, 21, 109, 255; "Body's Beauty," 36; and civic masculinity, 115–16; as *effeminatus*, 111, 116; "The House of Life" (1870, 1881), 116; as "nasty," 114; painting, 23; *Poems* (1870), 109; uxoriousness of, 116
Rossetti, William Michael, 110, 121n.45
Rowe, John Carlos, 202
Rowse, A. L., 230n.14
Royal Academy, 262
Rubin, Gayle, 5, 12n.8, 13n.15
Ruskin, John, 51; materialism of, 135; on production, 130, 134
Russell, Bertrand, 68
Russell, second earl (John Francis Stanley), 215–16, 221
Russo, Mary, 168n.42

sado-masochism, 6, 13n.19
sage: cultural authority of, 112–13; female, 113; and manhood, 113
Sainsbury, Maria Tuke, 256
sameness, 85, 94
same-sex desire, 1; and aesthetic theory, 22, 29, 33, 221; and beauty, 221; in

sexual dissidence (*continued*)
ture, 279; play as, 279; and purity, 25;
term, used by Dollimore, 10, 279; in
The Tragic Muse, 194; types of, 5, 71,
279–80; versus binary constructions,
71, 279–80; Wildean, 279–80; and
women's social identity, 46. *See also*
Aestheticism; androgyny; boy, adolescent; cross-dressing; dandy; decadence; Dionysus; dissidence; effeminacy; female body; female-female
desire; femininity; gay; homosexual;
homosexuality; lesbian; male body;
male-male desire; maenad; masculin-
ity; queer; same-sex desire; spinster;
Uranian; Wilde, Oscar
sexuality: and dance, 282, 293; and vi-
talism, 280. *See also* heterosexuality;
homosexual; homosexuality
Shand-Tucci, Douglass, 8–9
Shannon, Charles, 92
Shaw, George Bernard, 173
Shaw, Marion, 178
Sherard, Robert H., 169n.56
Shillito, Violet, 94
Showalter, Elaine, 21, 47
Sidgwick, Henry, 73n.4
Silver, Henry, 148
Simmel, Georg, 303n.6
Sinfield, Alan, 192, 194, 200, 256
Singer, Irving, 230n.14
Slade, Conrad, 217
Sloan, John, 160
SM. *See* sado-masochism
Small, Ian, 127
Smith, Edgar, 163
Smith, Logan Pearsall, 55, 60, 93
Smith, Timothy d'Arch, 102n.6, 253
Smyth, Ethel, 29, 38n.17, 100
snake: as positive symbol, 92
social body: as ill, 114; and male body, in
civic masculinity, 111–12, 114; and
purity, 38n.15
sodomy, 2, 224, 243
Solomon, Simeon, 1, 110; collaboration

with Swinburne, 117, 122n.67; gender
deviance of, 117–18; male body in
works of, 117–18
Somerville, Edith, 91
Sophocles, 74n.14; *Antigone*, 44
species: defined, 3
spectacle: society of, 128
Spectator, 58, 269
Spielmann, M. H., 165n.12
Spencer, Herbert, 137
Spenser, Edmund, 254
spinster, 46, 48; as independent woman,
73n.8; as maenad, 52–53, 60
Sprigge, Timothy L. S., 230n.14
Stanley, Alan, 253, 271–72
St. Denis, Ruth, 294
Stead, William T., 173
Stein, Gertrude, 105n.39
Stendhal (Henri Beyle), 211, 213
Stewart, Jessie G., 76n.40
Stimmung, 245, 253n.14
Stockton, Kathryn Bond, 12n.7
Stott, Rebecca, 102n.2
Strachey, James, 231n.15
Stray, Christopher A., 72n.2
Street, G. S., 166n.18, 173
Sturge Moore, T., 73n.6
Sturgeon, Mary, 103n.14
Stutfield, Hugh E. M., 102n.3
style: and masculinity, 204–205; and
nature, 173. *See also* aesthetics
subject: autobiographical, 180–81; con-
fessional, 11; deviant, 84; modern gay,
11; postmodern, 10; schizophrenic,
10–11; sexual, 250n.1; specular, in *De
Profundis*, 177–84
sublimation: and aesthetics, 36, 211; in
works of Santayana, 216
Sutcliffe, Frank Meadow, 276n.41
Swinburne, Algernon Charles, 1–2, 21,
109–10, 198, 255, 267, 274n.22;
collaboration with Solomon, 117,
122n.67; denunciation of Whitman,
261–62; as *effeminatus*, 111, 115;
friendship with Symonds, 261–62; as